D•N•ANGEL

BY YUKIRU SUGISAKI

VOLUME 6

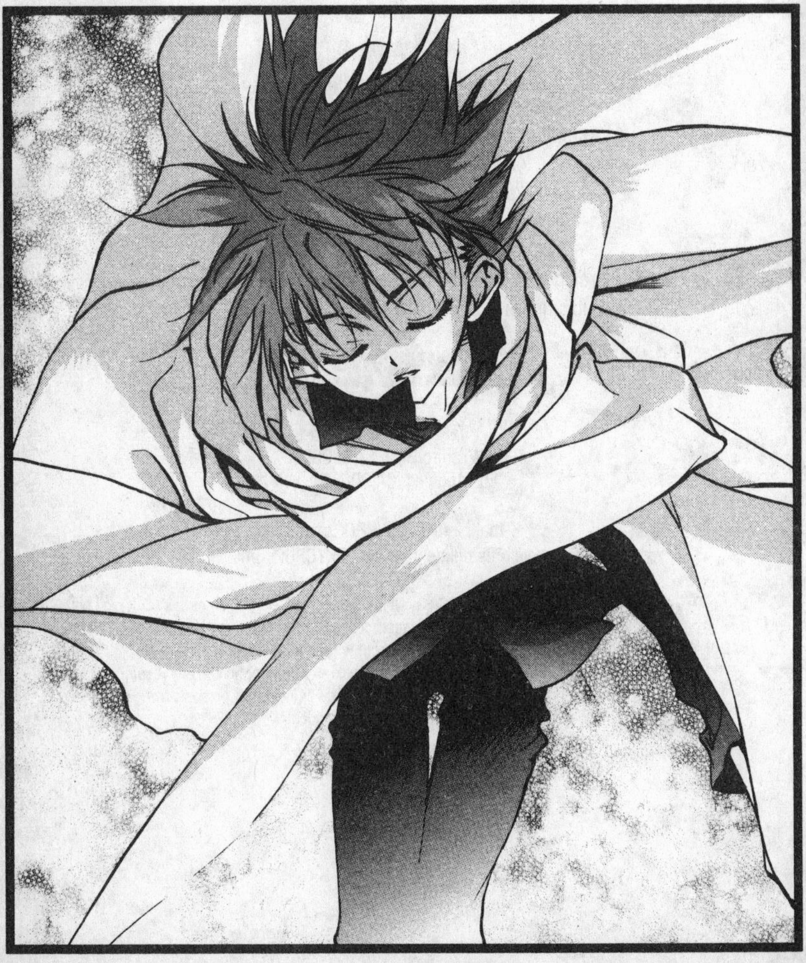

D•N•ANGEL Vol. 6
Created by Yukiru Sugisaki

Translation - Alethea and Athena Nibley
English Adaptation - Sarah Dyer
Copy Editor - Peter Ahlstrom
Retouch and Lettering - Jose Macasocol, Jr. and Abelardo Bigting
Production Artists - Angelica Perez and Eric Pineda
Cover Layout - Gary Shum

Editor - Bryce P. Coleman
Digital Imaging Manager - Chris Buford
Pre-Press Manager - Antonio DePietro
Production Managers - Jennifer Miller and Mutsumi Miyazaki
Art Director - Matt Alford
Managing Editor - Jill Freshney
VP of Production - Ron Klamert
Editor-in-Chief - Mike Kiley
President and C.O.O. - John Parker
Publisher and C.E.O. - Stuart Levy

A  Manga

TOKYOPOP Inc.
5900 Wilshire Blvd. Suite 2000
Los Angeles, CA 90036

E-mail: info@TOKYOPOP.com
Come visit us online at www.TOKYOPOP.com

ISBN: 1-59182-955-0

First TOKYOPOP printing: February 2005
10 9 8 7
Printed in the USA

D·N·ANGEL

Volume 6

By

Yukiru Sugisaki

HAMBURG // LONDON // LOS ANGELES // TOKYO

& STORY

Daisuke and Riku, the girl he loves, were finally able to confess their feelings for one another. But on their class trip, misunderstandings developed when Riku kept finding Daisuke with her twin sister, Risa. And if that wasn't bad enough, Satoshi trapped Dark inside a mirror called "the Sage of Sleep" and transformed into Krad, who attacked Daisuke! Daisuke escaped from Krad, and with the help of To-to (the Towa no Shirube), was able to rescue Dark. However, when he returned, he found out that Riku had run off and was now missing! He searched the island and finally found her deep in the woods...

Wiz

A mysterious animal who acts as Dark's familiar and who can transform into many things, including Dark's black wings. He can also transform himself into Dark or Daisuke.

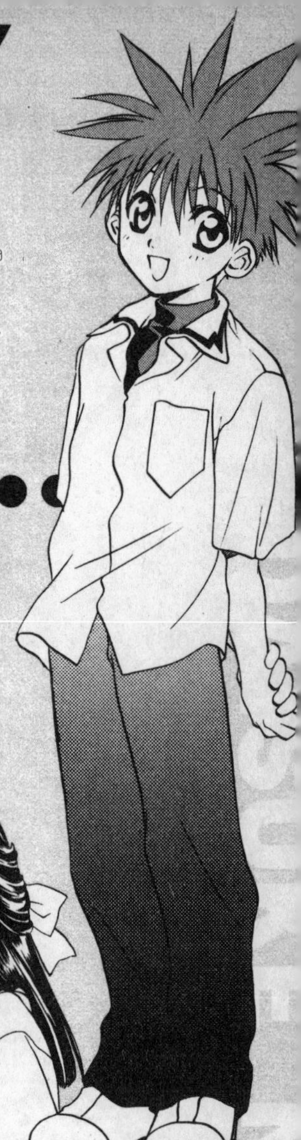

Risa Harada (younger sister)

Daisuke's first crush. Daisuke confessed his love to her...but she rejected him. She's been in love with Dark since the first time she saw him on TV.

Riku Harada (older sister)

Risa's identical twin sister. She and Daisuke have fallen for each other.

Daisuke Niwa

A 14-year-old student at Azumano Middle School. He has a unique genetic condition that causes him to transform into the infamous Phantom Thief Dark whenever he has romantic feelings.

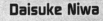

CHARACTERS

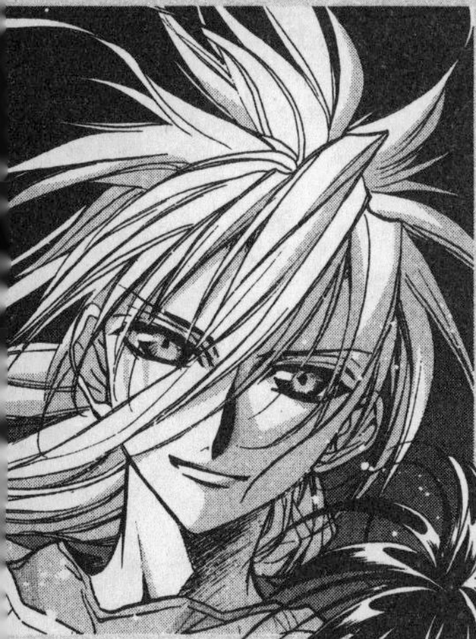

Krad

The form Satoshi Hiwatari transforms into because of his Hikari DNA. He has pure white wings. He sees the Niwa family and Dark as enemies.

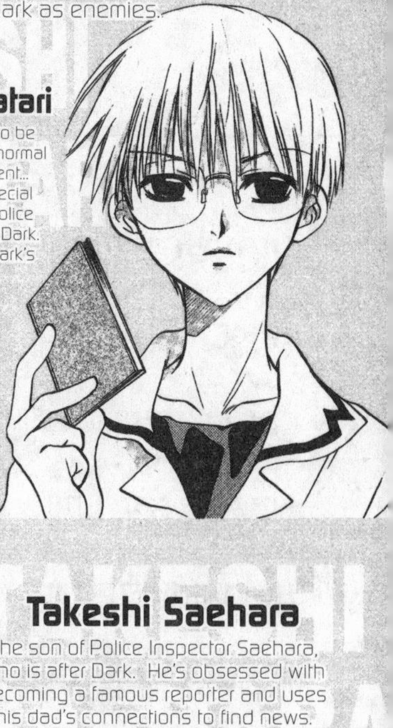

Satoshi Hiwatari

His last name used to be Hikari. Supposedly a normal middle school student... but he's also the special commander of the police operation to capture Dark. He transforms into Dark's enemy, Krad.

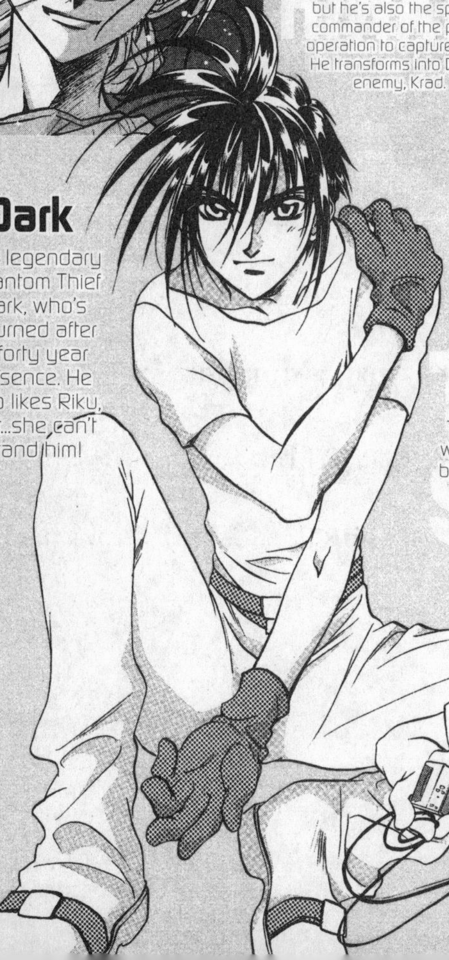

Dark

The legendary Phantom Thief Dark, who's returned after a forty year absence. He also likes Riku, but...she can't stand him!

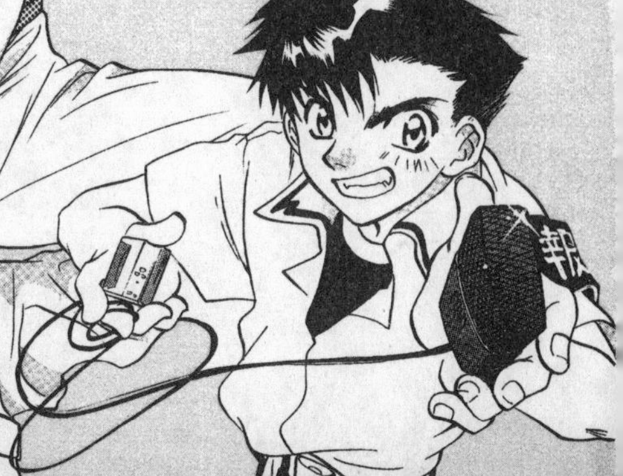

Takeshi Saehara

The son of Police Inspector Saehara, who is after Dark. He's obsessed with becoming a famous reporter and uses his dad's connections to find news.

CONTENTS

CHARACTERS & STORY..4

STAGE 2, PART 9 7

STAGE 2, PART 10 33

STAGE 2, PART 11..49

SPECIAL BONUS CHAPTER: RIKU AND RISA...........................73

THE SECOND HAND OF TIME PART 1...............................101

THE SECOND HAND OF TIME PART 2...............................137

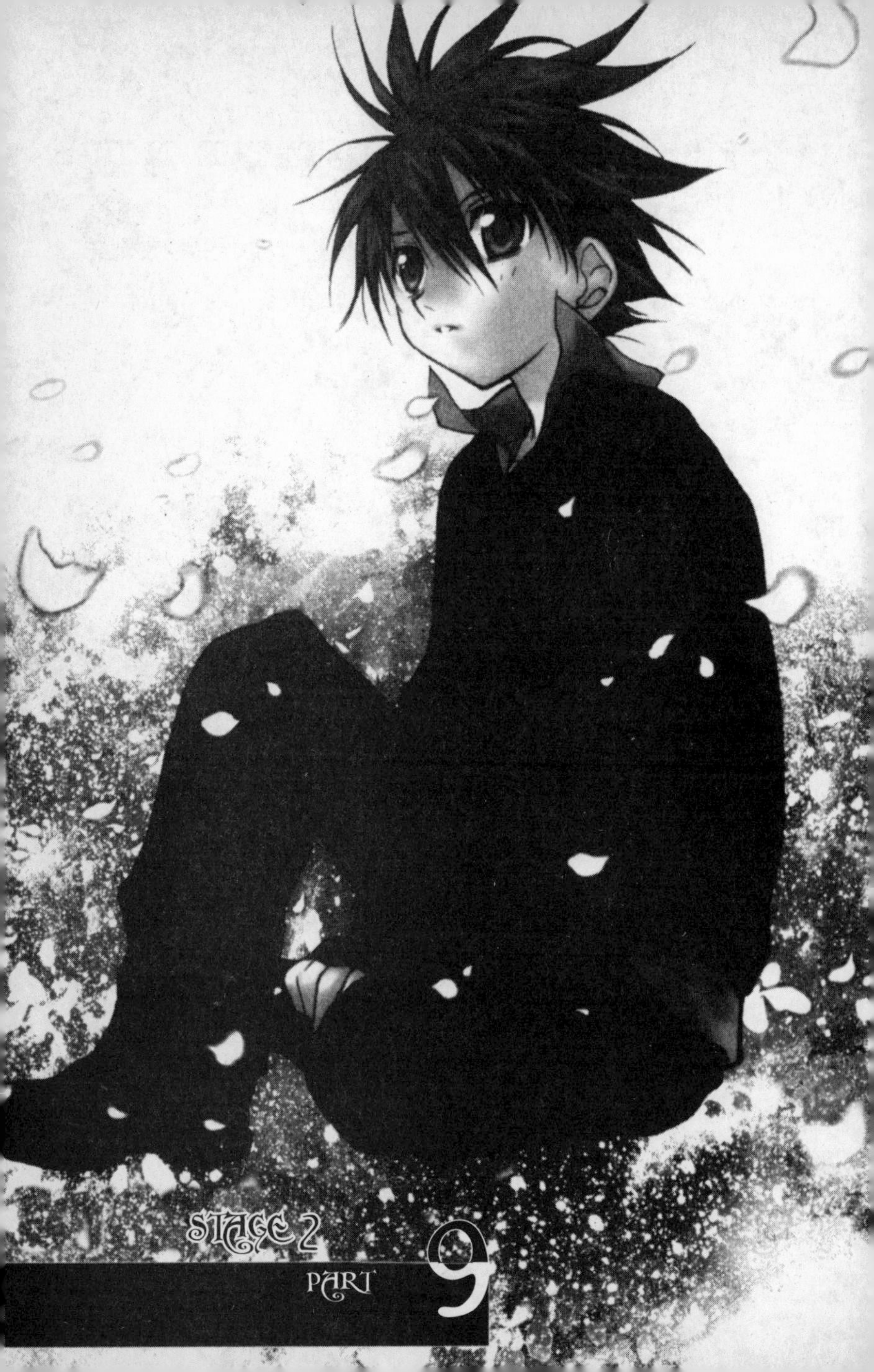
STAGE 2
PART 9

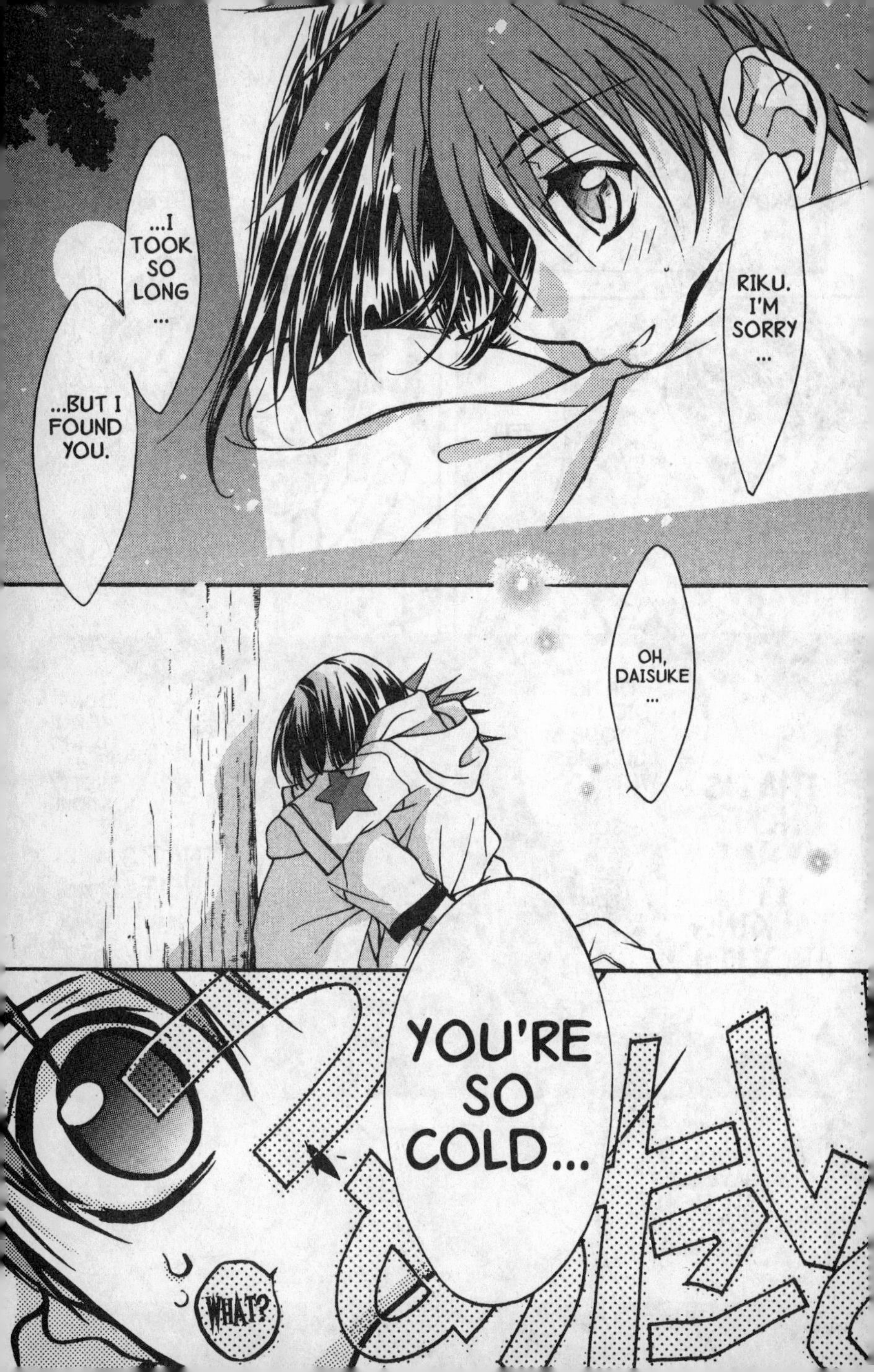
RIKU. I'M SORRY ...
...I TOOK SO LONG ...
...BUT I FOUND YOU.
OH, DAISUKE ...
YOU'RE SO COLD...
WHAT?

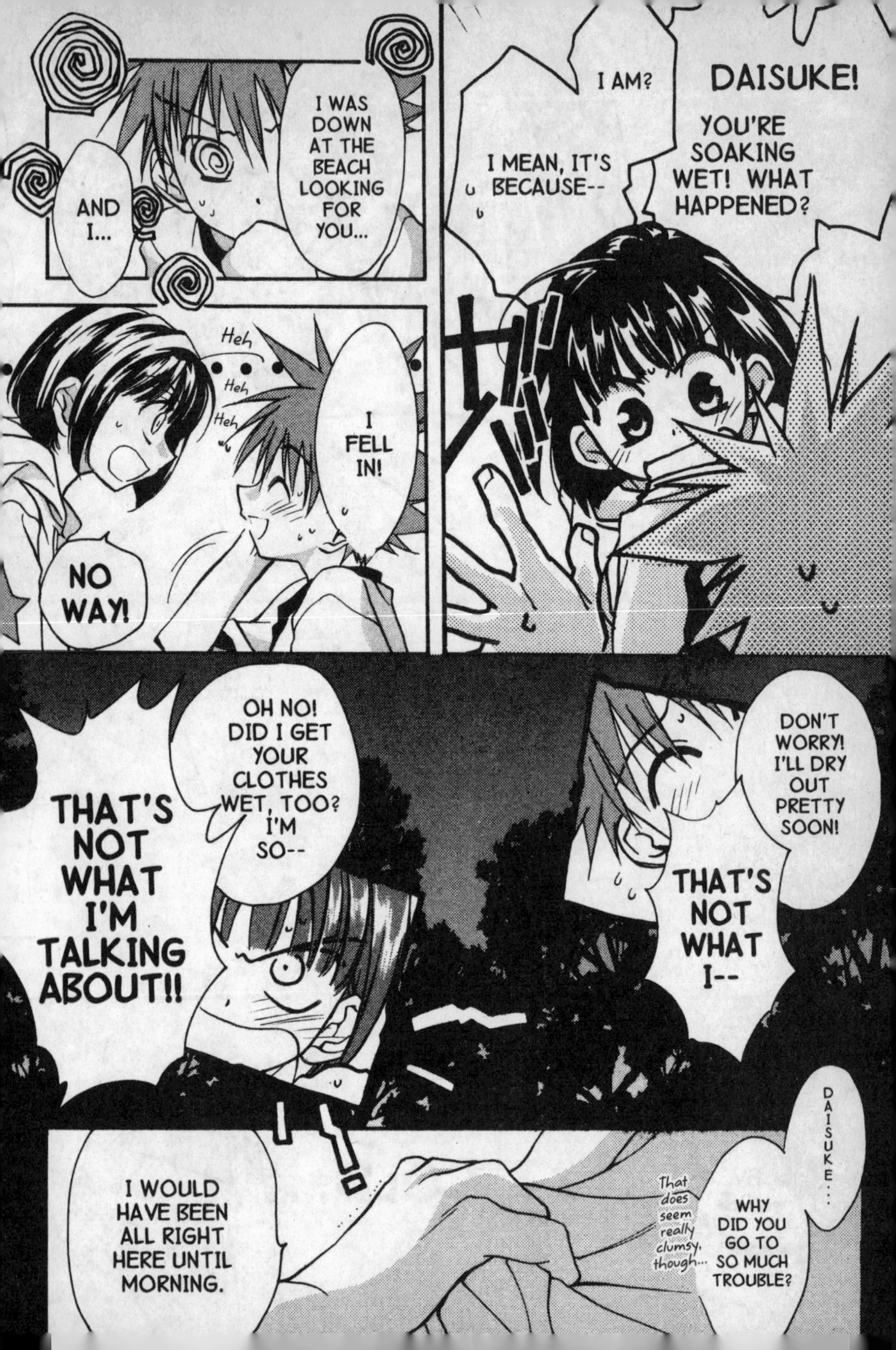
DAISUKE!
YOU'RE SOAKING WET! WHAT HAPPENED?
I AM?
I MEAN, IT'S BECAUSE--
I WAS DOWN AT THE BEACH LOOKING FOR YOU...
AND I...
I FELL IN!
Heh Heh Heh
NO WAY!
DON'T WORRY! I'LL DRY OUT PRETTY SOON!
THAT'S NOT WHAT I--
OH NO! DID I GET YOUR CLOTHES WET, TOO? I'M SO--
THAT'S NOT WHAT I'M TALKING ABOUT!!
DAISUKE...
WHY DID YOU GO TO SO MUCH TROUBLE?
That does seem really clumsy, though...
I WOULD HAVE BEEN ALL RIGHT HERE UNTIL MORNING.

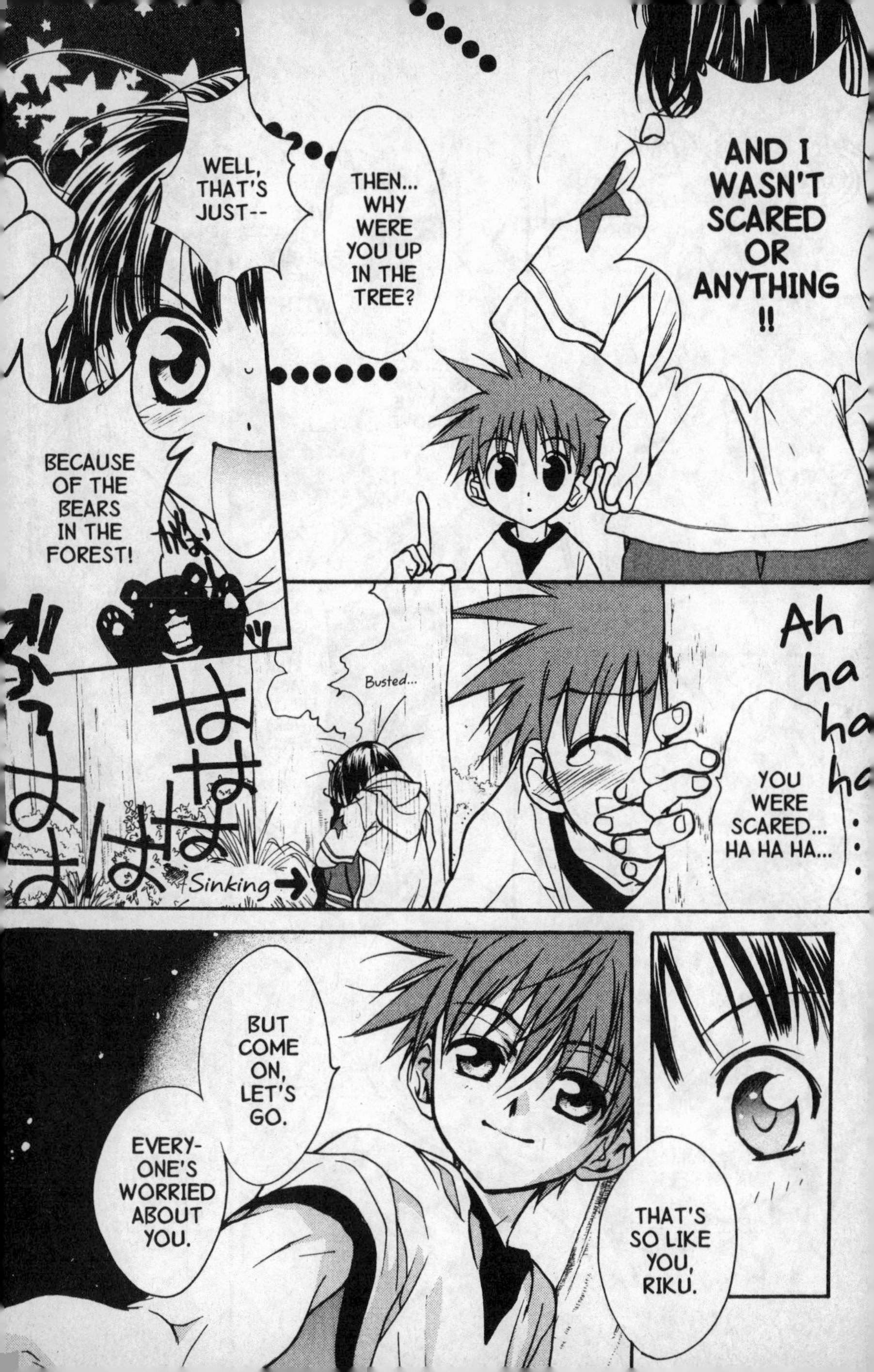
AND I WASN'T SCARED OR ANYTHING !!
THEN... WHY WERE YOU UP IN THE TREE?
WELL, THAT'S JUST--
BECAUSE OF THE BEARS IN THE FOREST!
Ah ha ha ha
YOU WERE SCARED... HA HA HA...
Busted...
Sinking
THAT'S SO LIKE YOU, RIKU.
BUT COME ON, LET'S GO.
EVERY-ONE'S WORRIED ABOUT YOU.

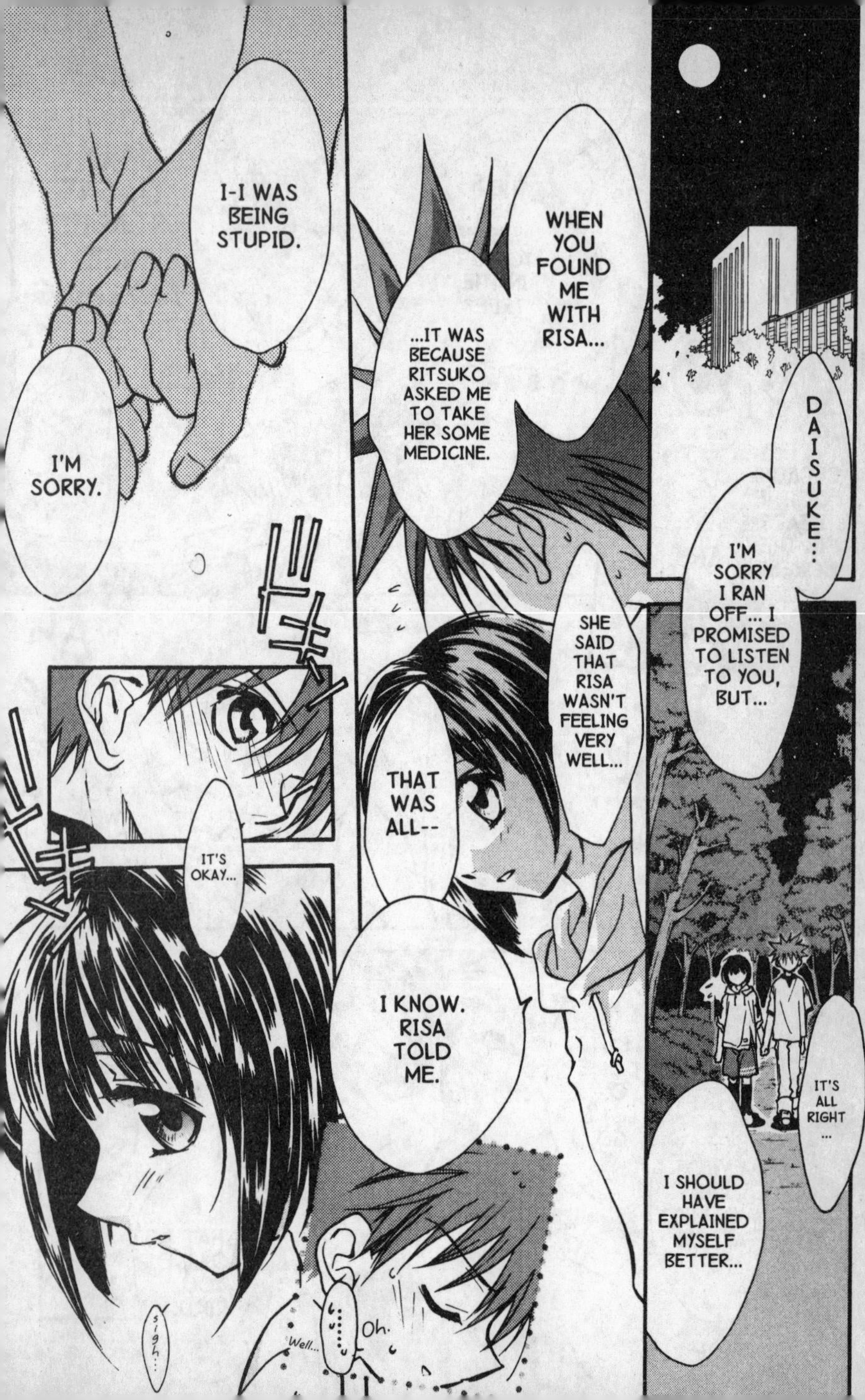
DAISUKE...
I'M SORRY I RAN OFF... I PROMISED TO LISTEN TO YOU, BUT...
IT'S ALL RIGHT...
I SHOULD HAVE EXPLAINED MYSELF BETTER...
WHEN YOU FOUND ME WITH RISA...
...IT WAS BECAUSE RITSUKO ASKED ME TO TAKE HER SOME MEDICINE.
SHE SAID THAT RISA WASN'T FEELING VERY WELL...
THAT WAS ALL--
I KNOW. RISA TOLD ME.
Oh.
Well...
I-I WAS BEING STUPID.
I'M SORRY.
IT'S OKAY...
sigh...

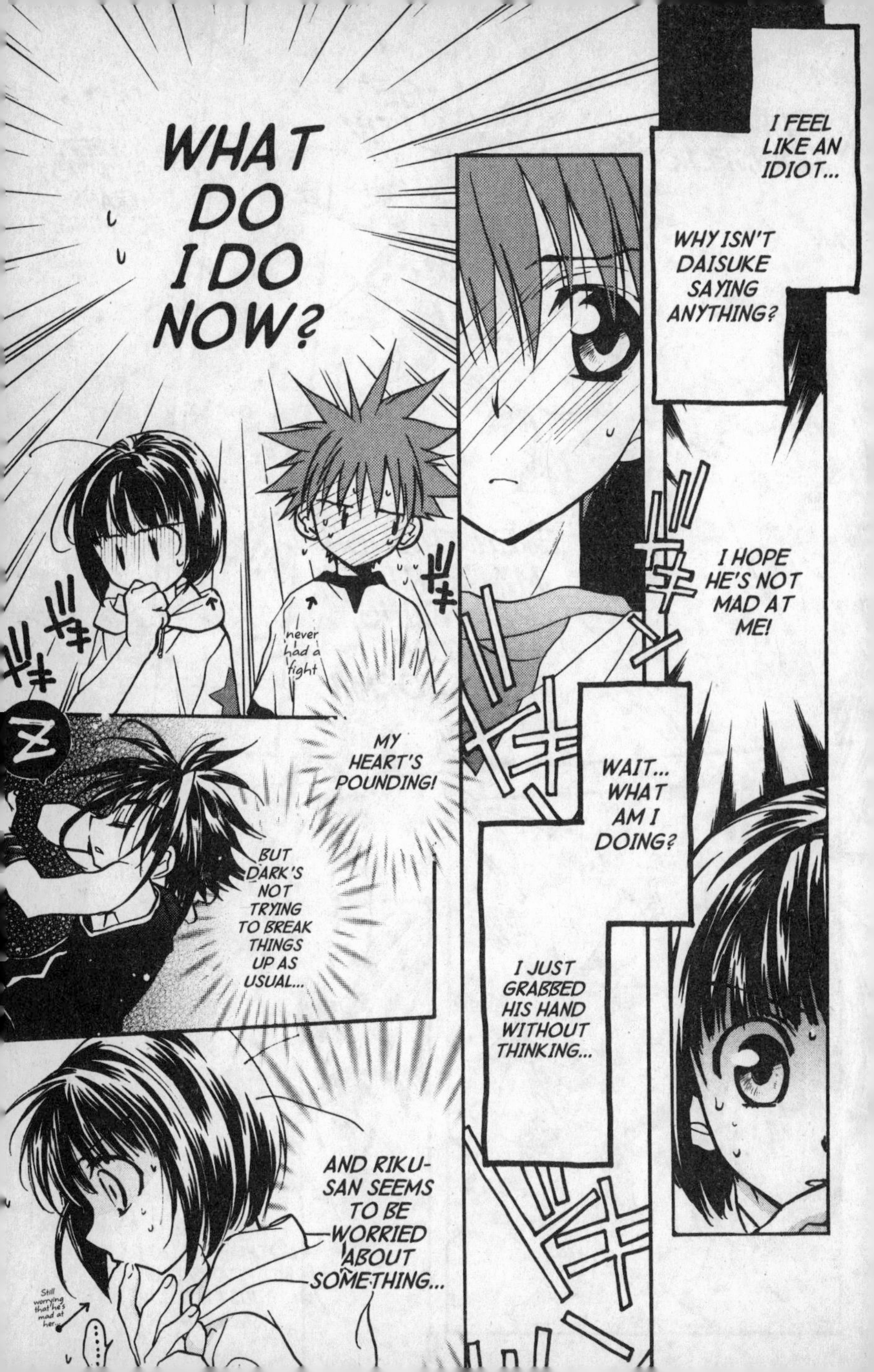
I FEEL LIKE AN IDIOT...
WHY ISN'T DAISUKE SAYING ANYTHING?
I HOPE HE'S NOT MAD AT ME!
WAIT... WHAT AM I DOING?
I JUST GRABBED HIS HAND WITHOUT THINKING...
WHAT DO I DO NOW?
never had a fight
MY HEART'S POUNDING!
BUT DARK'S NOT TRYING TO BREAK THINGS UP AS USUAL...
AND RIKU-SAN SEEMS TO BE WORRIED ABOUT SOMETHING...
Still worrying that he's mad at her.

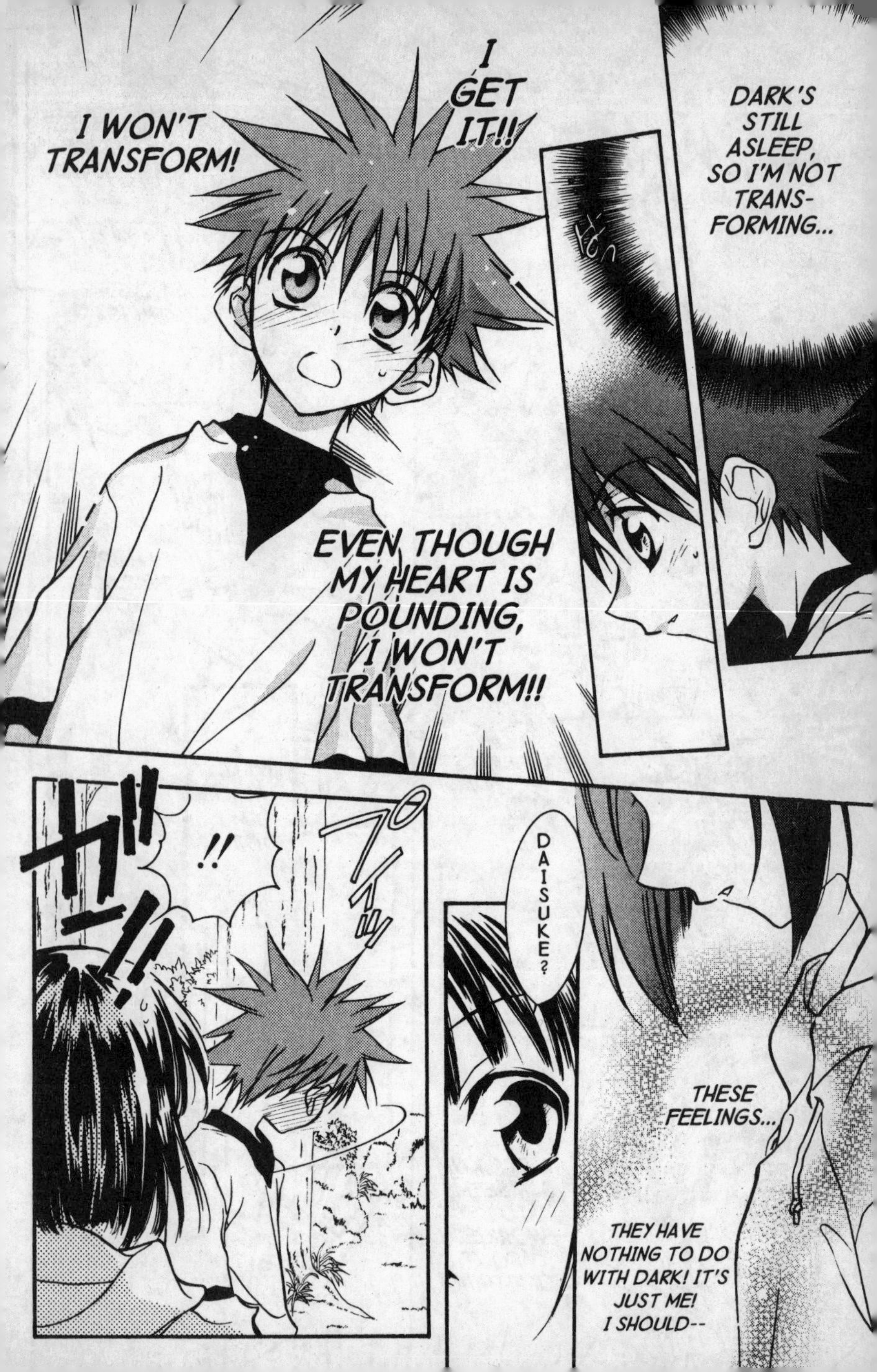
DARK'S STILL ASLEEP, SO I'M NOT TRANS-FORMING...
I GET IT!!
I WON'T TRANSFORM!
EVEN THOUGH MY HEART IS POUNDING, I WON'T TRANSFORM!!
DAISUKE?
THESE FEELINGS...
THEY HAVE NOTHING TO DO WITH DARK! IT'S JUST ME! I SHOULD--
!!

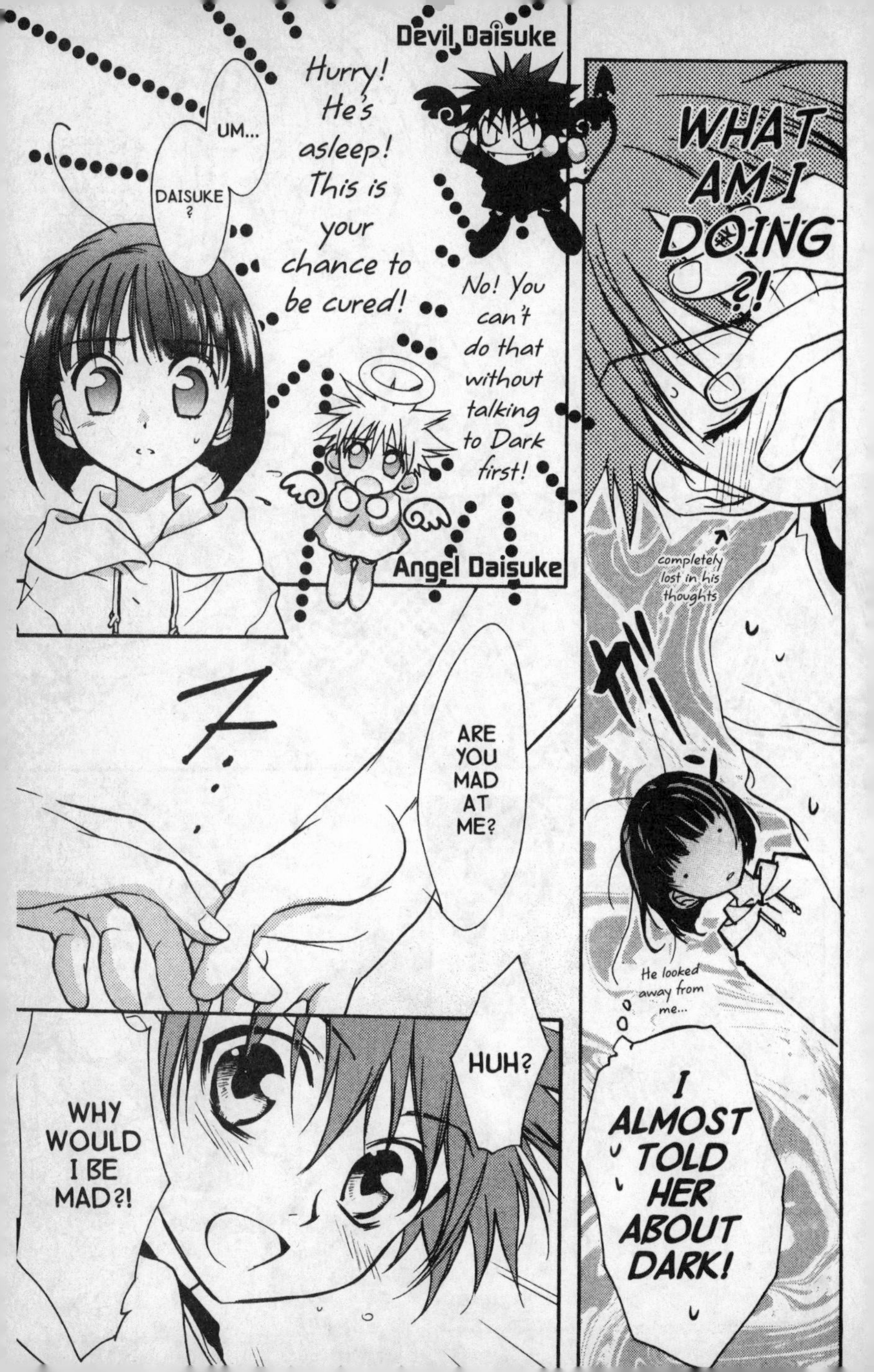
WHAT AM I DOING ?!
completely lost in his thoughts
He looked away from me...
I ALMOST TOLD HER ABOUT DARK!
Devil Daisuke
Hurry! He's asleep! This is your chance to be cured!
No! You can't do that without talking to Dark first!
Angel Daisuke
UM...
DAISUKE ?
ARE YOU MAD AT ME?
HUH?
WHY WOULD I BE MAD?!

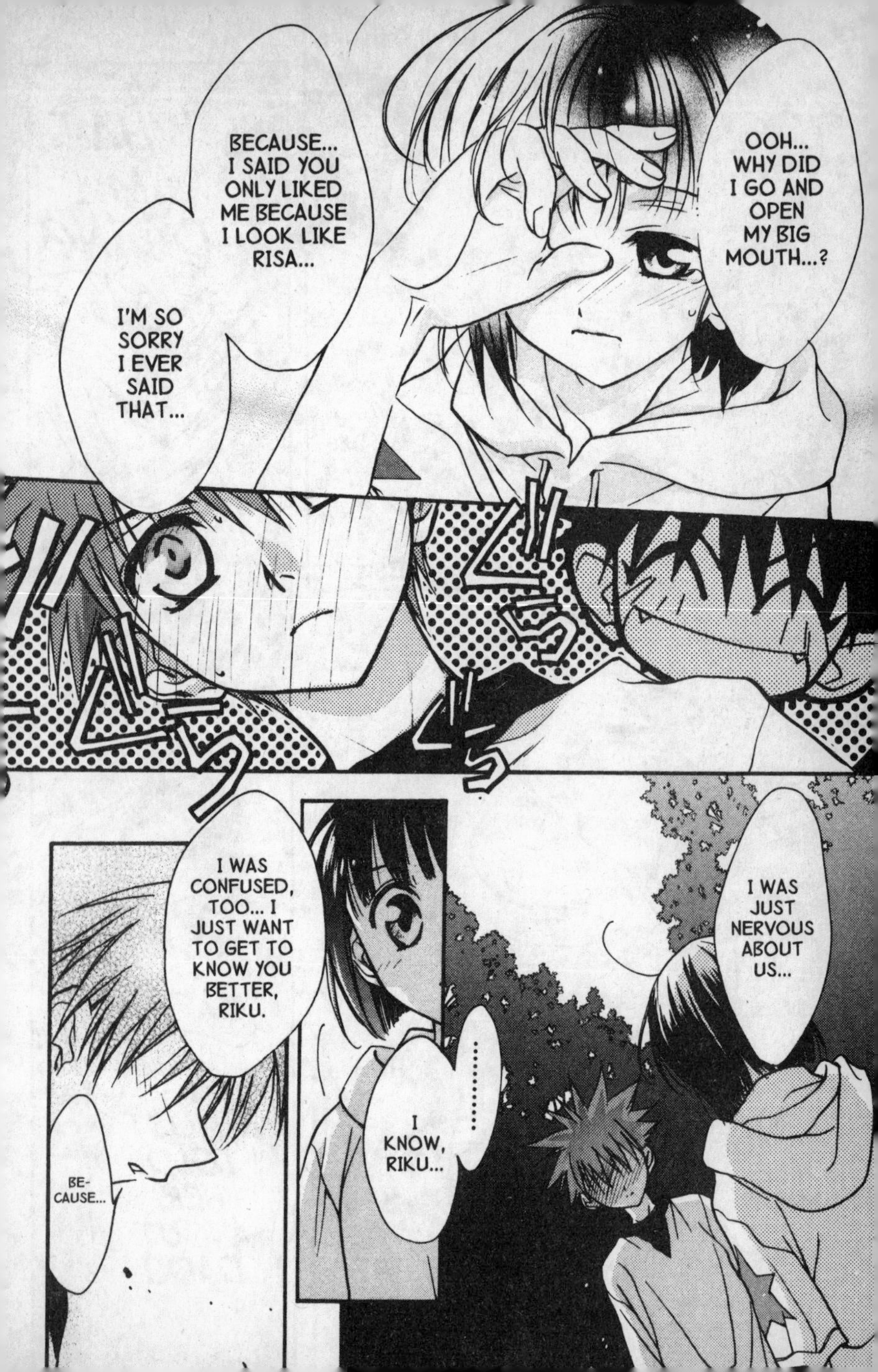
OOH... WHY DID I GO AND OPEN MY BIG MOUTH...?
BECAUSE... I SAID YOU ONLY LIKED ME BECAUSE I LOOK LIKE RISA...
I'M SO SORRY I EVER SAID THAT...
I WAS JUST NERVOUS ABOUT US...
......
I KNOW, RIKU...
I WAS CONFUSED, TOO... I JUST WANT TO GET TO KNOW YOU BETTER, RIKU.
BE-CAUSE...

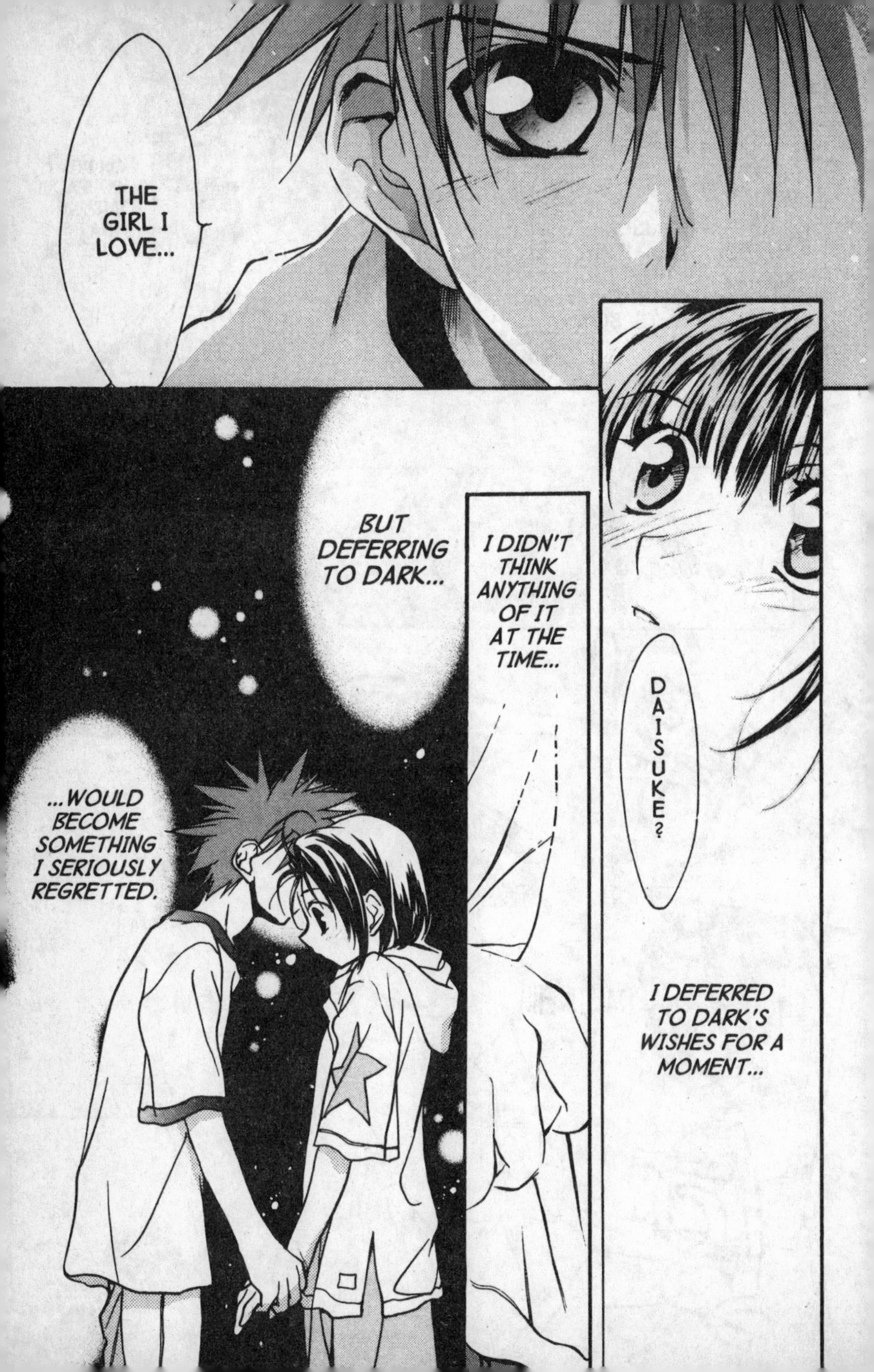
THE GIRL I LOVE...
DAISUKE?
I DEFERRED TO DARK'S WISHES FOR A MOMENT...
I DIDN'T THINK ANYTHING OF IT AT THE TIME...
BUT DEFERRING TO DARK...
...WOULD BECOME SOMETHING I SERIOUSLY REGRETTED.

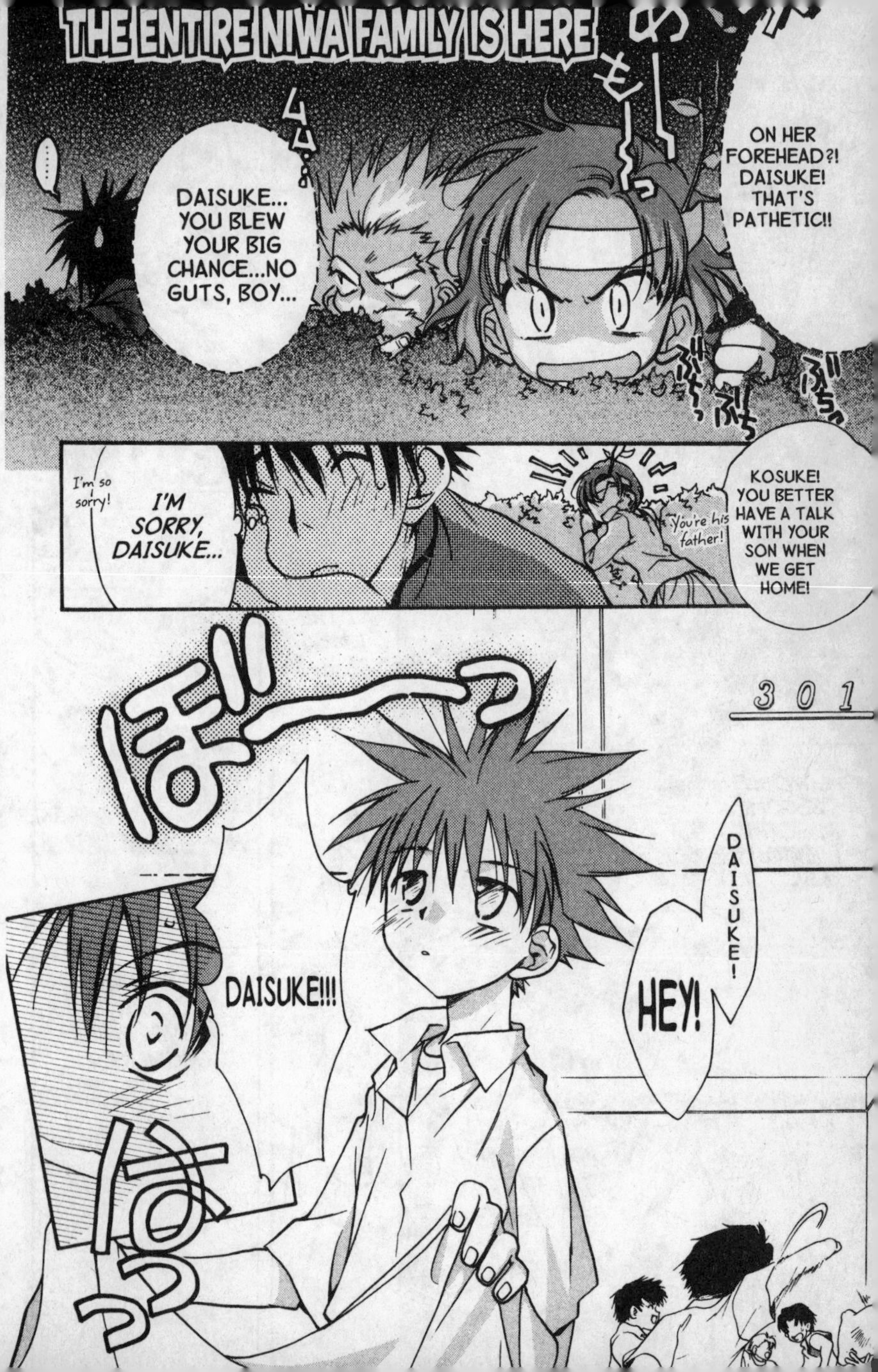
THE ENTIRE NIWA FAMILY IS HERE
ON HER FOREHEAD?! DAISUKE! THAT'S PATHETIC!!
DAISUKE... YOU BLEW YOUR BIG CHANCE...NO GUTS, BOY...
......
KOSUKE! YOU BETTER HAVE A TALK WITH YOUR SON WHEN WE GET HOME!
You're his father!
I'M SORRY, DAISUKE...
I'm so sorry!
301
DAISUKE!
HEY!
DAISUKE!!!

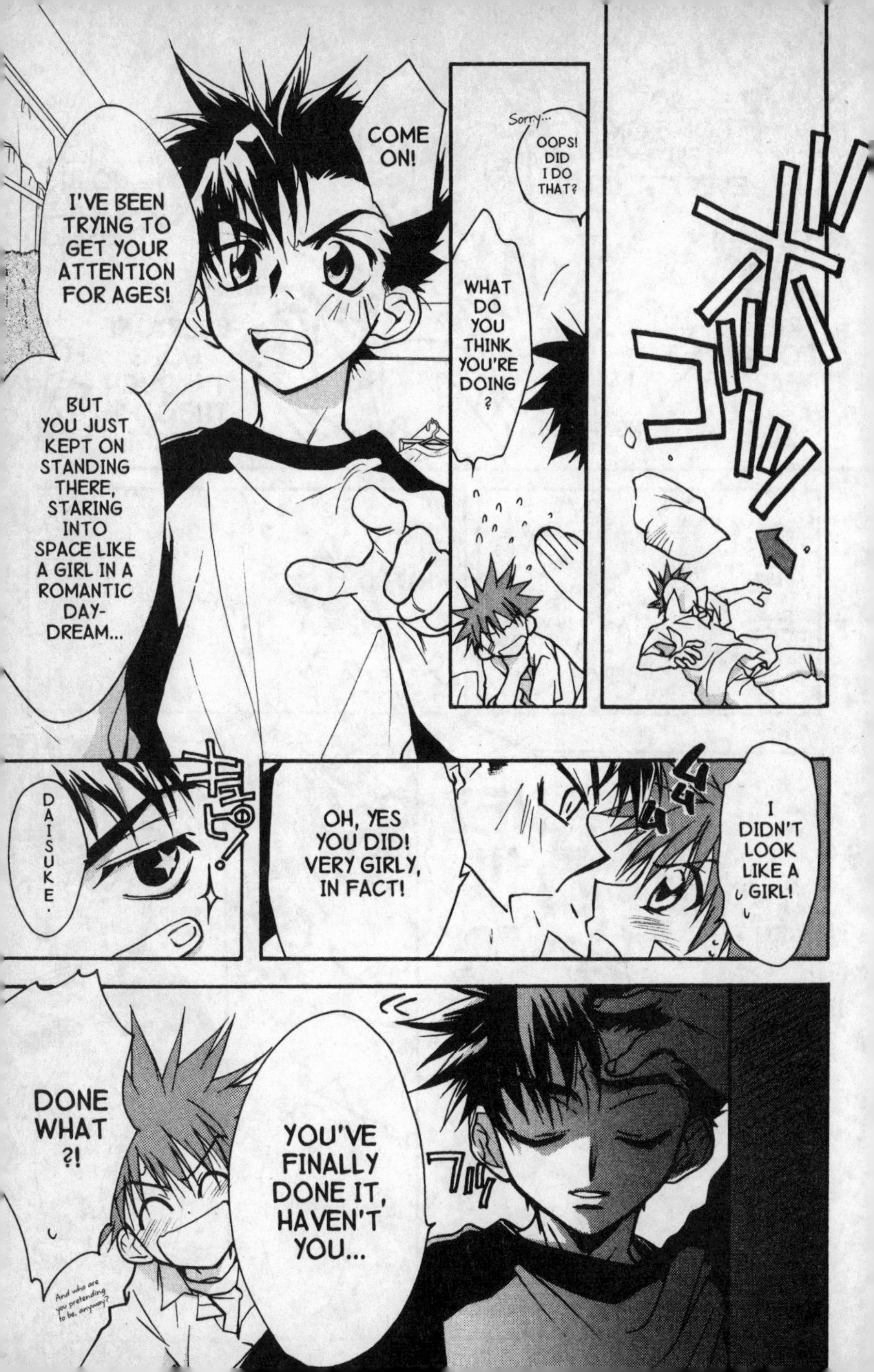
Sorry...
OOPS! DID I DO THAT?
WHAT DO YOU THINK YOU'RE DOING?
COME ON!
I'VE BEEN TRYING TO GET YOUR ATTENTION FOR AGES!
BUT YOU JUST KEPT ON STANDING THERE, STARING INTO SPACE LIKE A GIRL IN A ROMANTIC DAY-DREAM...
I DIDN'T LOOK LIKE A GIRL!
OH, YES YOU DID! VERY GIRLY, IN FACT!
DAISUKE.
YOU'VE FINALLY DONE IT, HAVEN'T YOU...
DONE WHAT?!
And who are you pretending to be, anyway?

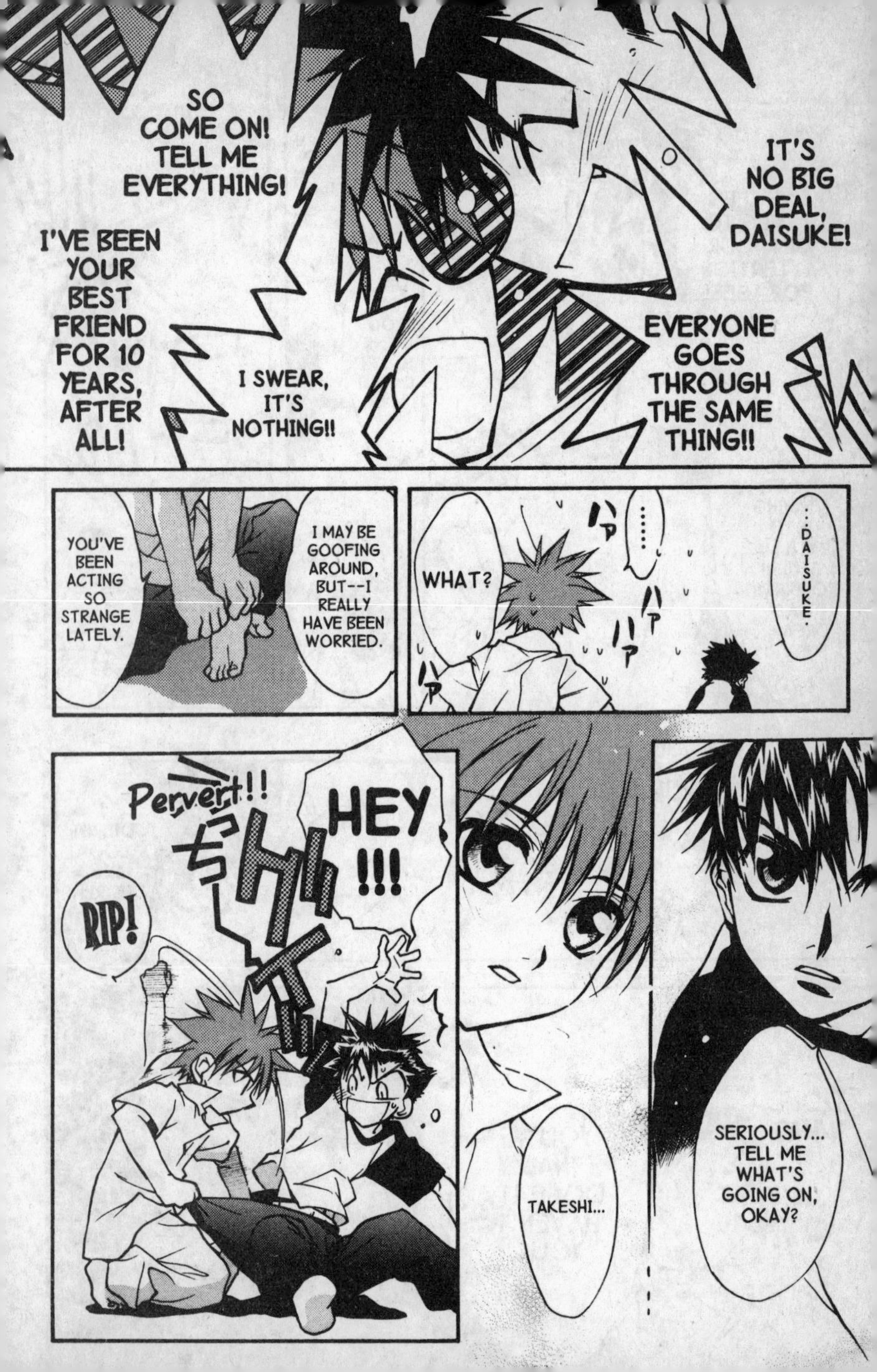
IT'S NO BIG DEAL, DAISUKE!
EVERYONE GOES THROUGH THE SAME THING!!
SO COME ON! TELL ME EVERYTHING!
I SWEAR, IT'S NOTHING!!
I'VE BEEN YOUR BEST FRIEND FOR 10 YEARS, AFTER ALL!
...DAISUKE.
......
WHAT?
I MAY BE GOOFING AROUND, BUT--I REALLY HAVE BEEN WORRIED.
YOU'VE BEEN ACTING SO STRANGE LATELY.
SERIOUSLY... TELL ME WHAT'S GOING ON, OKAY?
TAKESHI...
HEY !!!
Pervert!!
RIP!

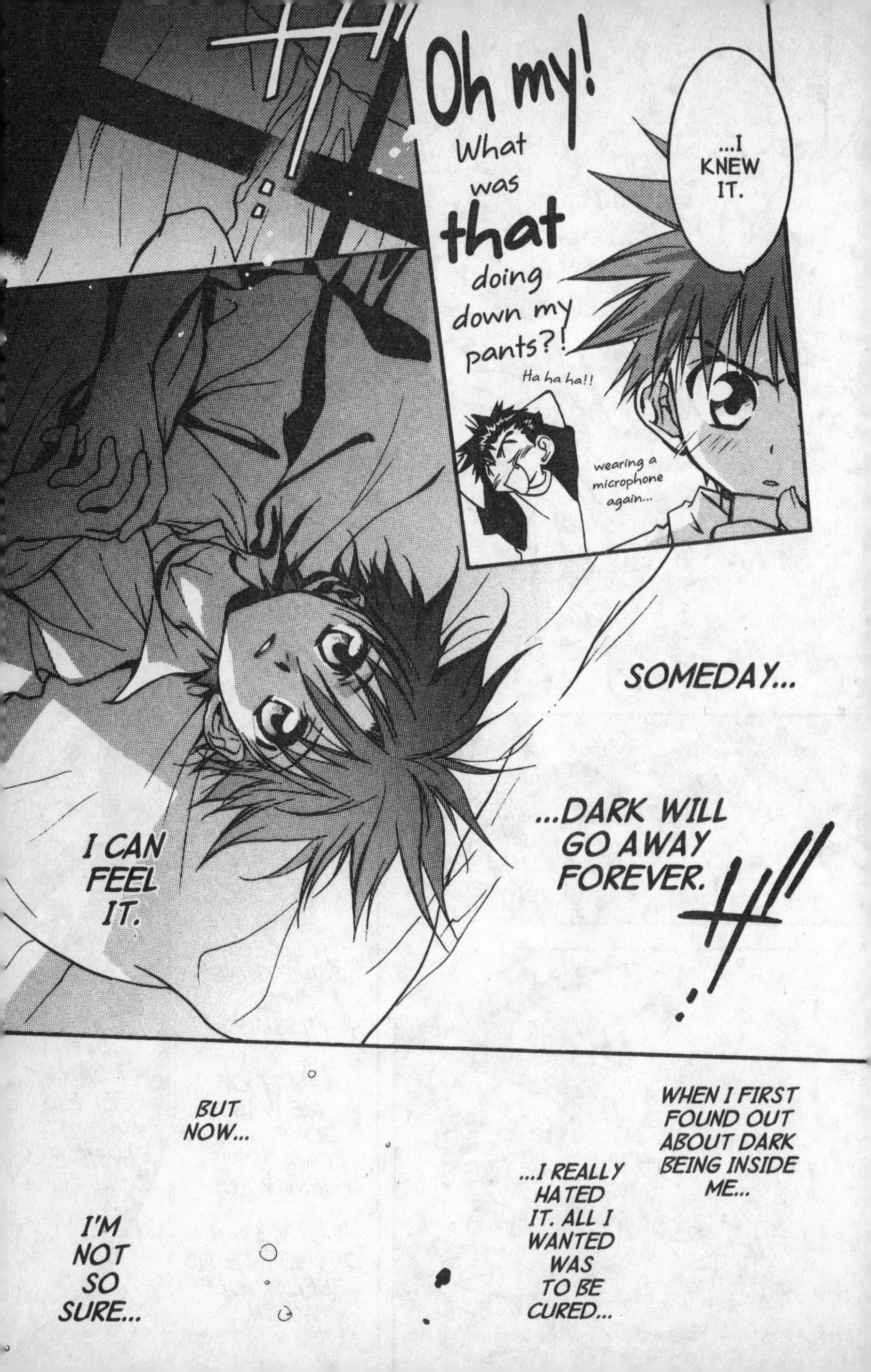
...I KNEW IT.
Oh my!
What was that doing down my pants?!
Ha ha ha!!
wearing a microphone again...
SOMEDAY...
...DARK WILL GO AWAY FOREVER.
I CAN FEEL IT.
WHEN I FIRST FOUND OUT ABOUT DARK BEING INSIDE ME...
...I REALLY HATED IT. ALL I WANTED WAS TO BE CURED...
BUT NOW...
I'M NOT SO SURE...

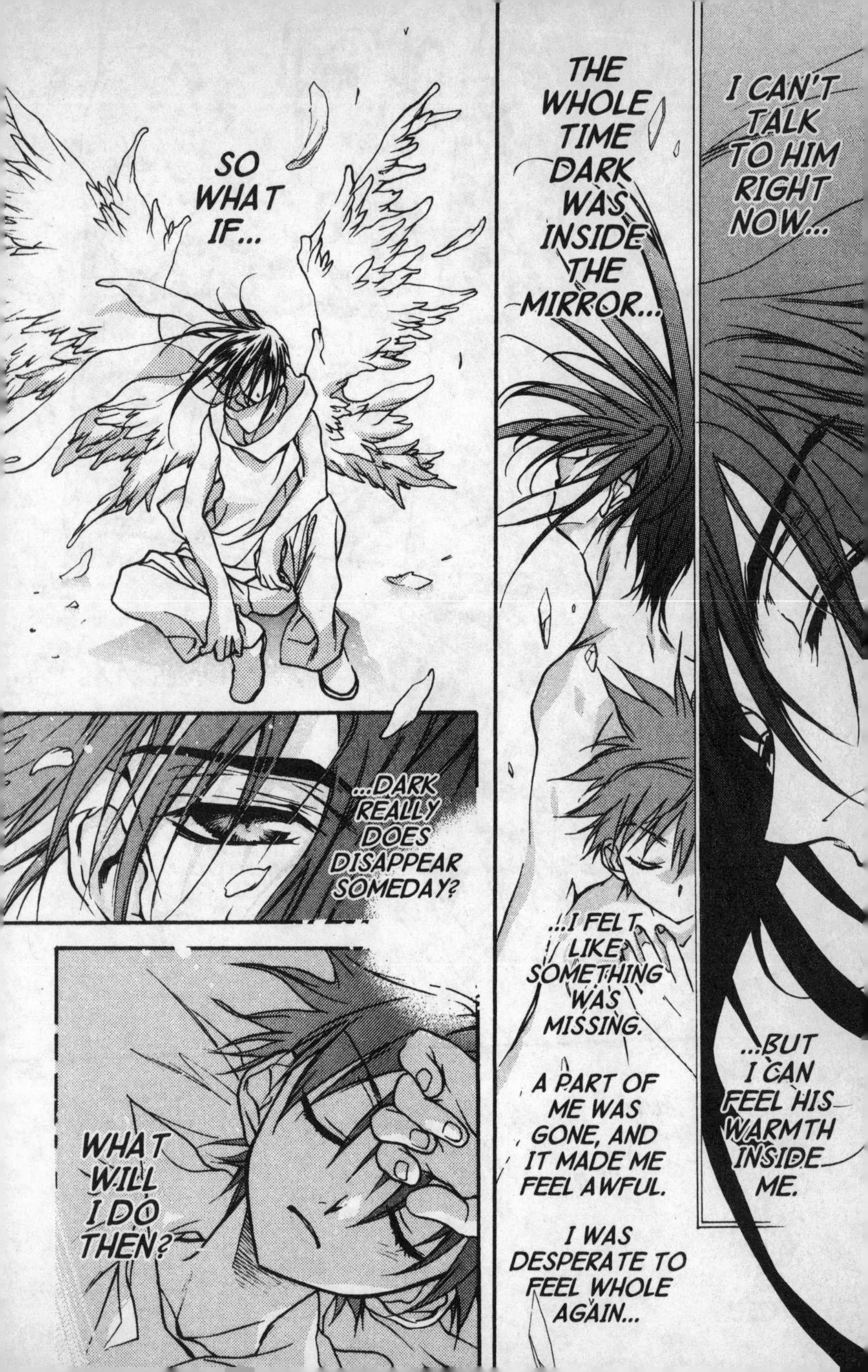
I CAN'T TALK TO HIM RIGHT NOW...
...BUT I CAN FEEL HIS WARMTH INSIDE ME.
THE WHOLE TIME DARK WAS INSIDE THE MIRROR...
...I FELT LIKE SOMETHING WAS MISSING.
A PART OF ME WAS GONE, AND IT MADE ME FEEL AWFUL.
I WAS DESPERATE TO FEEL WHOLE AGAIN...
SO WHAT IF...
...DARK REALLY DOES DISAPPEAR SOMEDAY?
WHAT WILL I DO THEN?

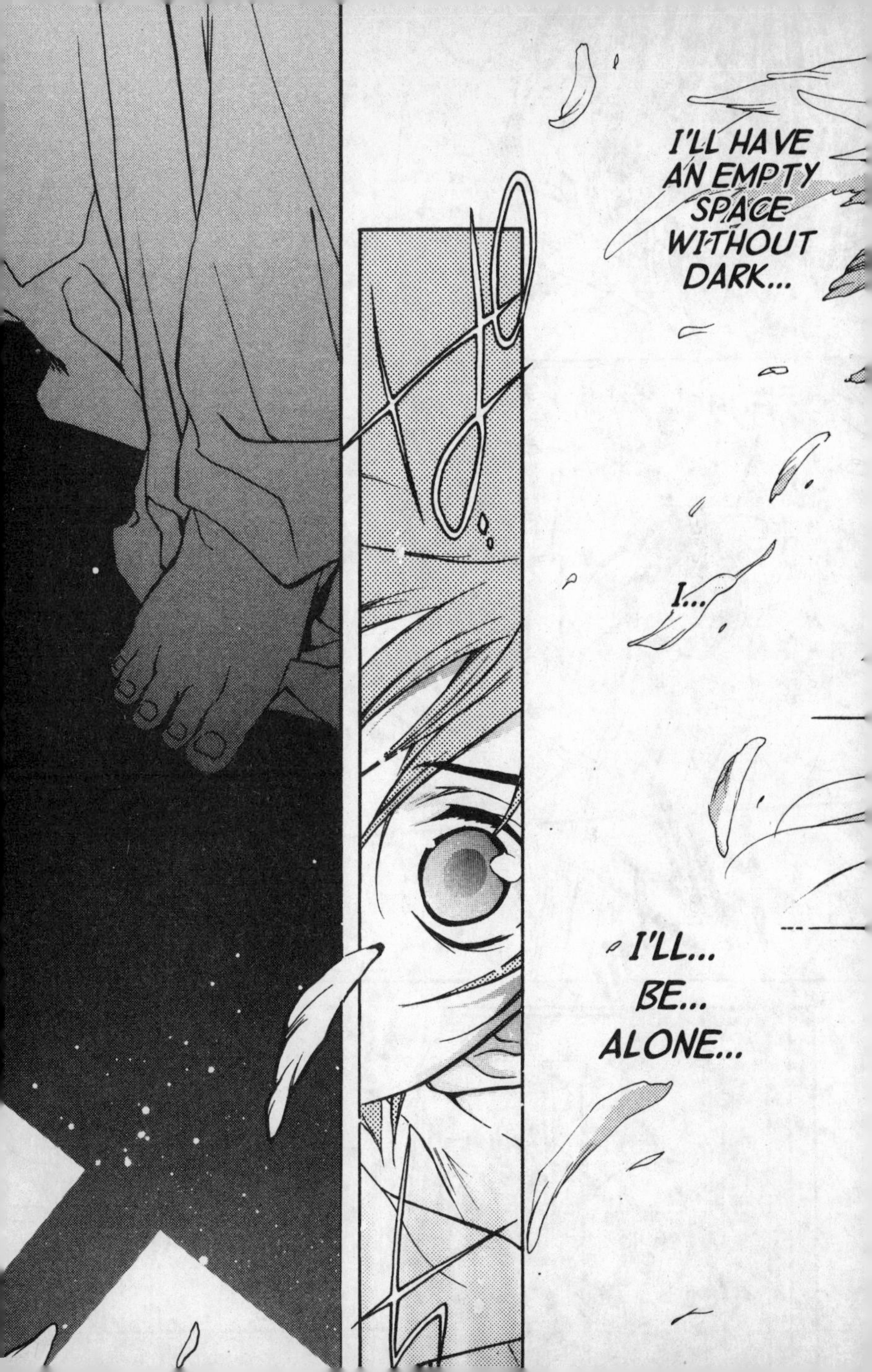
I'LL HAVE AN EMPTY SPACE WITHOUT DARK...
I...
I'LL... BE... ALONE...

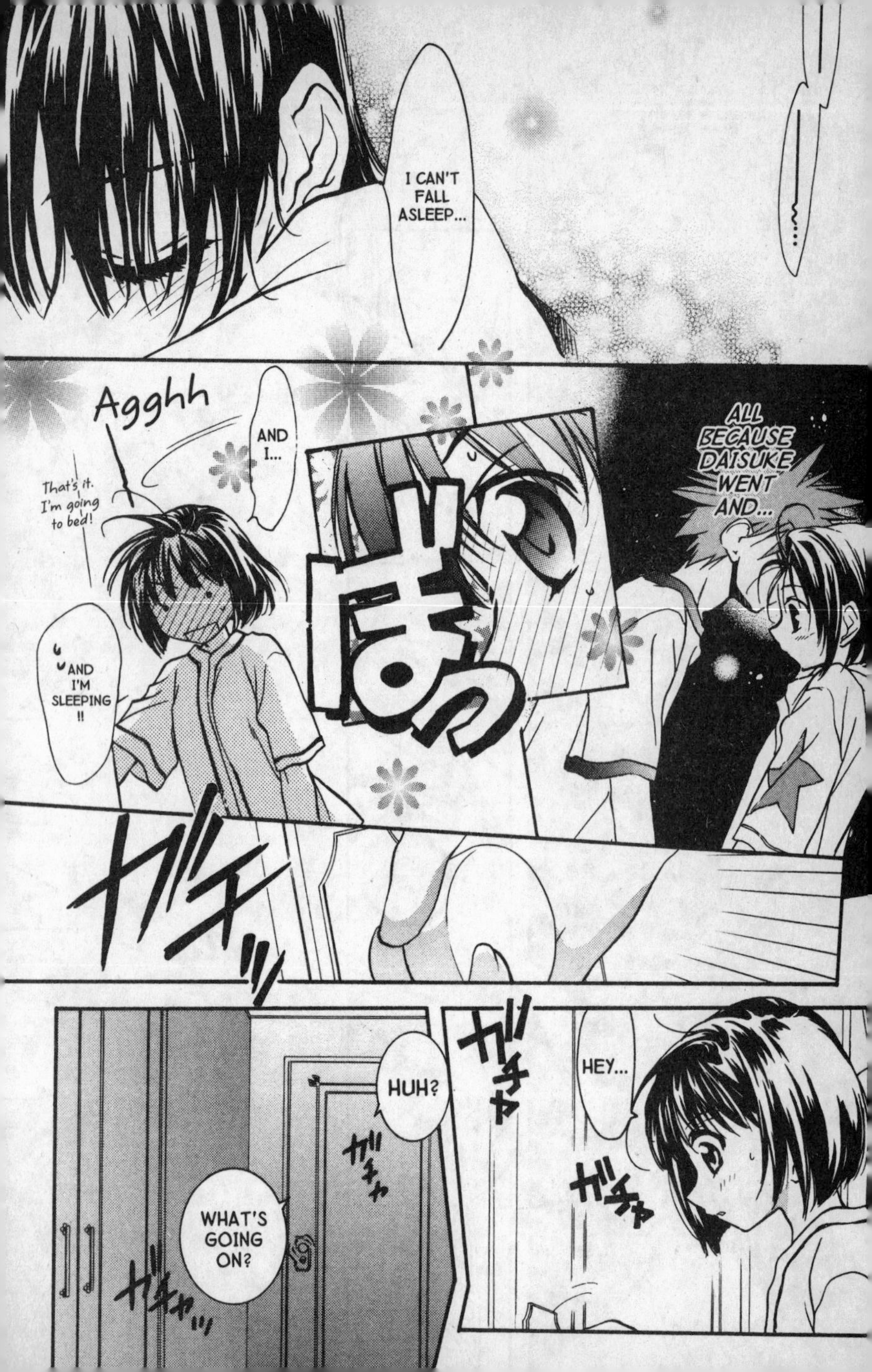
I CAN'T FALL ASLEEP...
ALL BECAUSE DAISUKE WENT AND...
ぼっ
AND I...
Agghh
That's it. I'm going to bed!
AND I'M SLEEPING !!
ガチャッ
HEY...
ガチャ
ガチャ
HUH?
ガチャ
WHAT'S GOING ON?
ガチャッ

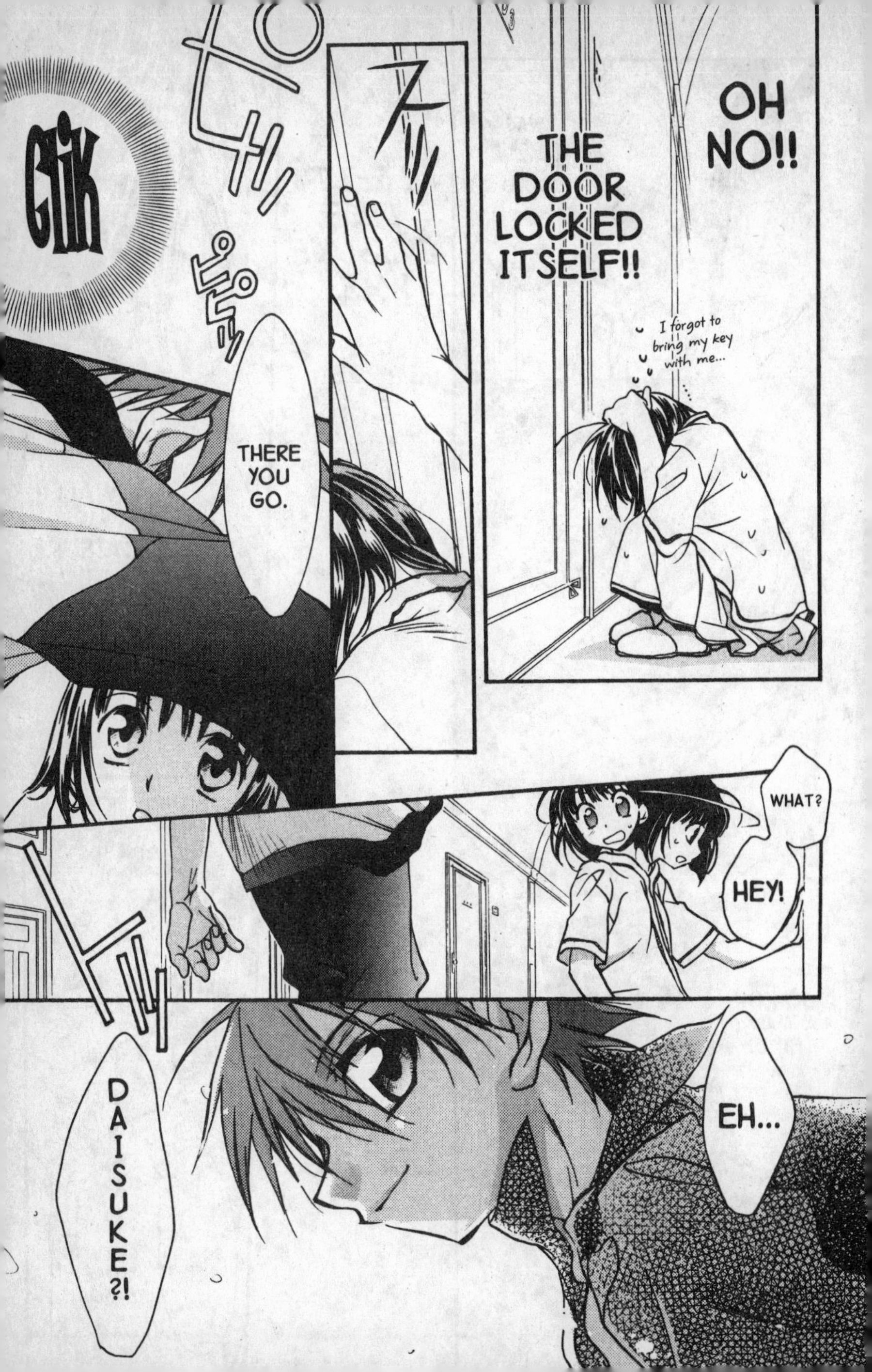
OH NO!!
THE DOOR LOCKED ITSELF!!
I forgot to bring my key with me...
GIK
THERE YOU GO.
WHAT?
HEY!
EH...
DAISUKE?!

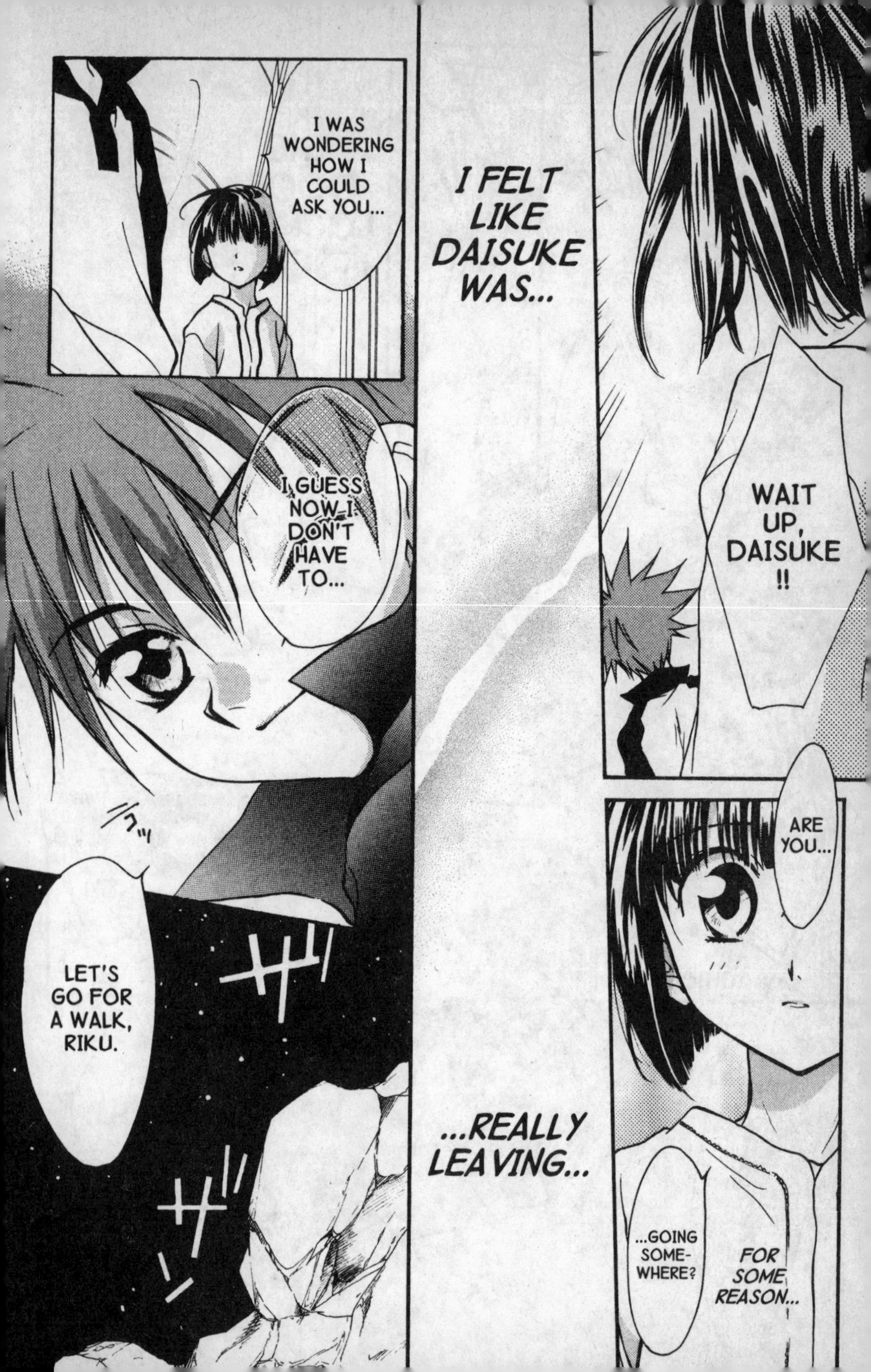
WAIT UP, DAISUKE!!
ARE YOU...
...GOING SOME-WHERE?
FOR SOME REASON...
I FELT LIKE DAISUKE WAS...
...REALLY LEAVING...
I WAS WONDERING HOW I COULD ASK YOU...
I GUESS NOW I DON'T HAVE TO...
LET'S GO FOR A WALK, RIKU.

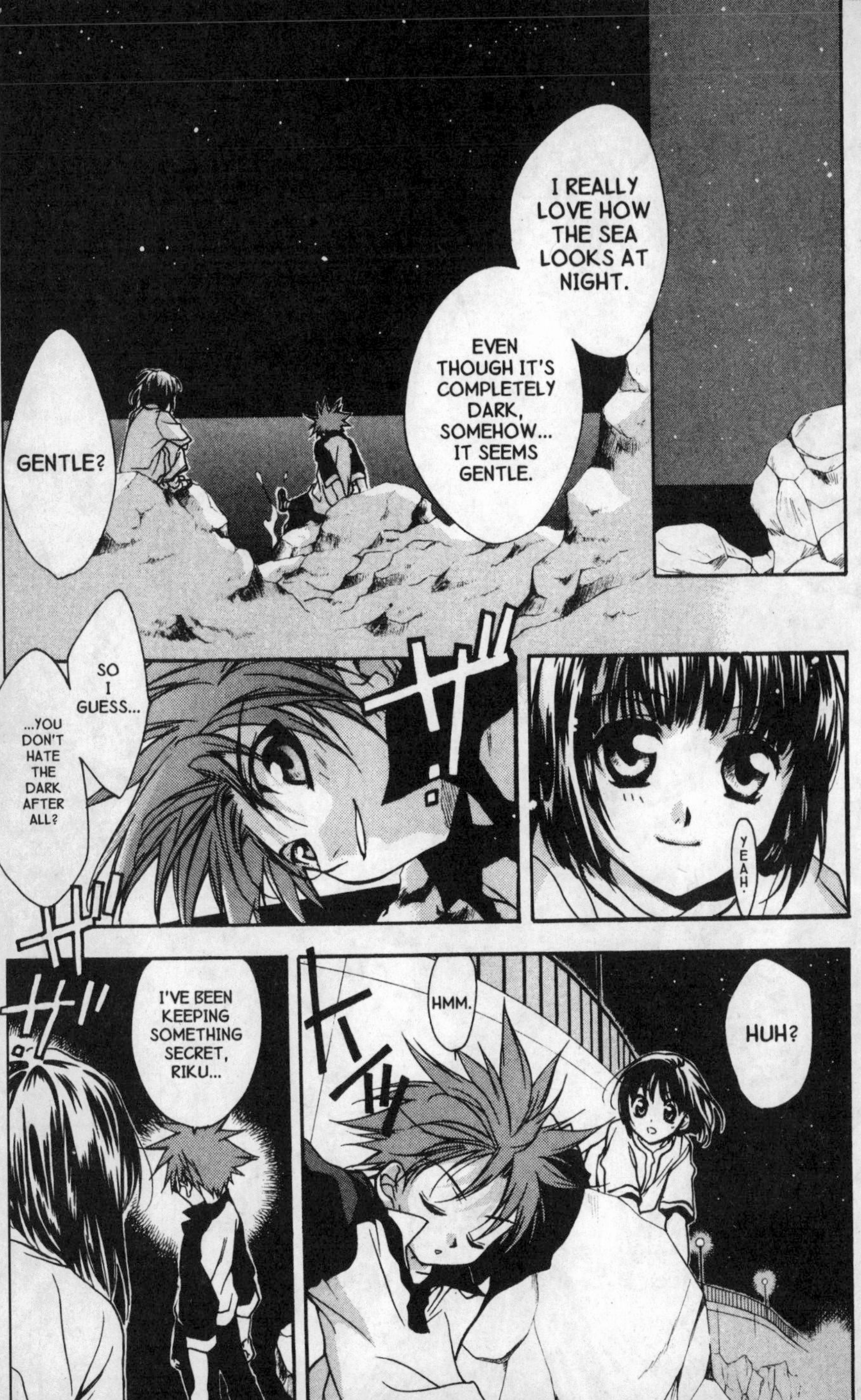
I REALLY LOVE HOW THE SEA LOOKS AT NIGHT.
EVEN THOUGH IT'S COMPLETELY DARK, SOMEHOW... IT SEEMS GENTLE.
GENTLE?
YEAH.
SO I GUESS...
...YOU DON'T HATE THE DARK AFTER ALL?
HUH?
HMM.
I'VE BEEN KEEPING SOMETHING SECRET, RIKU...

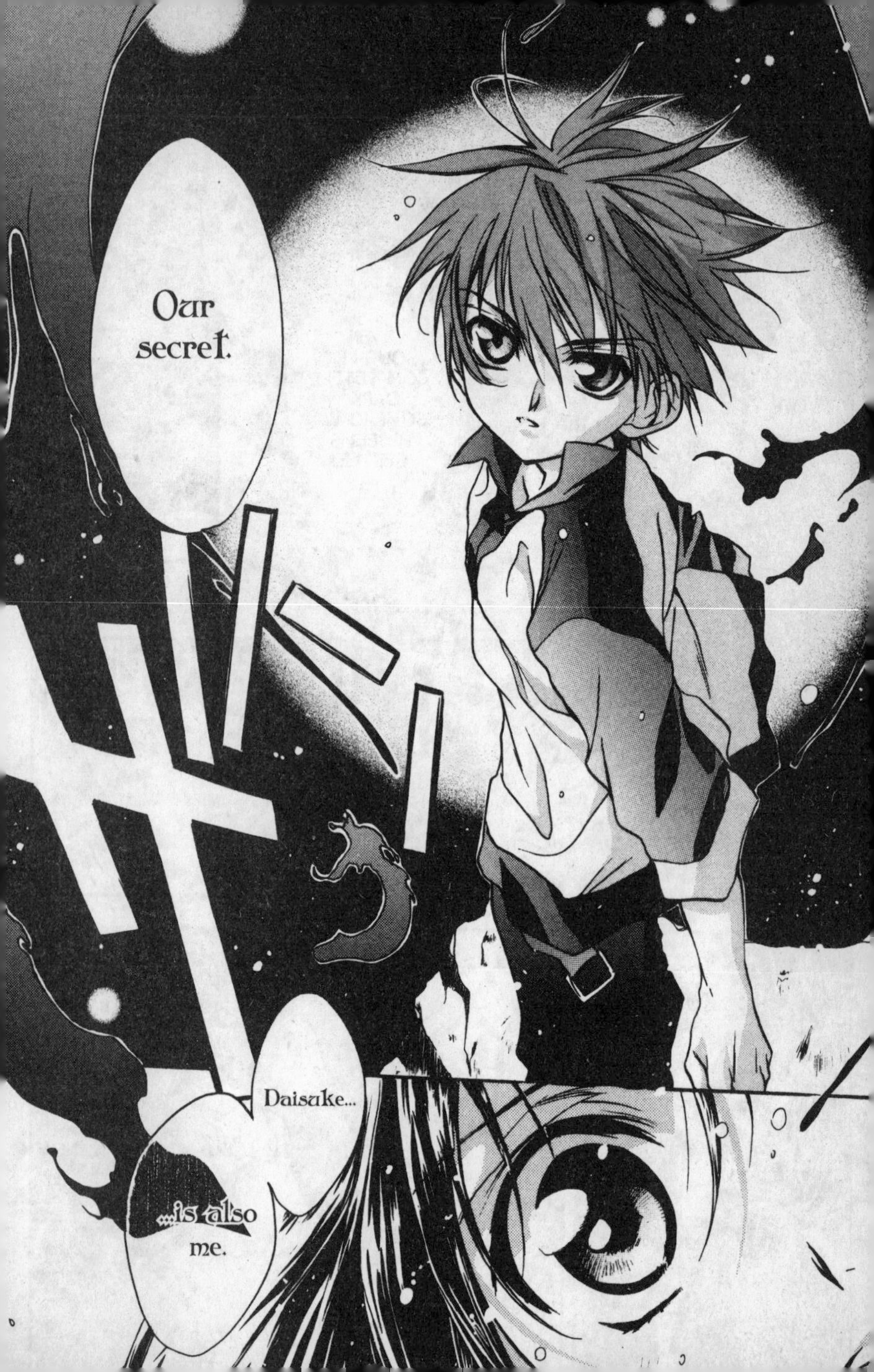
Our secret.
Daisuke...
...is also me.

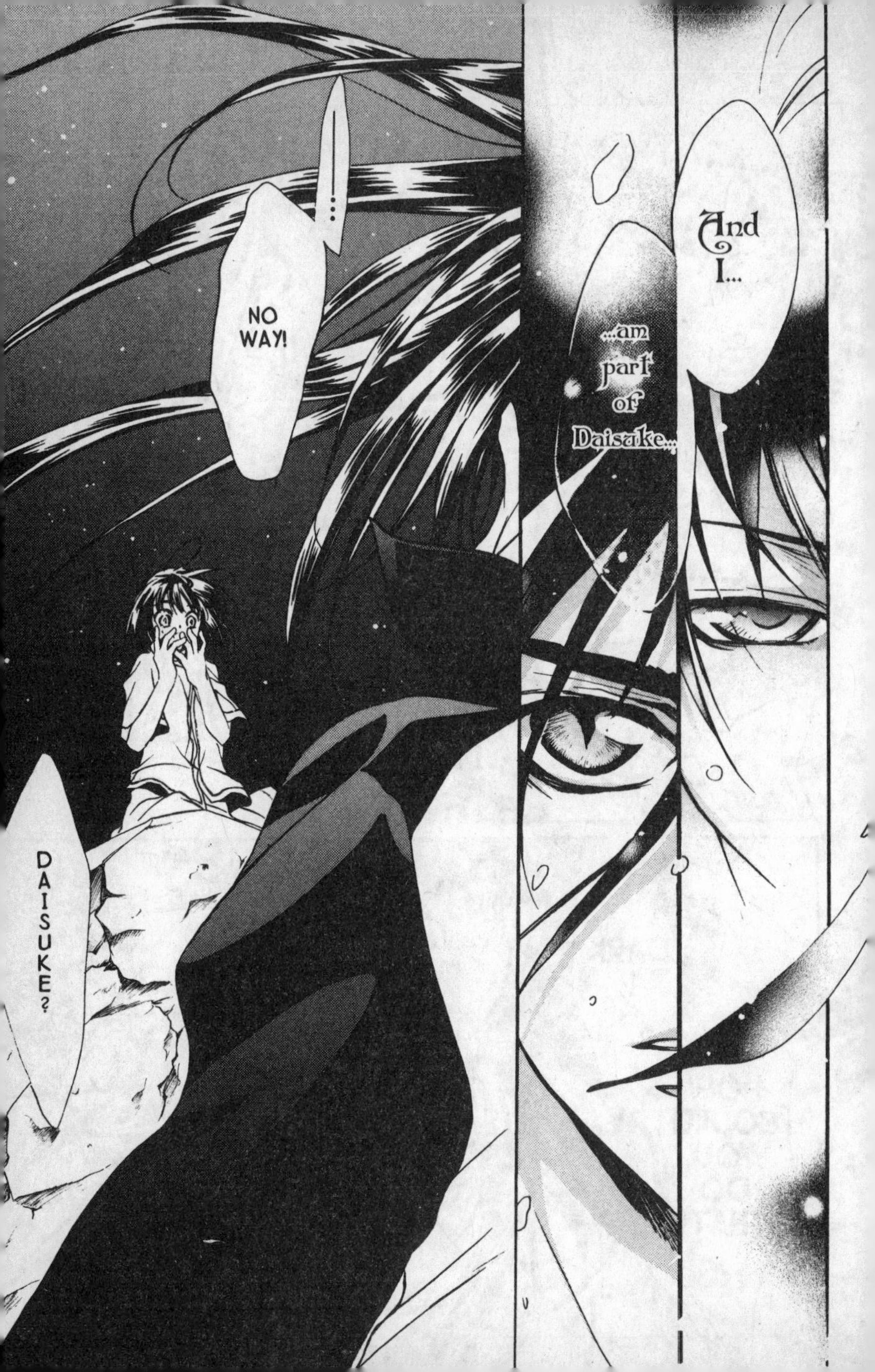
And I...
...am part of Daisuke...
NO WAY!
DAISUKE?

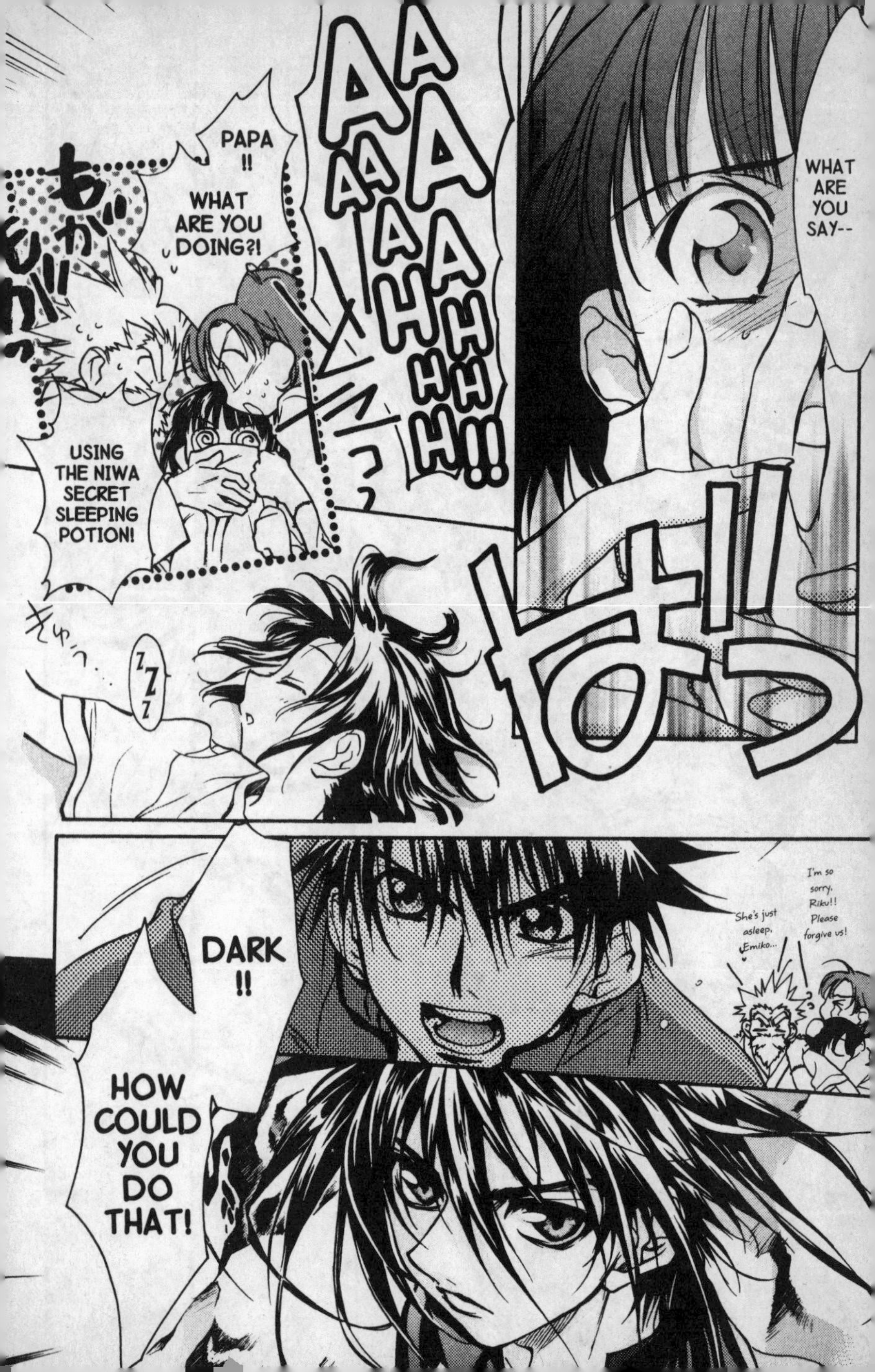
WHAT ARE YOU SAY--
はっ!!
AAAAAHHHHH!!
PAPA!!
WHAT ARE YOU DOING?!
USING THE NIWA SECRET SLEEPING POTION!
ZZZ
I'm so sorry, Riku!! Please forgive us!
She's just asleep, Emiko...
DARK!!
HOW COULD YOU DO THAT!

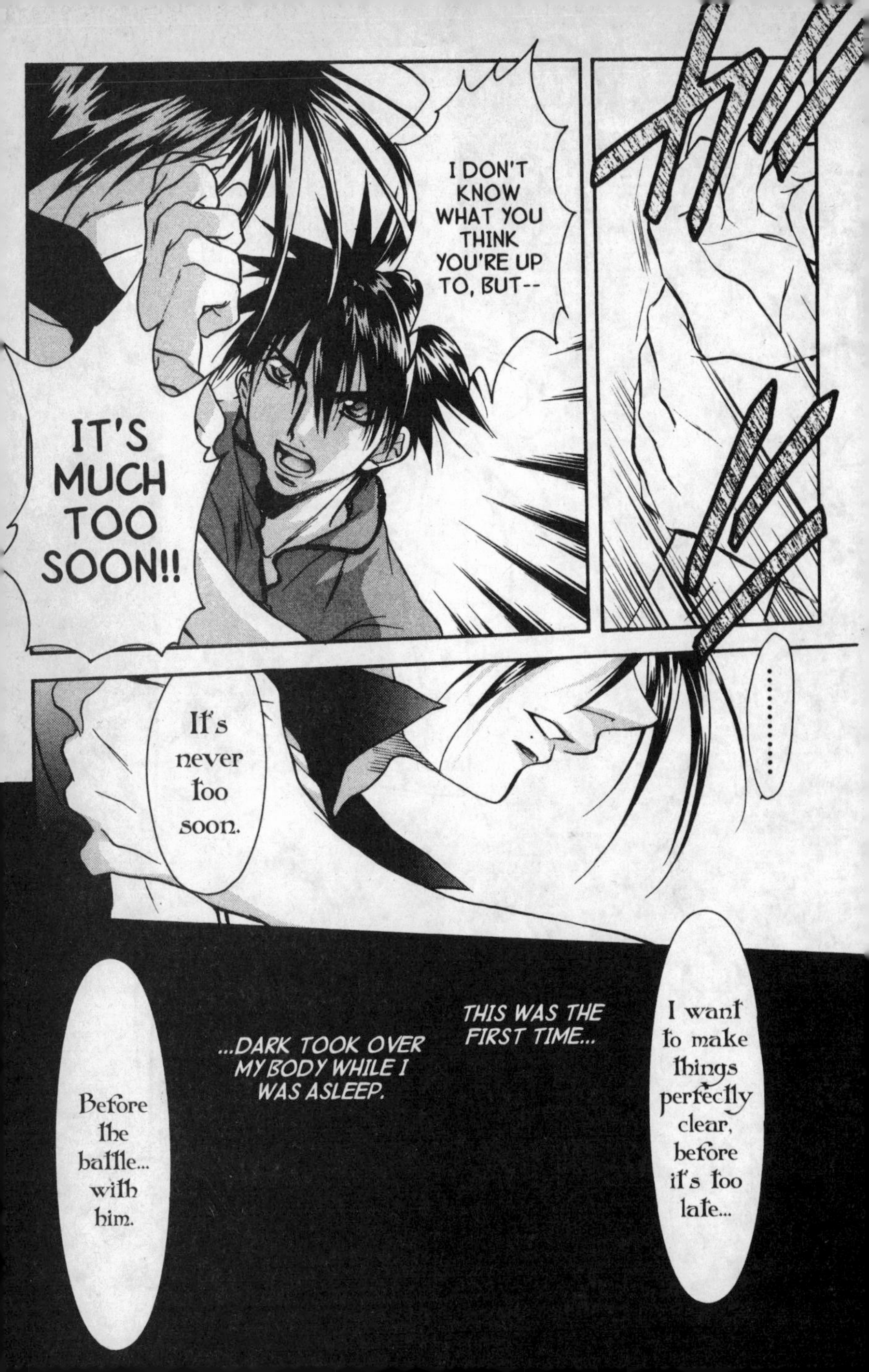
I DON'T KNOW WHAT YOU THINK YOU'RE UP TO, BUT--
IT'S MUCH TOO SOON!!
......
It's never too soon.
I want to make things perfectly clear, before it's too late...
THIS WAS THE FIRST TIME...
...DARK TOOK OVER MY BODY WHILE I WAS ASLEEP.
Before the battle... with him.

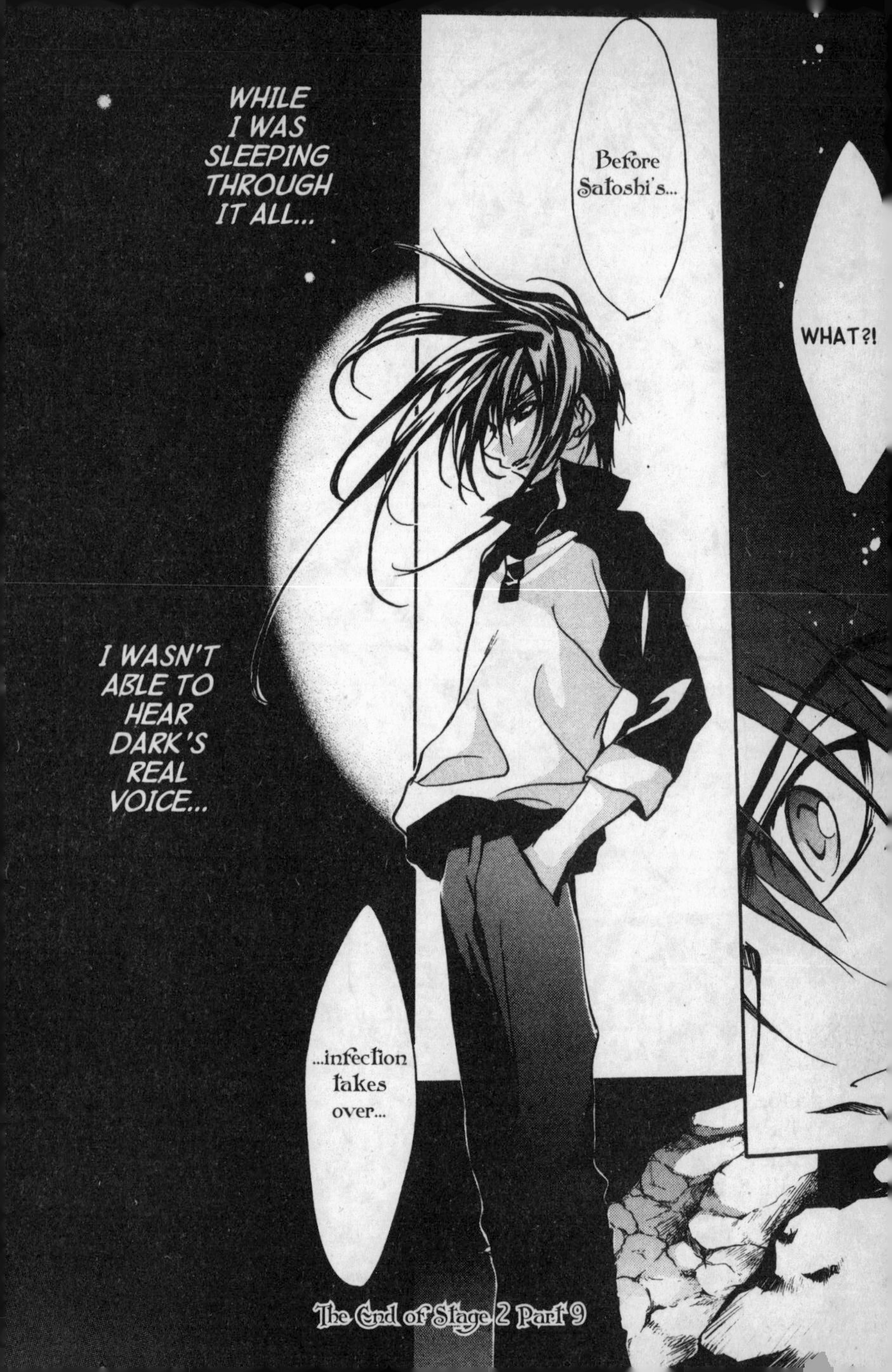
WHAT?!
Before Satoshi's...
...infection takes over...
WHILE I WAS SLEEPING THROUGH IT ALL...
I WASN'T ABLE TO HEAR DARK'S REAL VOICE...
The End of Stage 2 Part 9

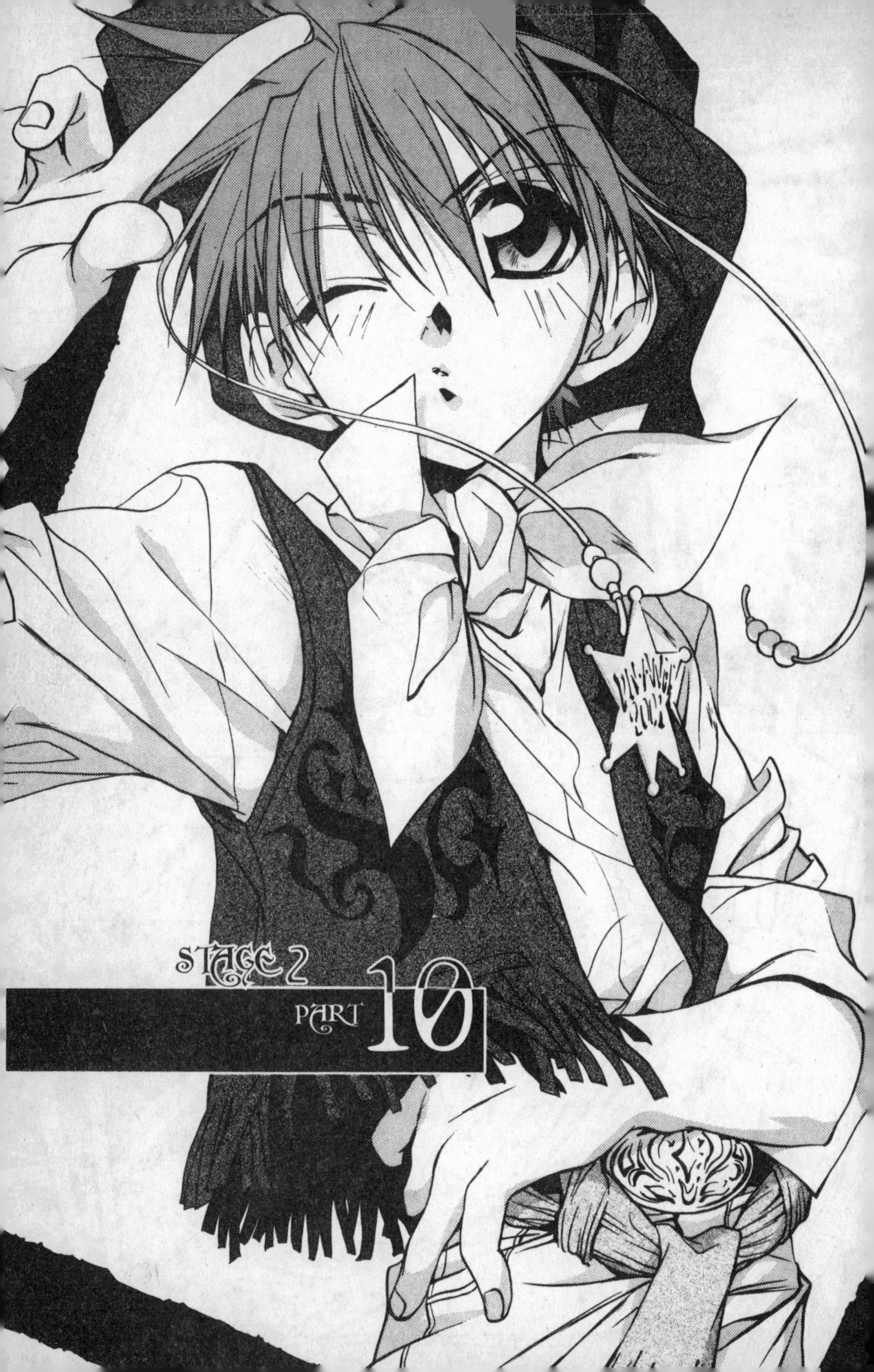
STAGE 2
PART 10

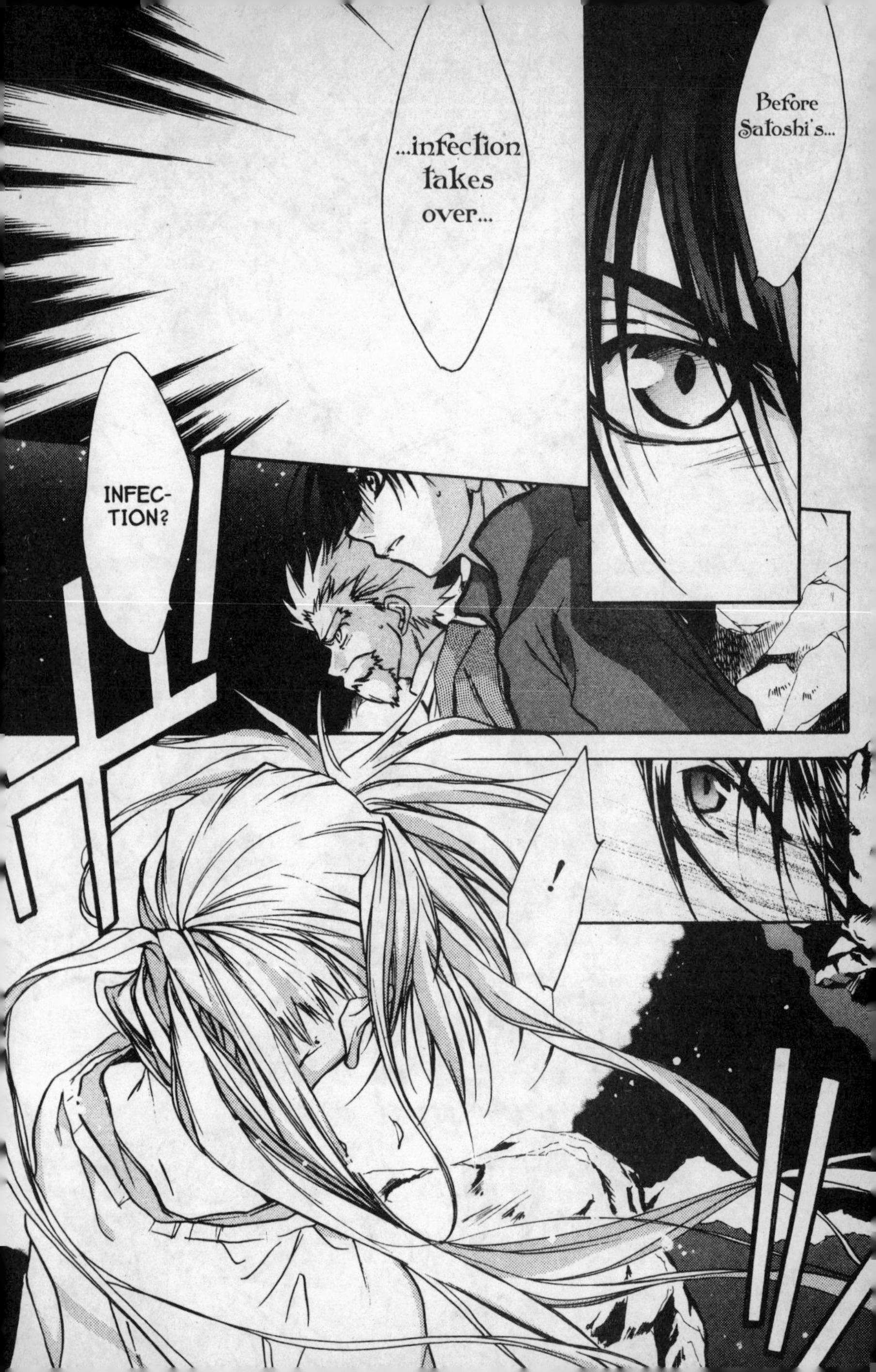
Before Satoshi's...
...infection takes over...
INFECTION?
!

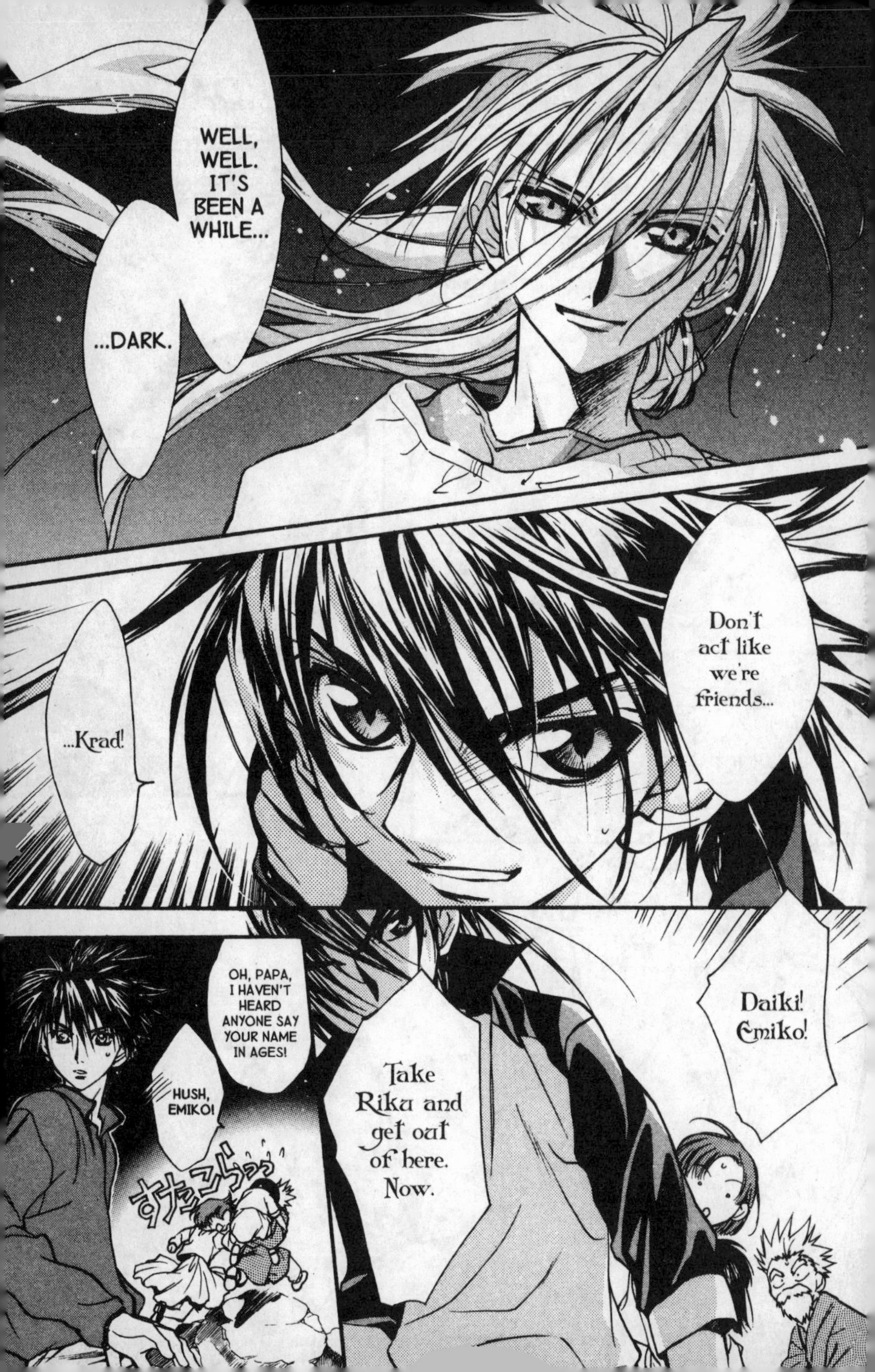
WELL, WELL. IT'S BEEN A WHILE...
...DARK.
Don't act like we're friends...
...Krad!
Daiki! Emiko!
Take Riku and get out of here. Now.
OH, PAPA, I HAVEN'T HEARD ANYONE SAY YOUR NAME IN AGES!
HUSH, EMIKO!

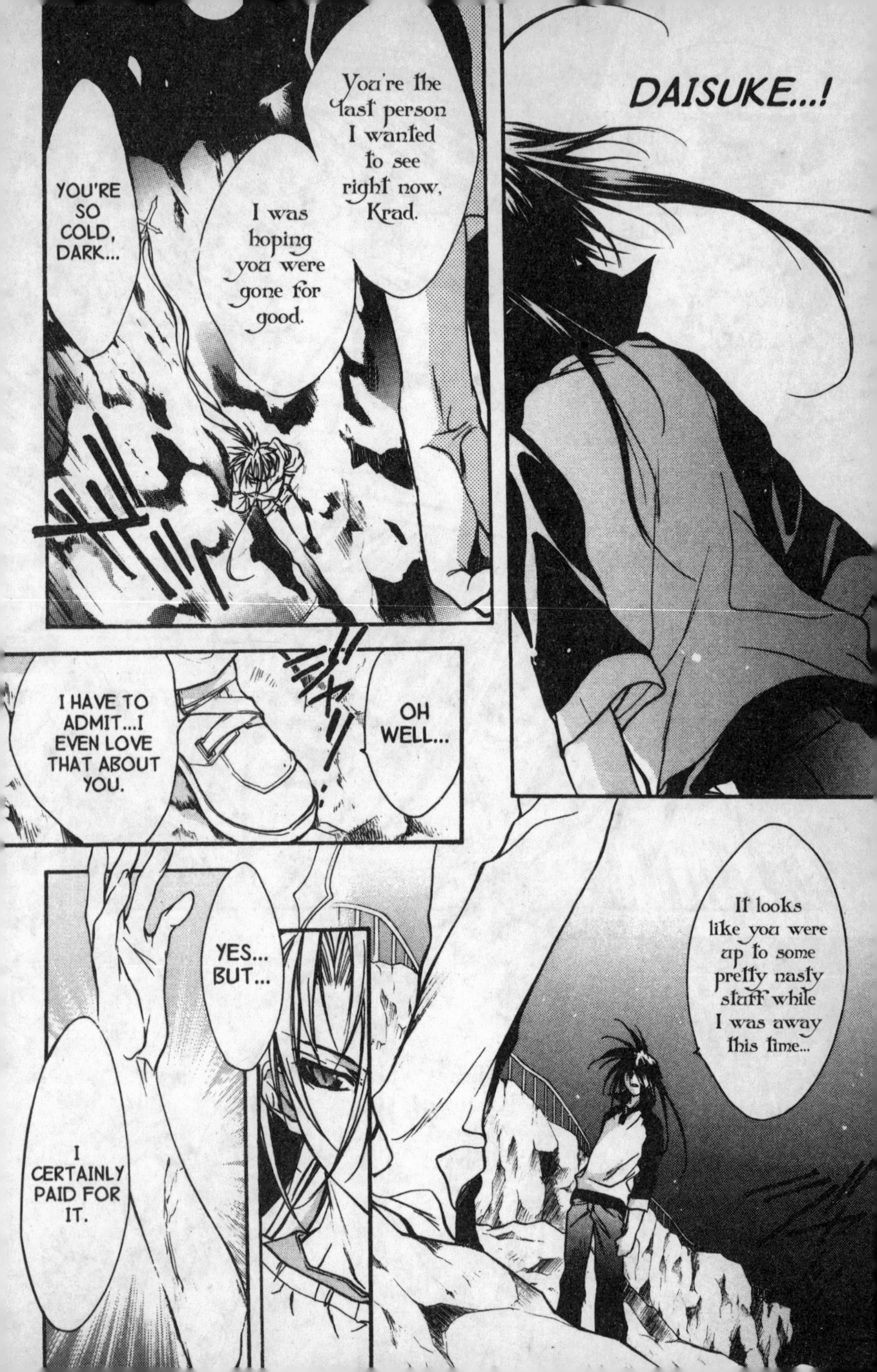
DAISUKE...!
You're the last person I wanted to see right now, Krad.
I was hoping you were gone for good.
YOU'RE SO COLD, DARK...
OH WELL...
I HAVE TO ADMIT...I EVEN LOVE THAT ABOUT YOU.
It looks like you were up to some pretty nasty stuff while I was away this time...
YES... BUT...
I CERTAINLY PAID FOR IT.

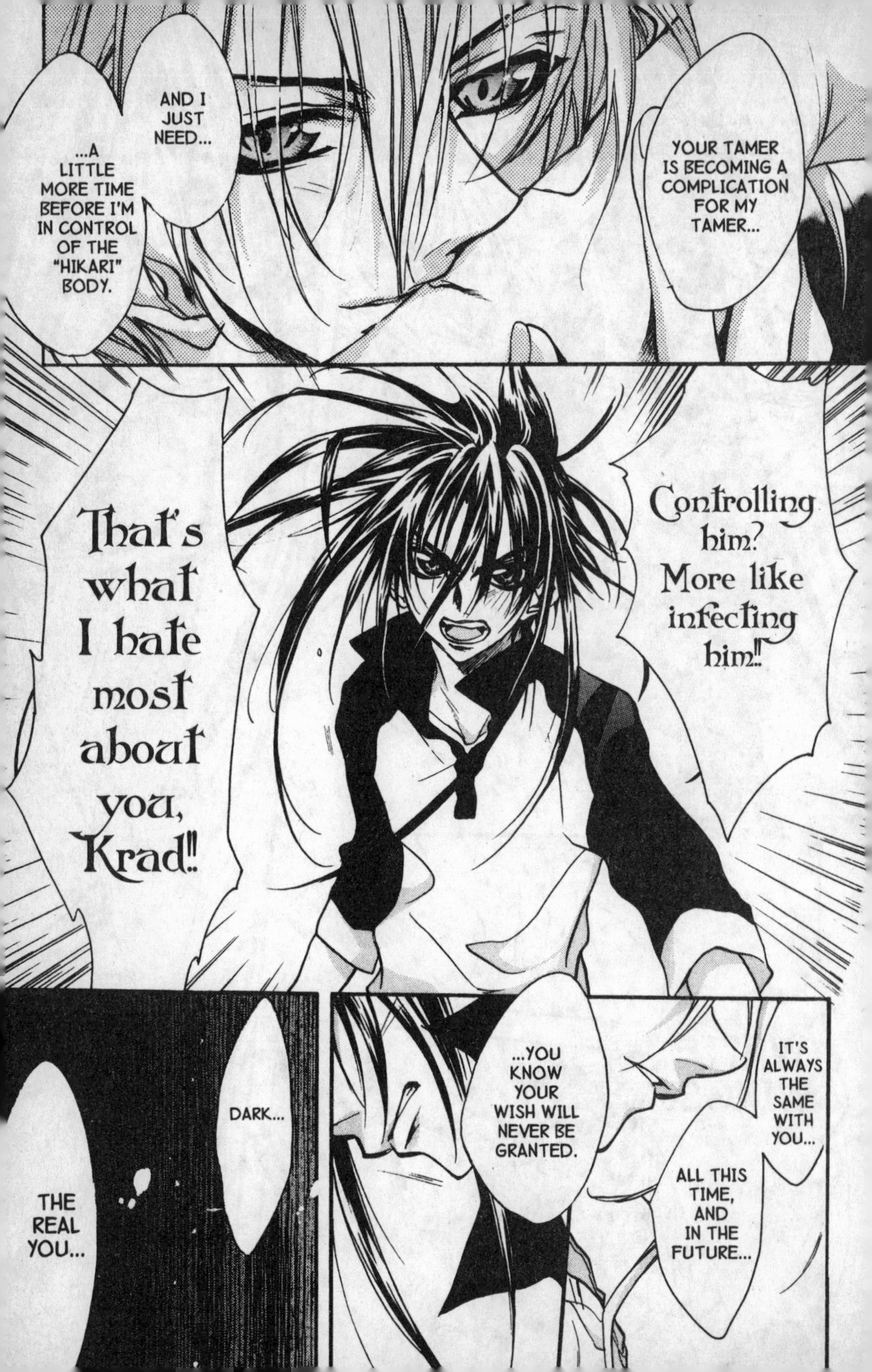
YOUR TAMER IS BECOMING A COMPLICATION FOR MY TAMER...
AND I JUST NEED...
...A LITTLE MORE TIME BEFORE I'M IN CONTROL OF THE "HIKARI" BODY.
Controlling him? More like infecting him!!
That's what I hate most about you, Krad!!
IT'S ALWAYS THE SAME WITH YOU...
ALL THIS TIME, AND IN THE FUTURE...
...YOU KNOW YOUR WISH WILL NEVER BE GRANTED.
DARK...
THE REAL YOU...

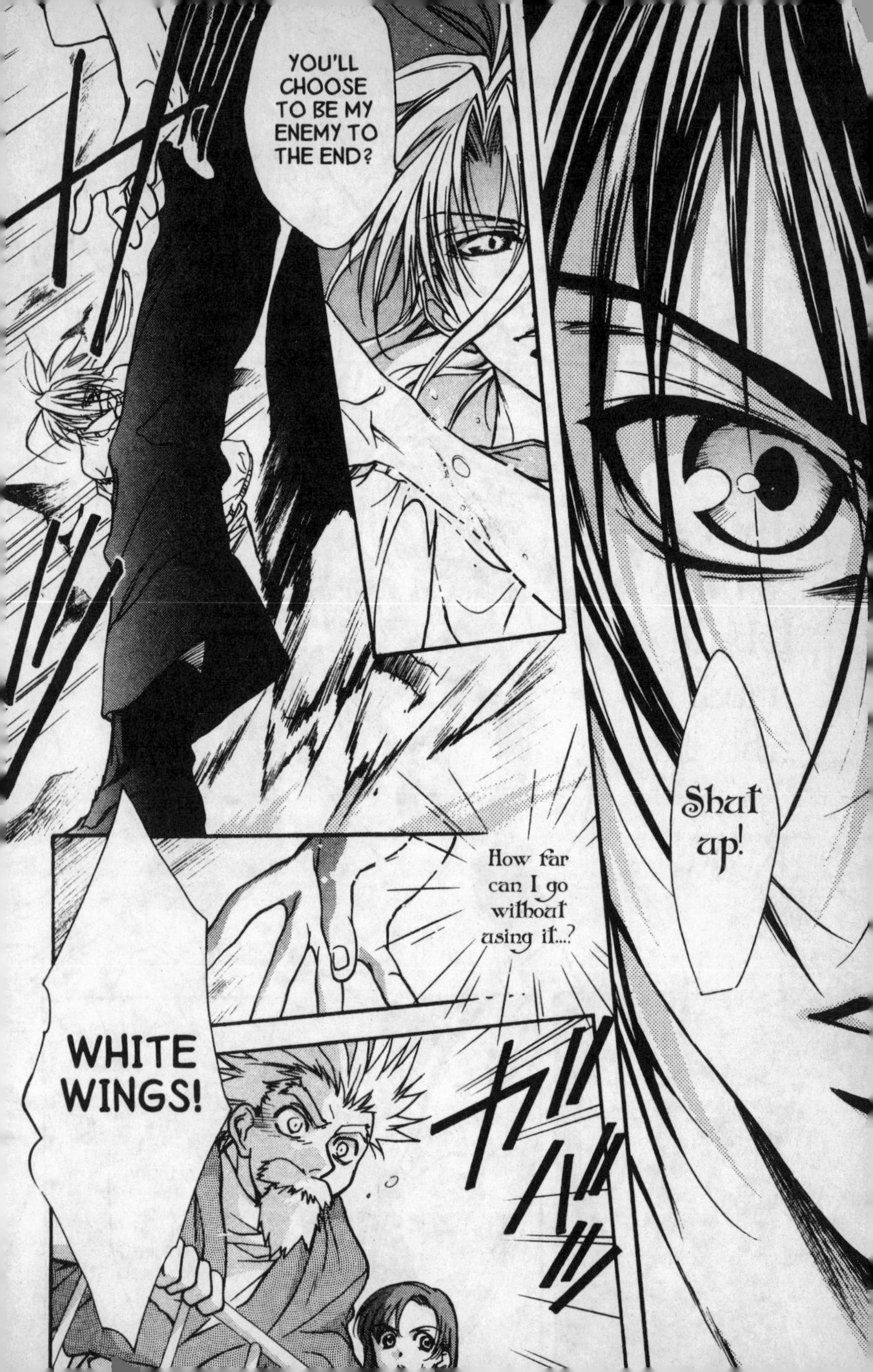
YOU'LL CHOOSE TO BE MY ENEMY TO THE END?
Shut up!
How far can I go without using it...?
WHITE WINGS!

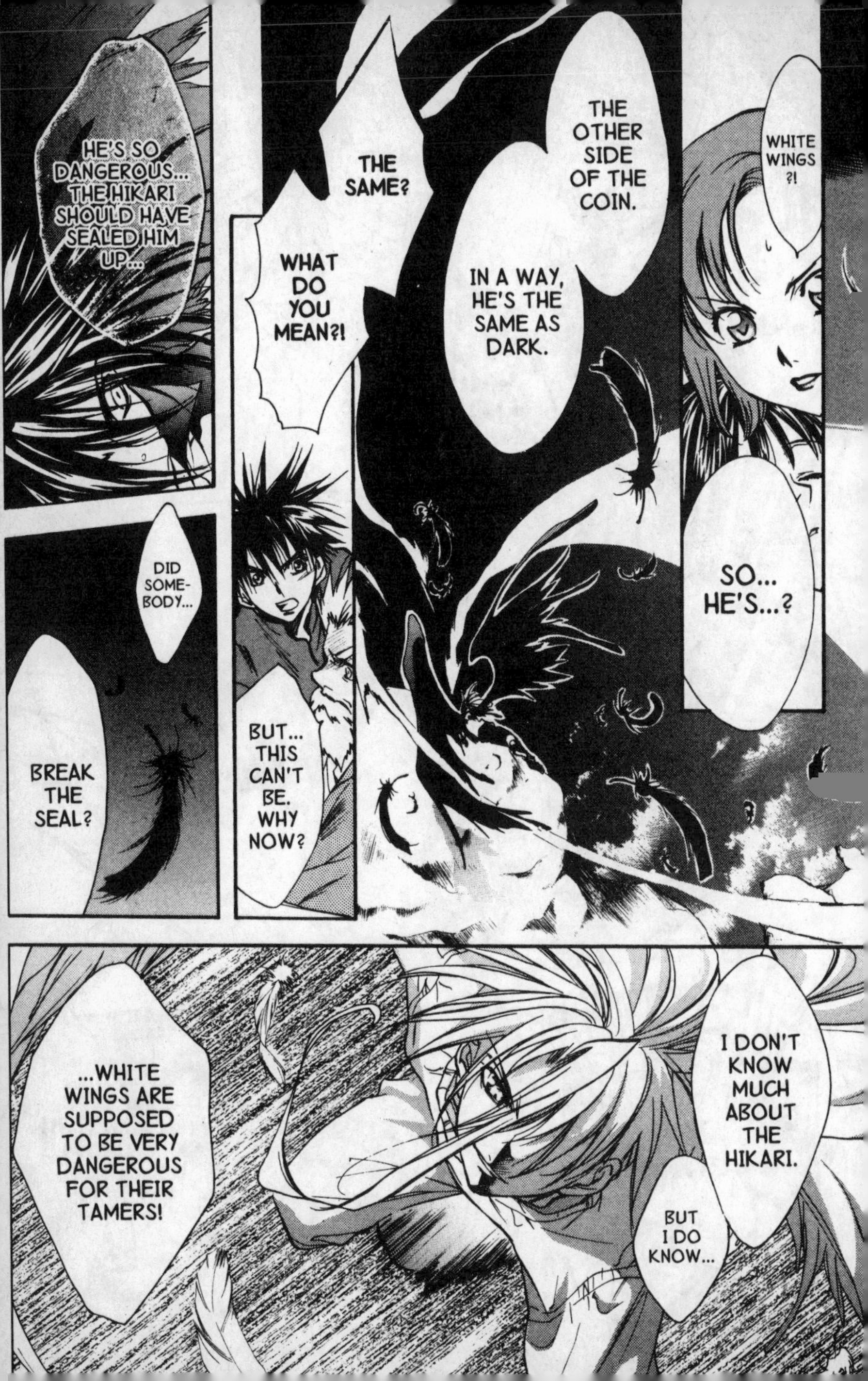
WHITE WINGS ?!
SO... HE'S...?
IN A WAY, HE'S THE SAME AS DARK.
THE SAME?
WHAT DO YOU MEAN?!
THE OTHER SIDE OF THE COIN.
BUT... THIS CAN'T BE. WHY NOW?
HE'S SO DANGEROUS... THE HIKARI SHOULD HAVE SEALED HIM UP...
DID SOME-BODY...
BREAK THE SEAL?
I DON'T KNOW MUCH ABOUT THE HIKARI.
BUT I DO KNOW...
...WHITE WINGS ARE SUPPOSED TO BE VERY DANGEROUS FOR THEIR TAMERS!

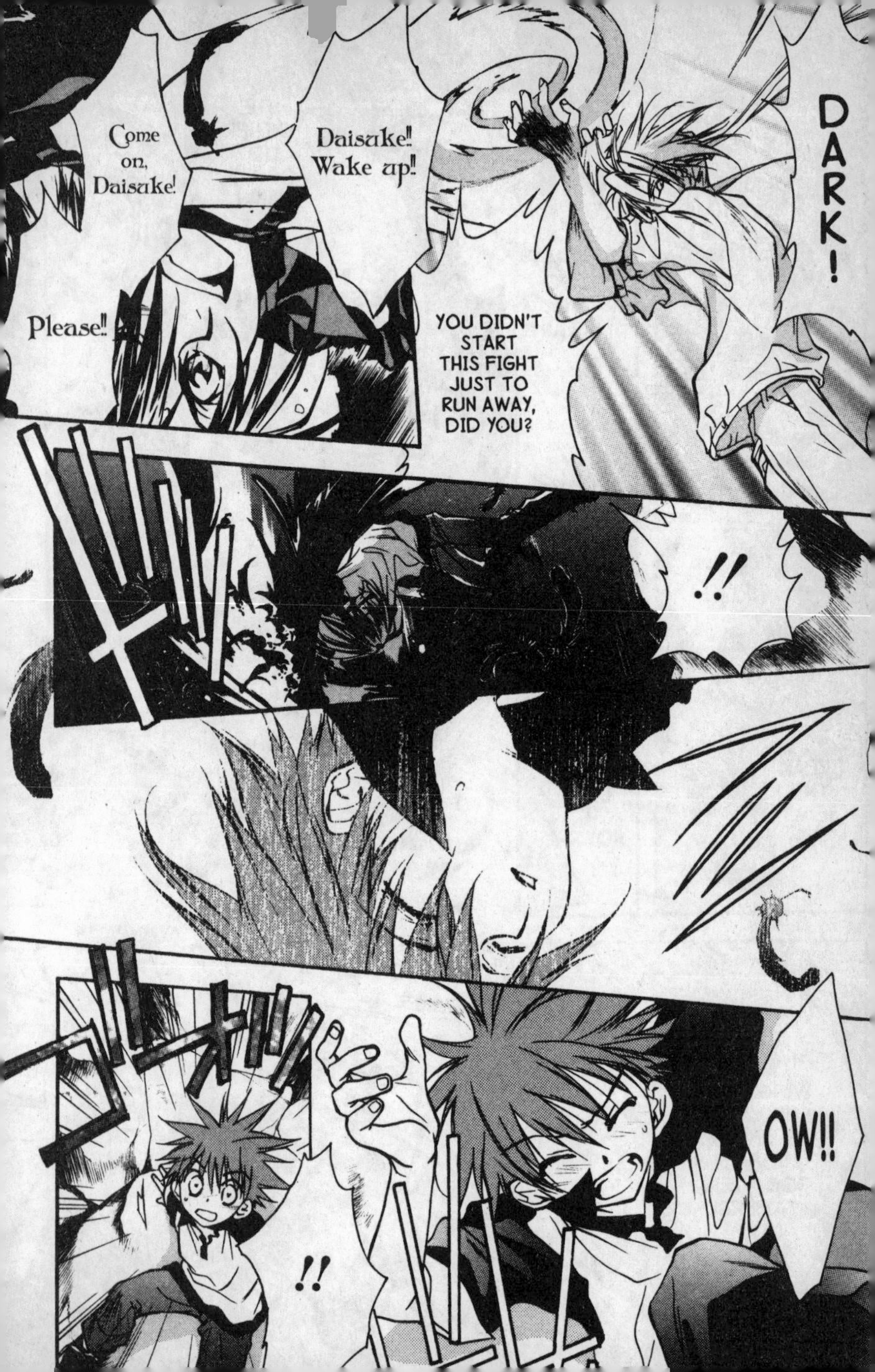
DARK!
Daisuke!! Wake up!!
Come on, Daisuke!
YOU DIDN'T START THIS FIGHT JUST TO RUN AWAY, DID YOU?
Please!!
!!
OW!!
!!

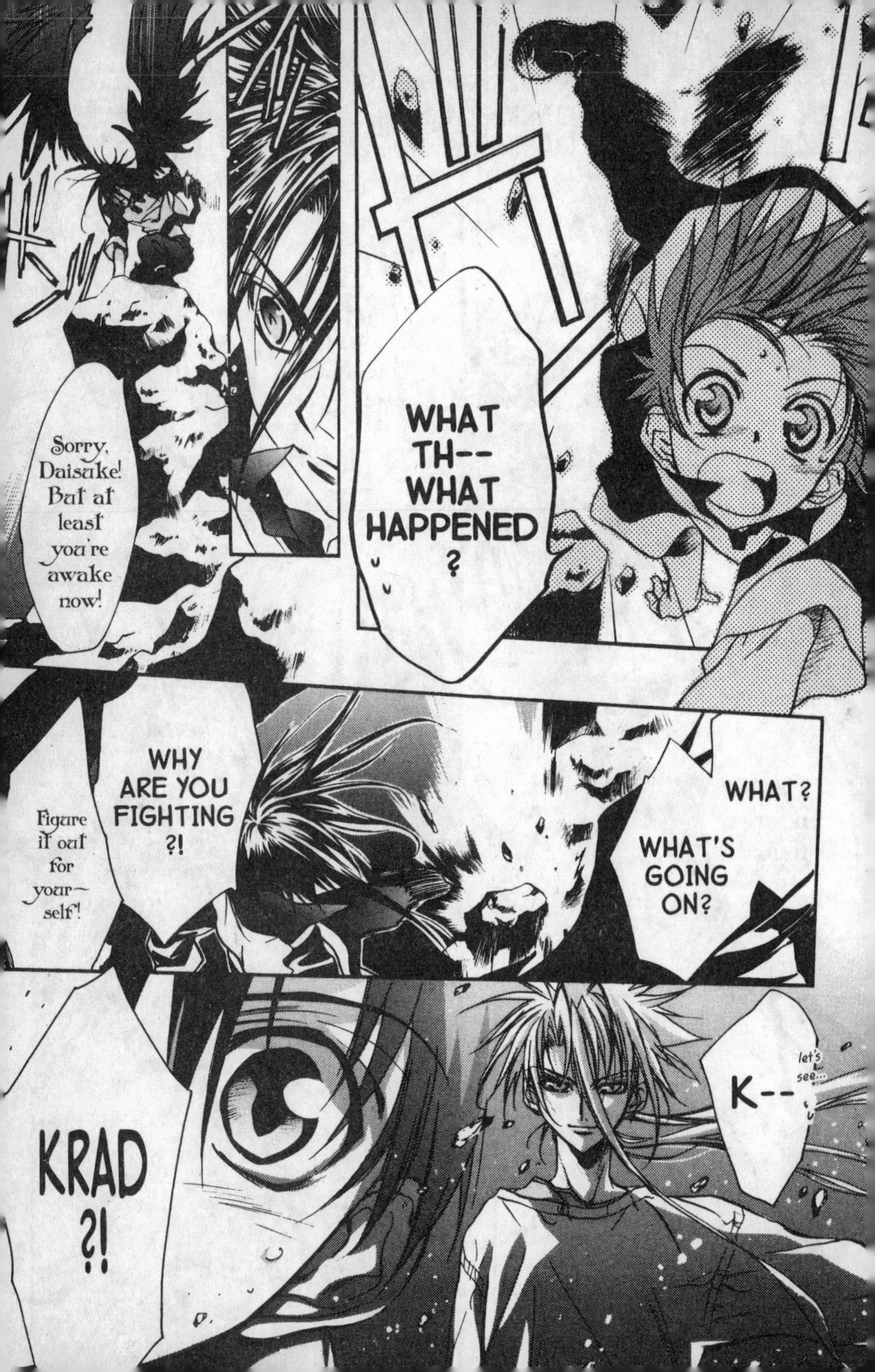
WHAT TH-- WHAT HAPPENED ?
Sorry, Daisuke! But at least you're awake now!
WHAT?
WHAT'S GOING ON?
WHY ARE YOU FIGHTING ?!
Figure it out for your-self!
K--
let's see...
KRAD ?!

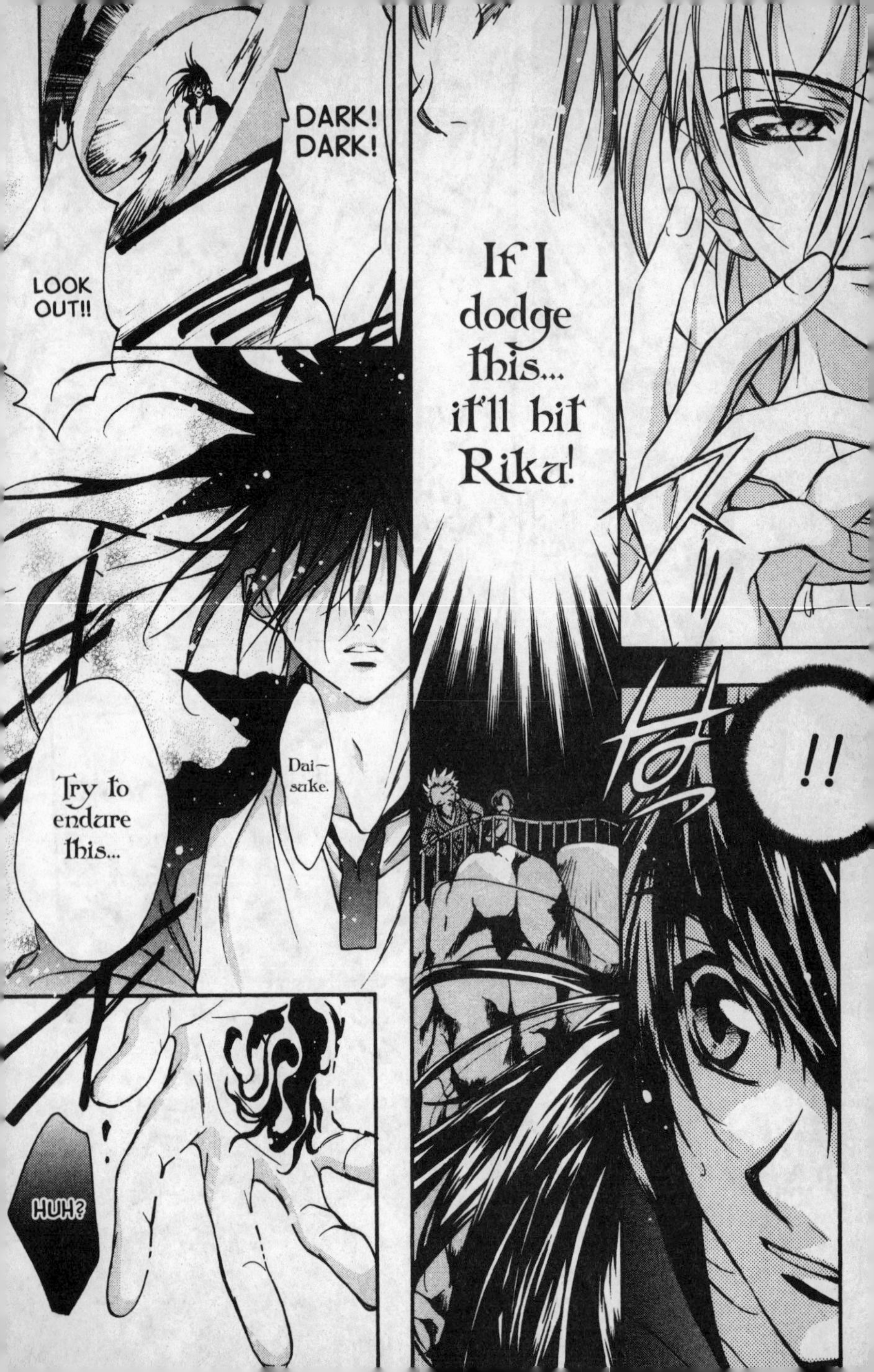
If I dodge this... it'll hit Riku!
!!
DARK! DARK!
LOOK OUT!!
Dai-suke.
Try to endure this...
HUH?

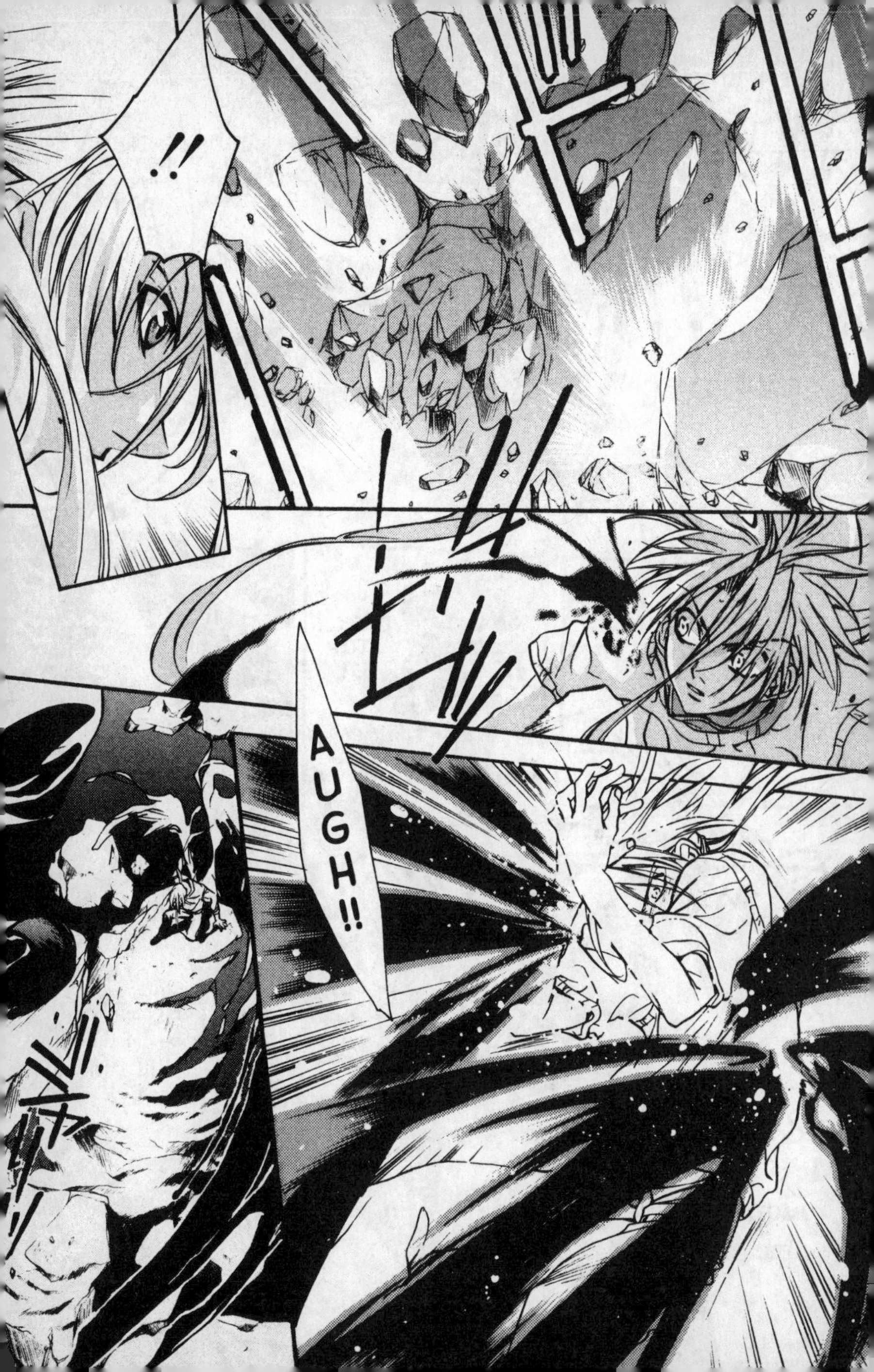
!!
AUGH!!

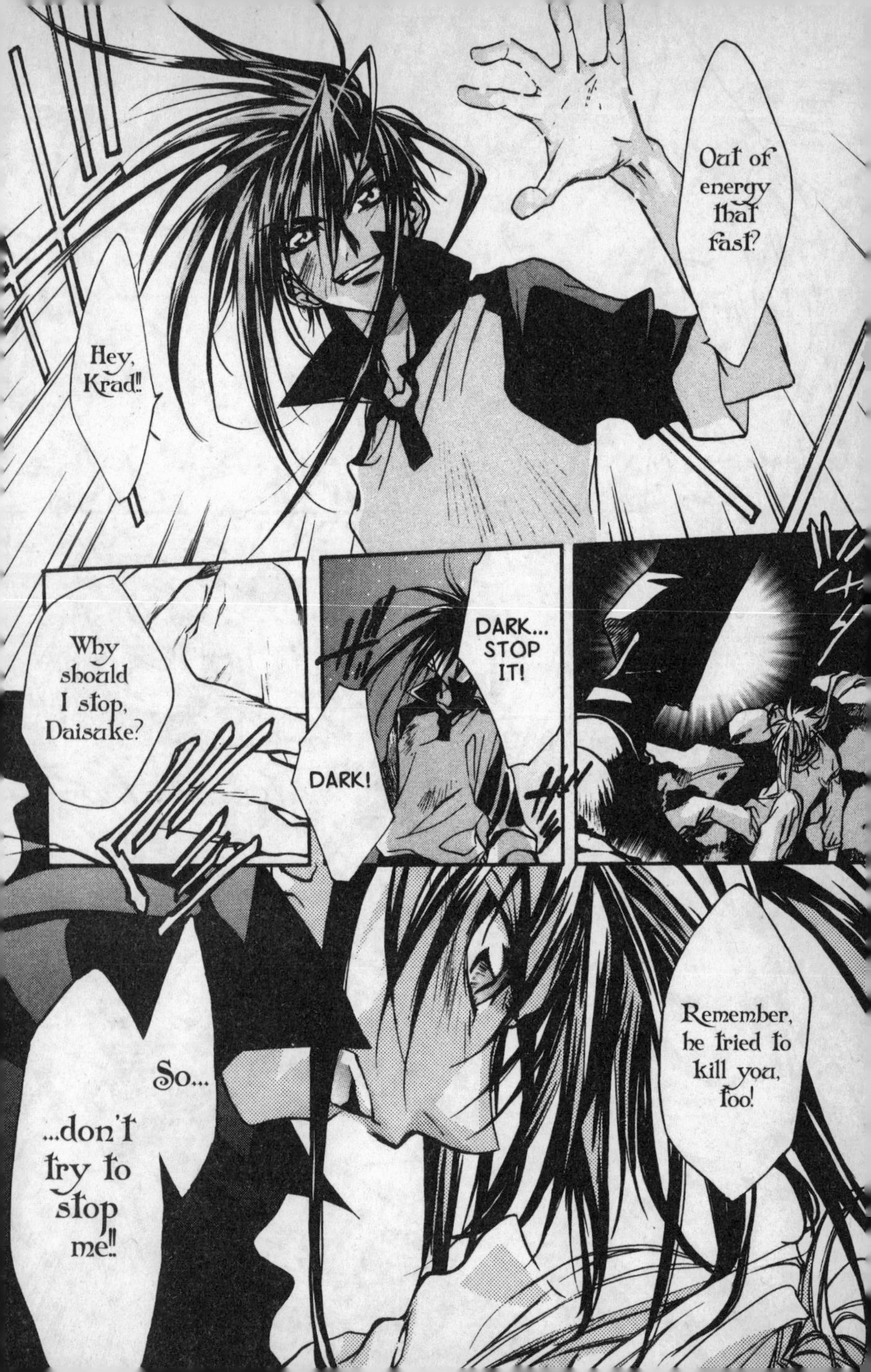
Out of energy that fast?
Hey, Krad!!
DARK... STOP IT!
DARK!
Why should I stop, Daisuke?
Remember, he tried to kill you, too!
So...
...don't try to stop me!!

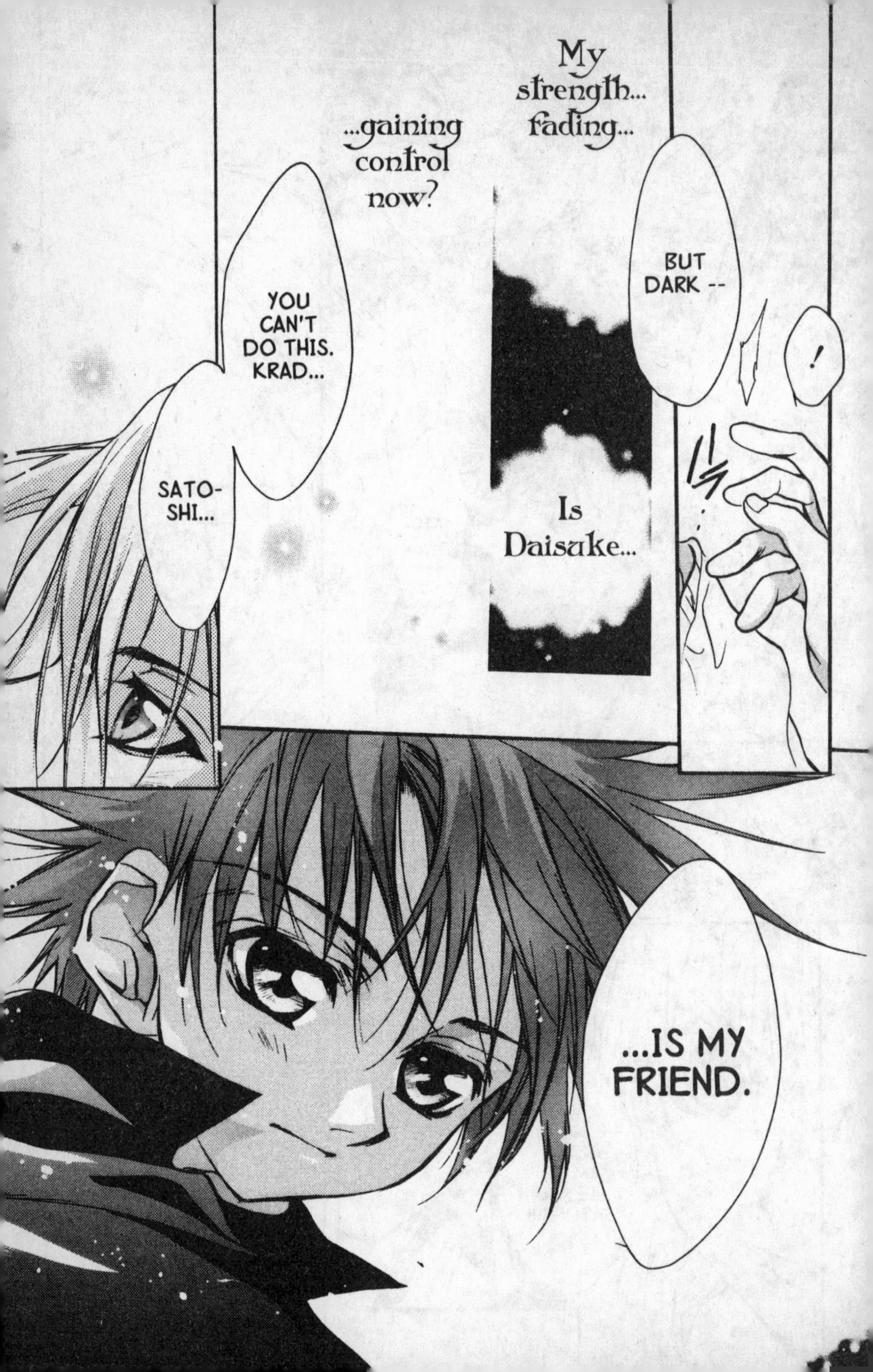
My strength... fading...
BUT DARK --
!
Is Daisuke...
...gaining control now?
YOU CAN'T DO THIS. KRAD...
SATO-SHI...
...IS MY FRIEND.

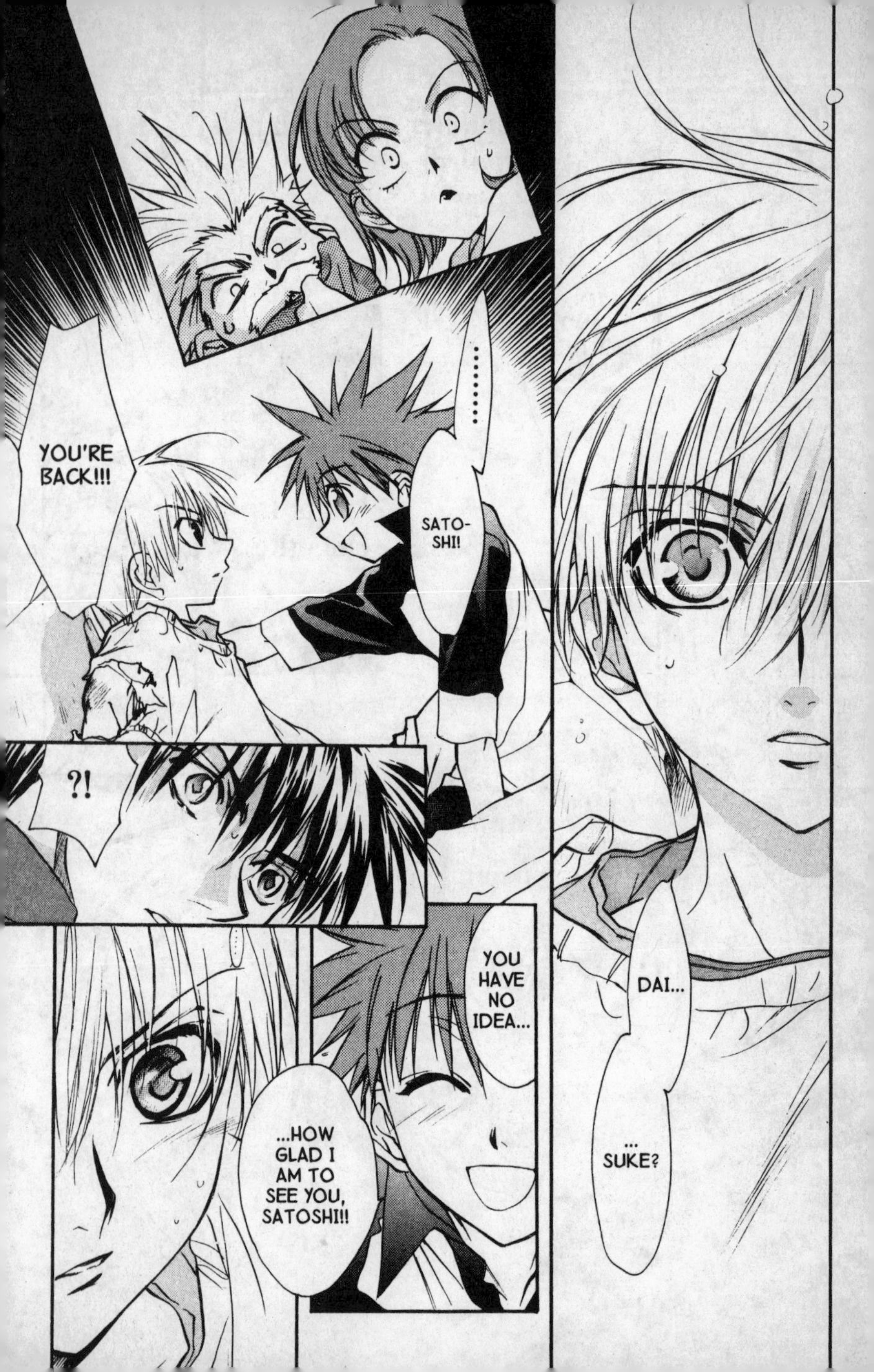
DAI...
...
SUKE?
......
SATO-
SHI!
YOU'RE BACK!!!
?!
YOU HAVE NO IDEA...
...HOW GLAD I AM TO SEE YOU, SATOSHI!!

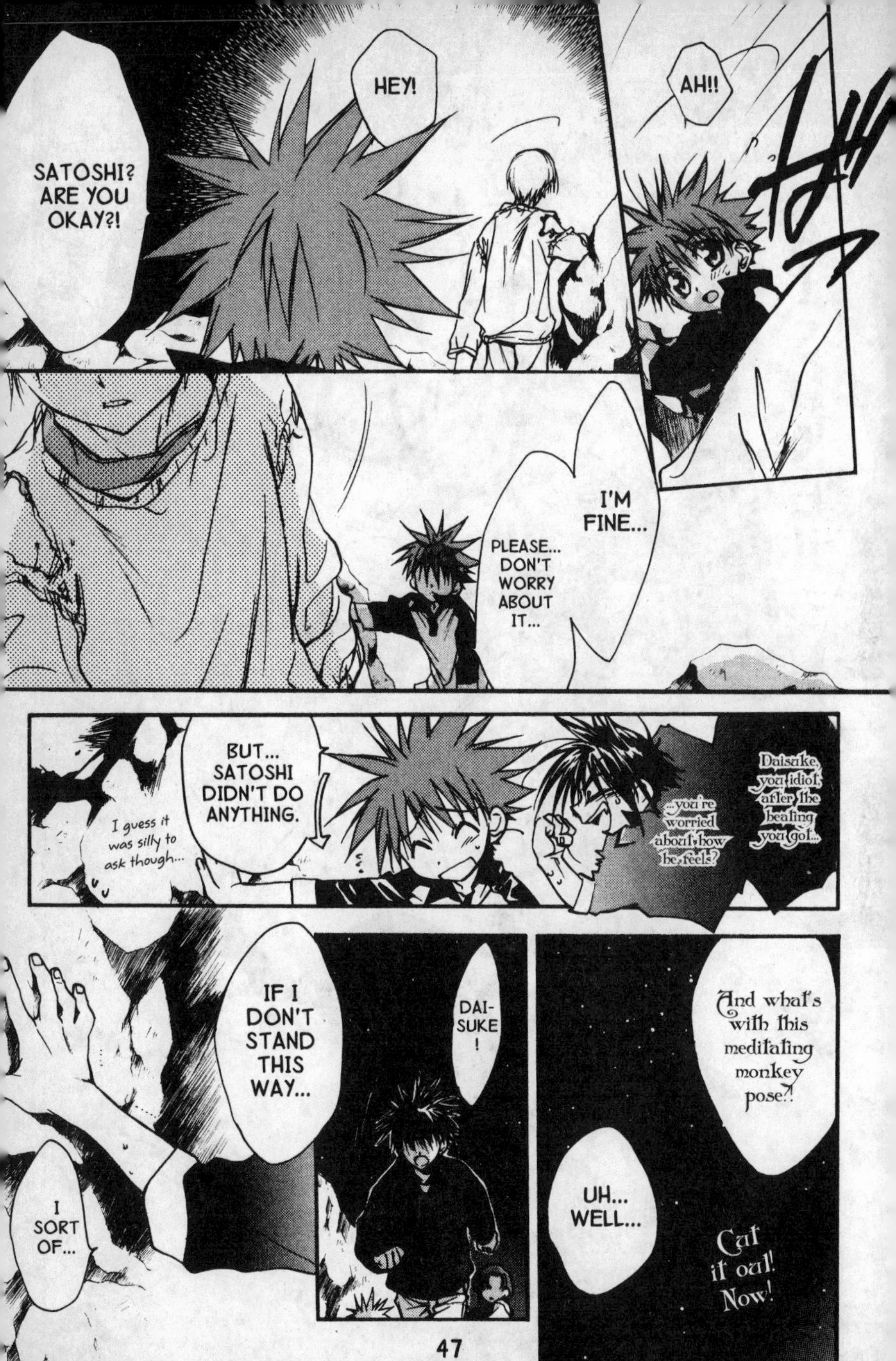
AH!!
HEY!
SATOSHI? ARE YOU OKAY?!
I'M FINE...
PLEASE... DON'T WORRY ABOUT IT...
Daisuke, you idiot, after the beating you got...
...you're worried about how he feels?
BUT... SATOSHI DIDN'T DO ANYTHING.
I guess it was silly to ask though...
And what's with this meditating monkey pose?!
UH... WELL...
Cut it out! Now!
DAI-SUKE!
IF I DON'T STAND THIS WAY...
I SORT OF...

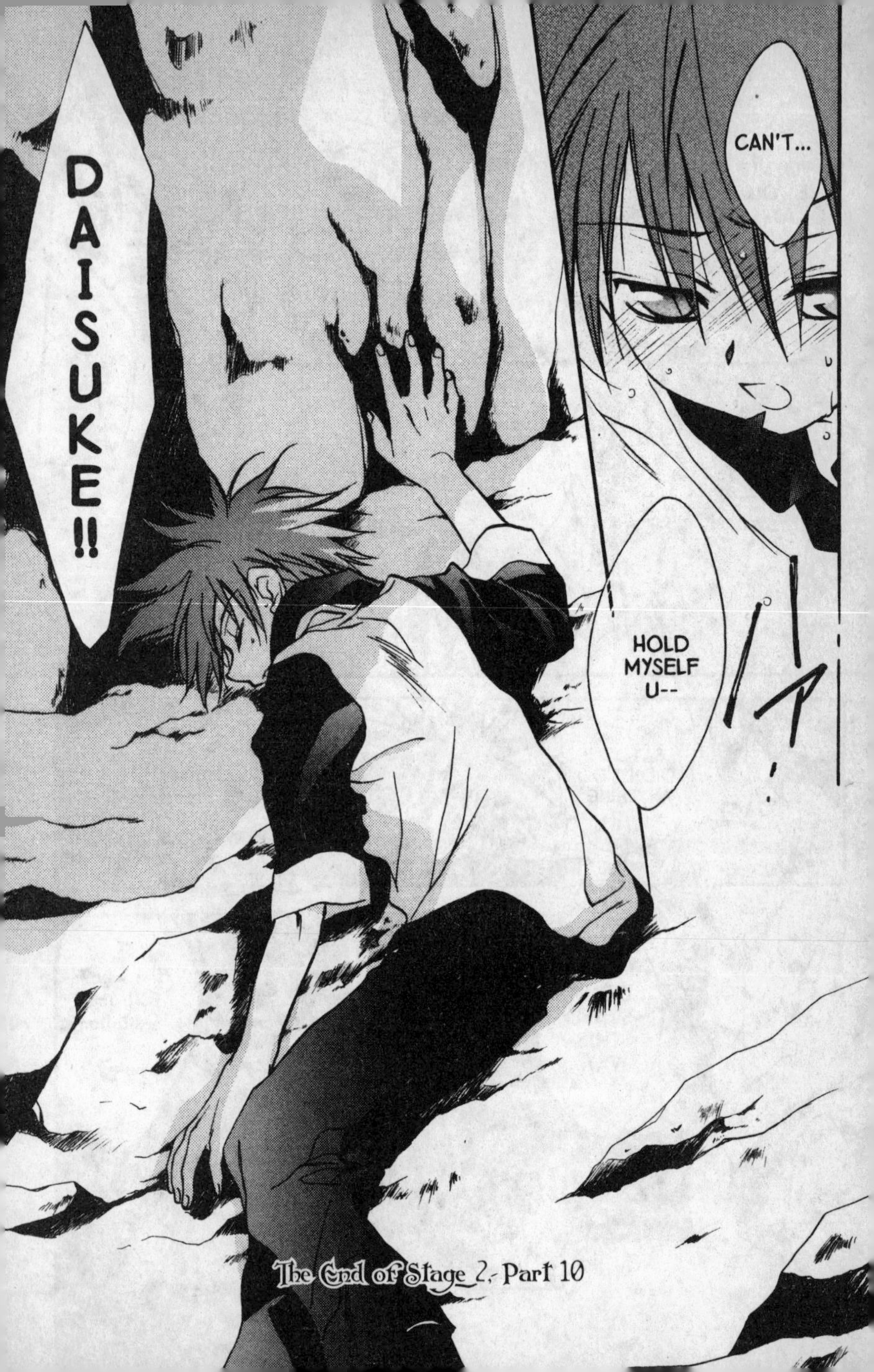
CAN'T...
HOLD MYSELF U--
DAISUKE!!
The End of Stage 2, Part 10

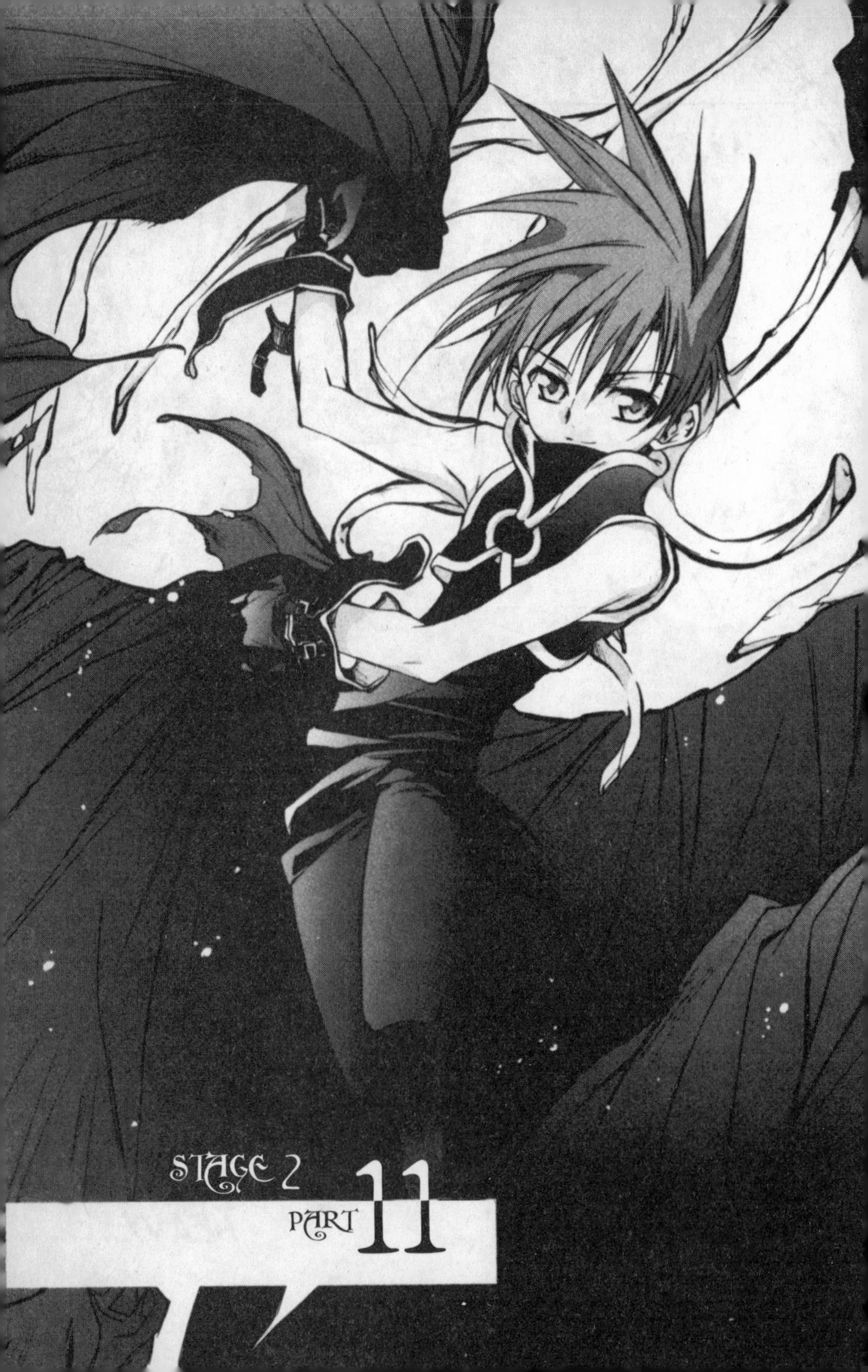
STAGE 2
PART 11

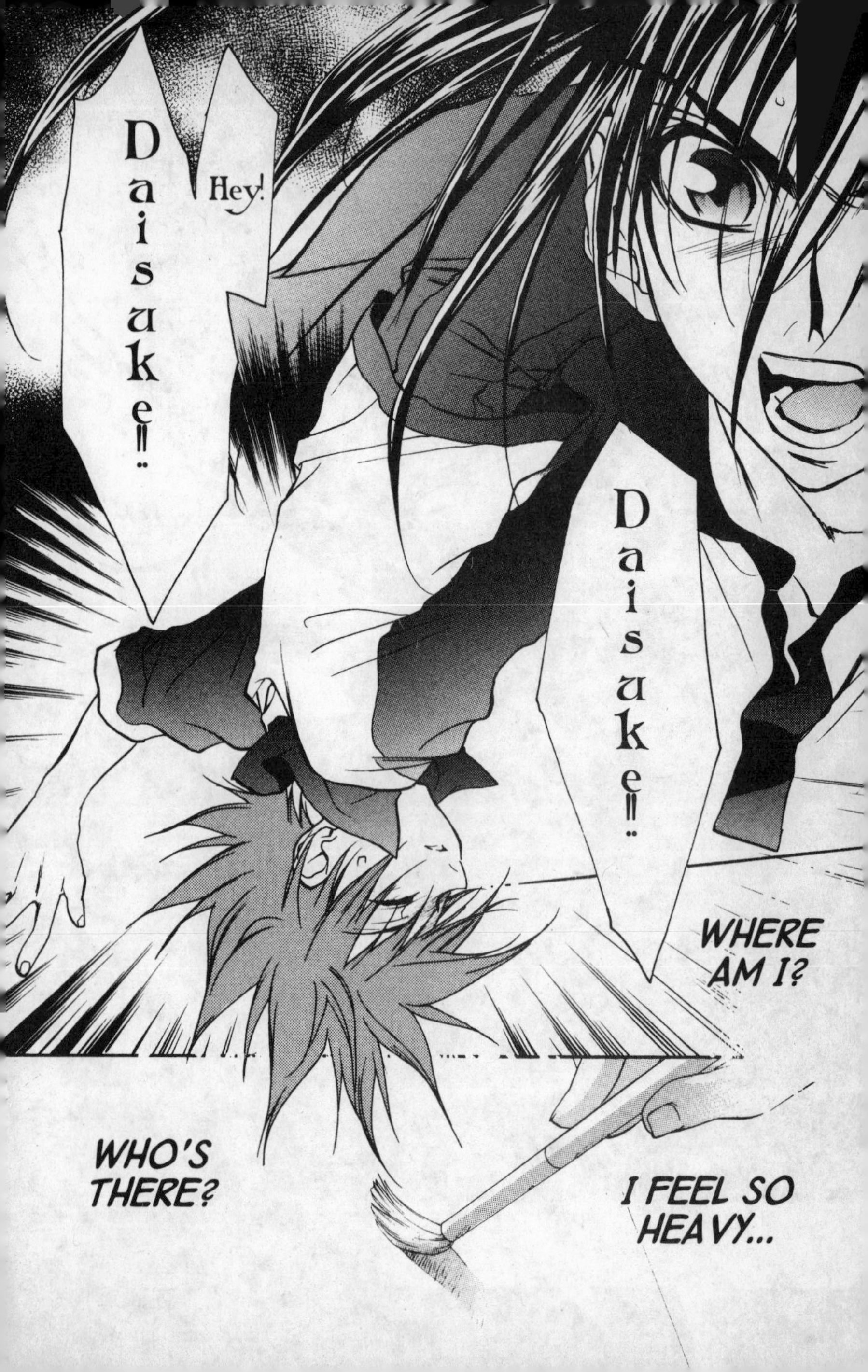
Daisuke!!
Hey! Daisuke!!
WHERE AM I?
I FEEL SO HEAVY...
WHO'S THERE?

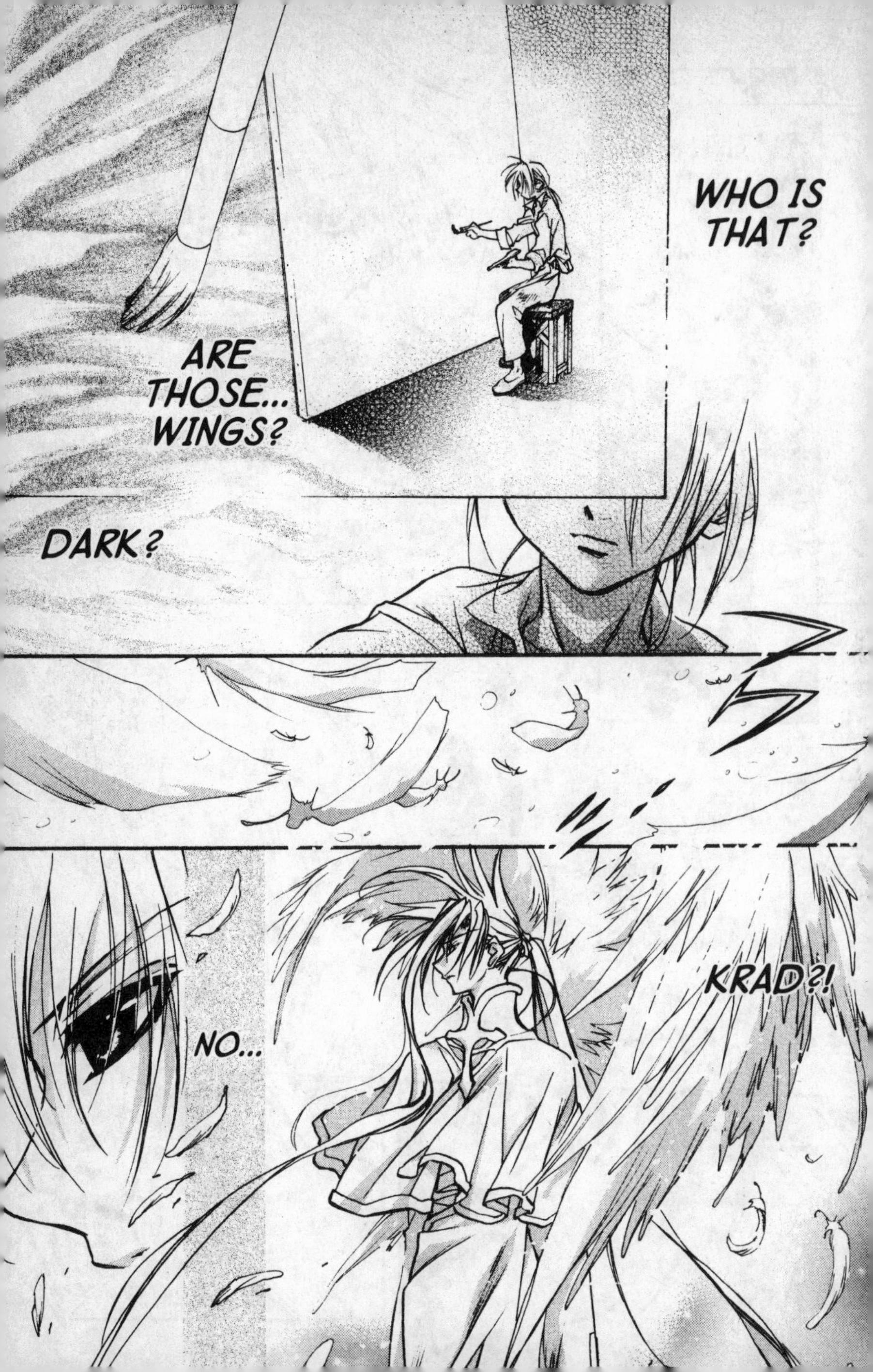
WHO IS THAT?
ARE THOSE... WINGS?
DARK?
KRAD?!
NO...

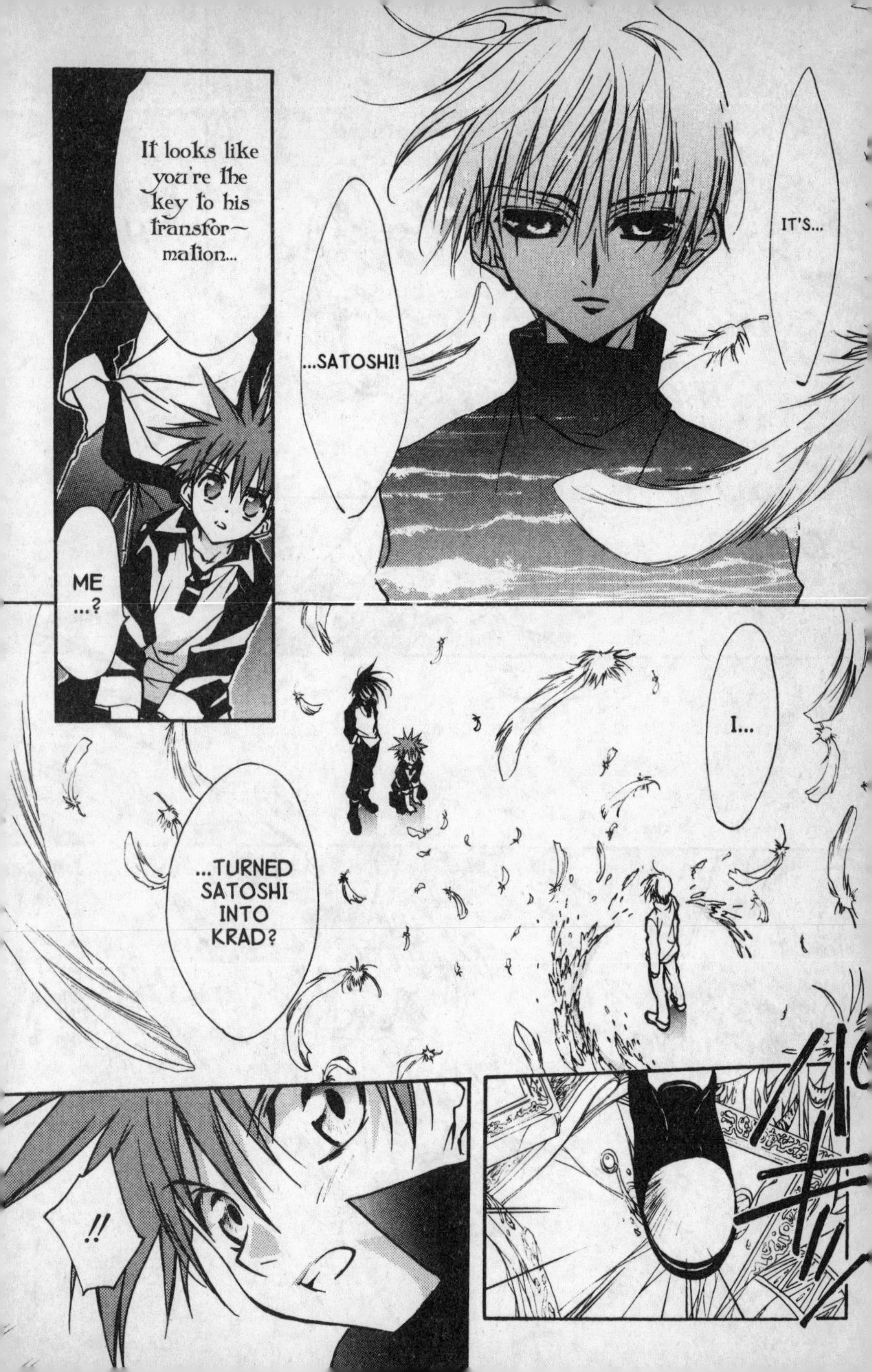
IT'S...
...SATOSHI!
It looks like you're the key to his transformation...
ME ...?
I...
...TURNED SATOSHI INTO KRAD?
!!

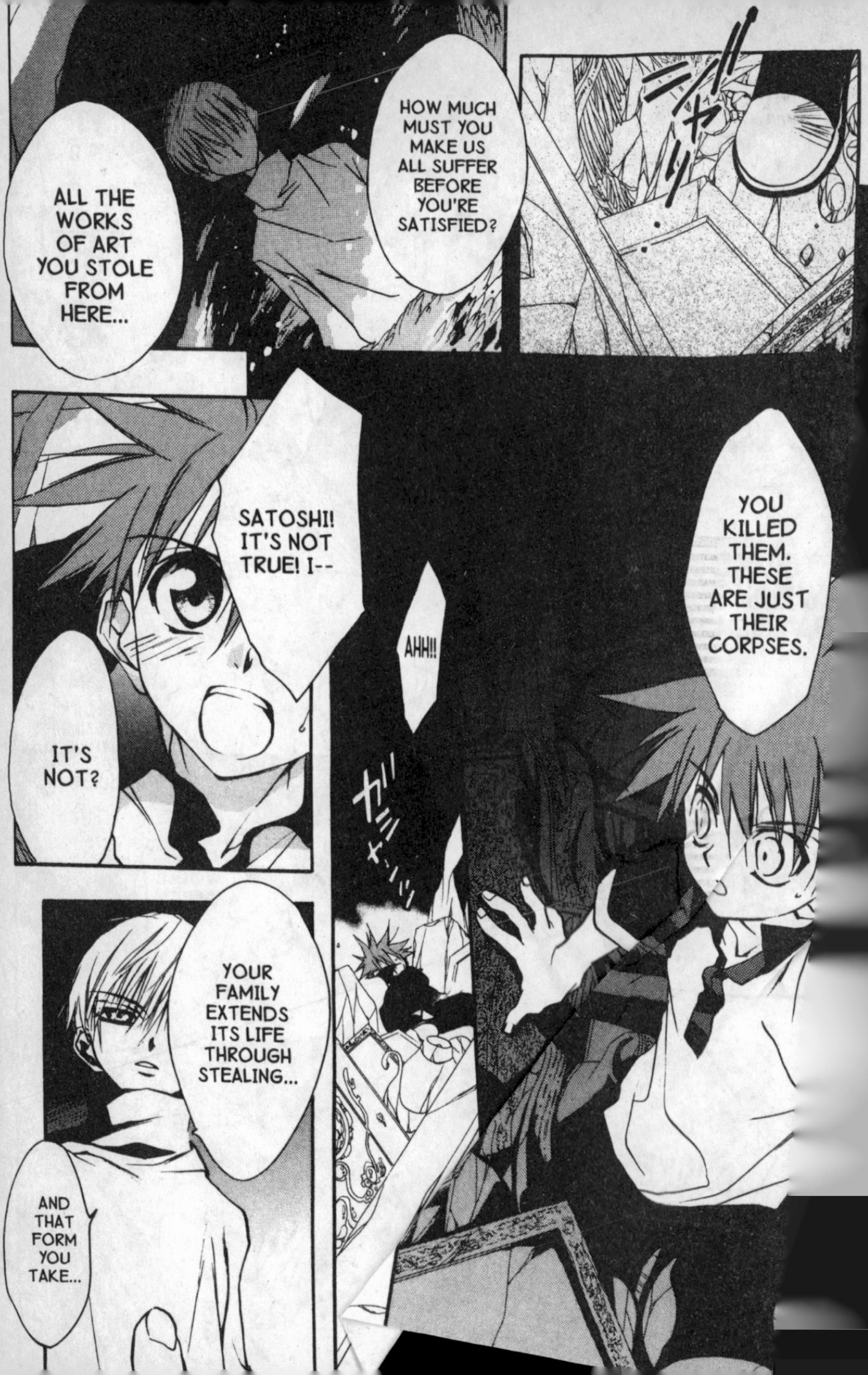
HOW MUCH MUST YOU MAKE US ALL SUFFER BEFORE YOU'RE SATISFIED?
ALL THE WORKS OF ART YOU STOLE FROM HERE...
YOU KILLED THEM. THESE ARE JUST THEIR CORPSES.
AHH!!
SATOSHI! IT'S NOT TRUE! I--
IT'S NOT?
YOUR FAMILY EXTENDS ITS LIFE THROUGH STEALING...
AND THAT FORM YOU TAKE...

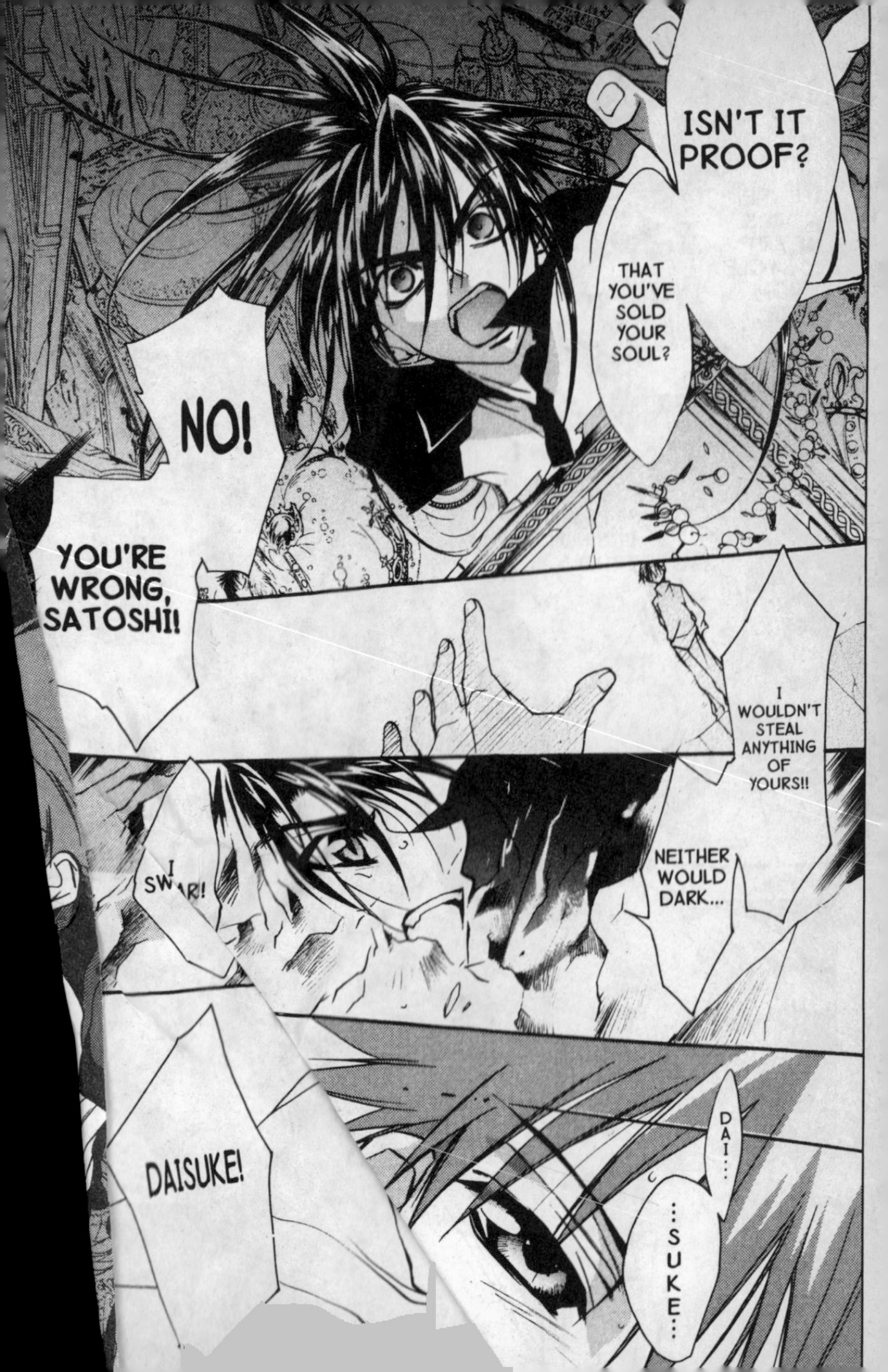

ISN'T IT PROOF?
THAT YOU'VE SOLD YOUR SOUL?
NO!
YOU'RE WRONG, SATOSHI!!
I WOULDN'T STEAL ANYTHING OF YOURS!!
NEITHER WOULD DARK...
I SW AR!
DAI...
...SUKE...
DAISUKE!

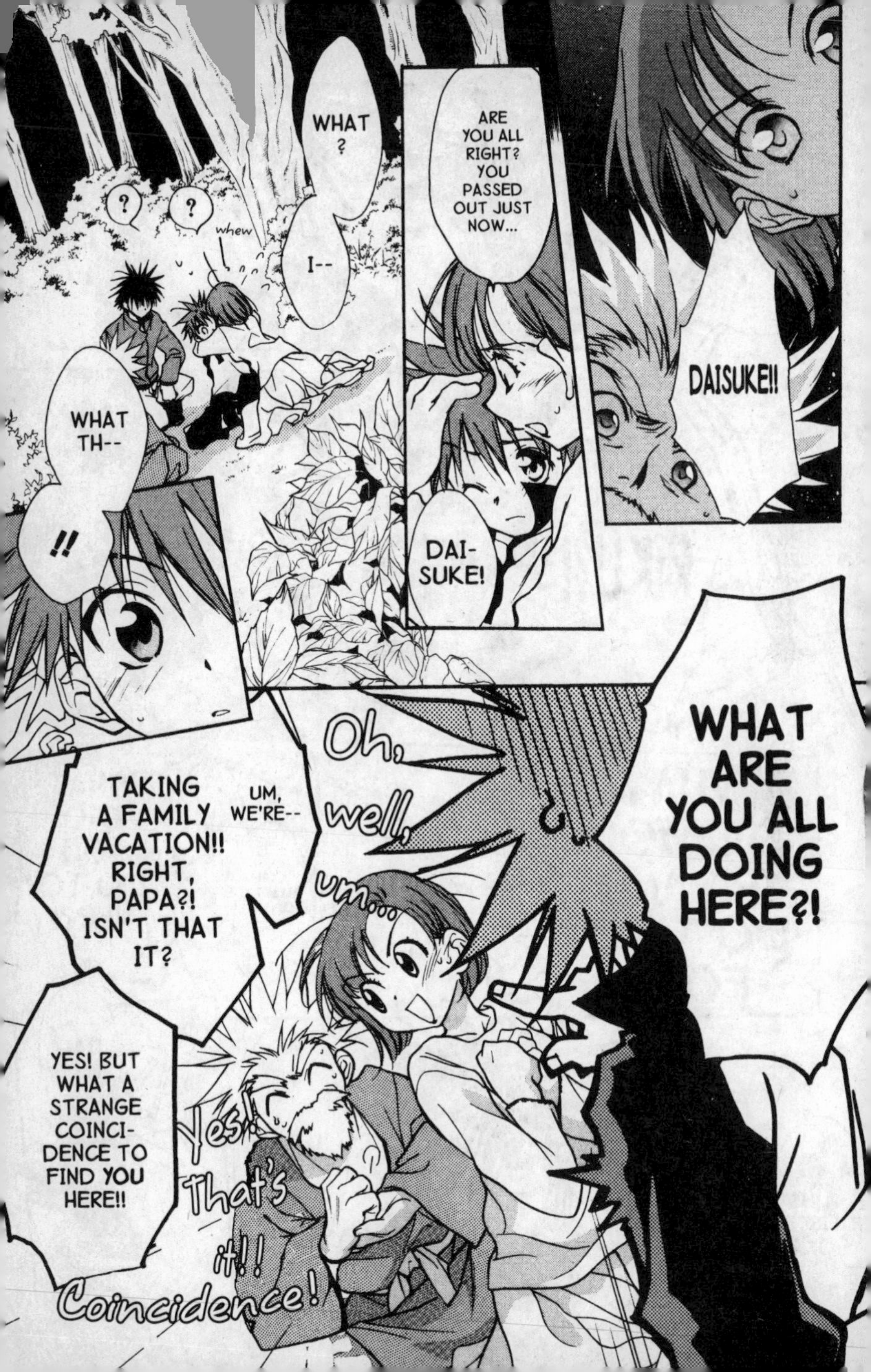
DAISUKE!!
ARE YOU ALL RIGHT? YOU PASSED OUT JUST NOW...
DAI-SUKE!
WHAT?
I--
?
?
whew
WHAT TH--
!!
WHAT ARE YOU ALL DOING HERE?!
Oh, well, um...
UM, WE'RE--
TAKING A FAMILY VACATION!! RIGHT, PAPA?! ISN'T THAT IT?
YES! BUT WHAT A STRANGE COINCIDENCE TO FIND YOU HERE!!
Yes! That's it!! Coincidence!

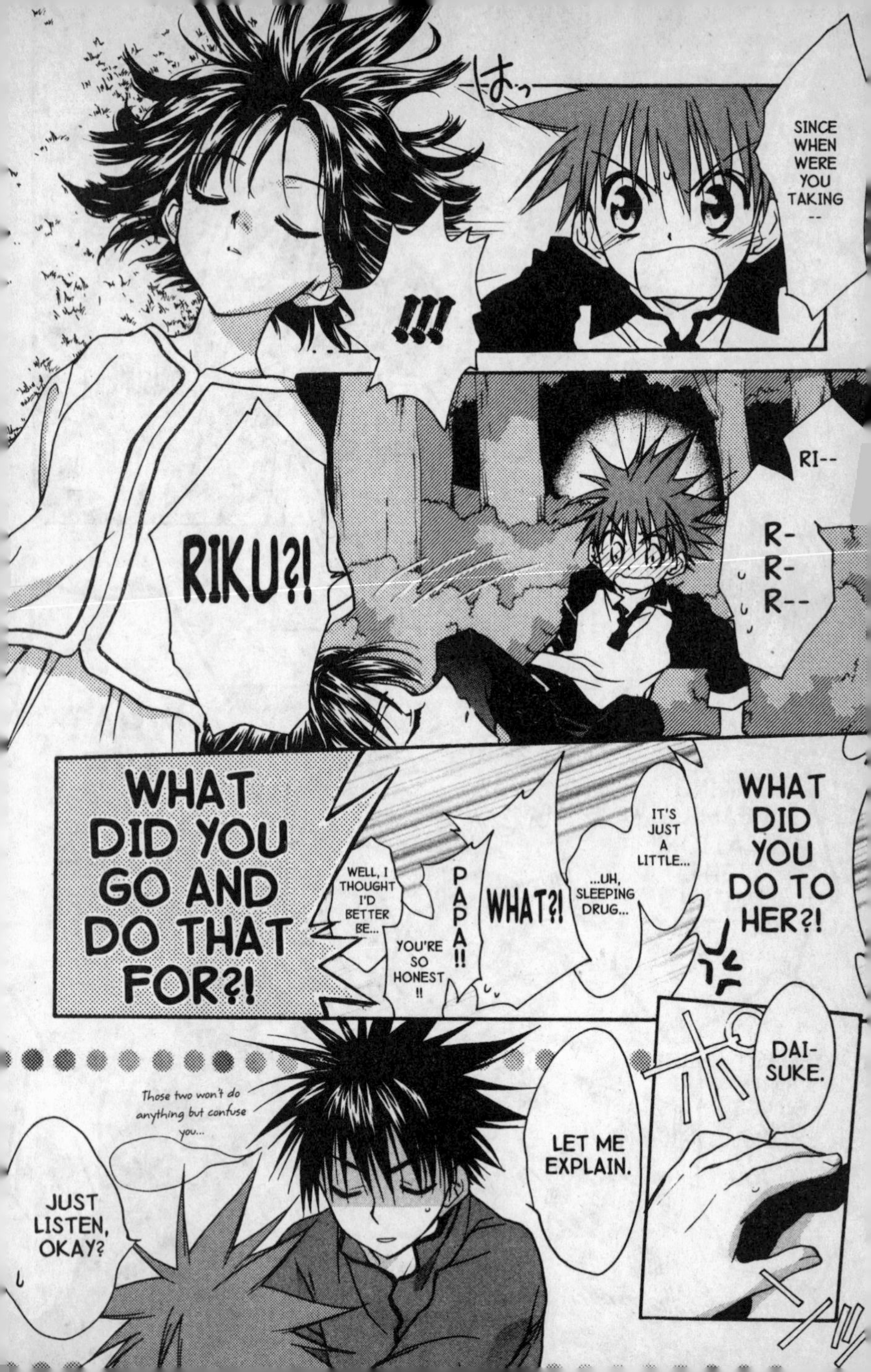
はっ
SINCE WHEN WERE YOU TAKING --
!!!
RI--
R- R- R--
RIKU?!
WHAT DID YOU DO TO HER?!
IT'S JUST A LITTLE...
...UH, SLEEPING DRUG...
WHAT?!
PAPA!!
WELL, I THOUGHT I'D BETTER BE...
YOU'RE SO HONEST !!
WHAT DID YOU GO AND DO THAT FOR?!
DAI- SUKE.
LET ME EXPLAIN.
Those two won't do anything but confuse you...
JUST LISTEN, OKAY?

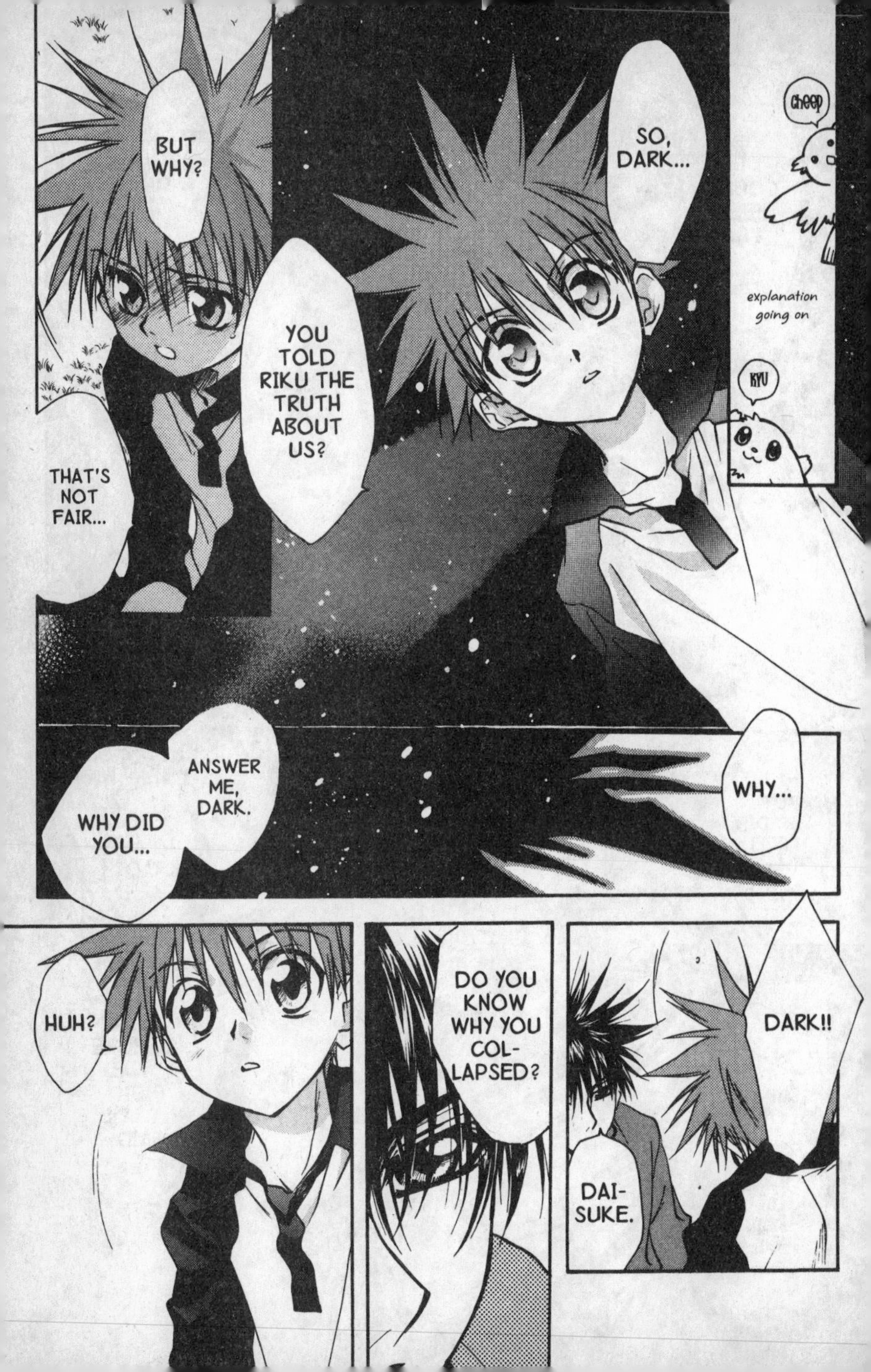
CHEEP
explanation going on
KYU
SO, DARK...
YOU TOLD RIKU THE TRUTH ABOUT US?
BUT WHY?
THAT'S NOT FAIR...
WHY...
ANSWER ME, DARK.
WHY DID YOU...
DARK!!
DAI-SUKE.
DO YOU KNOW WHY YOU COL-LAPSED?
HUH?

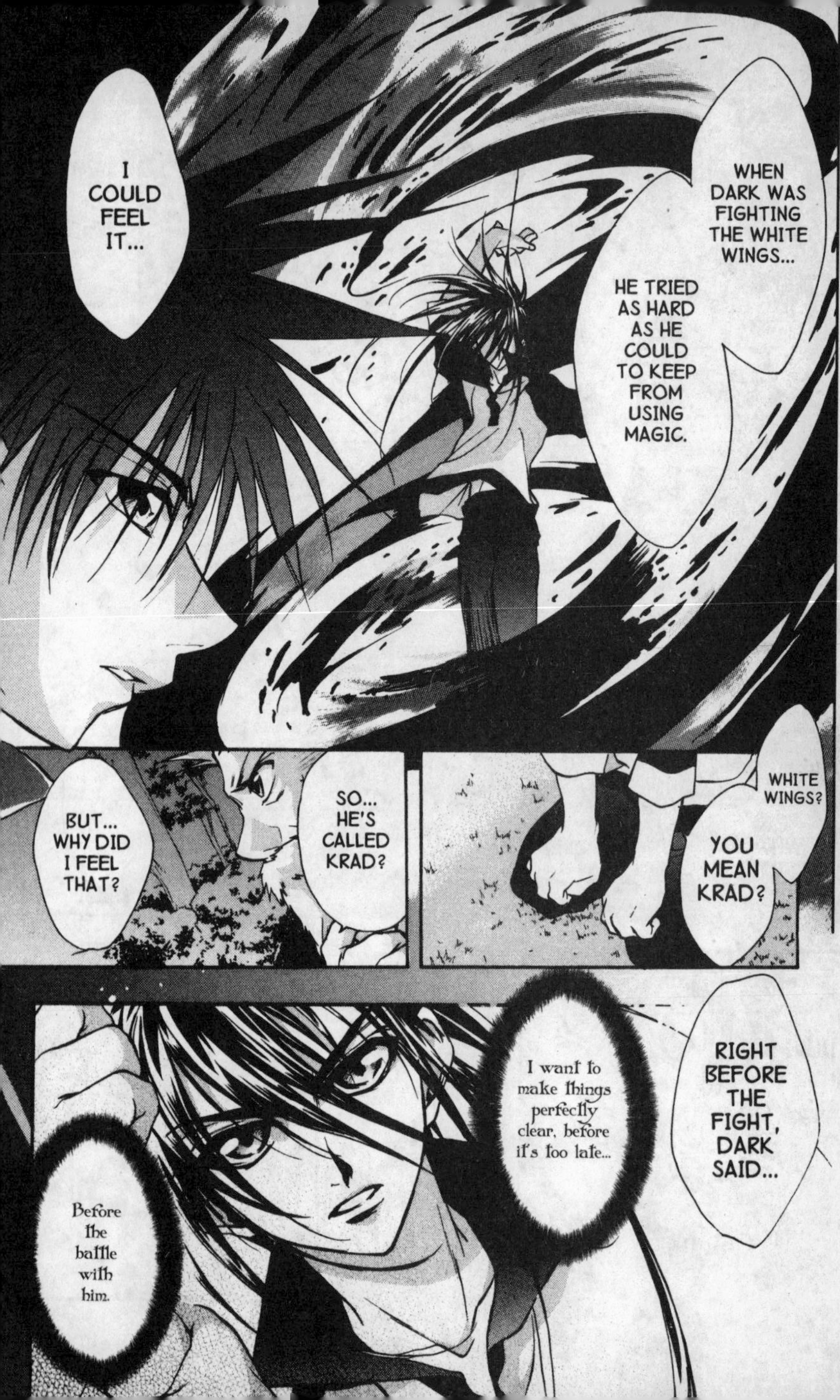
WHEN DARK WAS FIGHTING THE WHITE WINGS...
HE TRIED AS HARD AS HE COULD TO KEEP FROM USING MAGIC.
I COULD FEEL IT...
WHITE WINGS?
YOU MEAN KRAD?
SO... HE'S CALLED KRAD?
BUT... WHY DID I FEEL THAT?
RIGHT BEFORE THE FIGHT, DARK SAID...
I want to make things perfectly clear, before it's too late...
Before the battle with him.

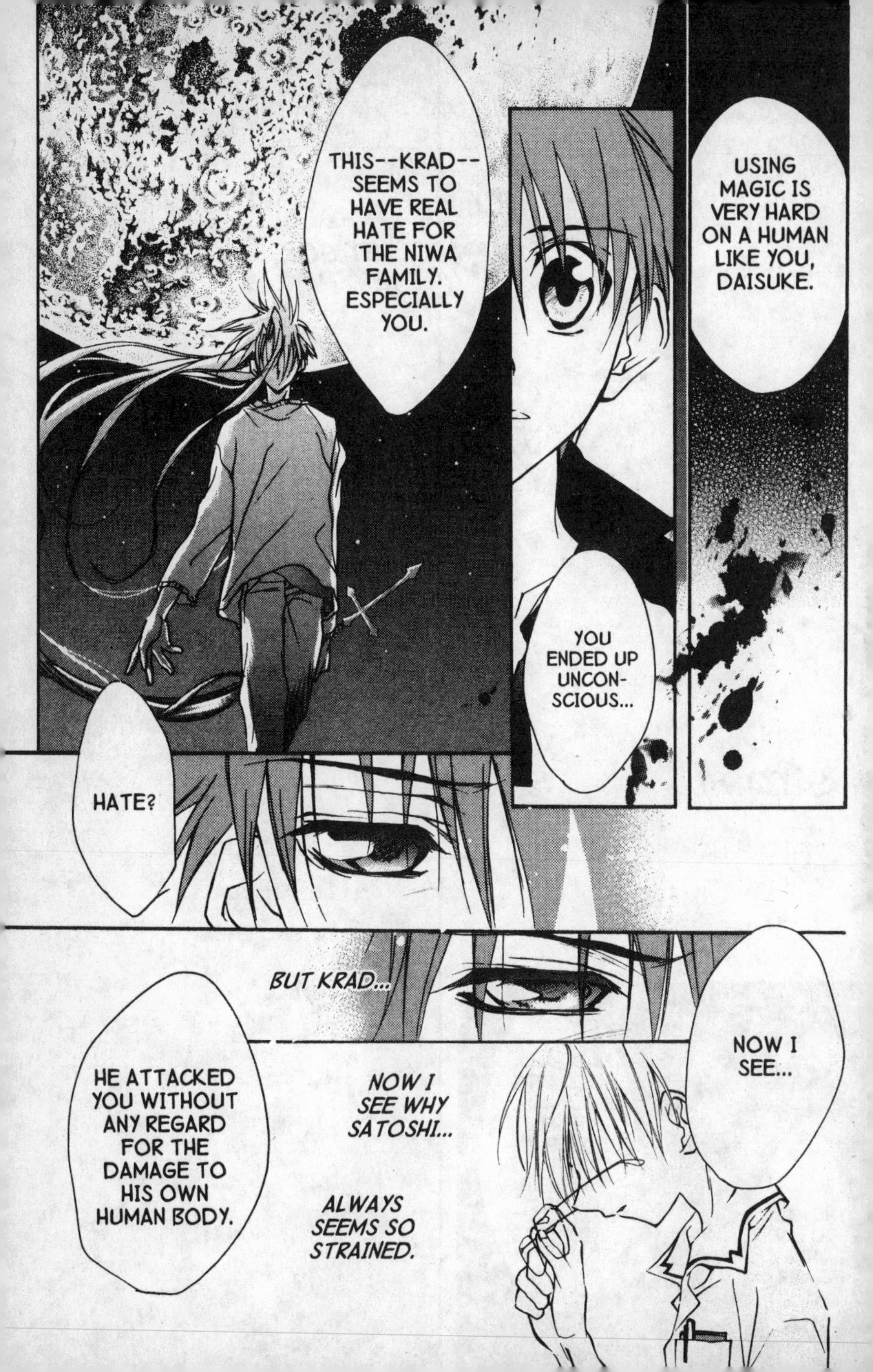
USING MAGIC IS VERY HARD ON A HUMAN LIKE YOU, DAISUKE.
YOU ENDED UP UNCON-SCIOUS...
THIS--KRAD--SEEMS TO HAVE REAL HATE FOR THE NIWA FAMILY. ESPECIALLY YOU.
HATE?
BUT KRAD...
HE ATTACKED YOU WITHOUT ANY REGARD FOR THE DAMAGE TO HIS OWN HUMAN BODY.
NOW I SEE...
NOW I SEE WHY SATOSHI...
ALWAYS SEEMS SO STRAINED.

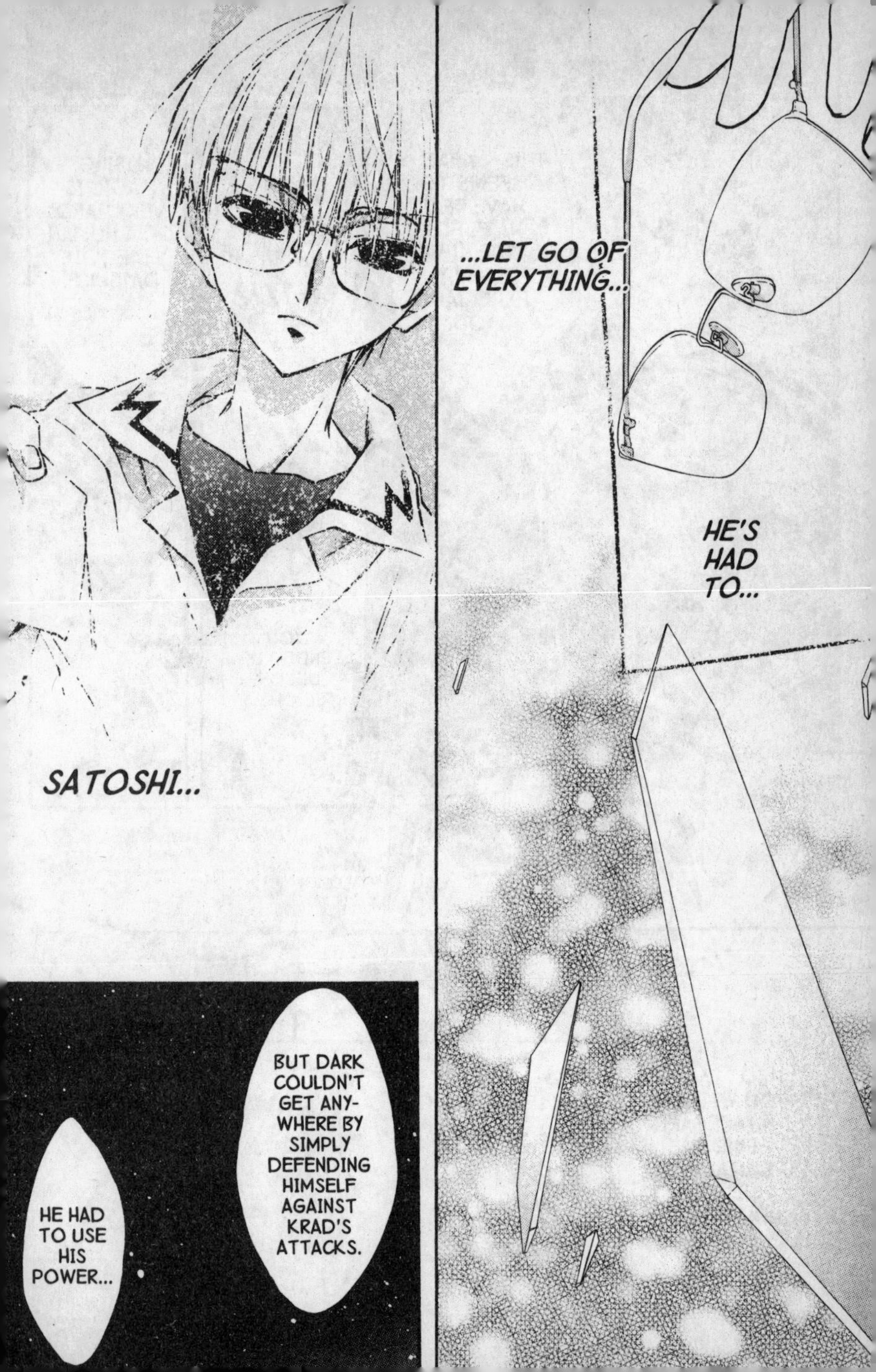
...LET GO OF EVERYTHING...
HE'S HAD TO...
SATOSHI...
BUT DARK COULDN'T GET ANYWHERE BY SIMPLY DEFENDING HIMSELF AGAINST KRAD'S ATTACKS.
HE HAD TO USE HIS POWER...

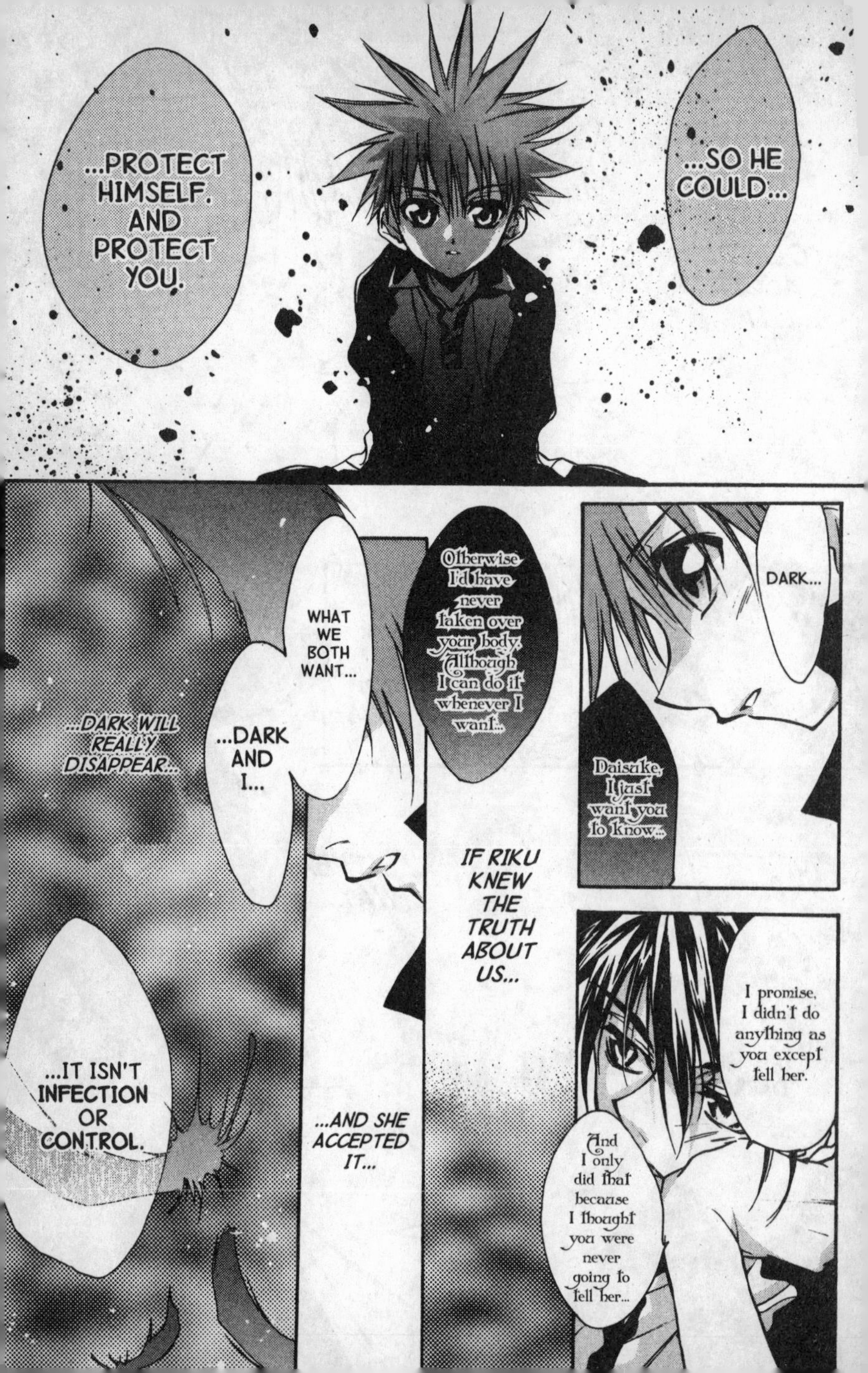
...SO HE COULD...
...PROTECT HIMSELF. AND PROTECT YOU.
DARK...
Daisuke, I just want you to know...
I promise, I didn't do anything as you except tell her.
And I only did that because I thought you were never going to tell her...
Otherwise I'd have never taken over your body. Although I can do it whenever I want...
IF RIKU KNEW THE TRUTH ABOUT US...
...AND SHE ACCEPTED IT...
WHAT WE BOTH WANT...
...DARK AND I...
...DARK WILL REALLY DISAPPEAR...
...IT ISN'T INFECTION OR CONTROL.

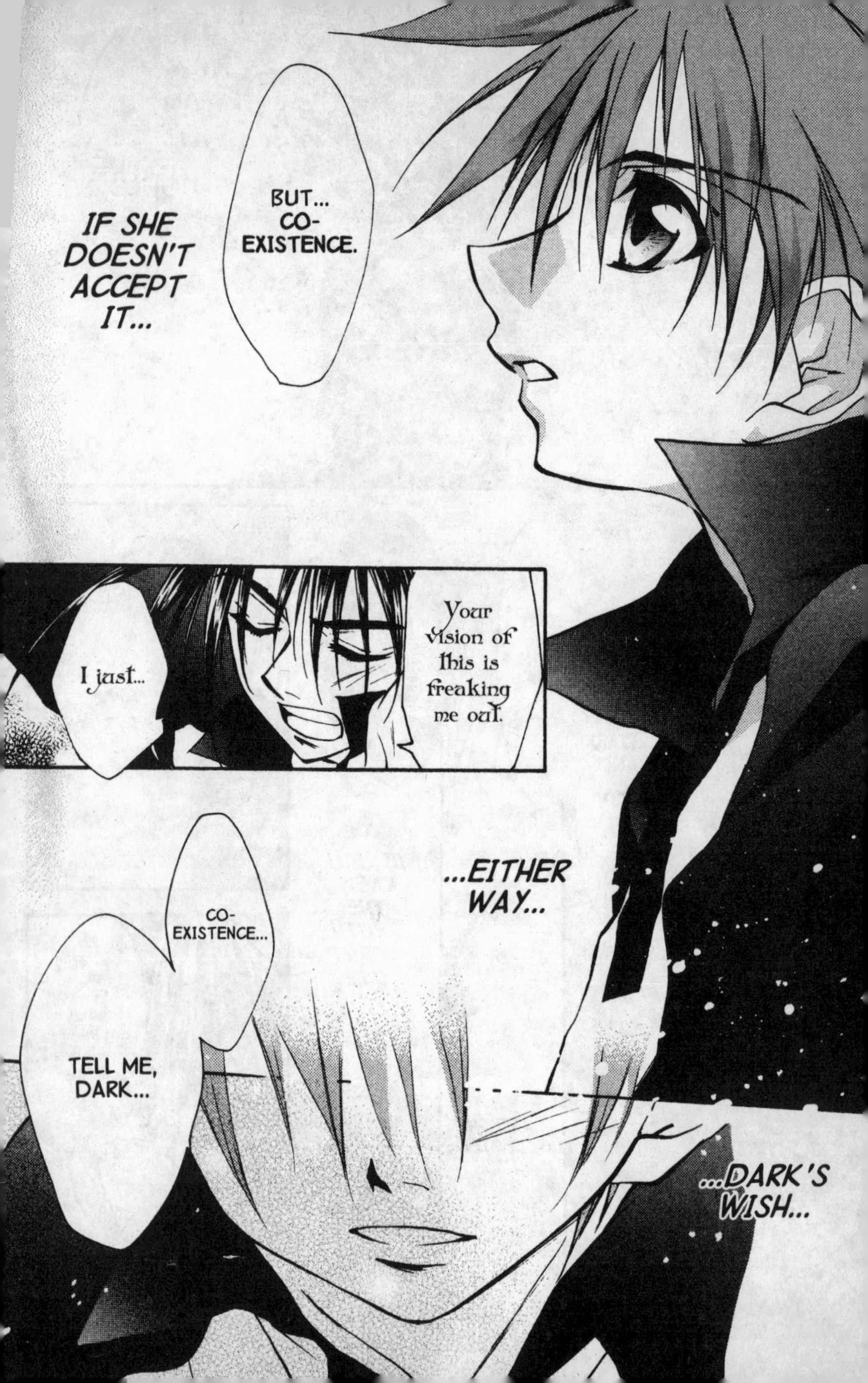
BUT... CO-EXISTENCE.
IF SHE DOESN'T ACCEPT IT...
Your vision of this is freaking me out.
I just...
...EITHER WAY...
CO-EXISTENCE...
TELL ME, DARK...
...DARK'S WISH...

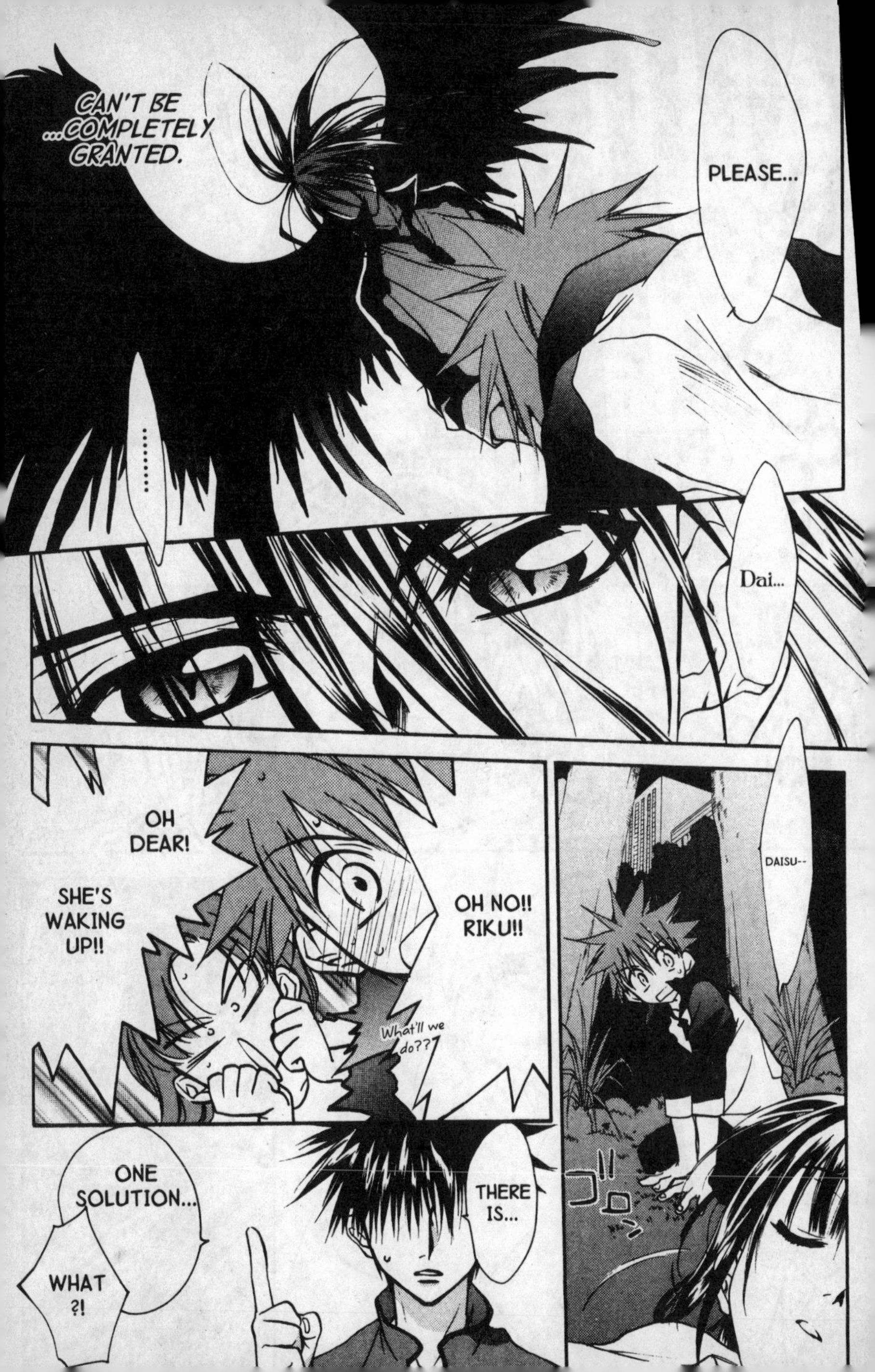
PLEASE...
CAN'T BE ...COMPLETELY GRANTED.
....
Dai...
DAISU--
OH NO!! RIKU!!
OH DEAR!
SHE'S WAKING UP!!
What'll we do??
THERE IS...
ONE SOLUTION...
WHAT ?!

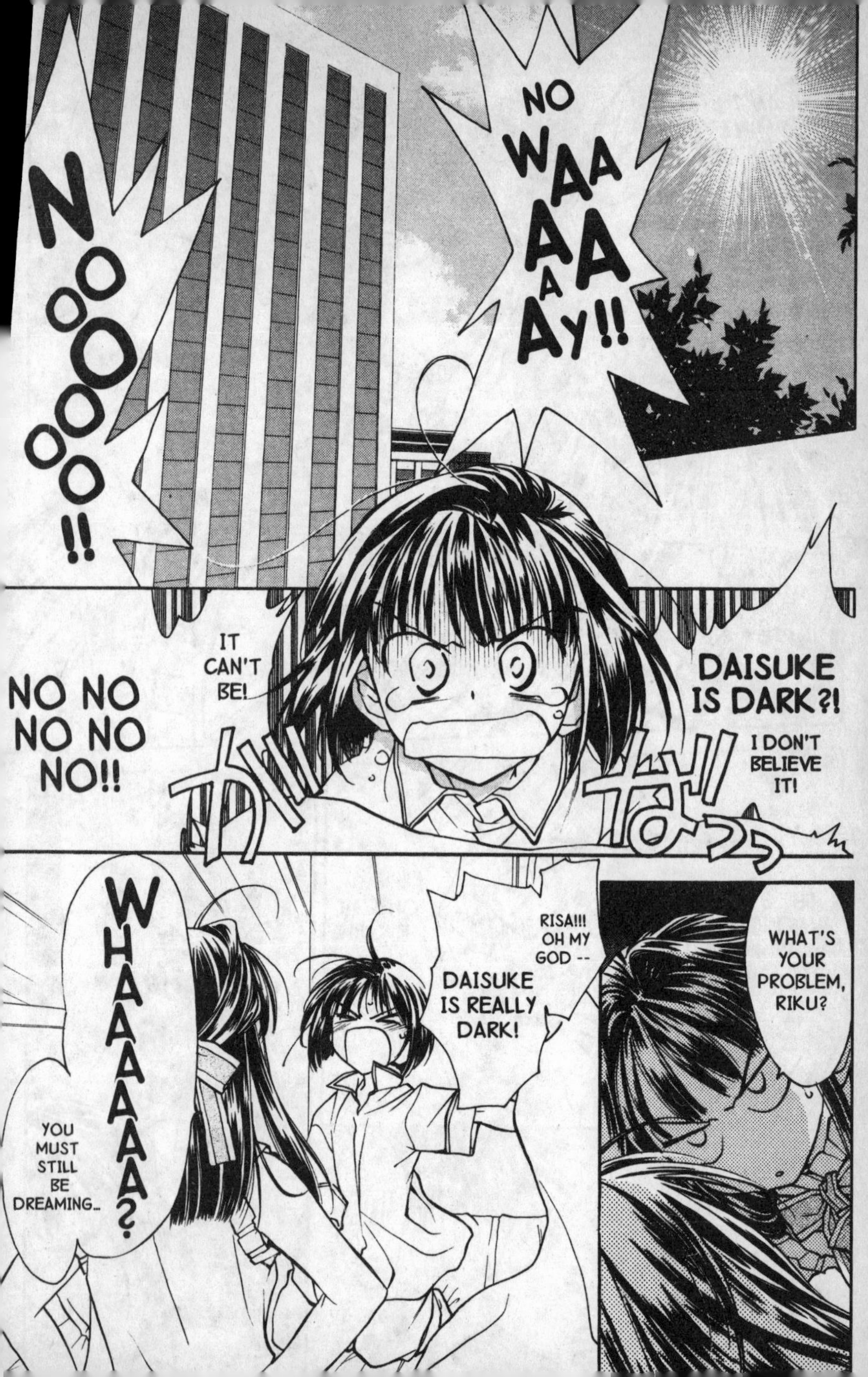
NO WAAAaAAY!!
NOOOOOOOOO!!
DAISUKE IS DARK?!
I DON'T BELIEVE IT!
なっ
IT CAN'T BE!
NO NO NO NO NO!!
わ
WHAT'S YOUR PROBLEM, RIKU?
RISA!!! OH MY GOD --
DAISUKE IS REALLY DARK!
WHAAAAAAA?
YOU MUST STILL BE DREAMING...

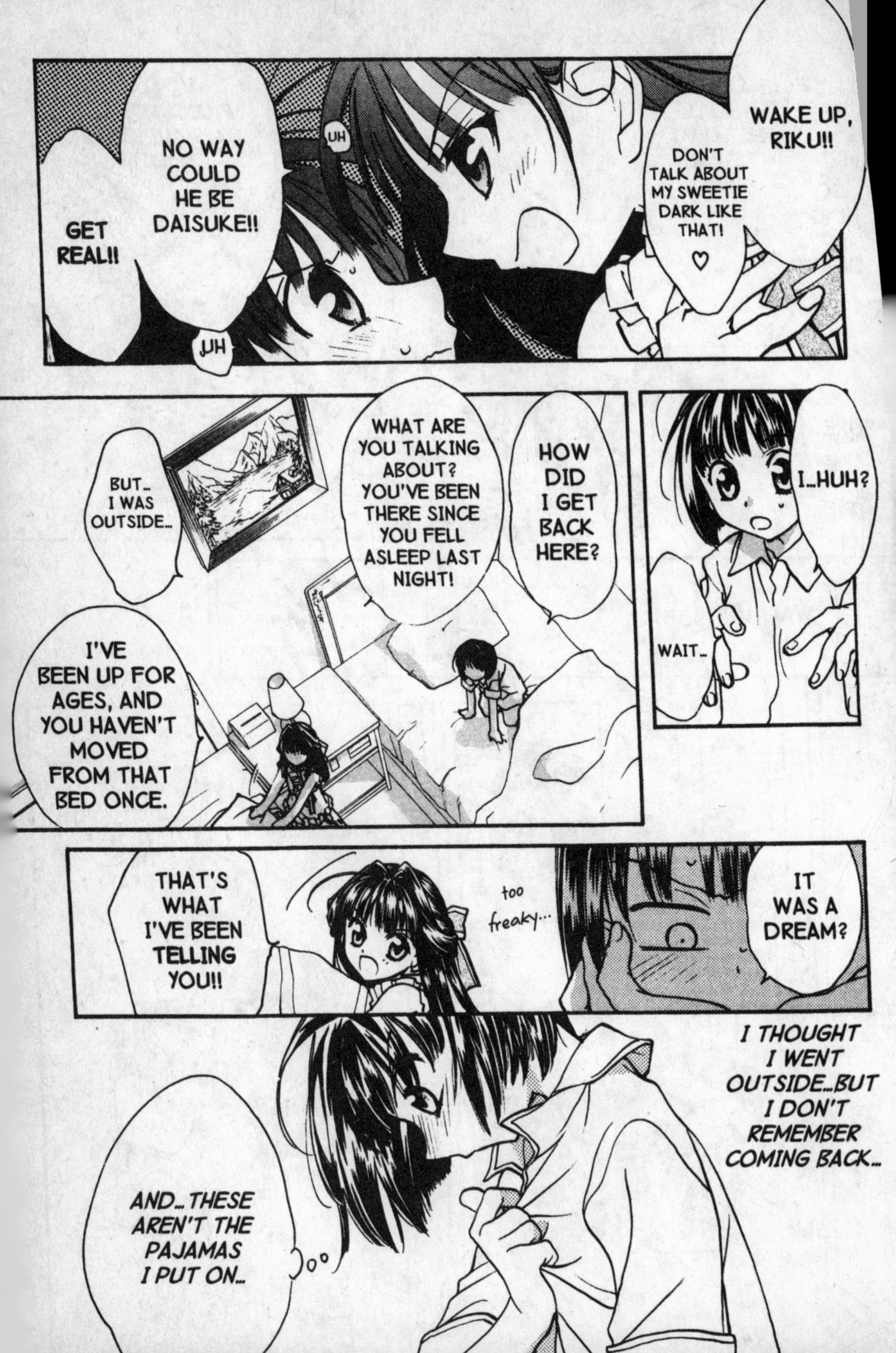
WAKE UP, RIKU!!
DON'T TALK ABOUT MY SWEETIE DARK LIKE THAT! ♡
UH
NO WAY COULD HE BE DAISUKE!!
GET REAL!!
UH
I...HUH?
WAIT...
HOW DID I GET BACK HERE?
WHAT ARE YOU TALKING ABOUT? YOU'VE BEEN THERE SINCE YOU FELL ASLEEP LAST NIGHT!
BUT... I WAS OUTSIDE...
I'VE BEEN UP FOR AGES, AND YOU HAVEN'T MOVED FROM THAT BED ONCE.
IT WAS A DREAM?
too freaky...
THAT'S WHAT I'VE BEEN TELLING YOU!!
I THOUGHT I WENT OUTSIDE...BUT I DON'T REMEMBER COMING BACK...
AND...THESE AREN'T THE PAJAMAS I PUT ON...

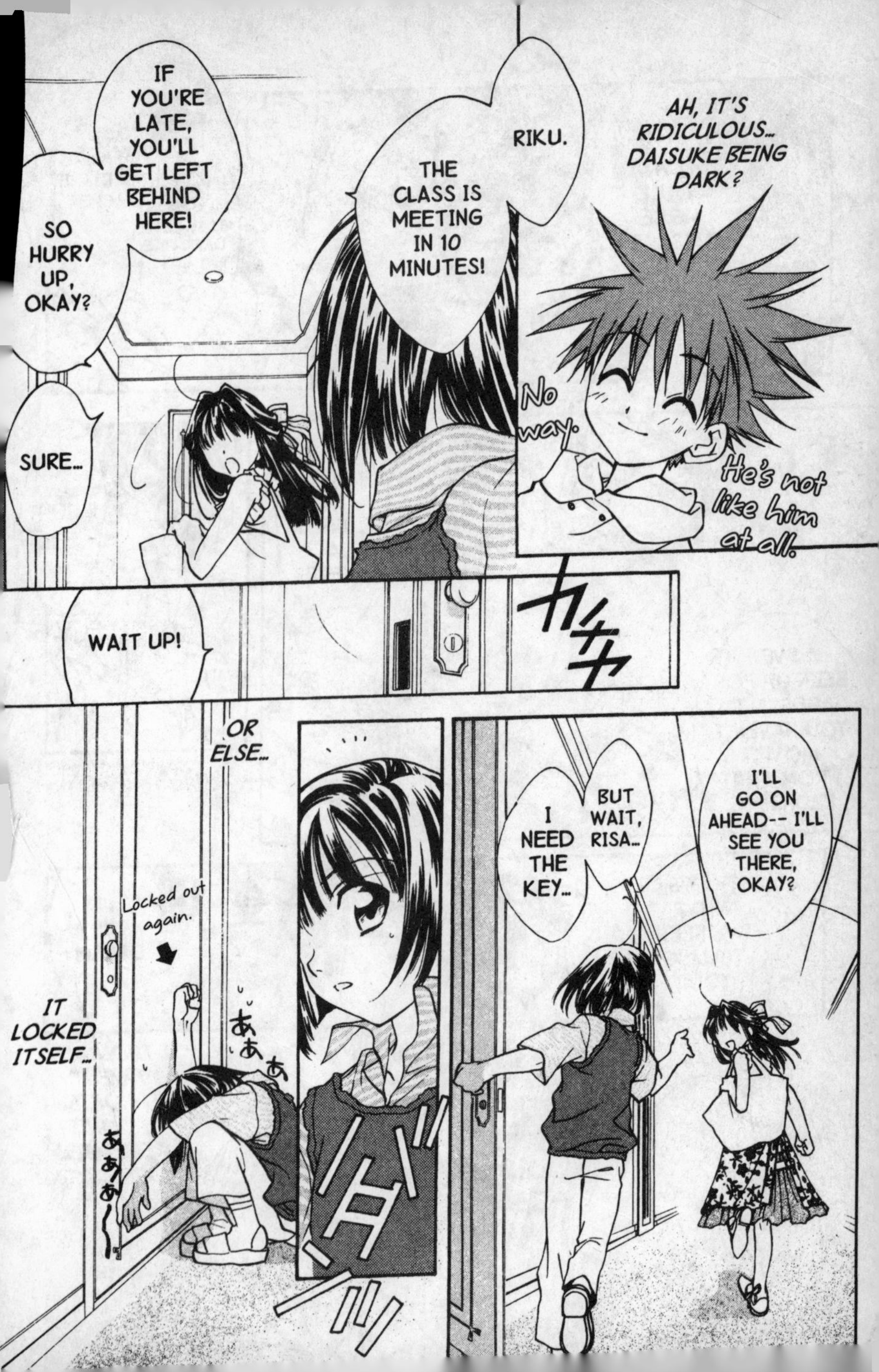
AH, IT'S RIDICULOUS... DAISUKE BEING DARK?
No way.
He's not like him at all.
RIKU.
THE CLASS IS MEETING IN 10 MINUTES!
IF YOU'RE LATE, YOU'LL GET LEFT BEHIND HERE!
SO HURRY UP, OKAY?
SURE...
カチャ
WAIT UP!
I'LL GO ON AHEAD-- I'LL SEE YOU THERE, OKAY?
BUT WAIT, RISA...
I NEED THE KEY...
...
OR ELSE...
IT LOCKED ITSELF...
Locked out again.
あああ
あああ~

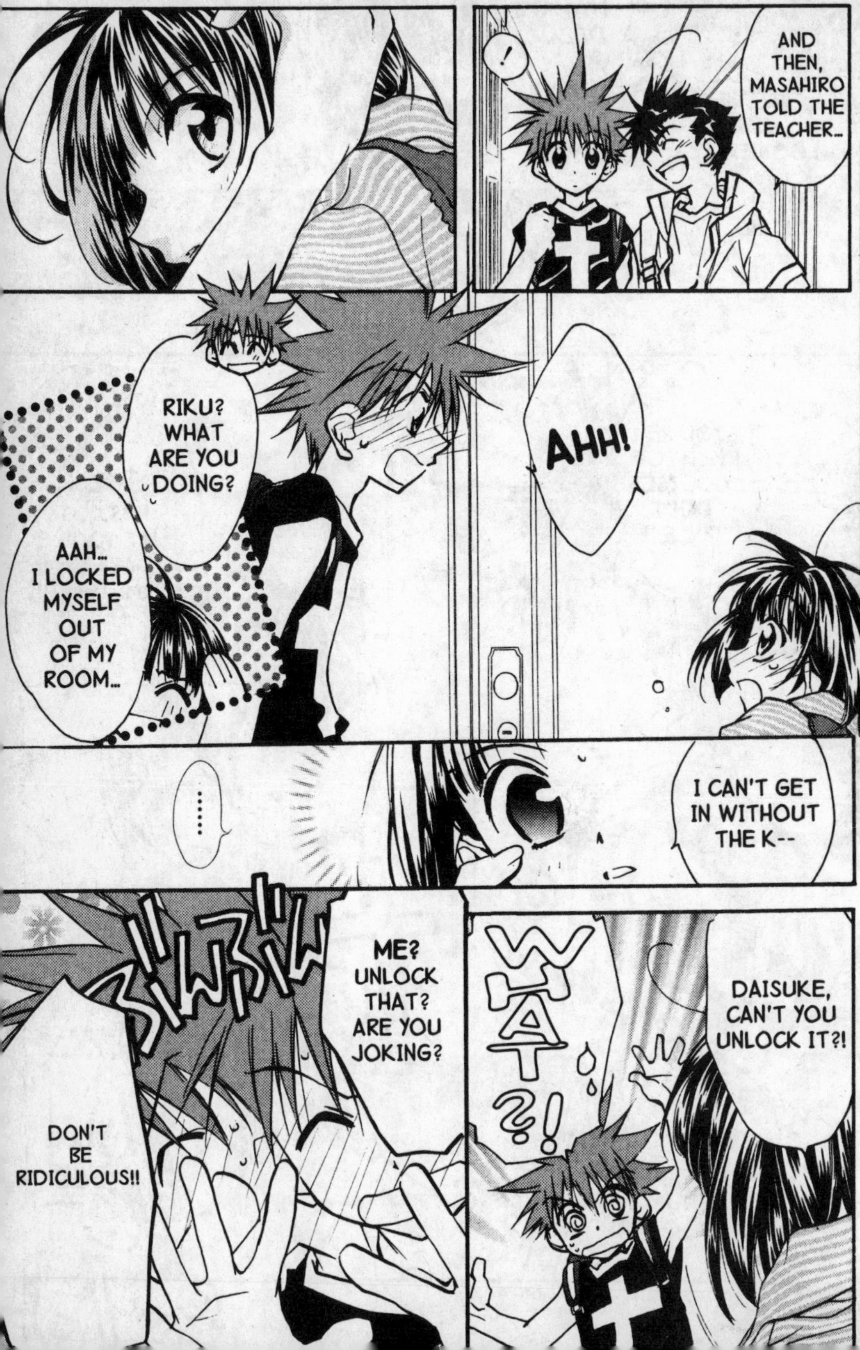
!
AND THEN, MASAHIRO TOLD THE TEACHER...
AHH!
RIKU? WHAT ARE YOU DOING?
AAH... I LOCKED MYSELF OUT OF MY ROOM...
I CAN'T GET IN WITHOUT THE K--
......
DAISUKE, CAN'T YOU UNLOCK IT?!
WHAT?!
ME? UNLOCK THAT? ARE YOU JOKING?
ぶんぶん
DON'T BE RIDICULOUS!!

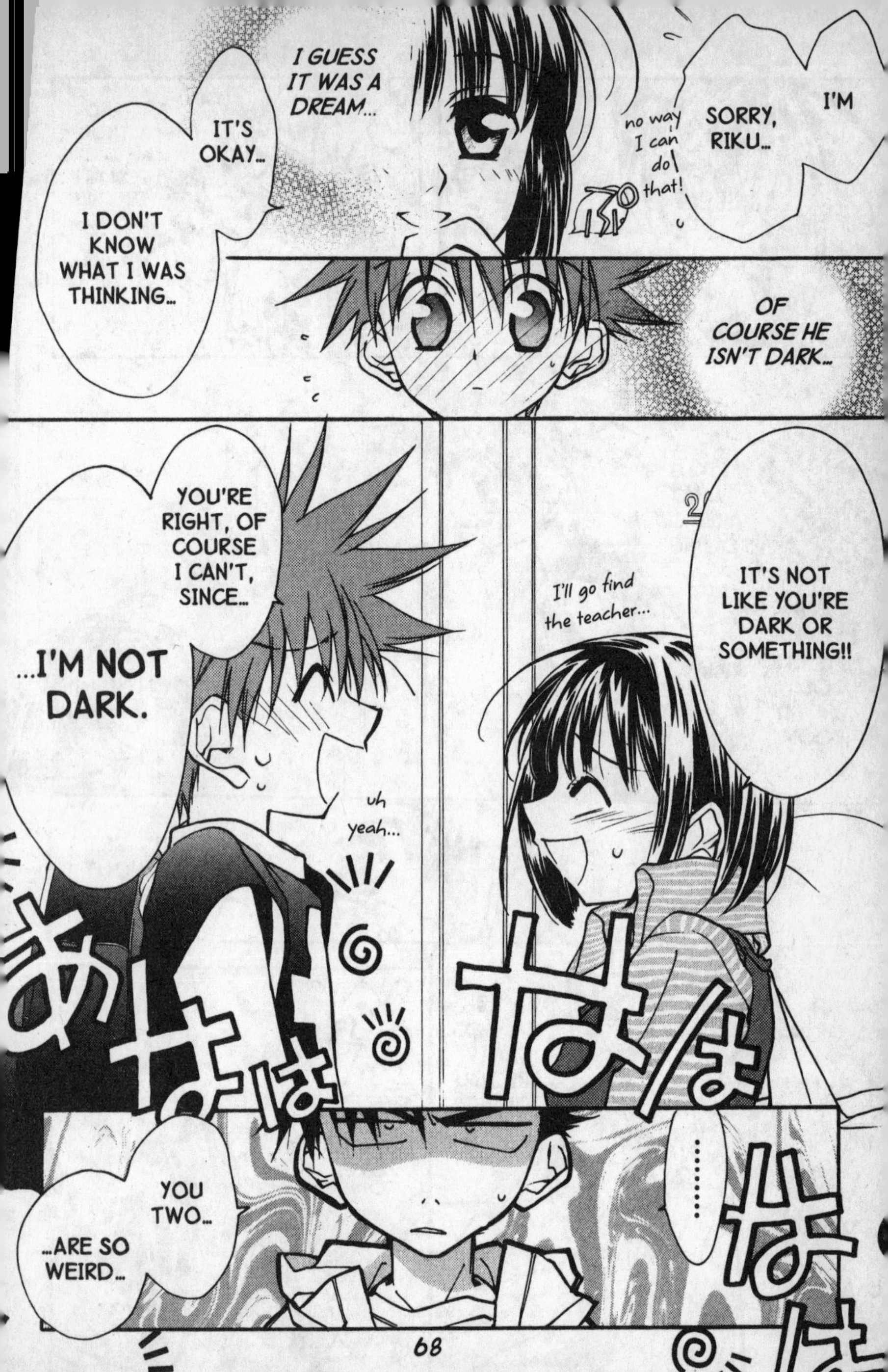
I'M SORRY, RIKU...
no way I can do that!
I GUESS IT WAS A DREAM...
IT'S OKAY... I DON'T KNOW WHAT I WAS THINKING...
OF COURSE HE ISN'T DARK...
IT'S NOT LIKE YOU'RE DARK OR SOMETHING!!
I'll go find the teacher...
YOU'RE RIGHT, OF COURSE I CAN'T, SINCE...
...I'M NOT DARK.
uh yeah...
あはは
はは
......
YOU TWO... ...ARE SO WEIRD...
はは

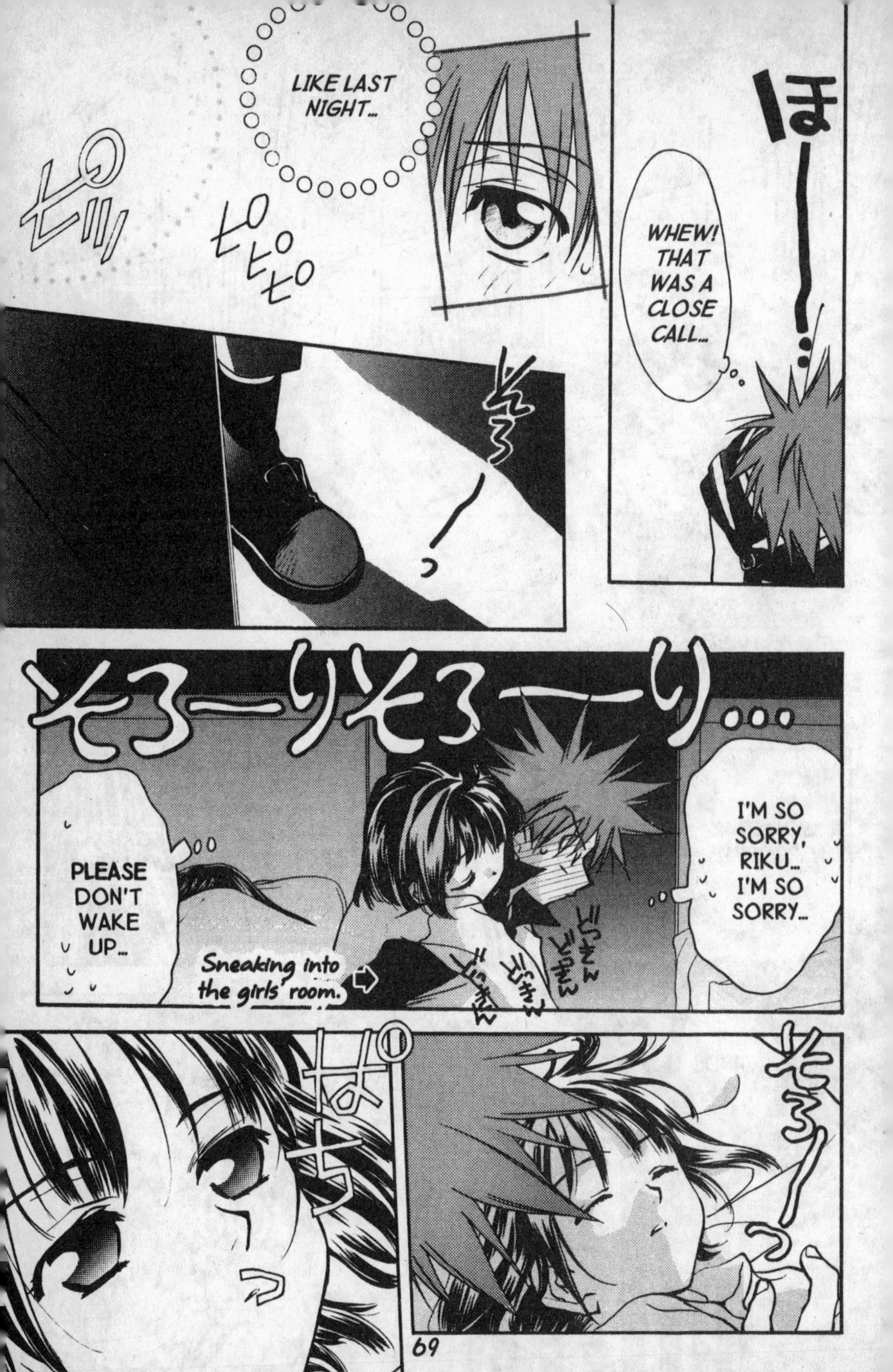
ほー…
WHEW! THAT WAS A CLOSE CALL...
LIKE LAST NIGHT...
ピロピロピロ
ピロ
そろーっ
そろーりそろーり…
I'M SO SORRY, RIKU... I'M SO SORRY...
PLEASE DON'T WAKE UP...
Sneaking into the girls' room.
どきどき
そろーっ
ぱちっ

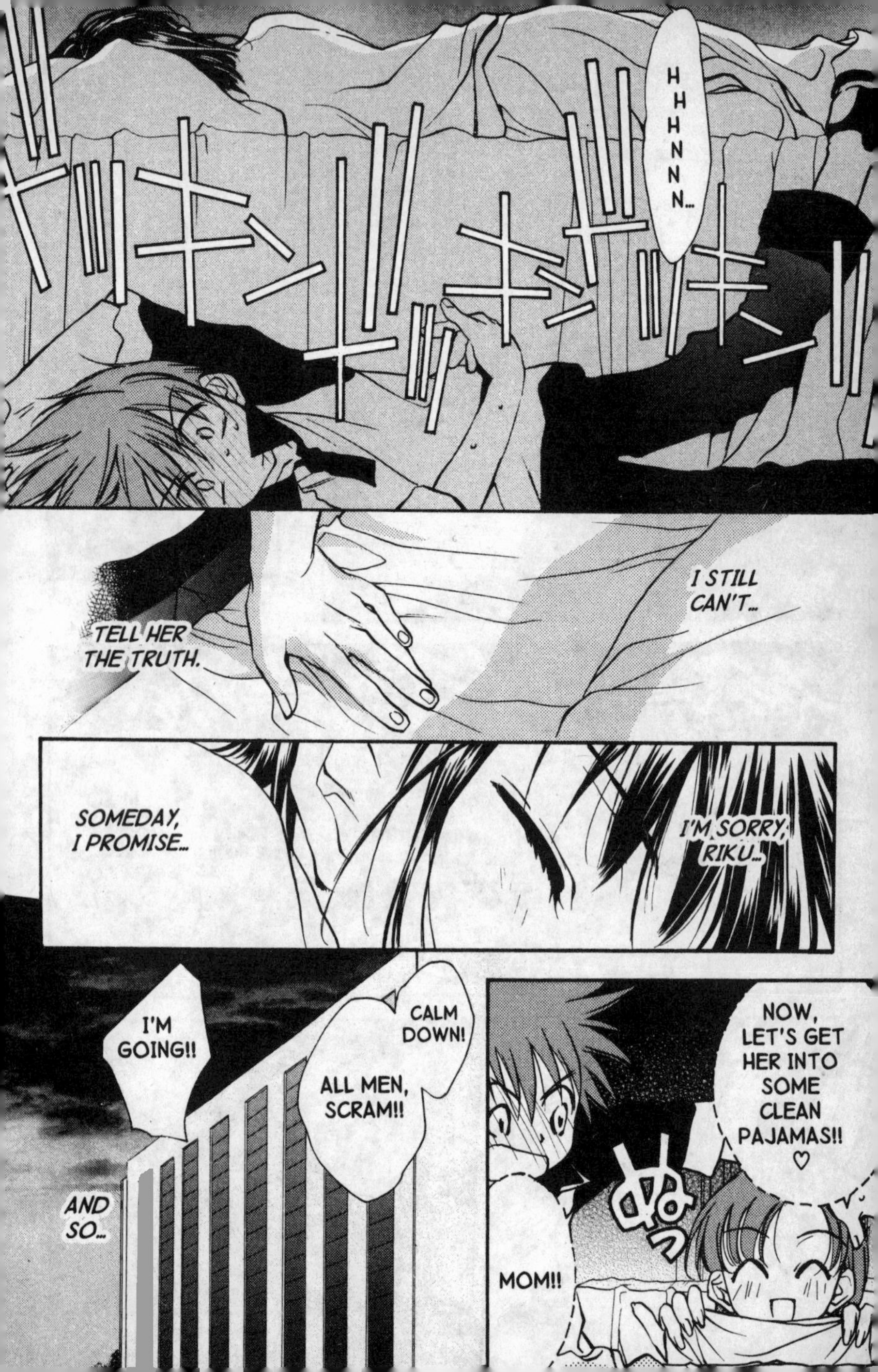
HHHNNN...
I STILL CAN'T...
TELL HER THE TRUTH.
I'M SORRY, RIKU...
SOMEDAY, I PROMISE...
NOW, LET'S GET HER INTO SOME CLEAN PAJAMAS!! ♡
ぬっ
MOM!!
CALM DOWN!
ALL MEN, SCRAM!!
I'M GOING!!
AND SO...

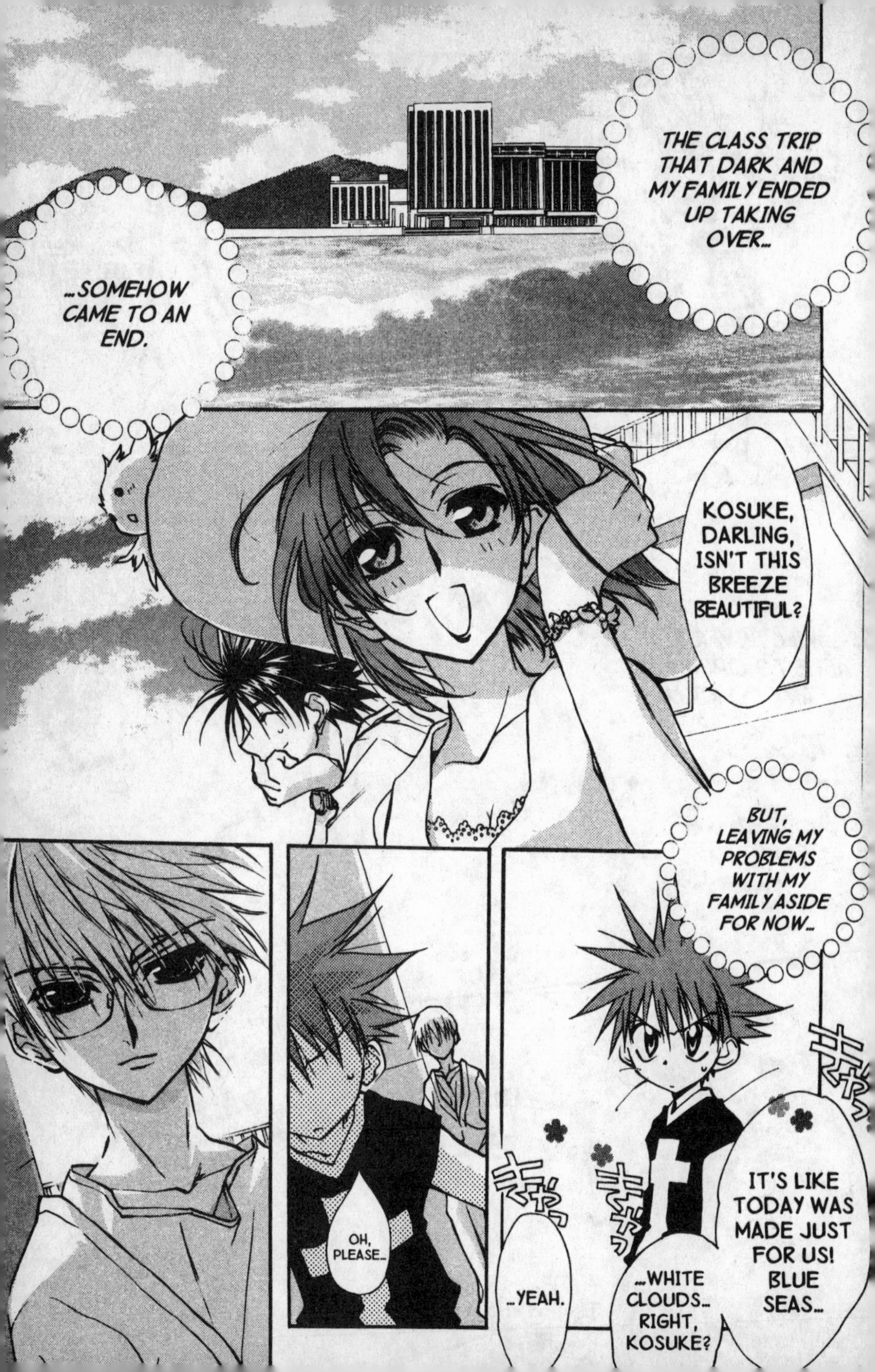
THE CLASS TRIP THAT DARK AND MY FAMILY ENDED UP TAKING OVER...
...SOMEHOW CAME TO AN END.
KOSUKE, DARLING, ISN'T THIS BREEZE BEAUTIFUL?
BUT, LEAVING MY PROBLEMS WITH MY FAMILY ASIDE FOR NOW...
IT'S LIKE TODAY WAS MADE JUST FOR US! BLUE SEAS...
...WHITE CLOUDS... RIGHT, KOSUKE?
...YEAH.
OH, PLEASE...

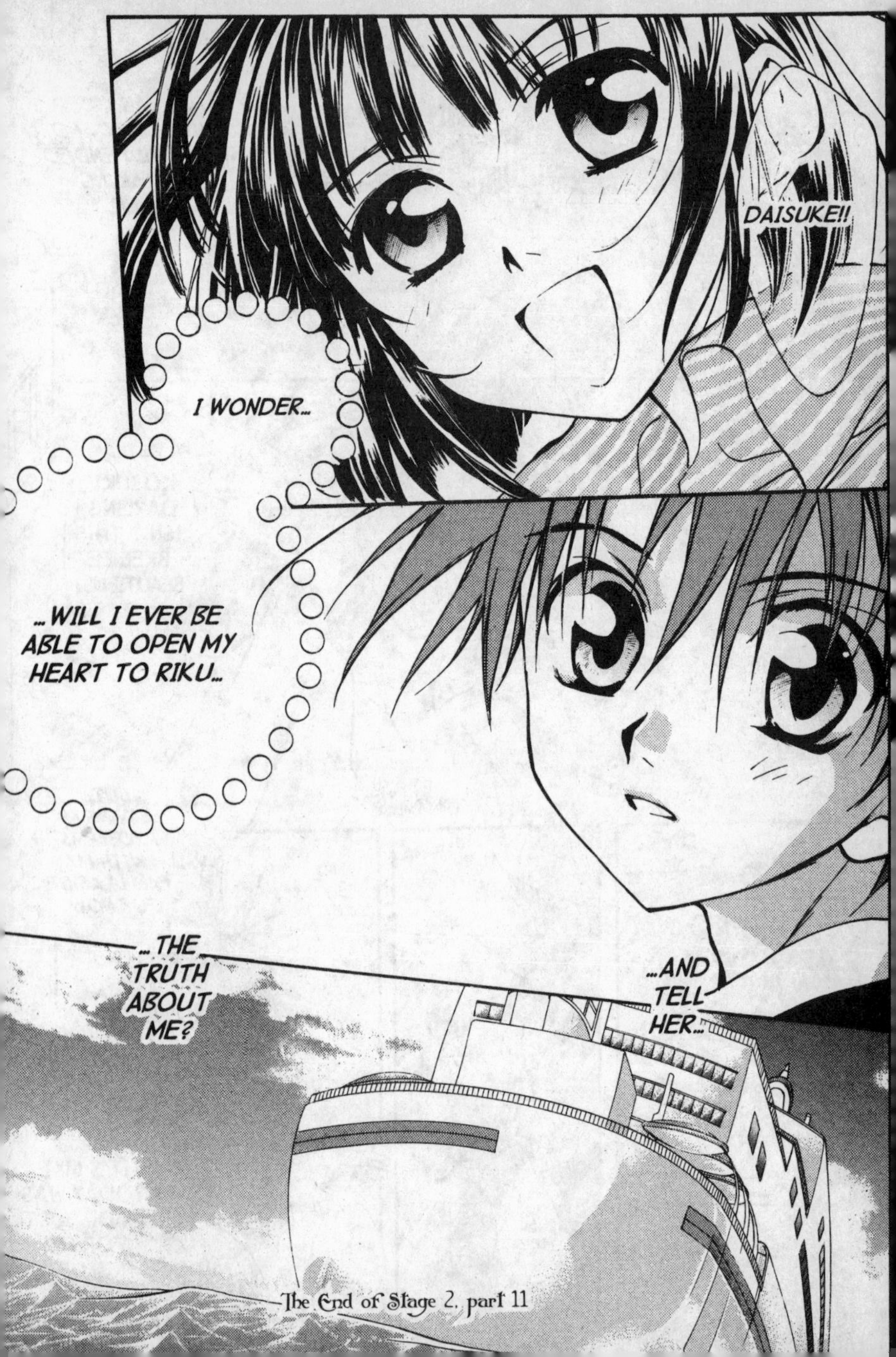
DAISUKE!!
I WONDER...
...WILL I EVER BE ABLE TO OPEN MY HEART TO RIKU...
...AND TELL HER...
...THE TRUTH ABOUT ME?
The End of Stage 2, part 11

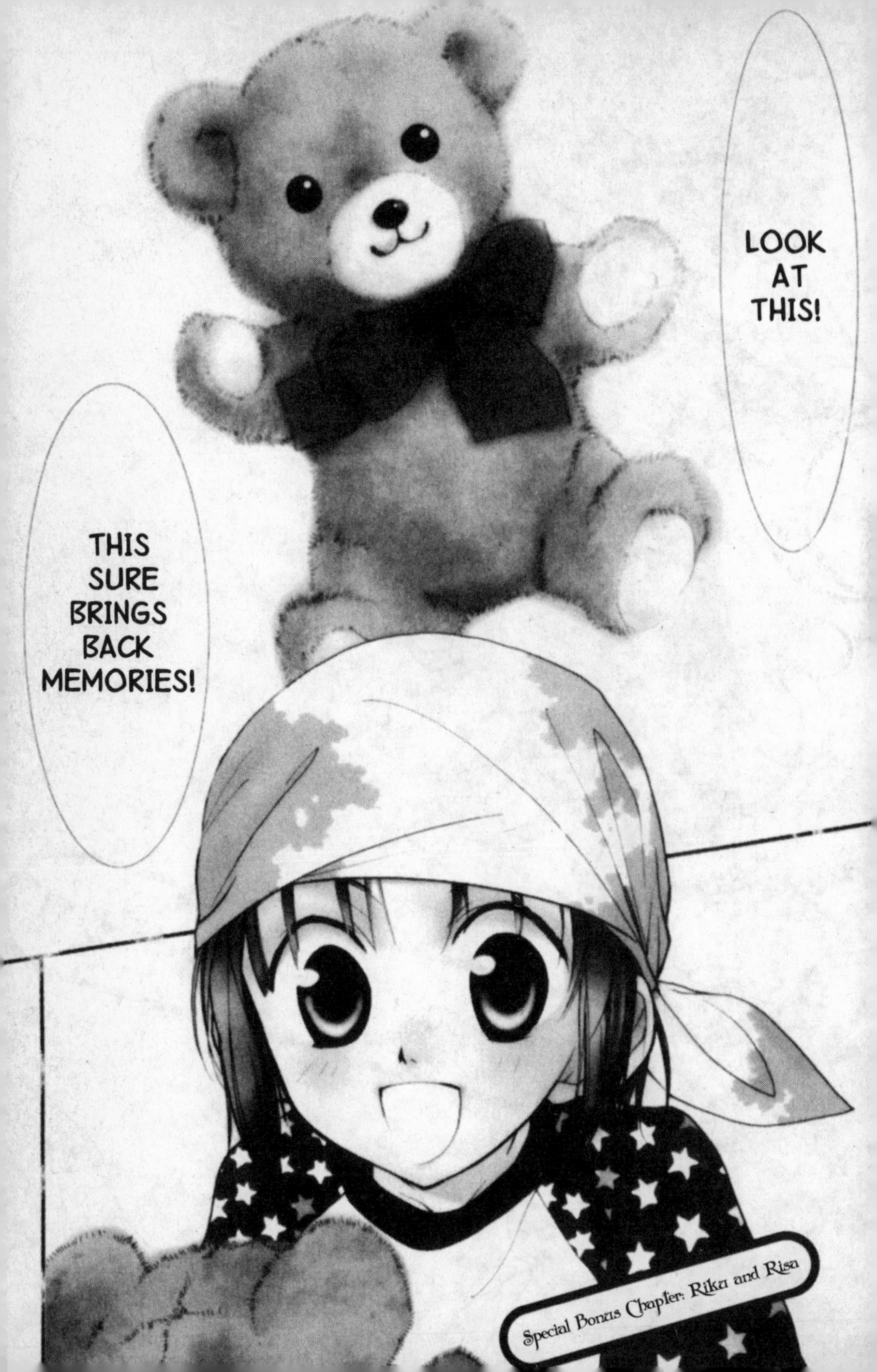
LOOK AT THIS!
THIS SURE BRINGS BACK MEMORIES!
Special Bonus Chapter: Riku and Risa

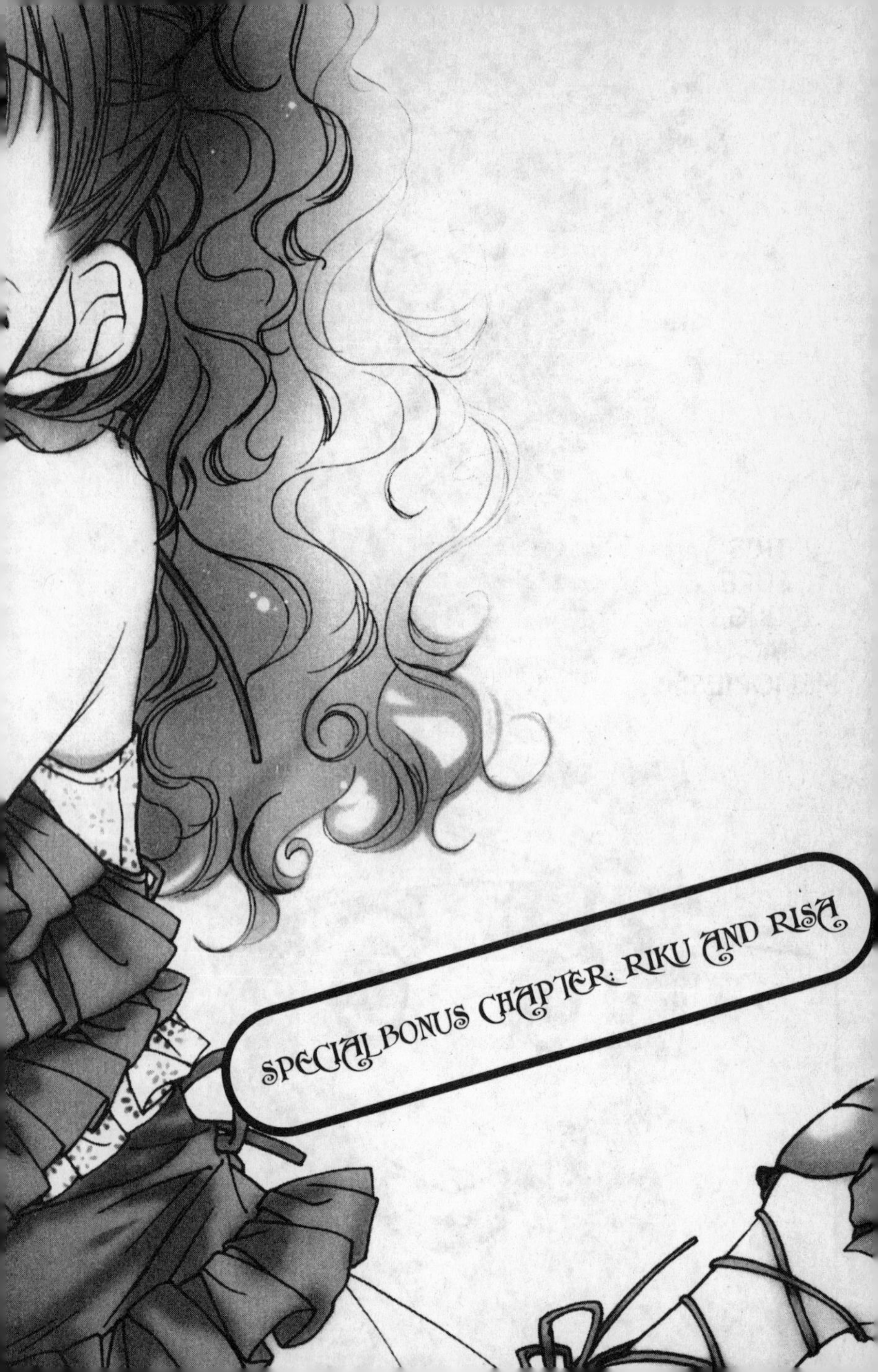
SPECIAL BONUS CHAPTER: RIKU AND RISA

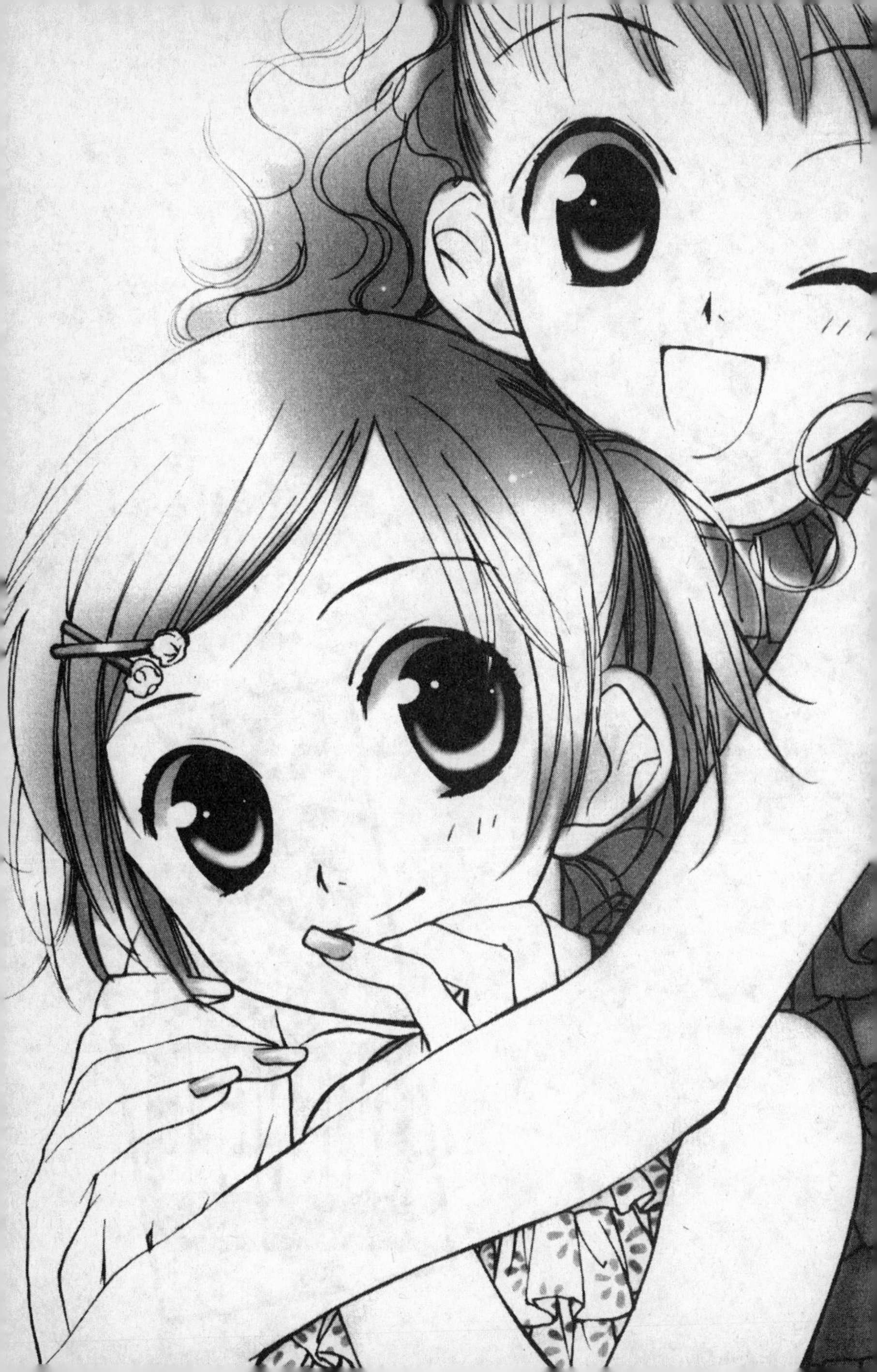

DNANGEL

DAISUKE&WIZ   YUKIRU SUGISAKI

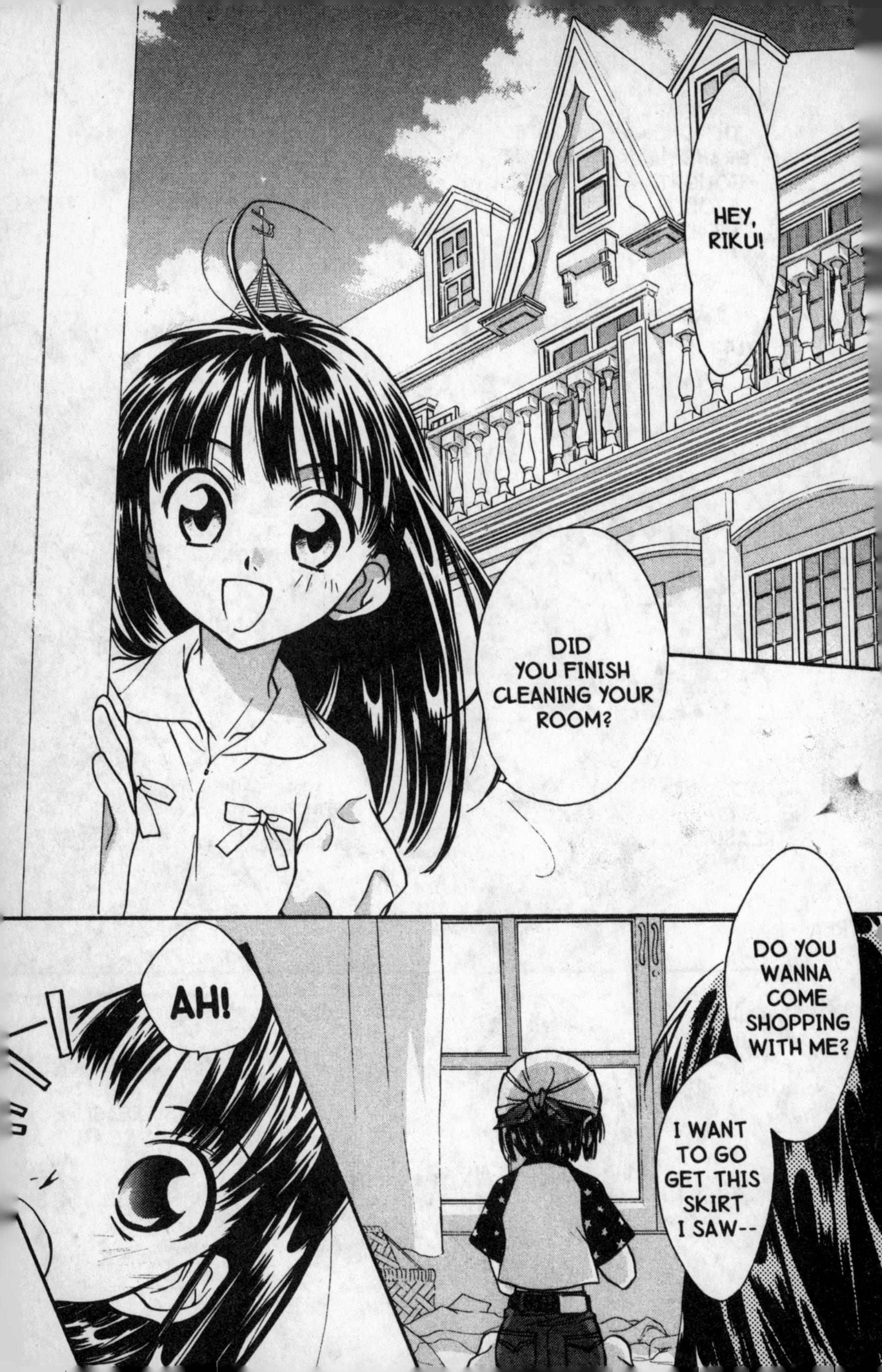
HEY, RIKU!
DID YOU FINISH CLEANING YOUR ROOM?
DO YOU WANNA COME SHOPPING WITH ME?
I WANT TO GO GET THIS SKIRT I SAW--
AH!

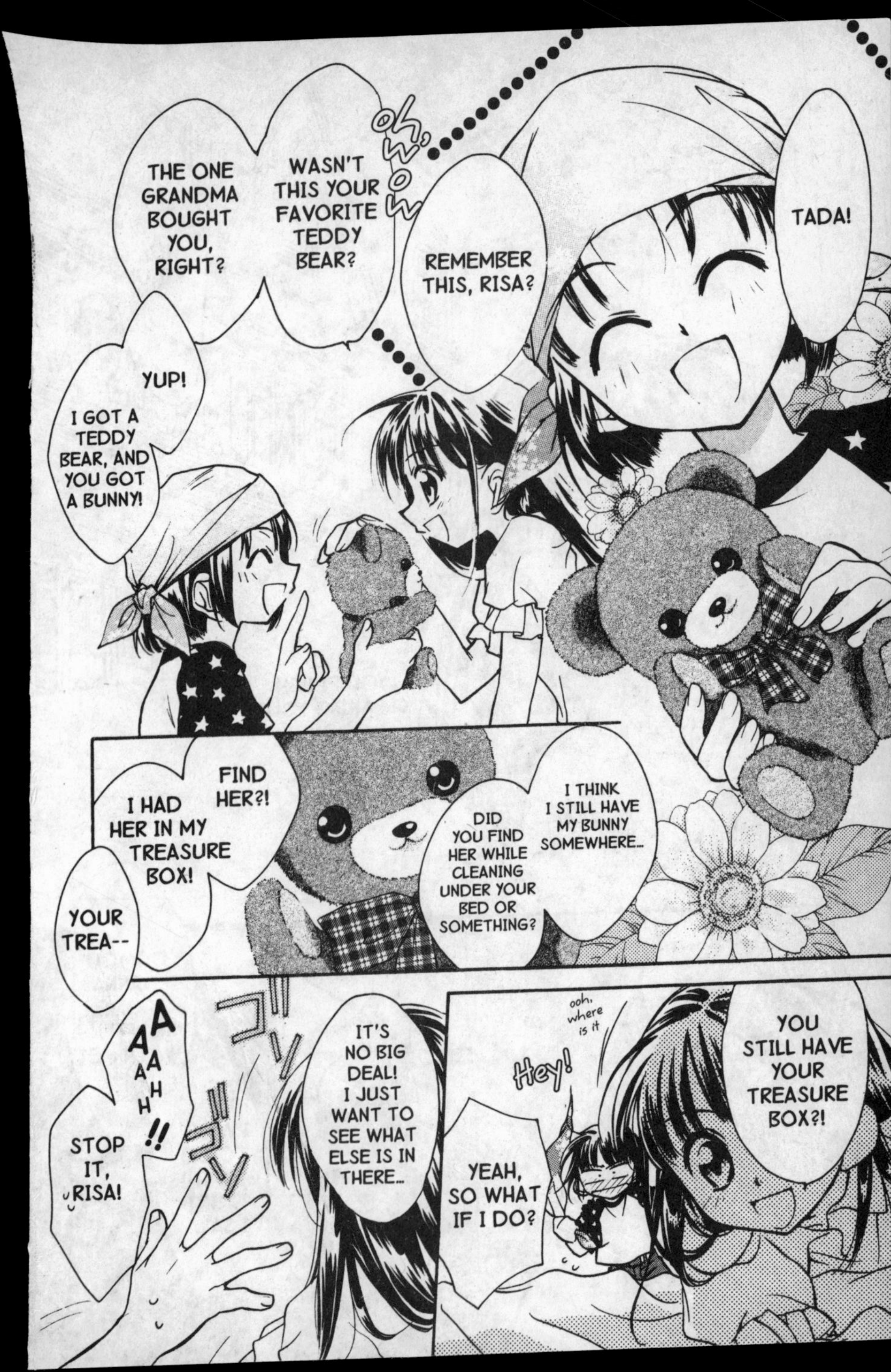
TADA!
REMEMBER THIS, RISA?
oh, wow
WASN'T THIS YOUR FAVORITE TEDDY BEAR?
THE ONE GRANDMA BOUGHT YOU, RIGHT?
YUP!
I GOT A TEDDY BEAR, AND YOU GOT A BUNNY!
I THINK I STILL HAVE MY BUNNY SOMEWHERE...
DID YOU FIND HER WHILE CLEANING UNDER YOUR BED OR SOMETHING?
FIND HER?!
I HAD HER IN MY TREASURE BOX!
YOUR TREA--
YOU STILL HAVE YOUR TREASURE BOX?!
ooh, where is it
Hey!
YEAH, SO WHAT IF I DO?
IT'S NO BIG DEAL! I JUST WANT TO SEE WHAT ELSE IS IN THERE...
AAAHH!!
STOP IT, RISA!

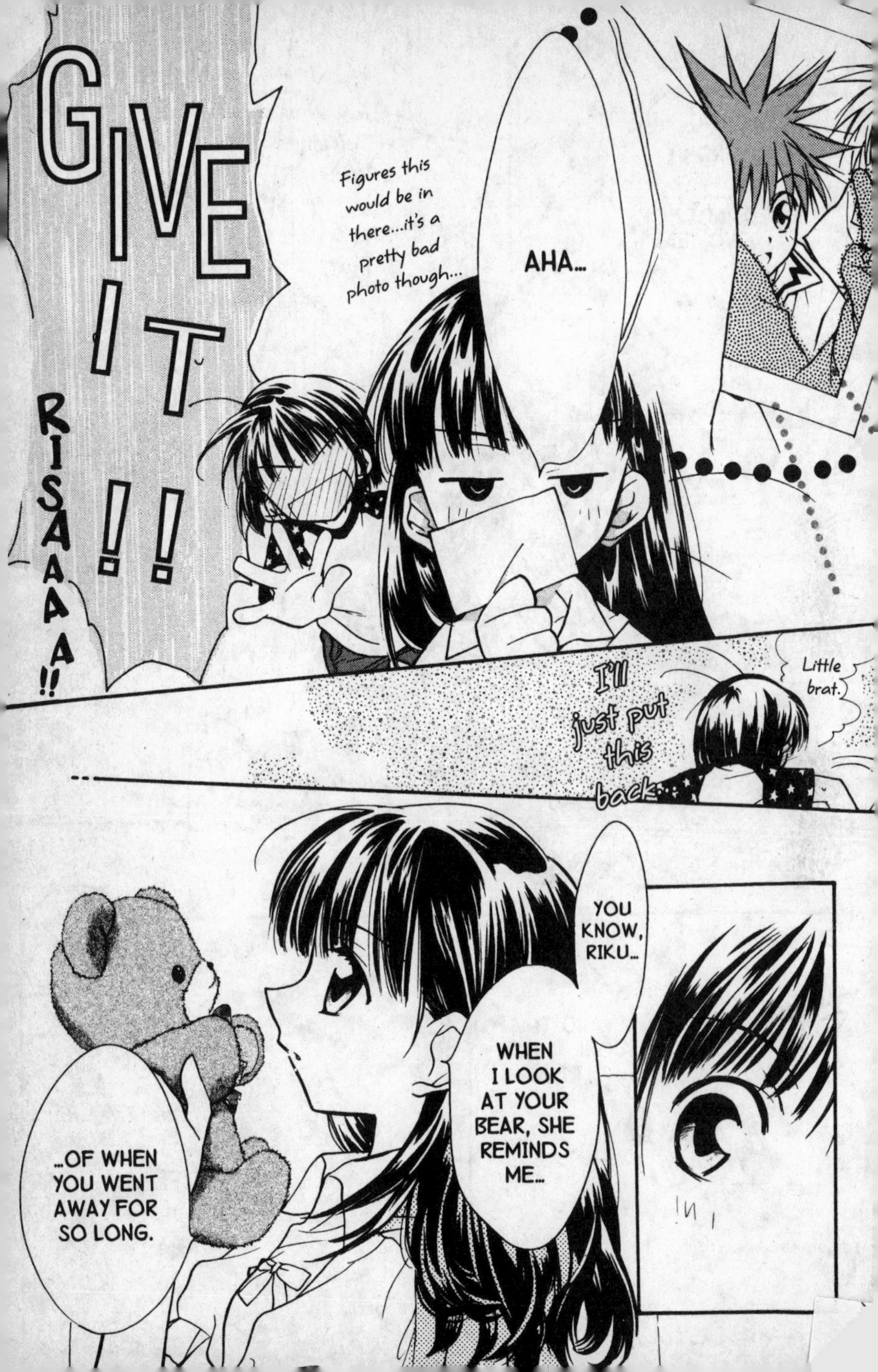
AHA...
Figures this would be in there...it's a pretty bad photo though...
GIVE IT!!
RISAAAA!!
Little brat.
I'll just put this back.
YOU KNOW, RIKU...
WHEN I LOOK AT YOUR BEAR, SHE REMINDS ME...
...OF WHEN YOU WENT AWAY FOR SO LONG.

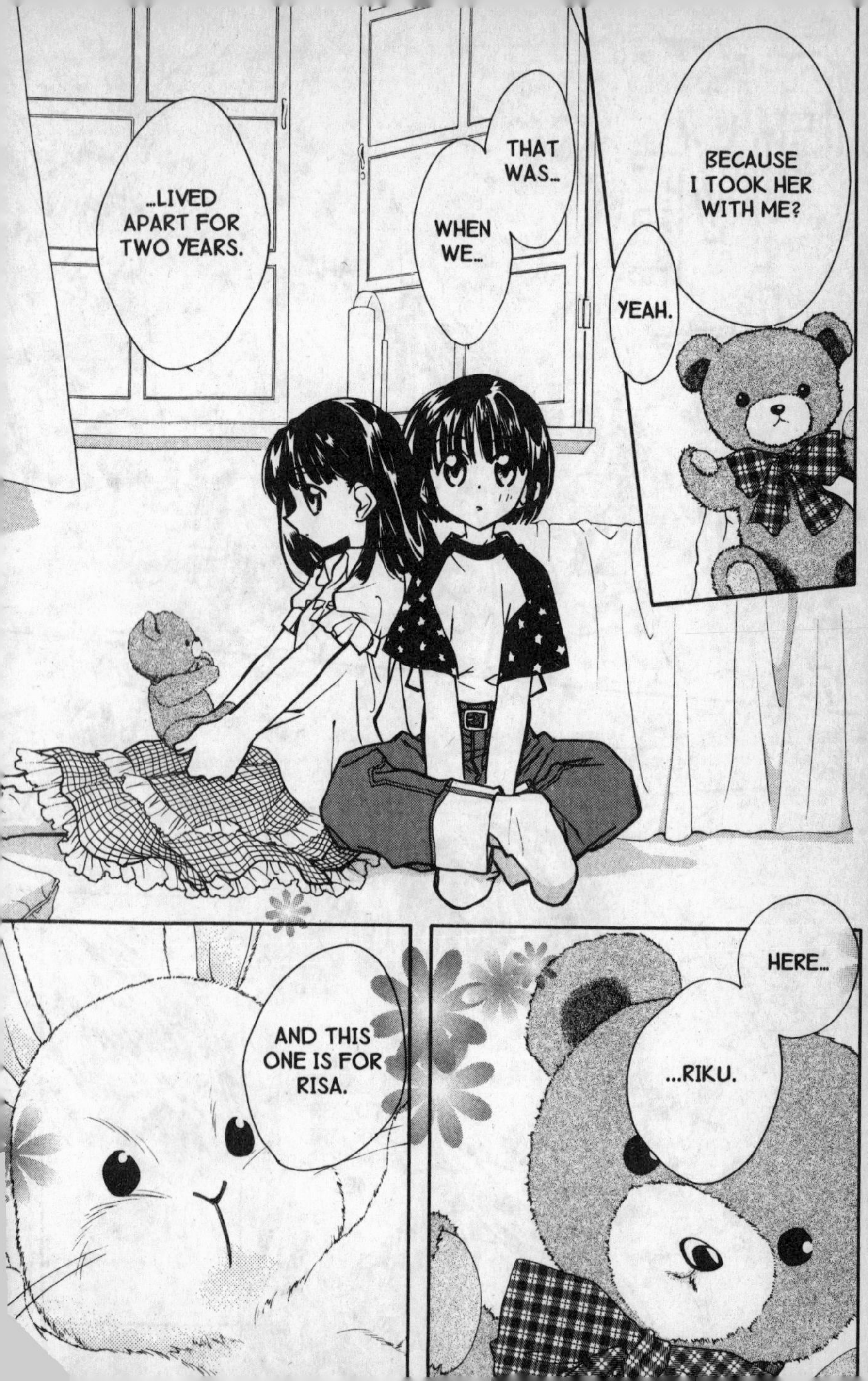
BECAUSE I TOOK HER WITH ME?
YEAH.
THAT WAS...
WHEN WE...
...LIVED APART FOR TWO YEARS.
HERE...
...RIKU.
AND THIS ONE IS FOR RISA.

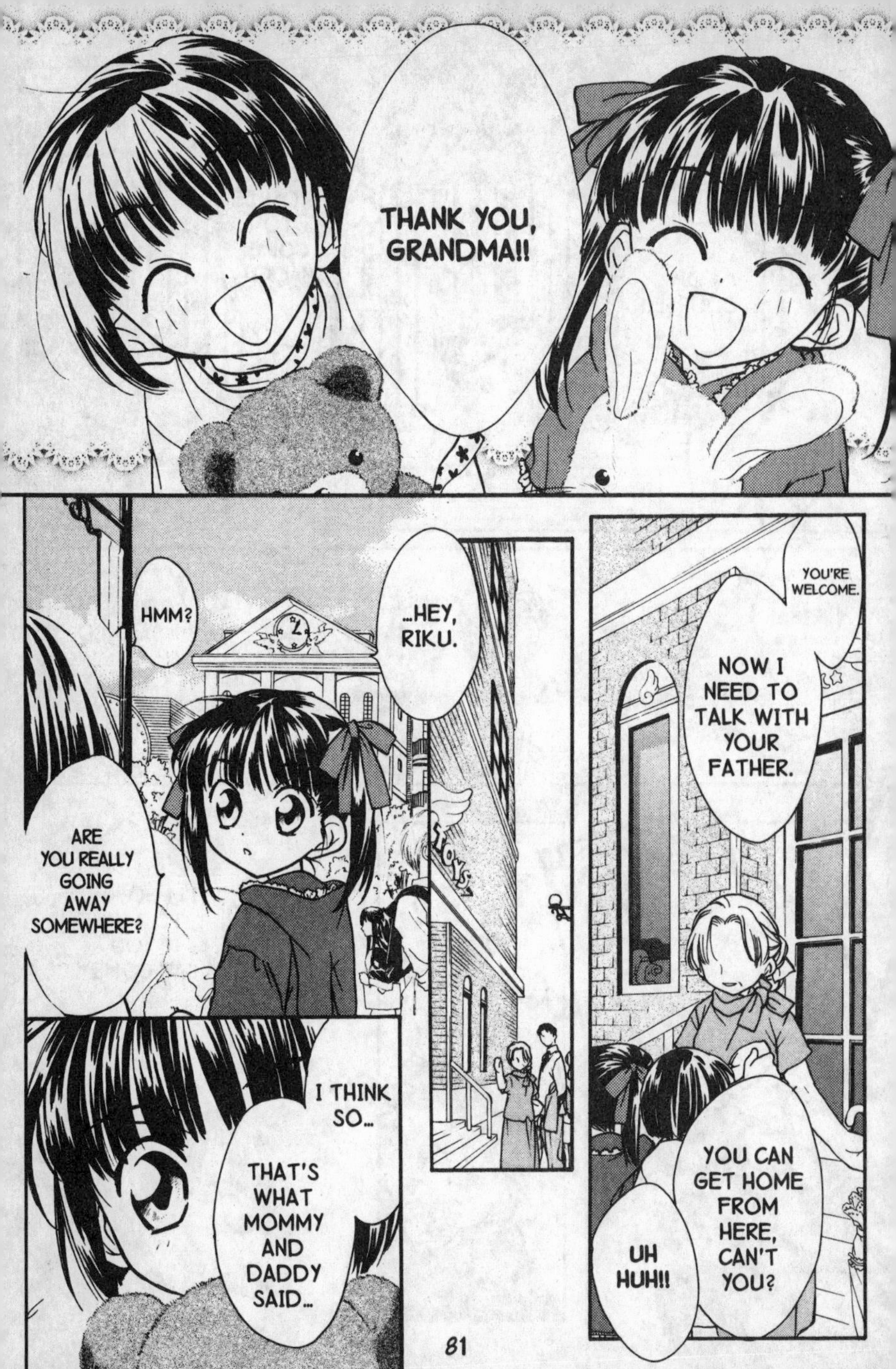
THANK YOU, GRANDMA!!
YOU'RE WELCOME.
NOW I NEED TO TALK WITH YOUR FATHER.
YOU CAN GET HOME FROM HERE, CAN'T YOU?
UH HUH!!
...HEY, RIKU.
HMM?
ARE YOU REALLY GOING AWAY SOMEWHERE?
I THINK SO...
THAT'S WHAT MOMMY AND DADDY SAID...

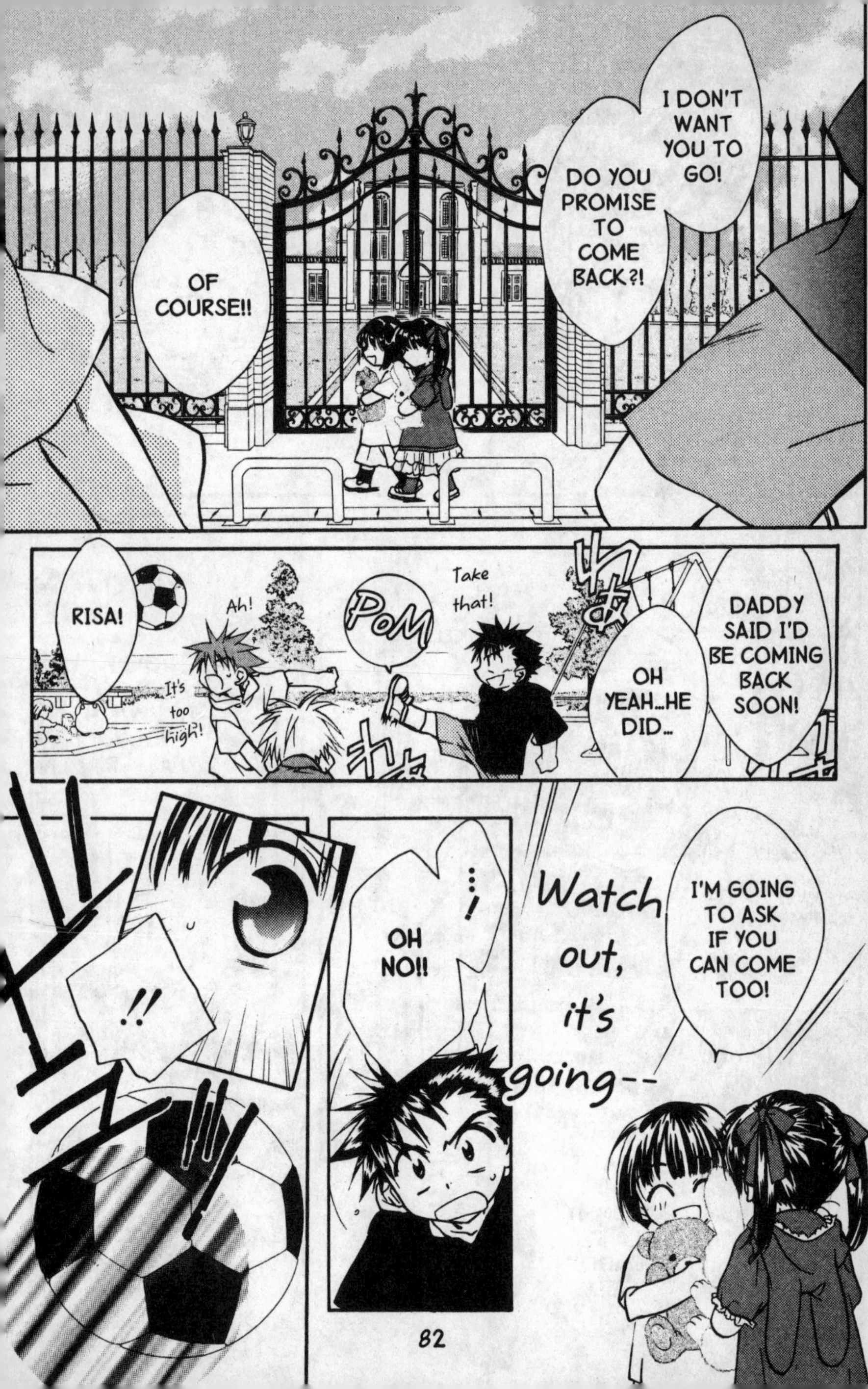
I DON'T WANT YOU TO GO!
DO YOU PROMISE TO COME BACK?!
OF COURSE!!
DADDY SAID I'D BE COMING BACK SOON!
OH YEAH...HE DID...
Take that!
PoM
Ah!
It's too high!
RISA!
I'M GOING TO ASK IF YOU CAN COME TOO!
Watch out, it's going--
...!
OH NO!!
!!

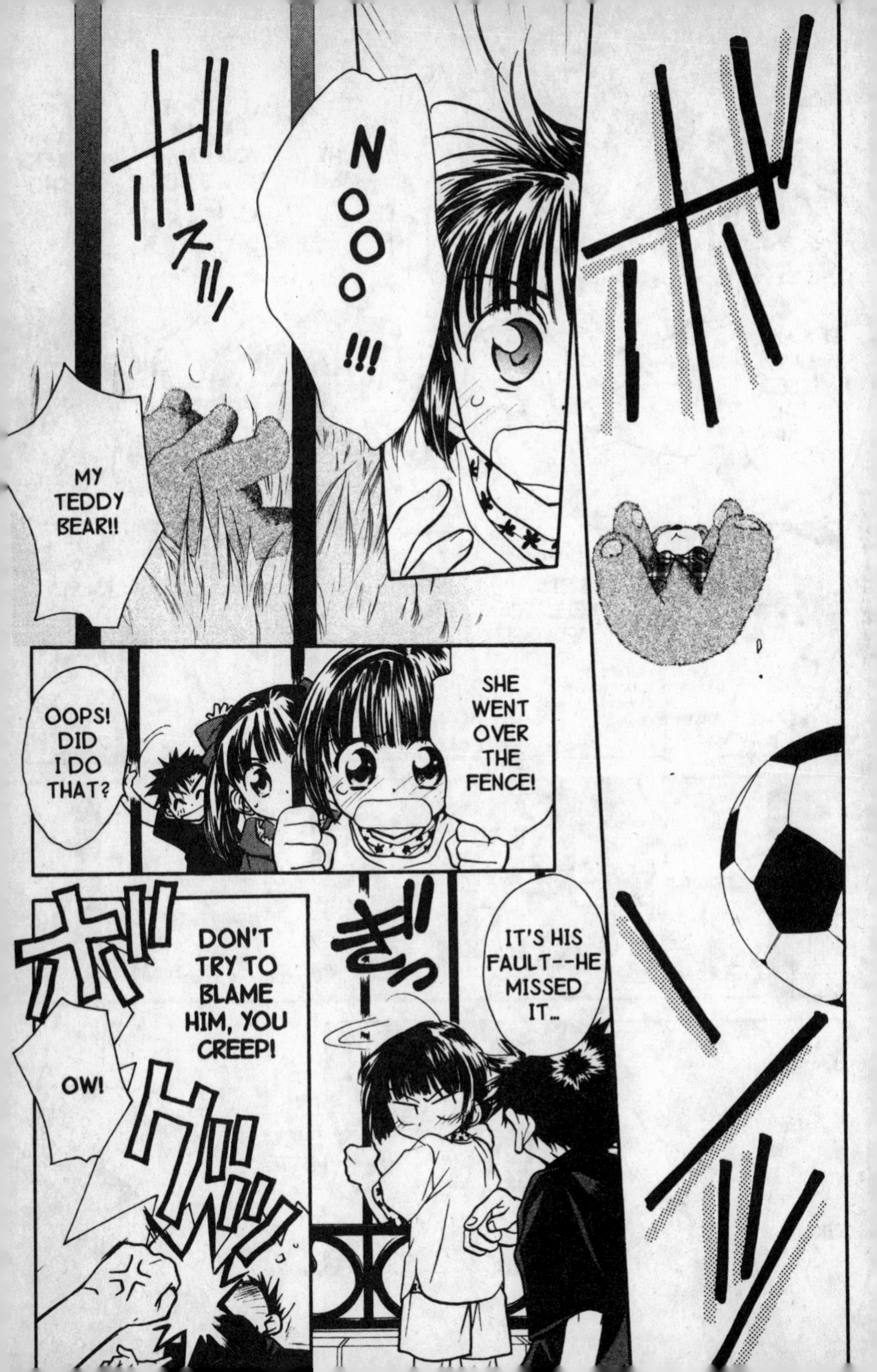
NOOO!!!
MY TEDDY BEAR!!
SHE WENT OVER THE FENCE!
OOPS! DID I DO THAT?
IT'S HIS FAULT--HE MISSED IT...
ぎっ
DON'T TRY TO BLAME HIM, YOU CREEP!
OW!

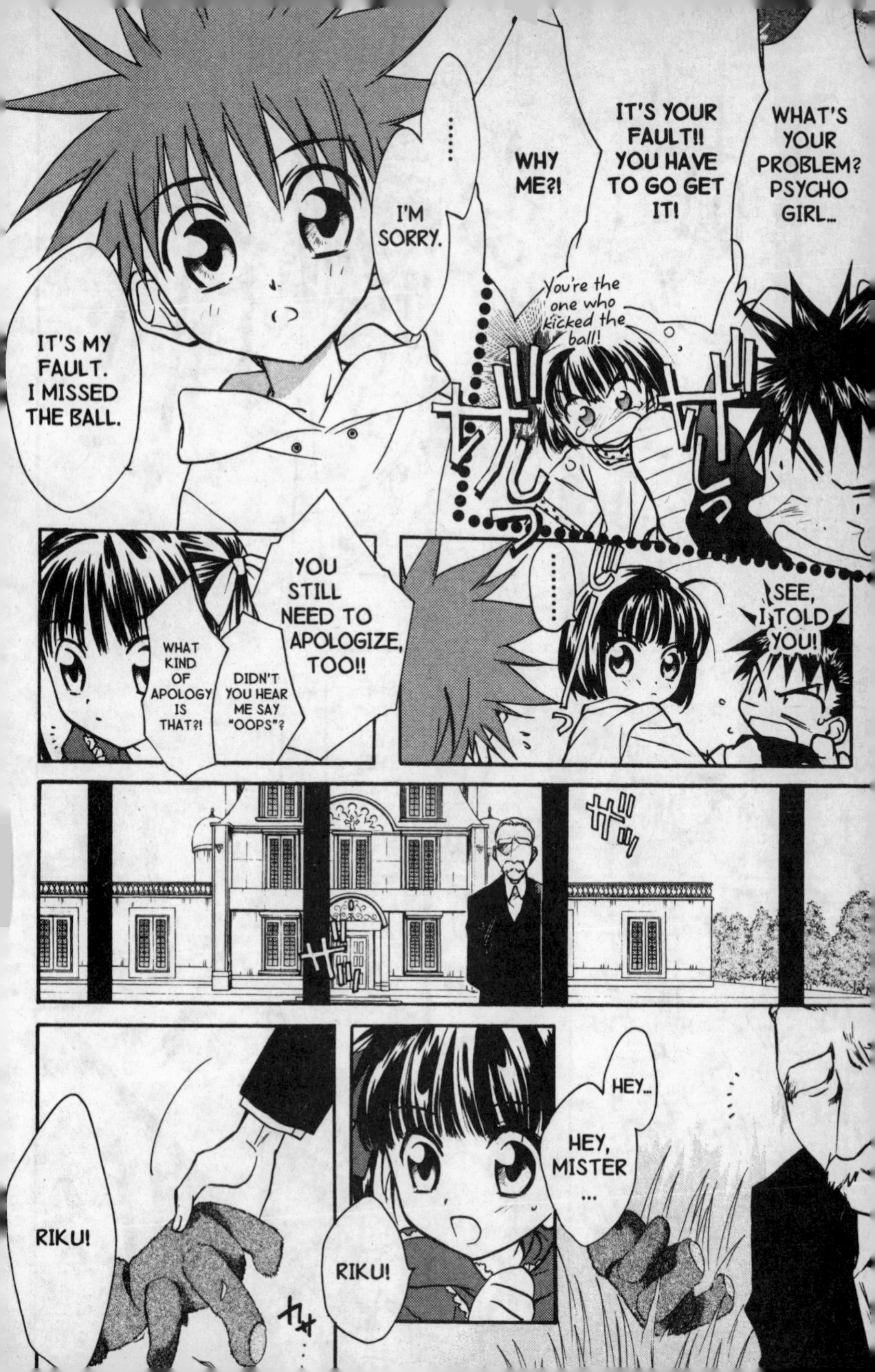

WHAT'S YOUR PROBLEM? PSYCHO GIRL...
IT'S YOUR FAULT!! YOU HAVE TO GO GET IT!
WHY ME?!
You're the one who kicked the ball!
......
I'M SORRY.
IT'S MY FAULT. I MISSED THE BALL.
SEE, I TOLD YOU!
......
YOU STILL NEED TO APOLOGIZE, TOO!!
DIDN'T YOU HEAR ME SAY "OOPS"?
WHAT KIND OF APOLOGY IS THAT?!
HEY...
HEY, MISTER ...
RIKU!
RIKU!

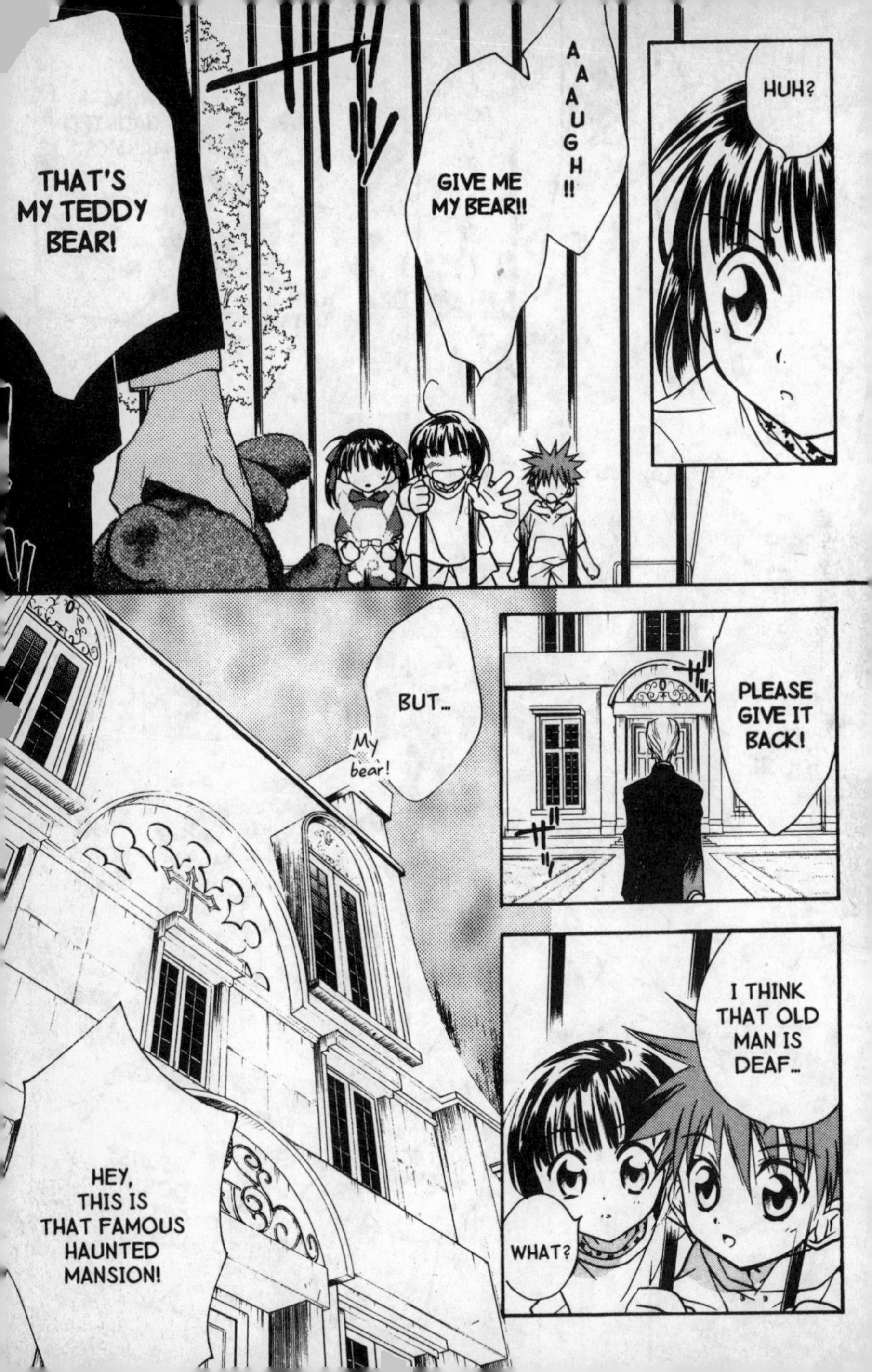
HUH?
AAAUGH!!
GIVE ME MY BEAR!!
THAT'S MY TEDDY BEAR!
PLEASE GIVE IT BACK!
I THINK THAT OLD MAN IS DEAF...
WHAT?
BUT...
My bear!
HEY, THIS IS THAT FAMOUS HAUNTED MANSION!

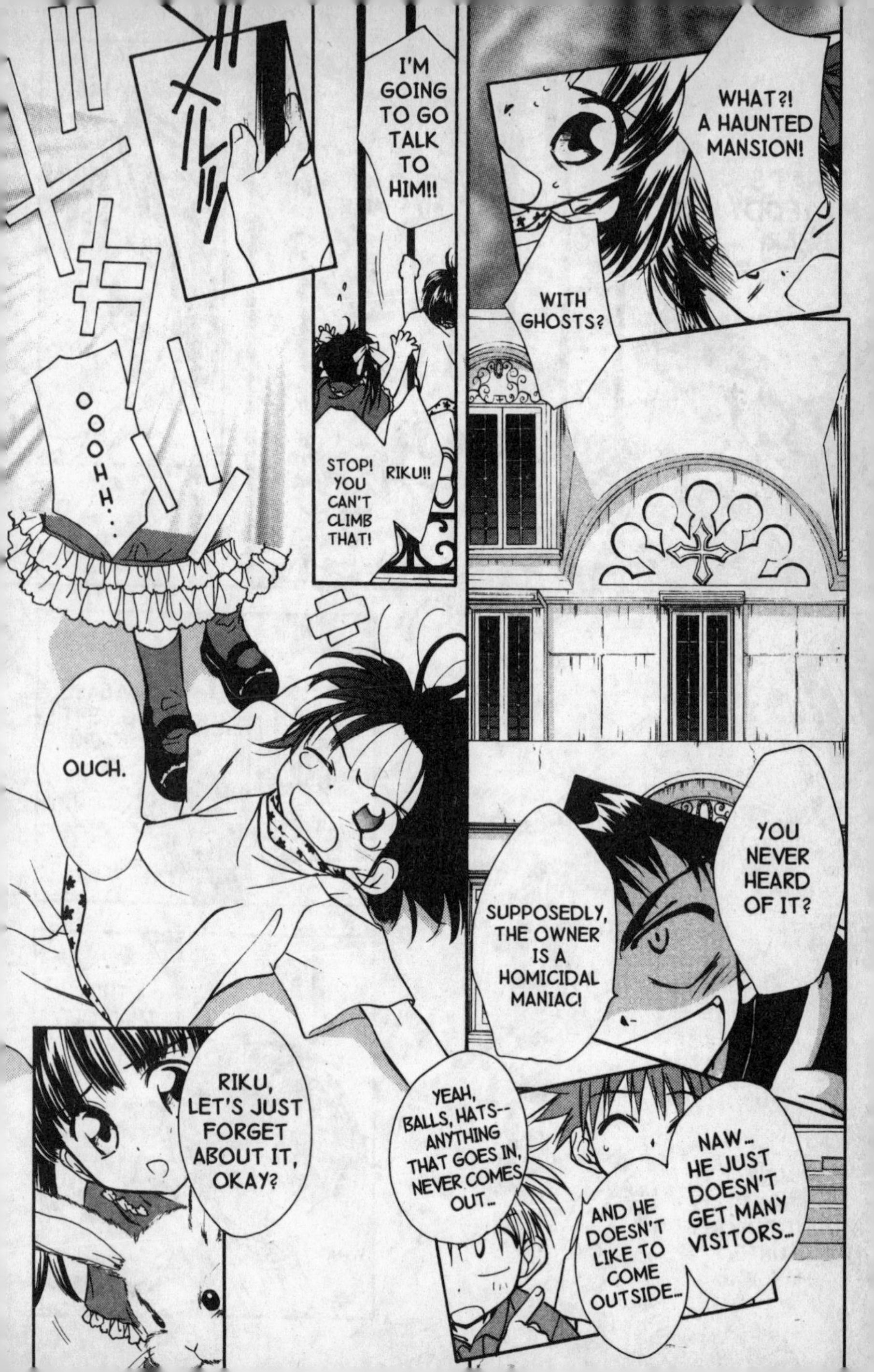
WHAT?! A HAUNTED MANSION!
WITH GHOSTS?
YOU NEVER HEARD OF IT?
SUPPOSEDLY, THE OWNER IS A HOMICIDAL MANIAC!
NAW... HE JUST DOESN'T GET MANY VISITORS...
AND HE DOESN'T LIKE TO COME OUTSIDE...
YEAH, BALLS, HATS--ANYTHING THAT GOES IN, NEVER COMES OUT...
RIKU, LET'S JUST FORGET ABOUT IT, OKAY?
I'M GOING TO GO TALK TO HIM!!
STOP! YOU CAN'T CLIMB THAT!
RIKU!!
OOOHH...
OUCH.

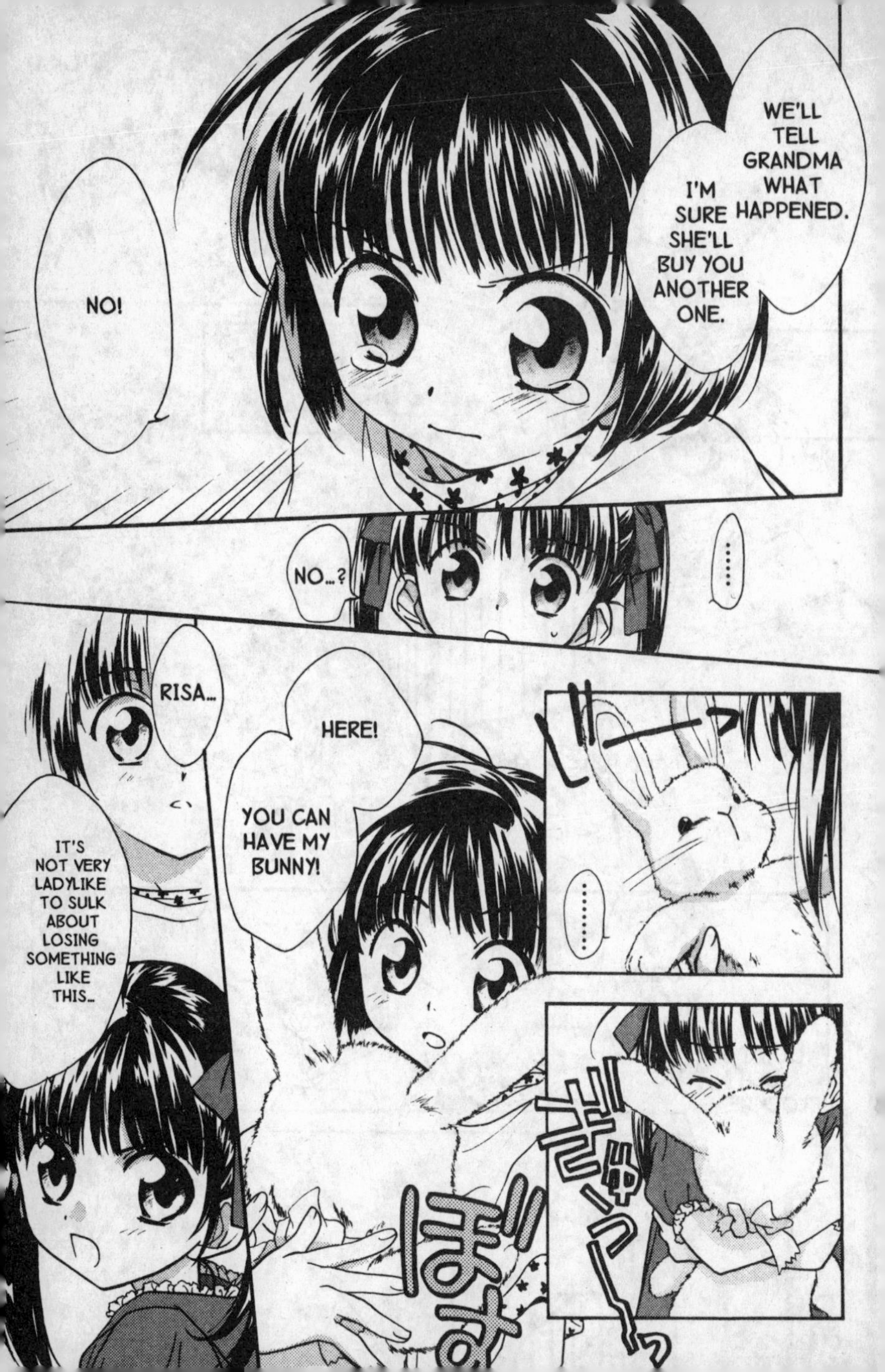
WE'LL TELL GRANDMA WHAT HAPPENED.
I'M SURE SHE'LL BUY YOU ANOTHER ONE.
NO!
......
NO...?
......
HERE!
YOU CAN HAVE MY BUNNY!
RISA...
IT'S NOT VERY LADYLIKE TO SULK ABOUT LOSING SOMETHING LIKE THIS...

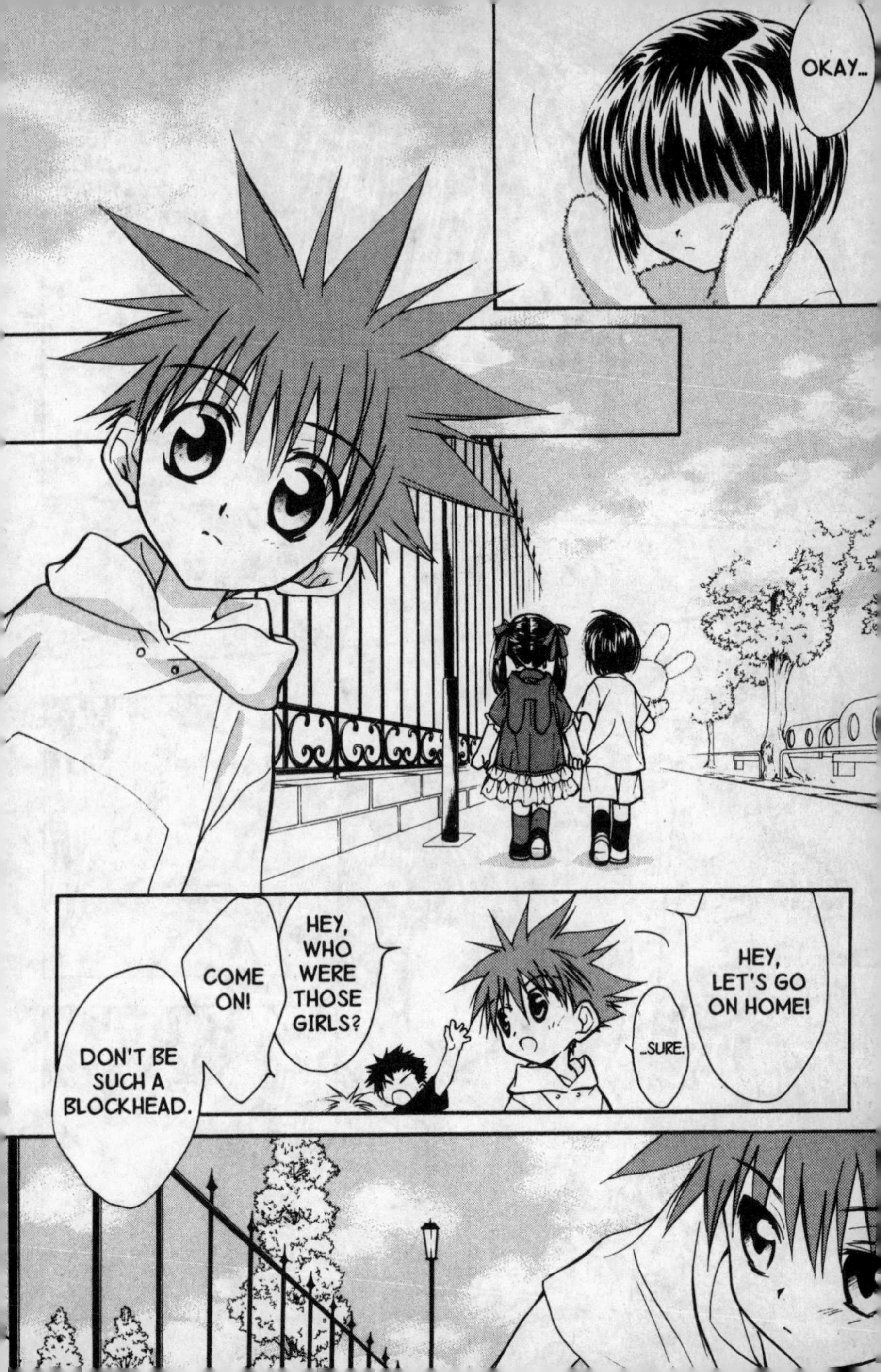
OKAY...
HEY, LET'S GO ON HOME!
...SURE.
HEY, WHO WERE THOSE GIRLS?
COME ON!
DON'T BE SUCH A BLOCKHEAD.

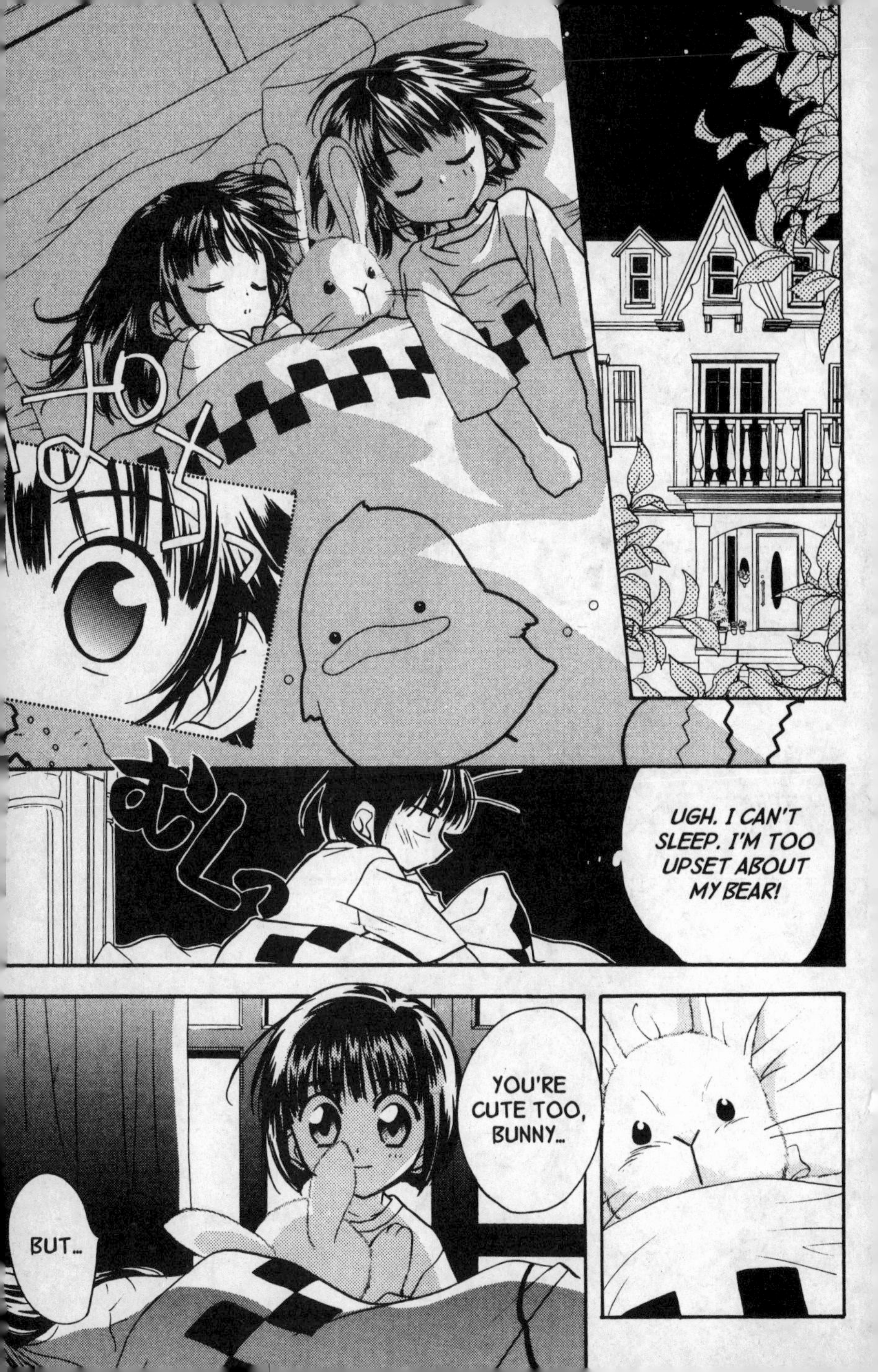
UGH. I CAN'T SLEEP. I'M TOO UPSET ABOUT MY BEAR!
YOU'RE CUTE TOO, BUNNY...
BUT...

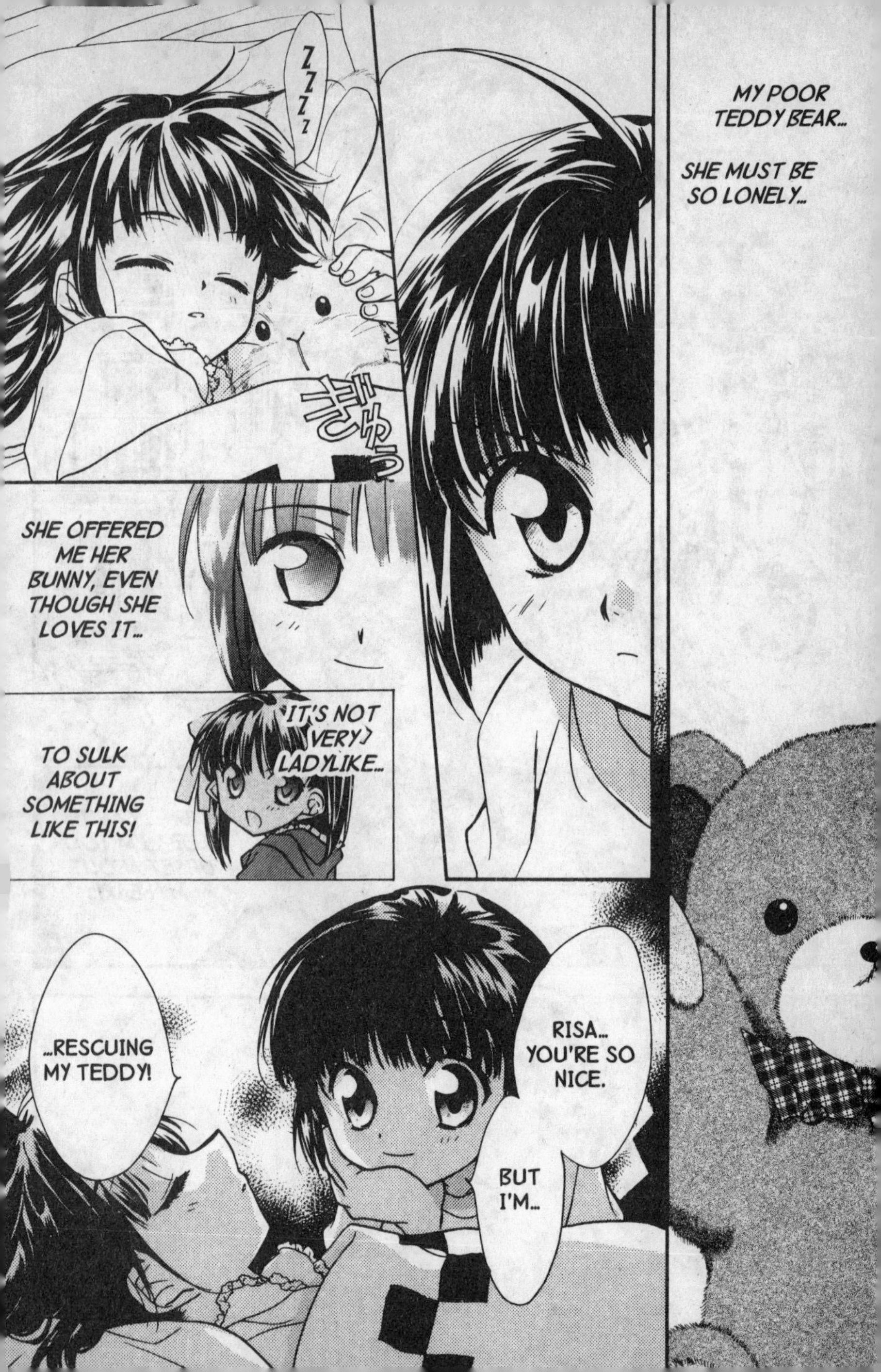
MY POOR TEDDY BEAR...
SHE MUST BE SO LONELY...
ZZZZ
ぎゅう
SHE OFFERED ME HER BUNNY, EVEN THOUGH SHE LOVES IT...
IT'S NOT VERY LADYLIKE...
TO SULK ABOUT SOMETHING LIKE THIS!
RISA... YOU'RE SO NICE.
BUT I'M...
...RESCUING MY TEDDY!

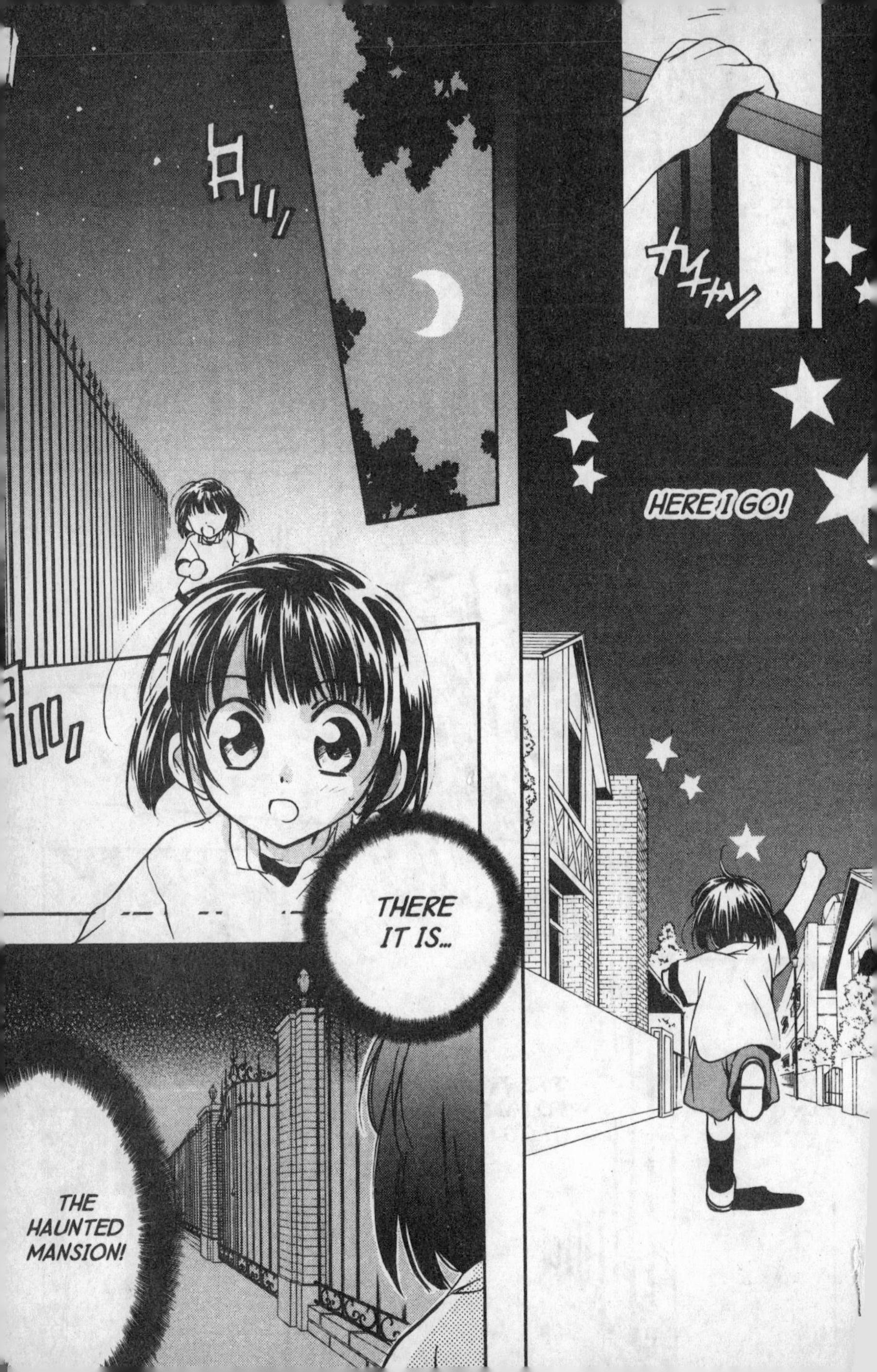
HERE I GO!
THERE IT IS...
THE HAUNTED MANSION!

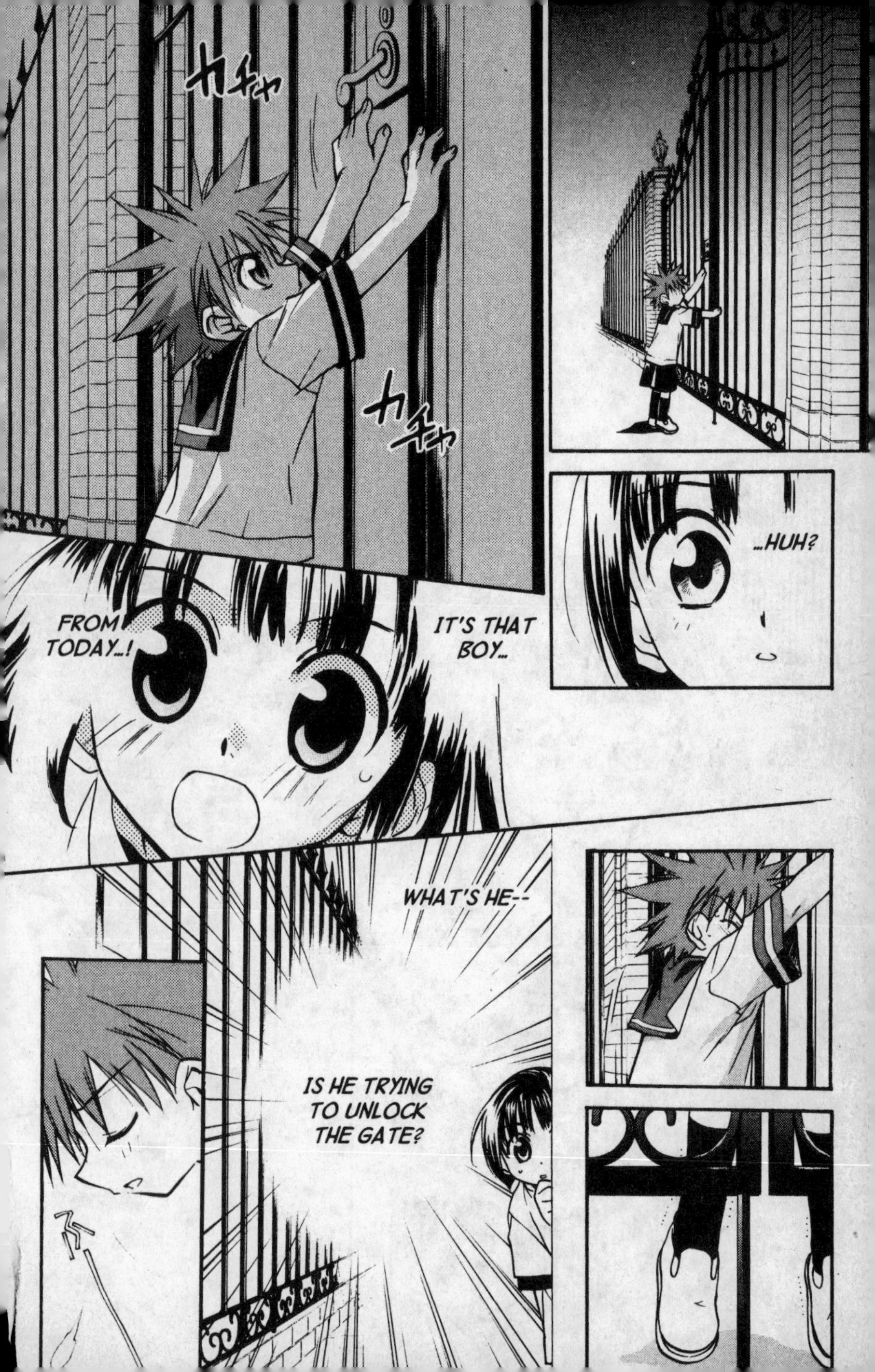
カチャ
カチャ
...HUH?
IT'S THAT BOY...
FROM TODAY...!
WHAT'S HE--
IS HE TRYING TO UNLOCK THE GATE?

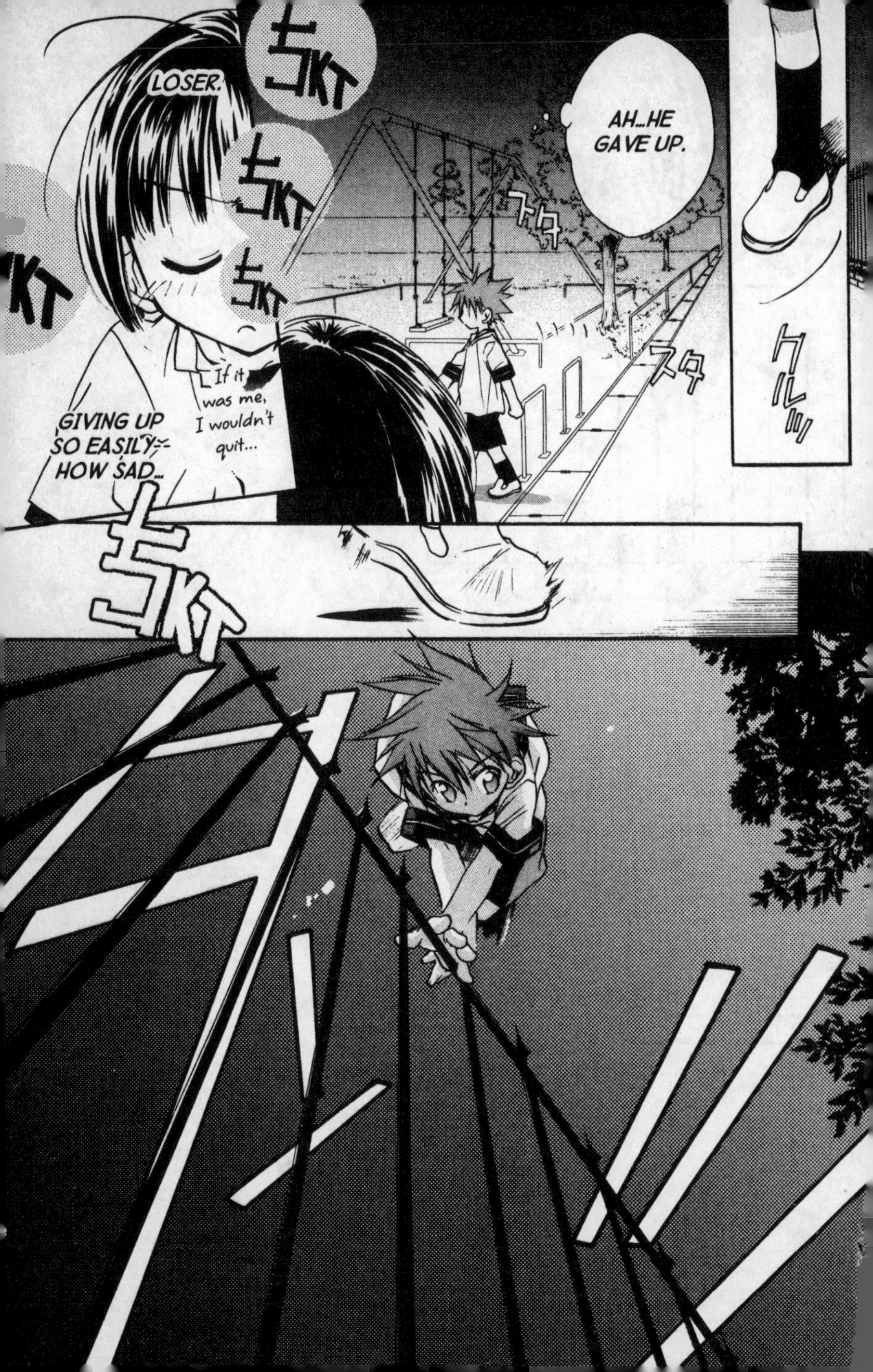

クルッ
AH...HE GAVE UP.
スタ
スタ
SKT
SKT
SKT
LOSER.
SKT
If it was me, I wouldn't quit...
GIVING UP SO EASILY~ HOW SAD...
SKT

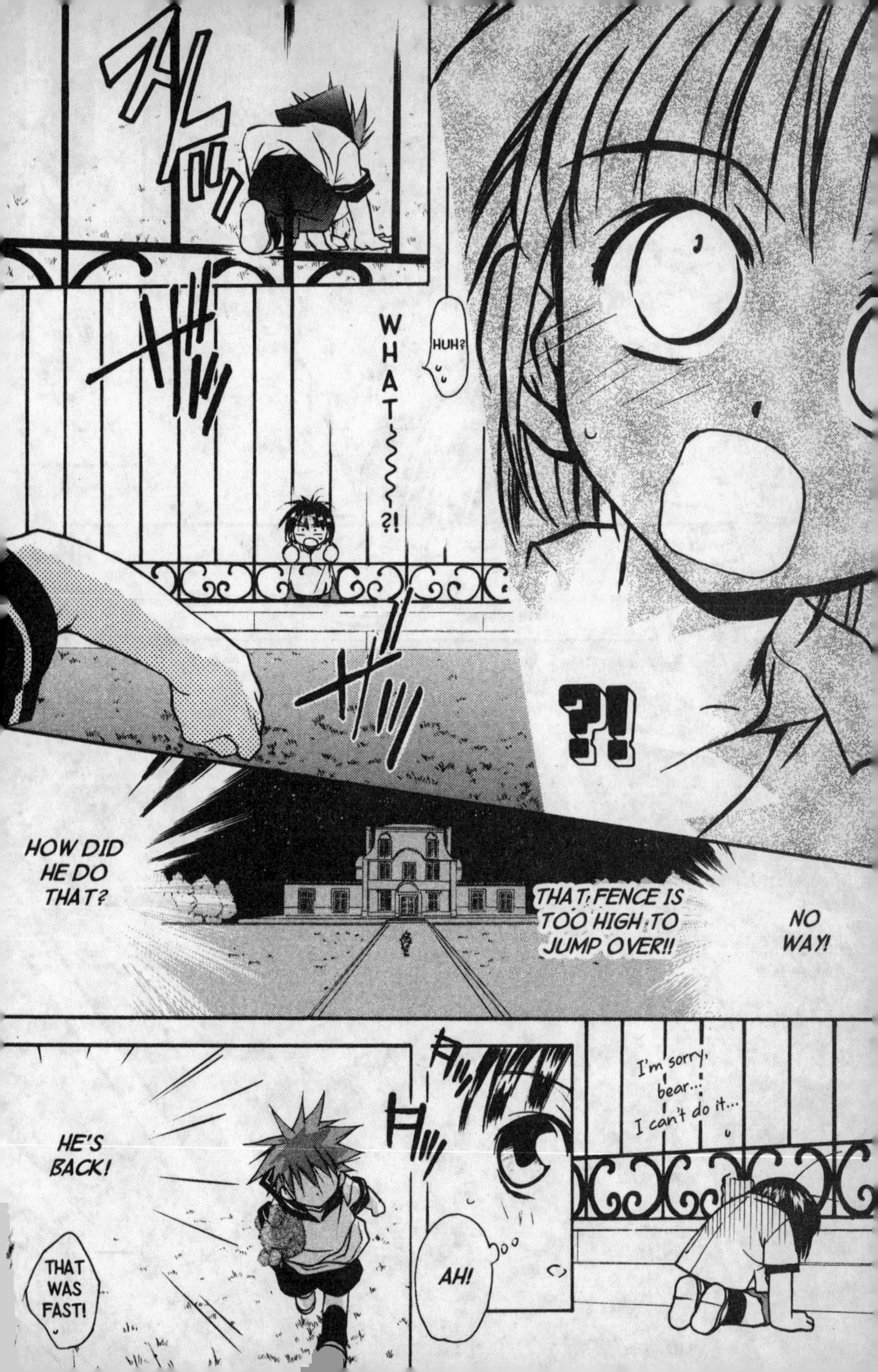
?!
WHAT~?!
HUH?
NO WAY!
THAT FENCE IS TOO HIGH TO JUMP OVER!!
HOW DID HE DO THAT?
I'm sorry, bear... I can't do it...
AH!
HE'S BACK!
THAT WAS FAST!

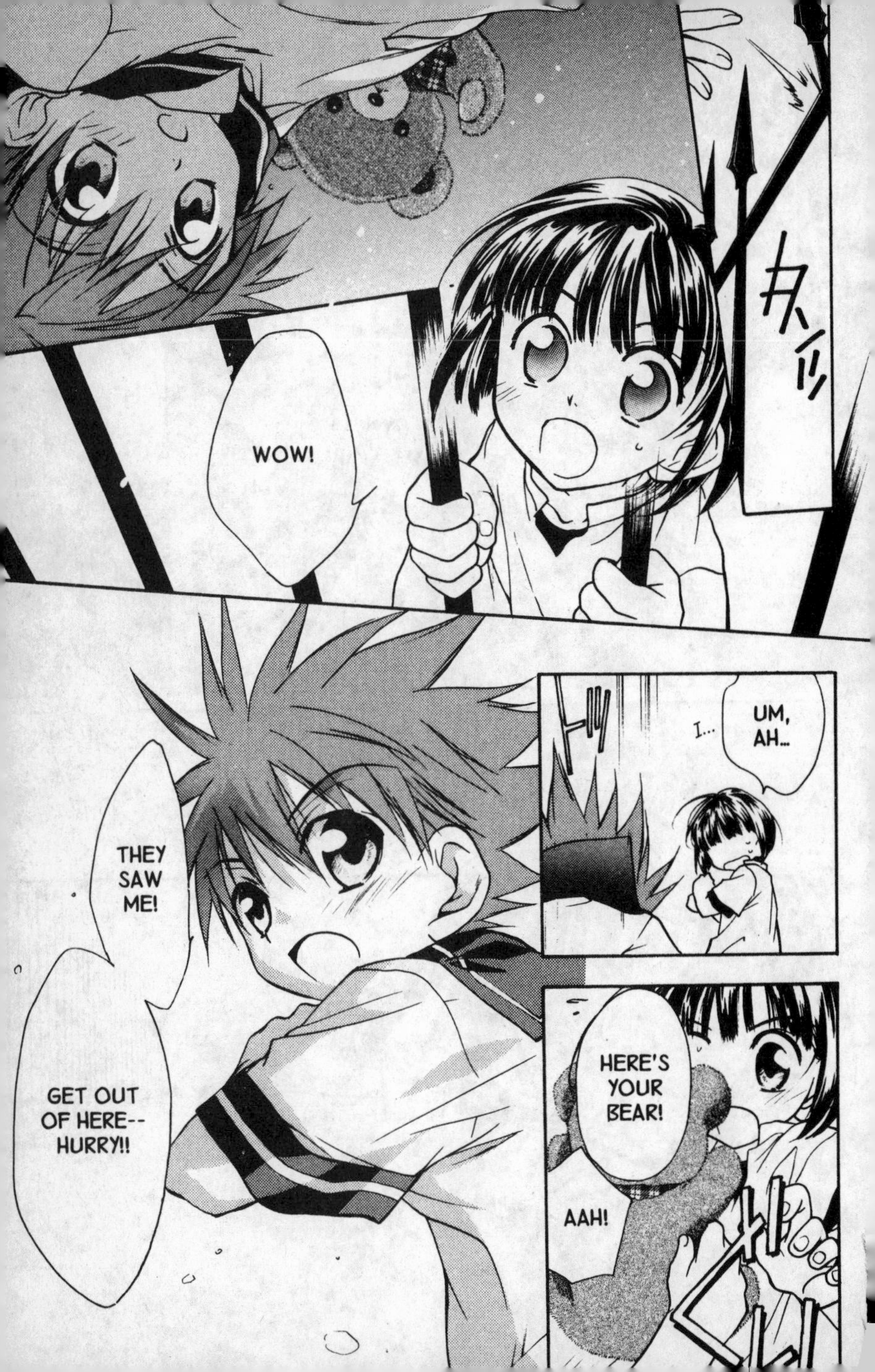
WOW!
UM, AH...
I...
HERE'S YOUR BEAR!
AAH!
THEY SAW ME!
GET OUT OF HERE--HURRY!!

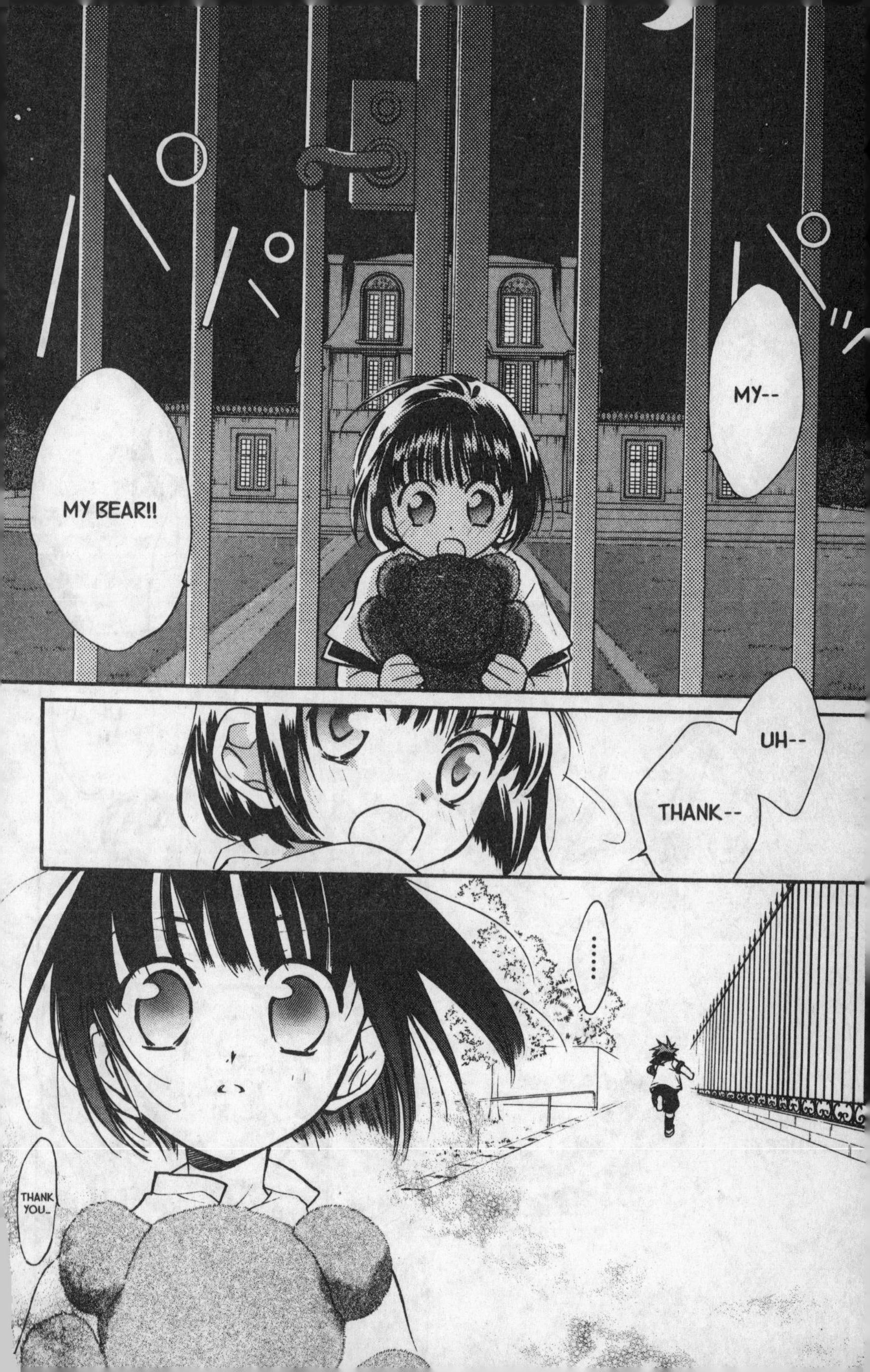
MY--
MY BEAR!!
UH--
THANK--
......
THANK YOU_

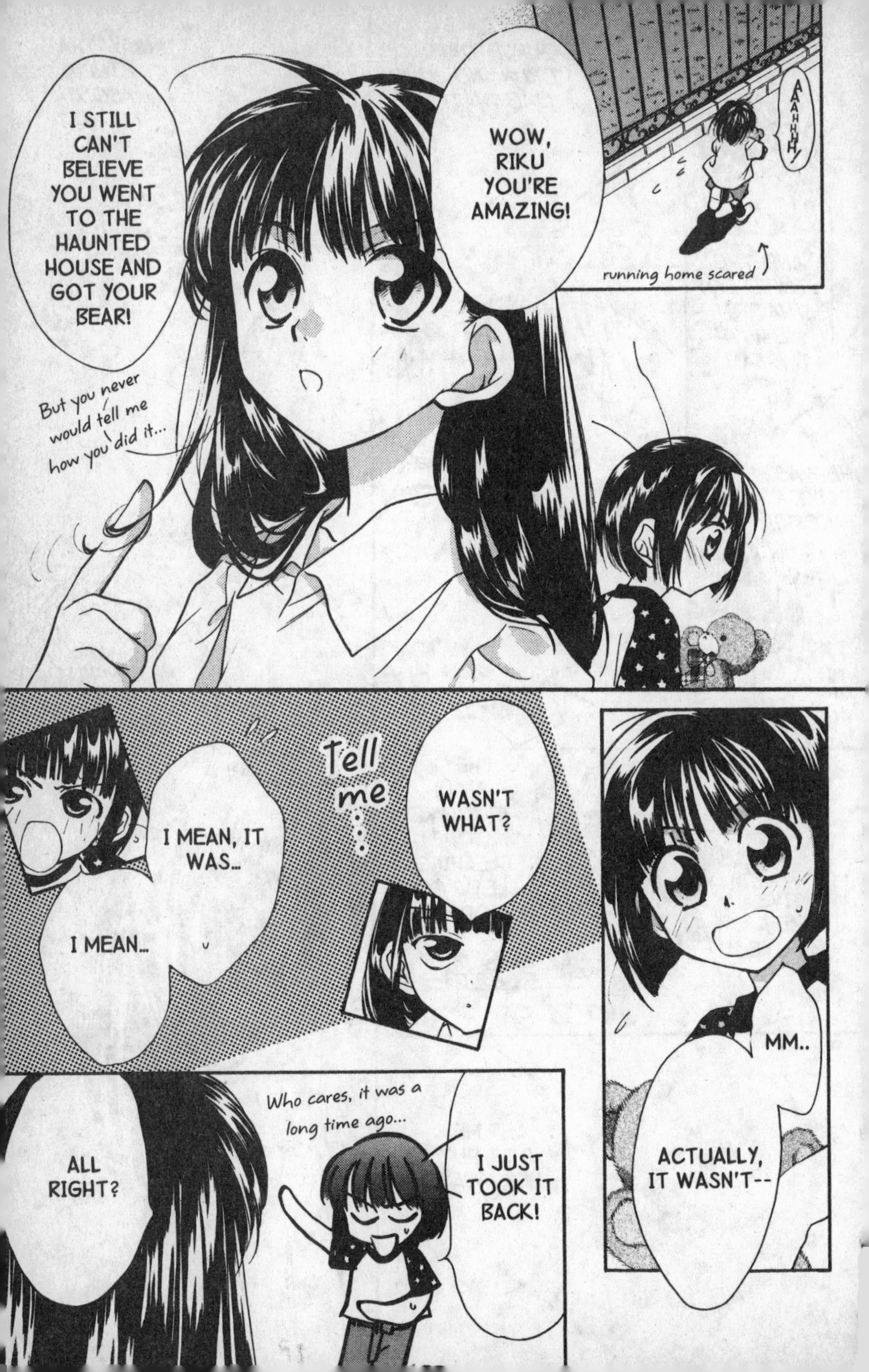
AAHHHH!
running home scared
WOW, RIKU YOU'RE AMAZING!
I STILL CAN'T BELIEVE YOU WENT TO THE HAUNTED HOUSE AND GOT YOUR BEAR!
But you never would tell me how you did it...
MM..
ACTUALLY, IT WASN'T--
WASN'T WHAT?
Tell me...
I MEAN, IT WAS...
I MEAN...
Who cares, it was a long time ago...
I JUST TOOK IT BACK!
ALL RIGHT?

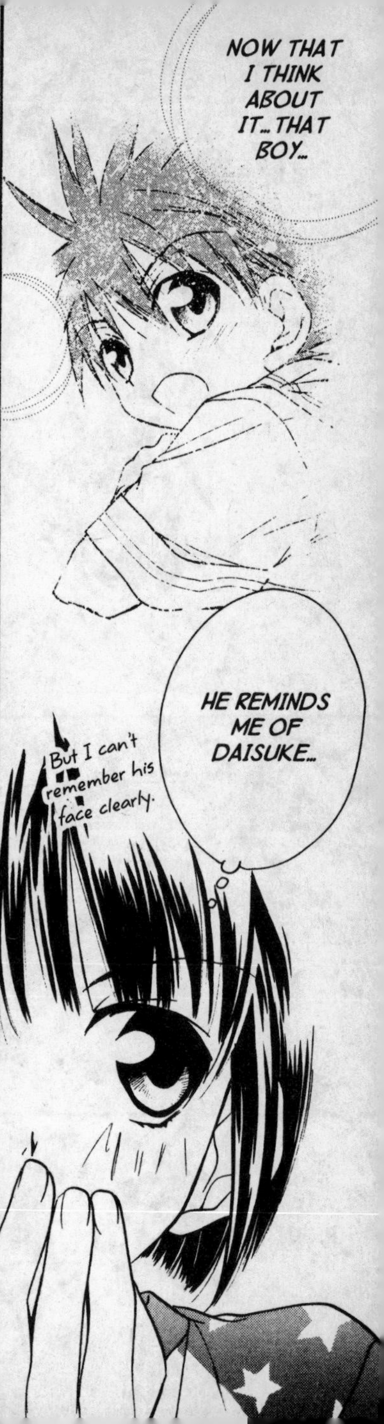
NOW THAT I THINK ABOUT IT...THAT BOY...
HE REMINDS ME OF DAISUKE...
But I can't remember his face clearly.

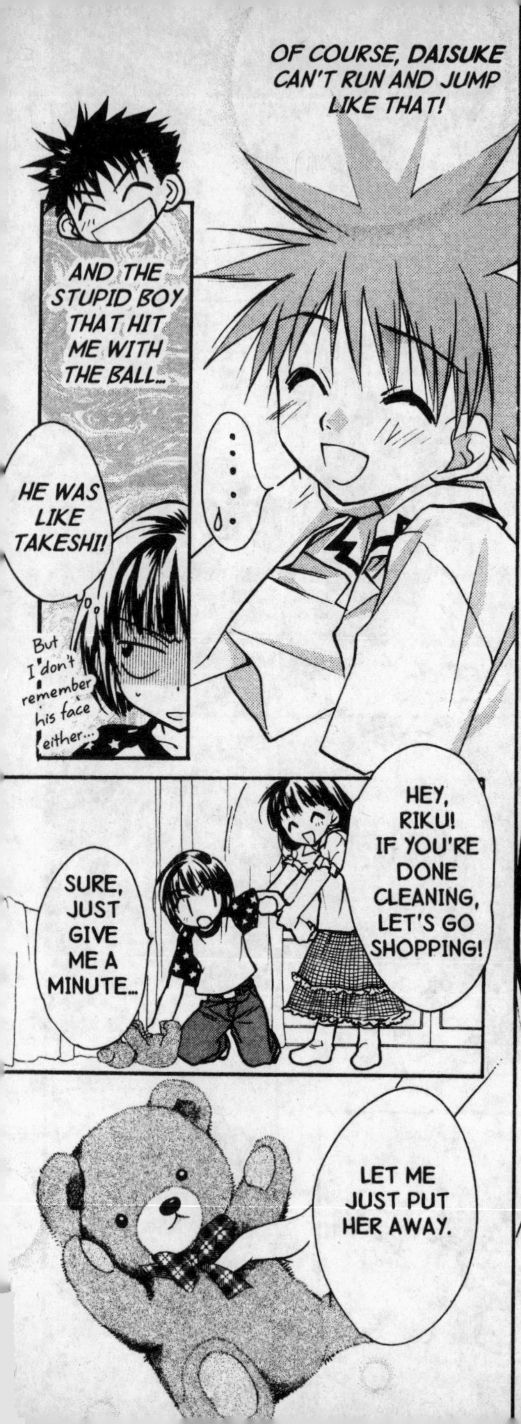
OF COURSE, DAISUKE CAN'T RUN AND JUMP LIKE THAT!
...
AND THE STUPID BOY THAT HIT ME WITH THE BALL...
HE WAS LIKE TAKESHI!
But I don't remember his face either...
HEY, RIKU! IF YOU'RE DONE CLEANING, LET'S GO SHOPPING!
SURE, JUST GIVE ME A MINUTE...
LET ME JUST PUT HER AWAY.

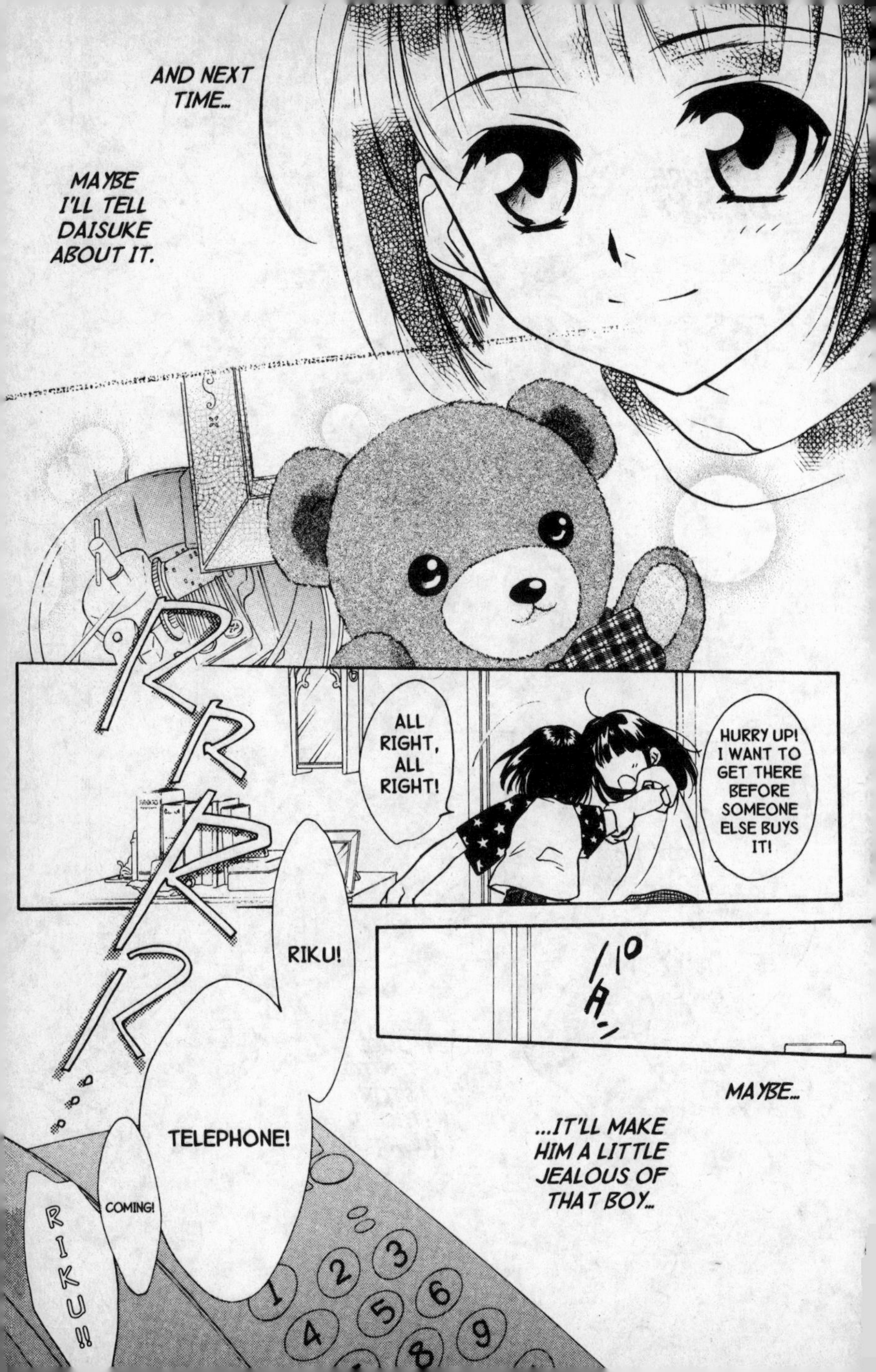
AND NEXT TIME...
MAYBE I'LL TELL DAISUKE ABOUT IT.
HURRY UP! I WANT TO GET THERE BEFORE SOMEONE ELSE BUYS IT!
ALL RIGHT, ALL RIGHT!
RRRR...
MAYBE...
...IT'LL MAKE HIM A LITTLE JEALOUS OF THAT BOY...
RIKU!
TELEPHONE!
COMING!
RIKU!!

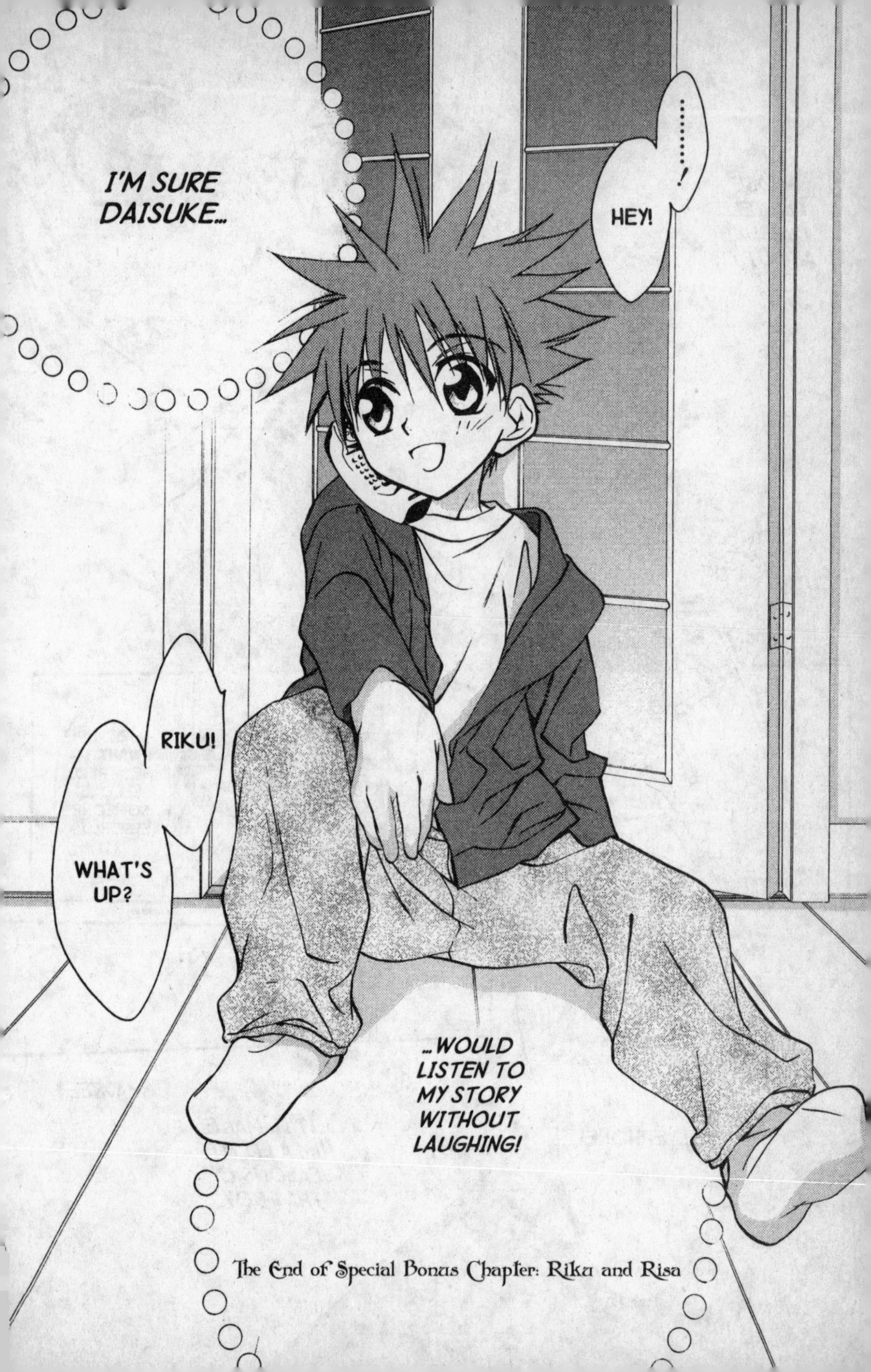
......!
HEY!
I'M SURE DAISUKE...
RIKU!
WHAT'S UP?
...WOULD LISTEN TO MY STORY WITHOUT LAUGHING!

The End of Special Bonus Chapter: Riku and Risa

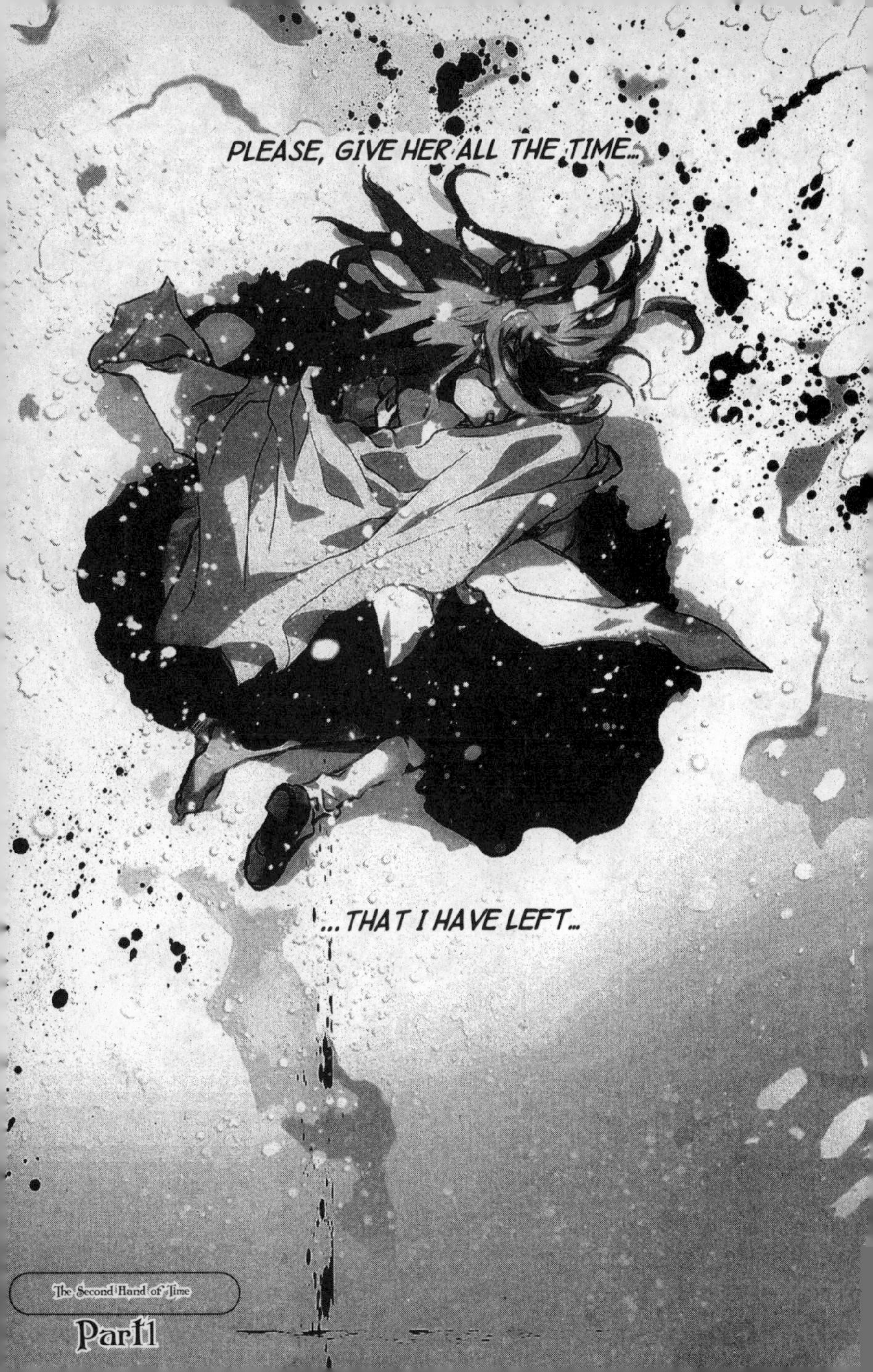
PLEASE, GIVE HER ALL THE TIME...
...THAT I HAVE LEFT...
The Second Hand of Time
Part 1

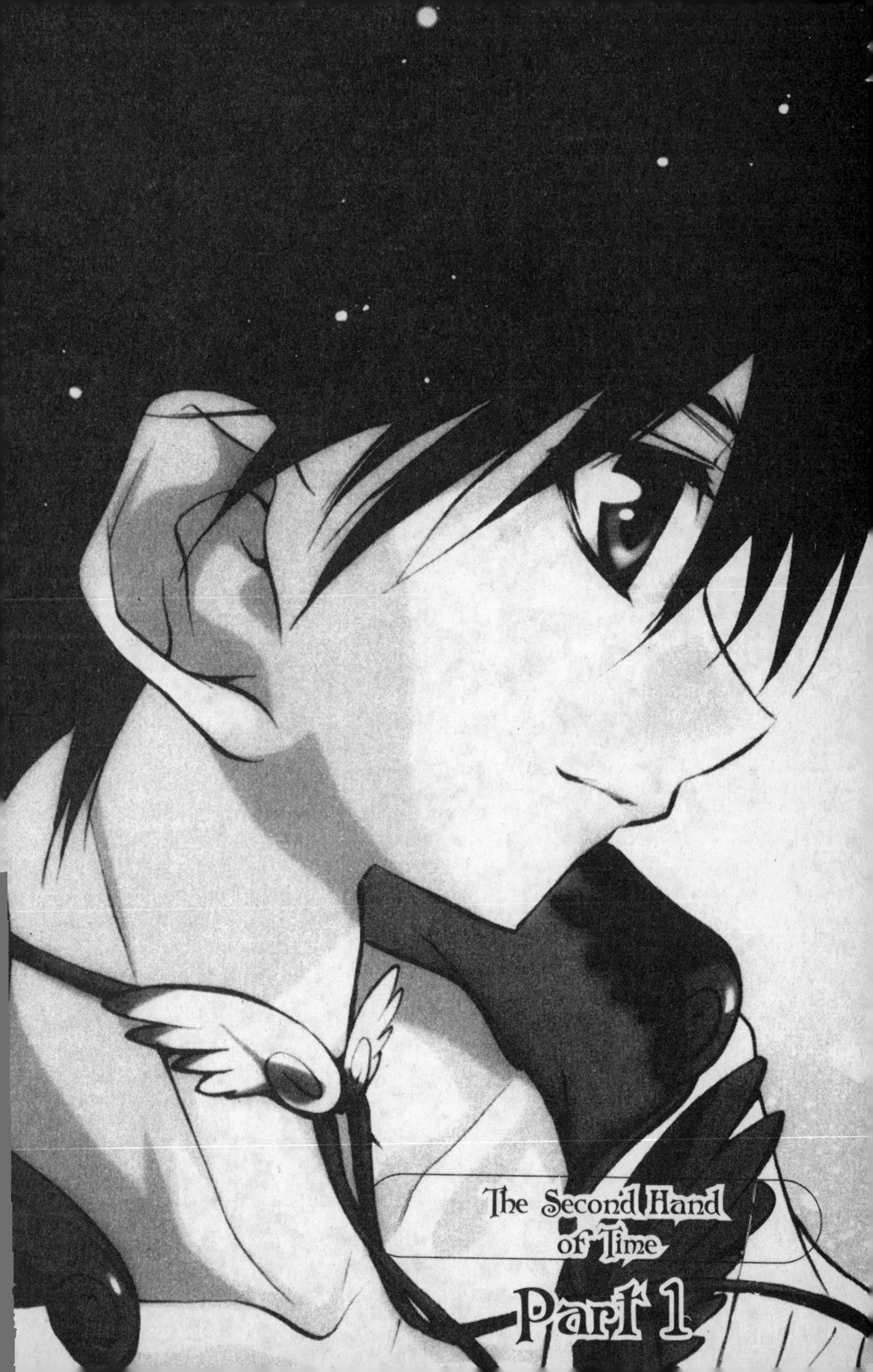
The Second Hand of Time
Part 1

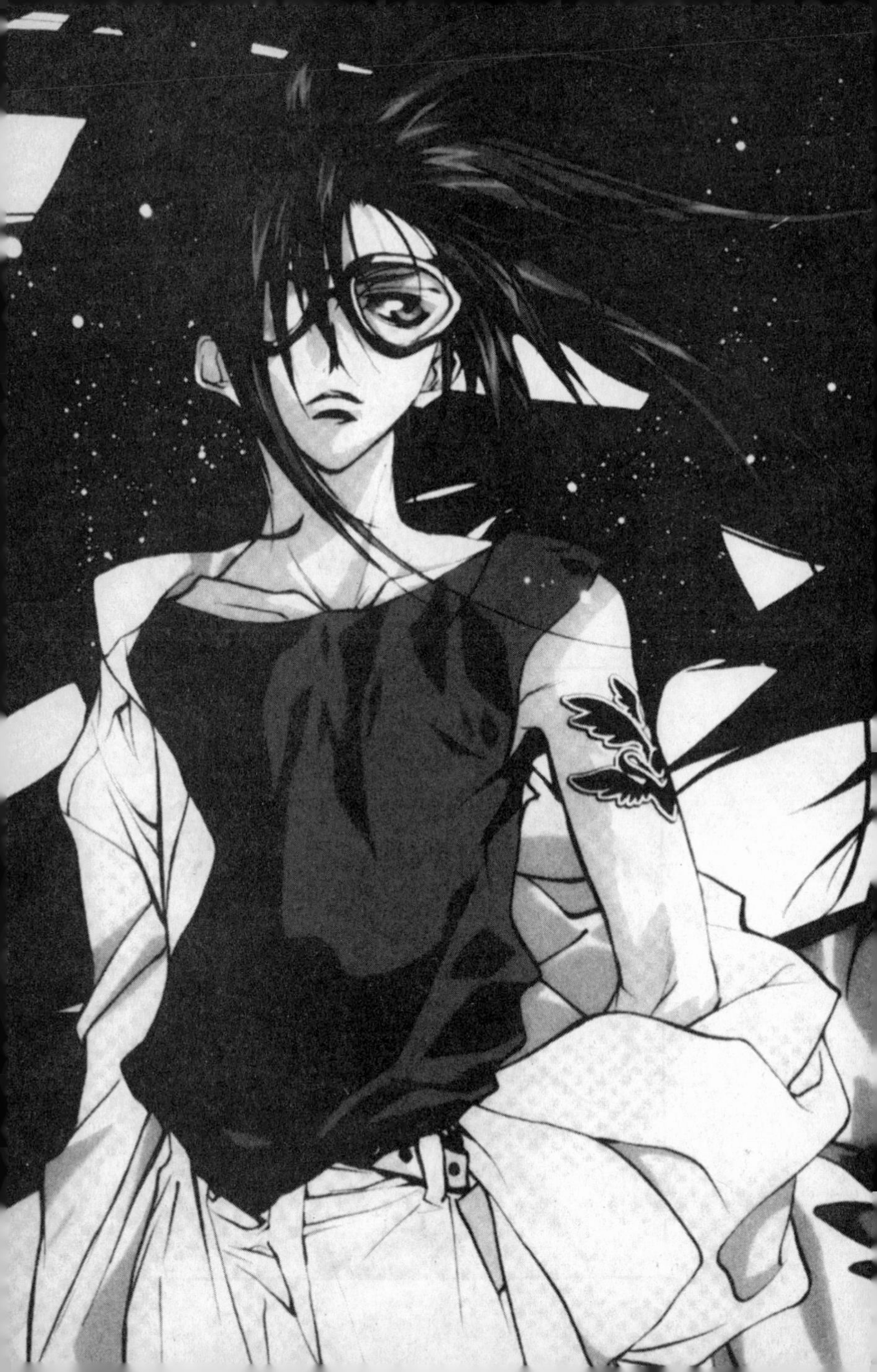

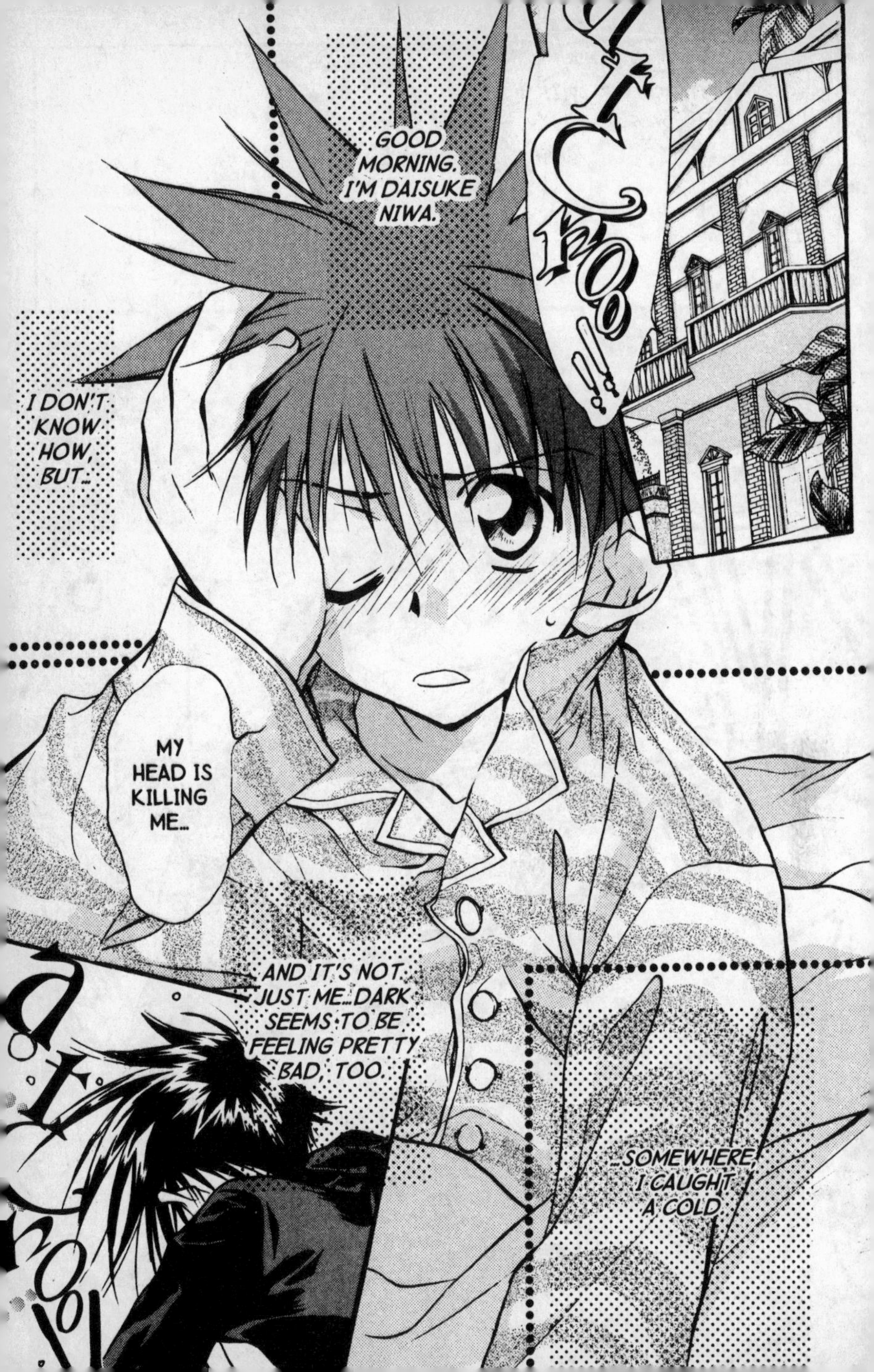
tchooo!!
GOOD MORNING. I'M DAISUKE NIWA.
I DON'T KNOW HOW, BUT...
...SOMEWHERE, I CAUGHT A COLD.
MY HEAD IS KILLING ME...
AND IT'S NOT JUST ME...DARK SEEMS TO BE FEELING PRETTY BAD, TOO.
atchooo!

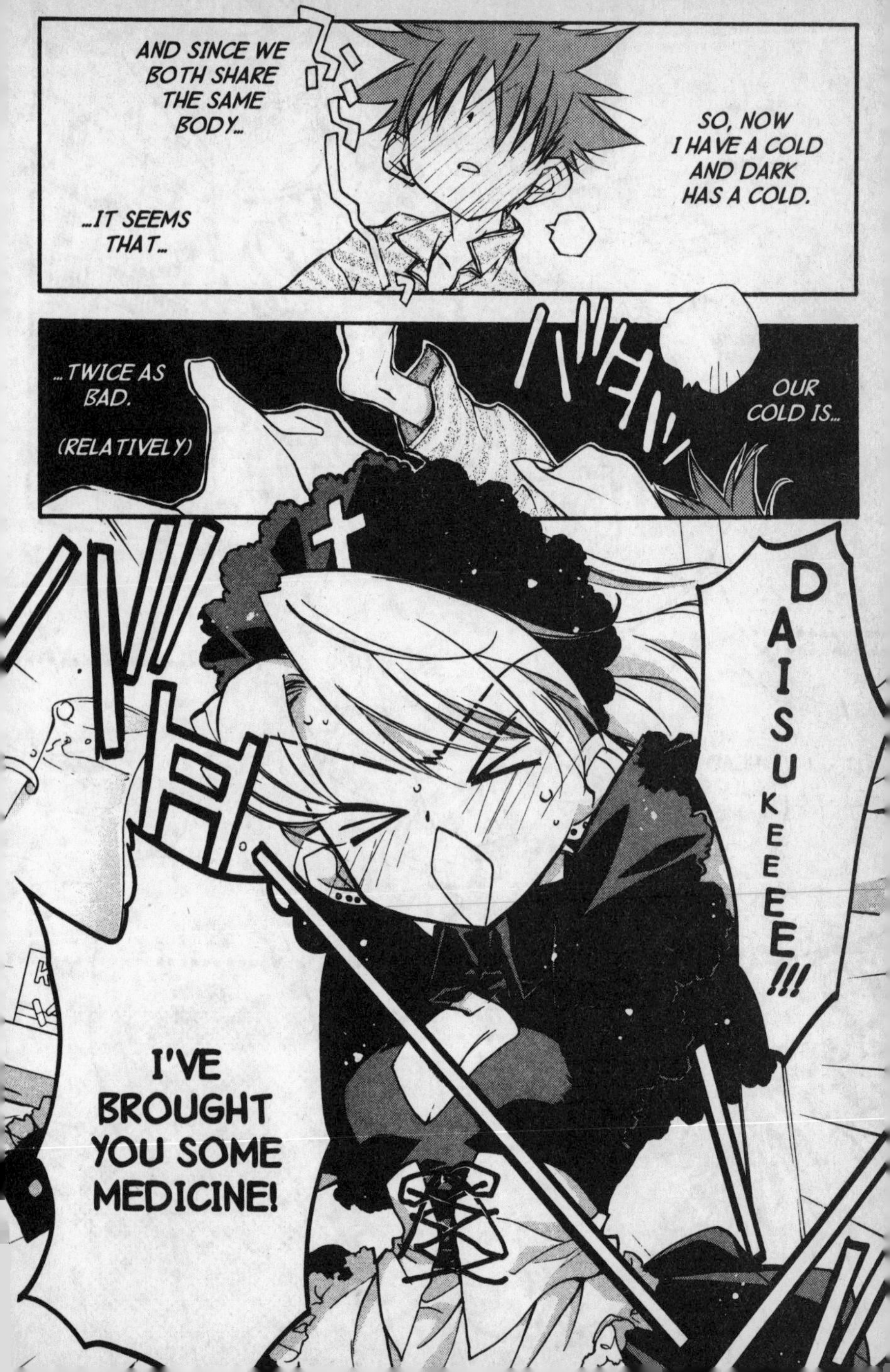
SO, NOW I HAVE A COLD AND DARK HAS A COLD.
AND SINCE WE BOTH SHARE THE SAME BODY...
...IT SEEMS THAT...
OUR COLD IS...
...TWICE AS BAD.
(RELATIVELY)
DAISUKEEEEE!!!
I'VE BROUGHT YOU SOME MEDICINE!

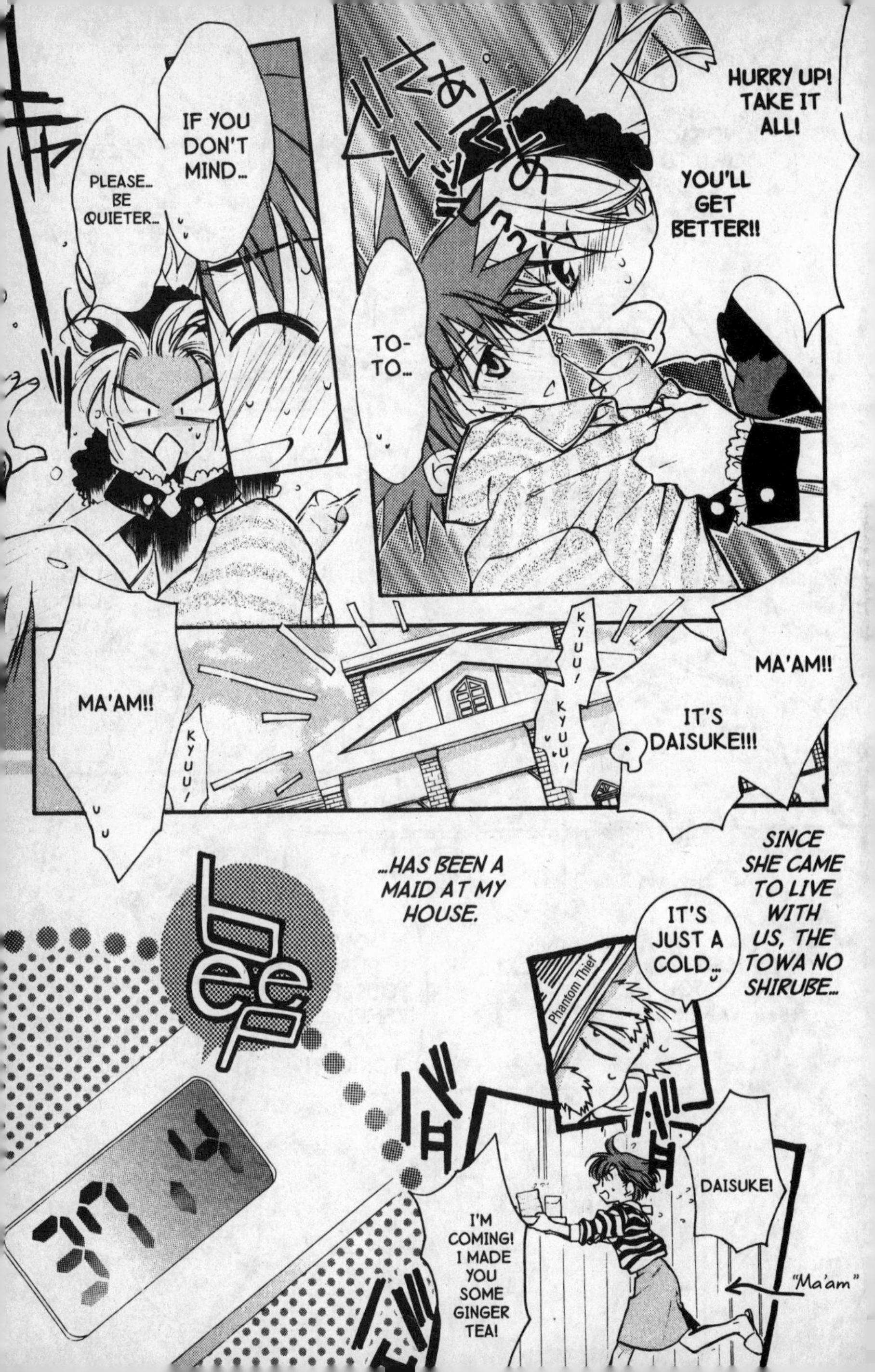
HURRY UP! TAKE IT ALL!
YOU'LL GET BETTER!!
TO-TO...
IF YOU DON'T MIND...
PLEASE... BE QUIETER...
MA'AM!!
IT'S DAISUKE!!!
KYUU! KYUU!
KYUU!
MA'AM!!
SINCE SHE CAME TO LIVE WITH US, THE TOWA NO SHIRUBE...
IT'S JUST A COLD...
...HAS BEEN A MAID AT MY HOUSE.
Phantom Thief
DAISUKE!
I'M COMING! I MADE YOU SOME GINGER TEA!
"Ma'am"
beep

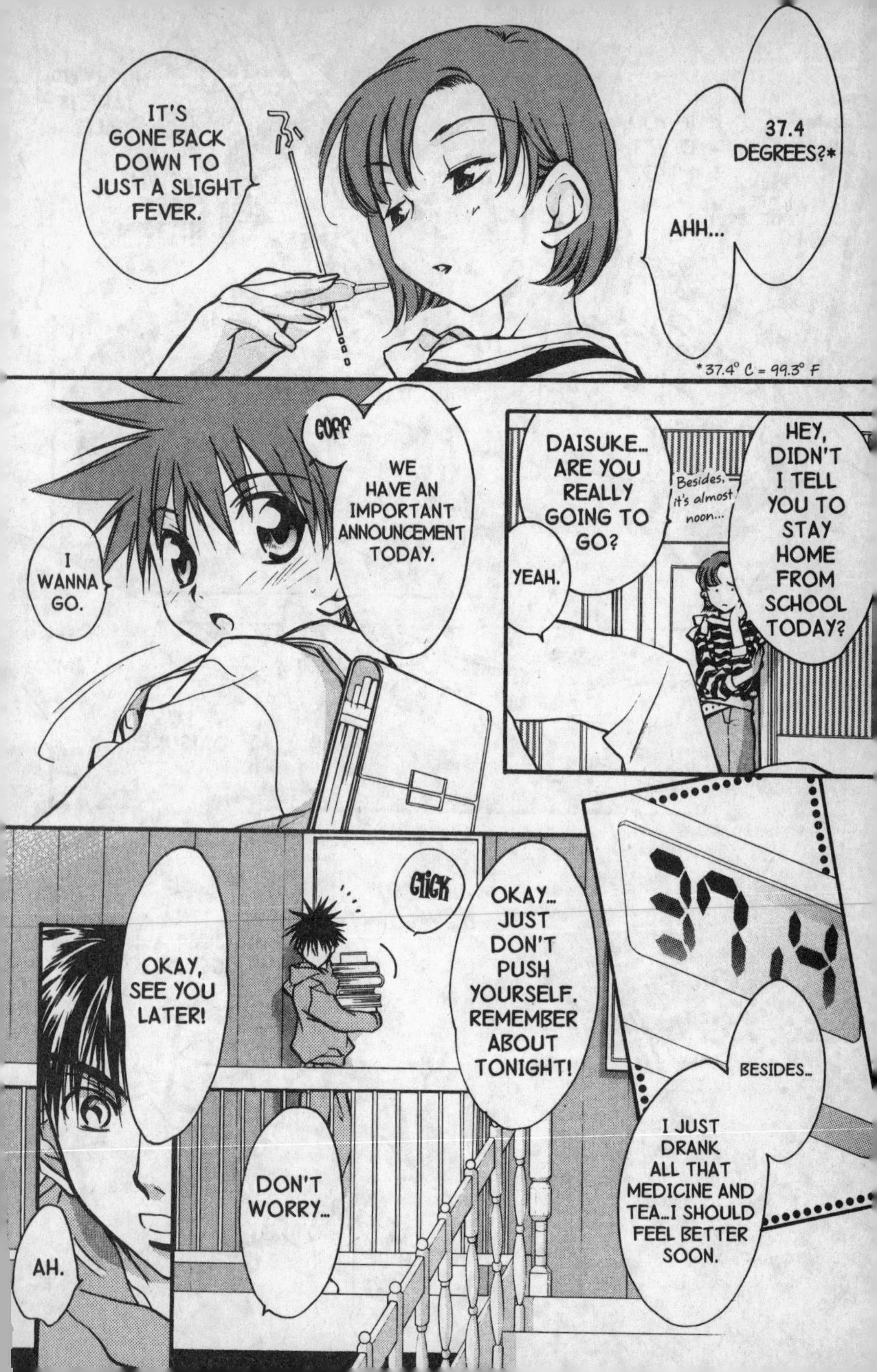
37.4 DEGREES?*
AHH...
IT'S GONE BACK DOWN TO JUST A SLIGHT FEVER.
HEY, DIDN'T I TELL YOU TO STAY HOME FROM SCHOOL TODAY?
Besides, it's almost noon...
DAISUKE... ARE YOU REALLY GOING TO GO?
YEAH.
COFF
WE HAVE AN IMPORTANT ANNOUNCEMENT TODAY.
I WANNA GO.
BESIDES...
I JUST DRANK ALL THAT MEDICINE AND TEA...I SHOULD FEEL BETTER SOON.
CLICK
OKAY... JUST DON'T PUSH YOURSELF. REMEMBER ABOUT TONIGHT!
DON'T WORRY...
OKAY, SEE YOU LATER!
AH.

*37.4° C = 99.3° F

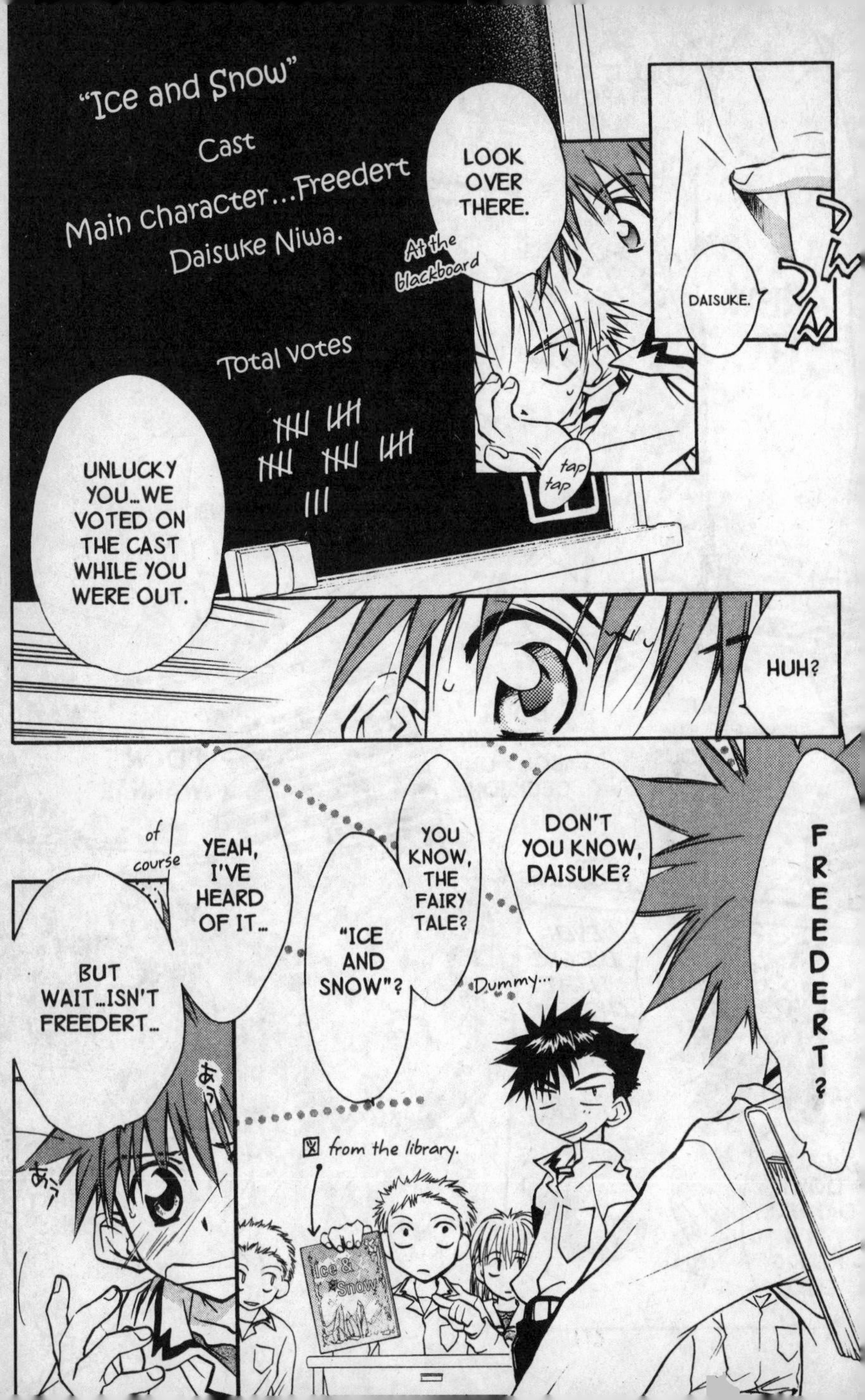
DAISUKE.
LOOK OVER THERE.
At the blackboard
tap tap
"Ice and Snow"
Cast
Main character...Freedert
Daisuke Niwa.
Total votes
UNLUCKY YOU...WE VOTED ON THE CAST WHILE YOU WERE OUT.
HUH?
FREEDERT?
DON'T YOU KNOW, DAISUKE?
YOU KNOW, THE FAIRY TALE?
Dummy...
"ICE AND SNOW"?
YEAH, I'VE HEARD OF IT...
of course
BUT WAIT...ISN'T FREEDERT...
あう
あう
図 from the library.
Ice & Snow

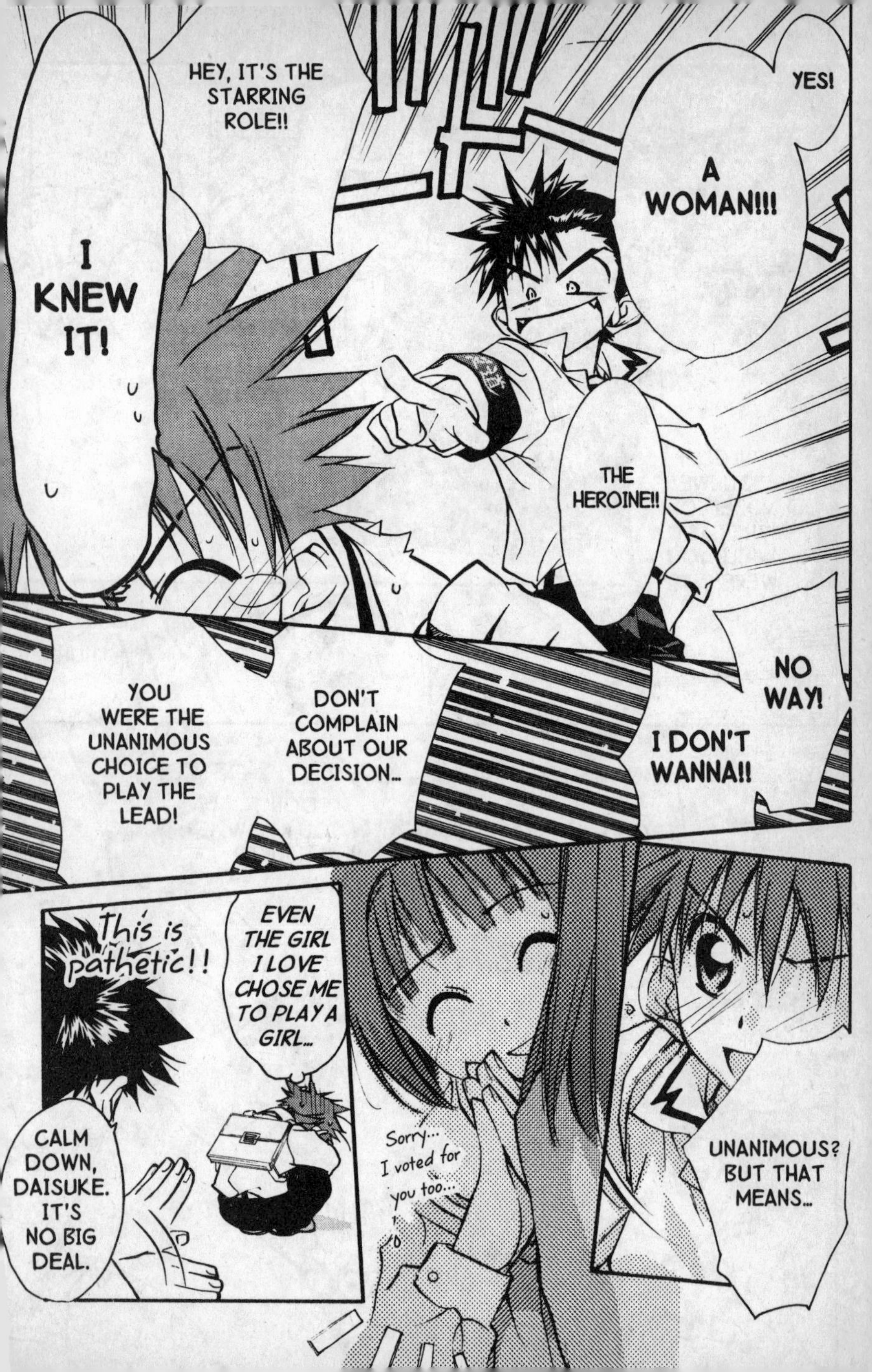
YES! A WOMAN!!!
THE HEROINE!!
HEY, IT'S THE STARRING ROLE!!
I KNEW IT!
NO WAY! I DON'T WANNA!!
DON'T COMPLAIN ABOUT OUR DECISION...
YOU WERE THE UNANIMOUS CHOICE TO PLAY THE LEAD!
UNANIMOUS? BUT THAT MEANS...
Sorry... I voted for you too...
EVEN THE GIRL I LOVE CHOSE ME TO PLAY A GIRL...
This is pathetic!!
CALM DOWN, DAISUKE. IT'S NO BIG DEAL.

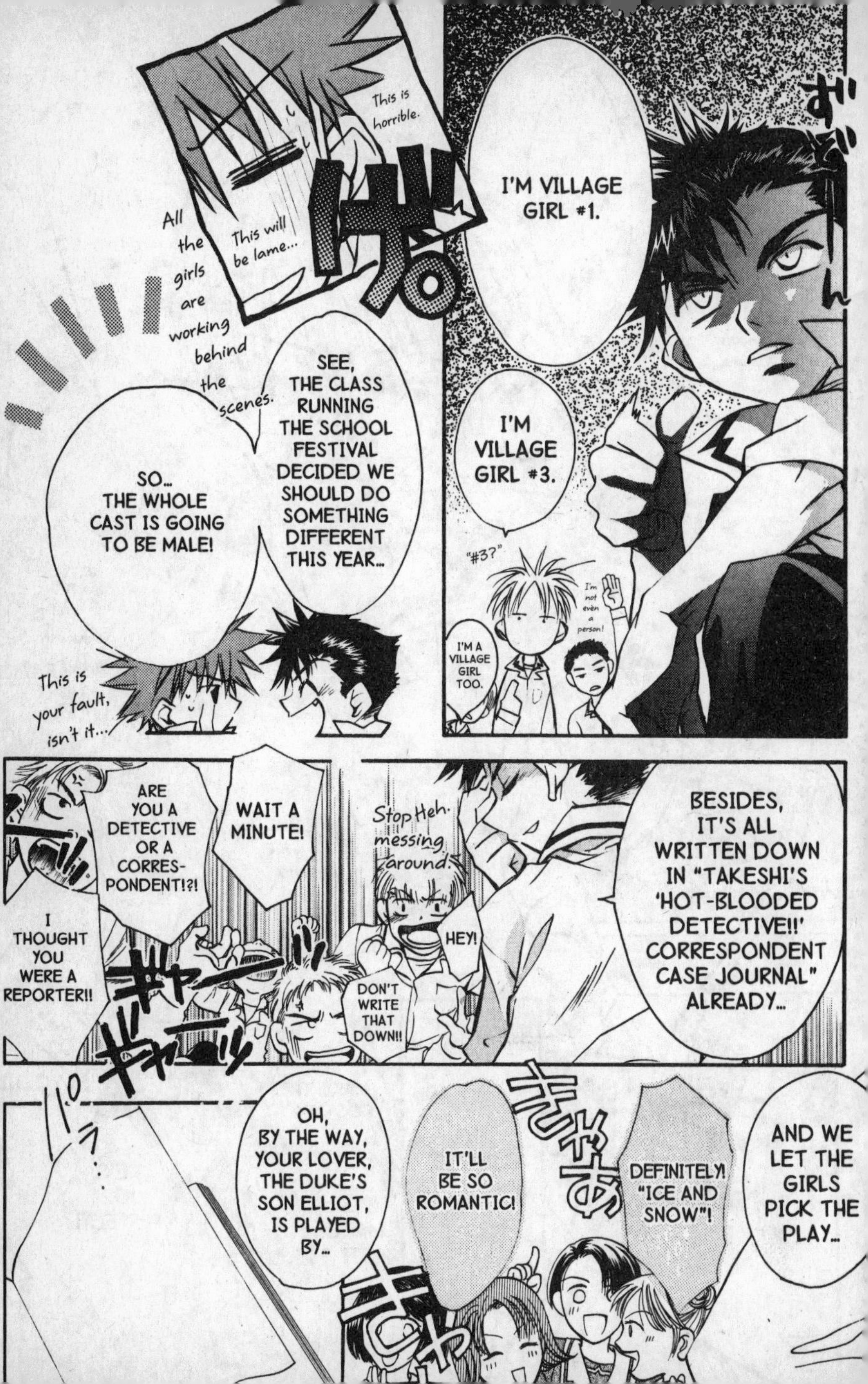
I'M VILLAGE GIRL #1.
I'M VILLAGE GIRL #3.
"#3?"
I'm not even a person!
I'M A VILLAGE GIRL TOO.
This is horrible.
This will be lame...
All the girls are working behind the scenes.
SEE, THE CLASS RUNNING THE SCHOOL FESTIVAL DECIDED WE SHOULD DO SOMETHING DIFFERENT THIS YEAR...
SO... THE WHOLE CAST IS GOING TO BE MALE!
This is your fault, isn't it...
BESIDES, IT'S ALL WRITTEN DOWN IN "TAKESHI'S 'HOT-BLOODED DETECTIVE!!' CORRESPONDENT CASE JOURNAL" ALREADY...
Heh.
Stop messing around.
HEY!
DON'T WRITE THAT DOWN!!
WAIT A MINUTE!
ARE YOU A DETECTIVE OR A CORRES- PONDENT!?!
I THOUGHT YOU WERE A REPORTER!!
AND WE LET THE GIRLS PICK THE PLAY...
DEFINITELY! "ICE AND SNOW"!
IT'LL BE SO ROMANTIC!
OH, BY THE WAY, YOUR LOVER, THE DUKE'S SON ELLIOT, IS PLAYED BY...

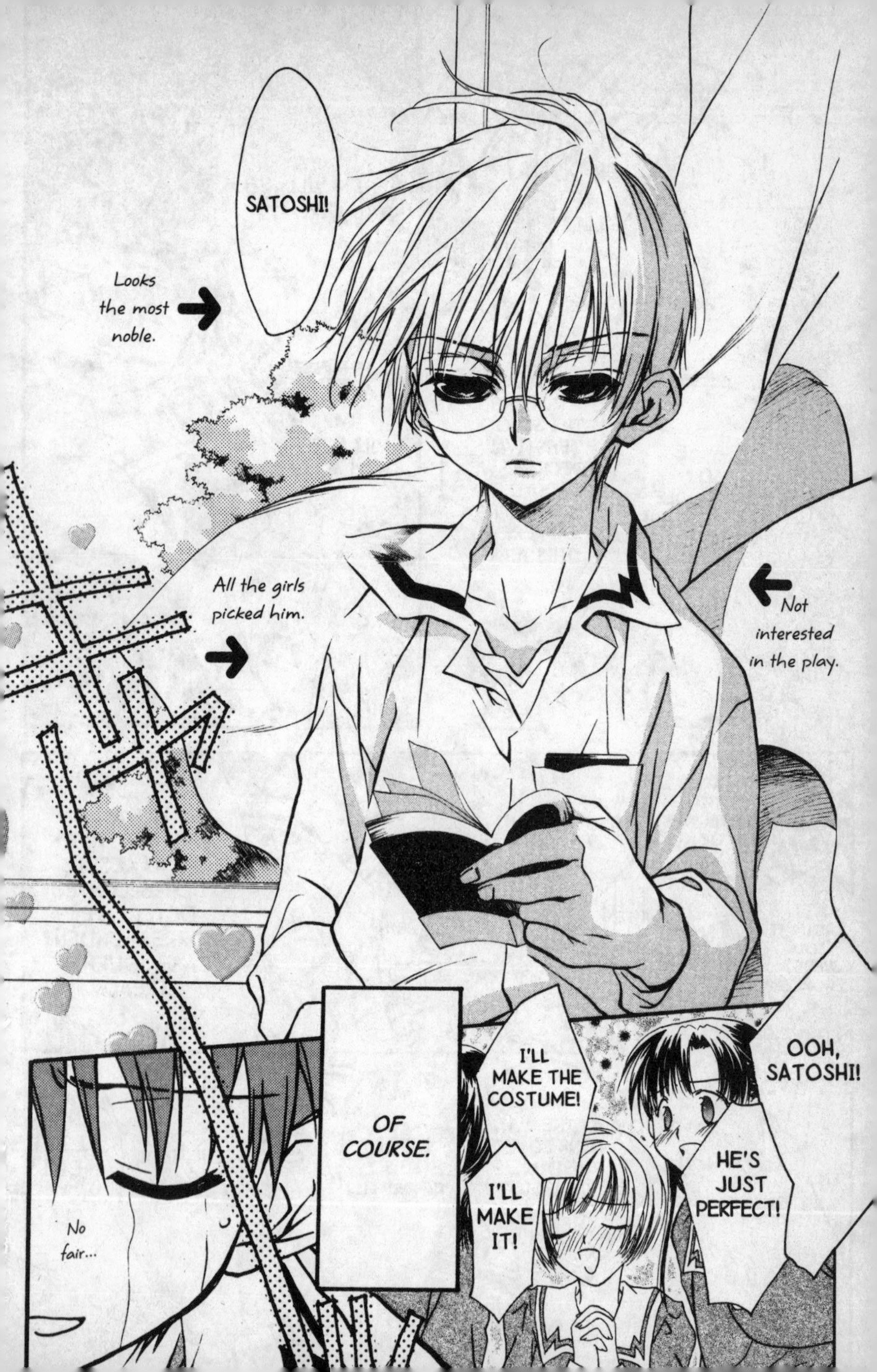
SATOSHI!
Looks the most noble.
Not interested in the play.
All the girls picked him.
OOH, SATOSHI!
I'LL MAKE THE COSTUME!
HE'S JUST PERFECT!
I'LL MAKE IT!
OF COURSE.
No fair...

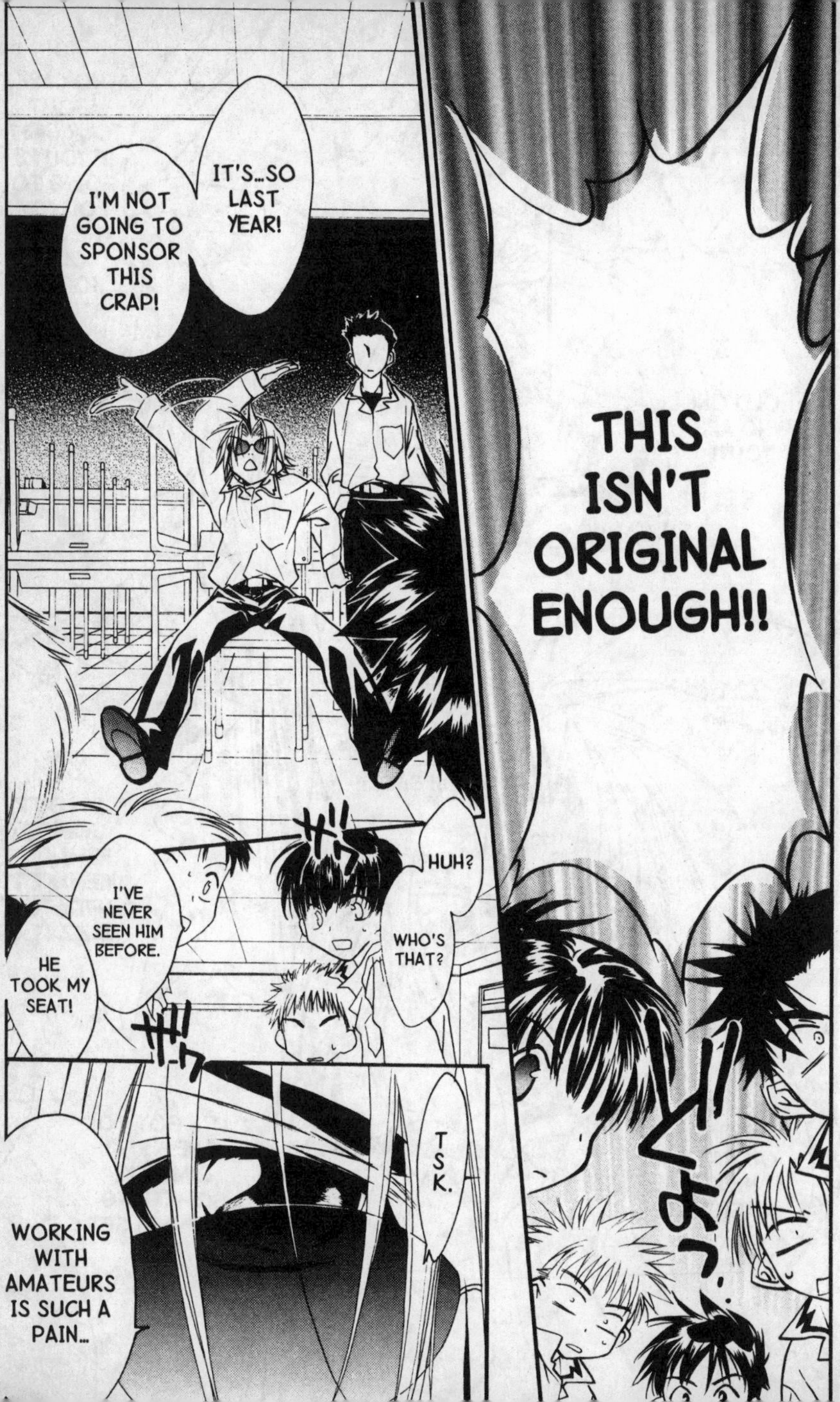
THIS ISN'T ORIGINAL ENOUGH!!
IT'S...SO LAST YEAR!
I'M NOT GOING TO SPONSOR THIS CRAP!
HUH?
WHO'S THAT?
I'VE NEVER SEEN HIM BEFORE.
HE TOOK MY SEAT!
TSK.
WORKING WITH AMATEURS IS SUCH A PAIN...

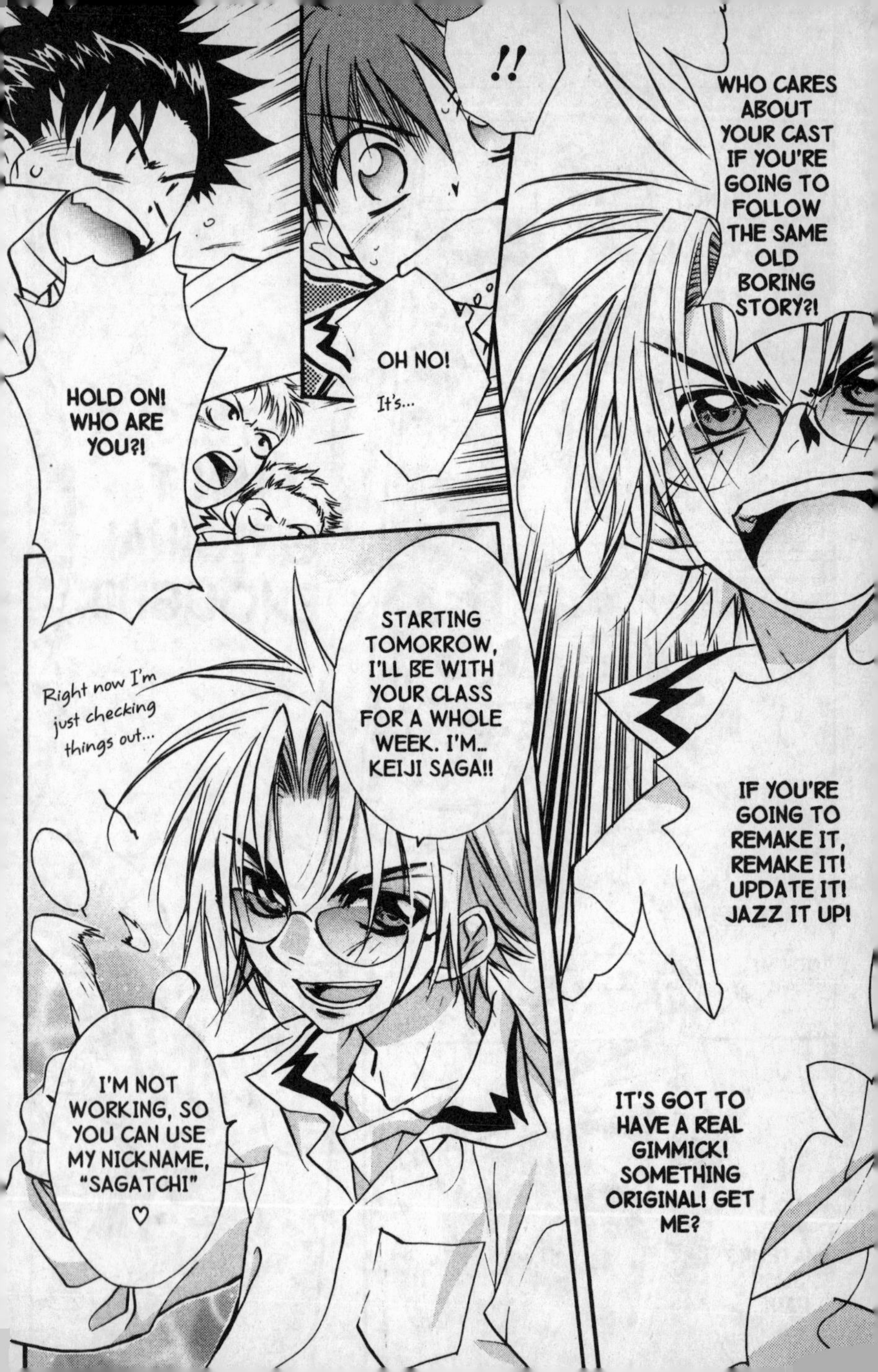
WHO CARES ABOUT YOUR CAST IF YOU'RE GOING TO FOLLOW THE SAME OLD BORING STORY?!
IF YOU'RE GOING TO REMAKE IT, REMAKE IT! UPDATE IT! JAZZ IT UP!
IT'S GOT TO HAVE A REAL GIMMICK! SOMETHING ORIGINAL! GET ME?
!!
OH NO!
It's...
HOLD ON! WHO ARE YOU?!
STARTING TOMORROW, I'LL BE WITH YOUR CLASS FOR A WHOLE WEEK. I'M... KEIJI SAGA!!
Right now I'm just checking things out...
I'M NOT WORKING, SO YOU CAN USE MY NICKNAME, "SAGATCHI" ♡

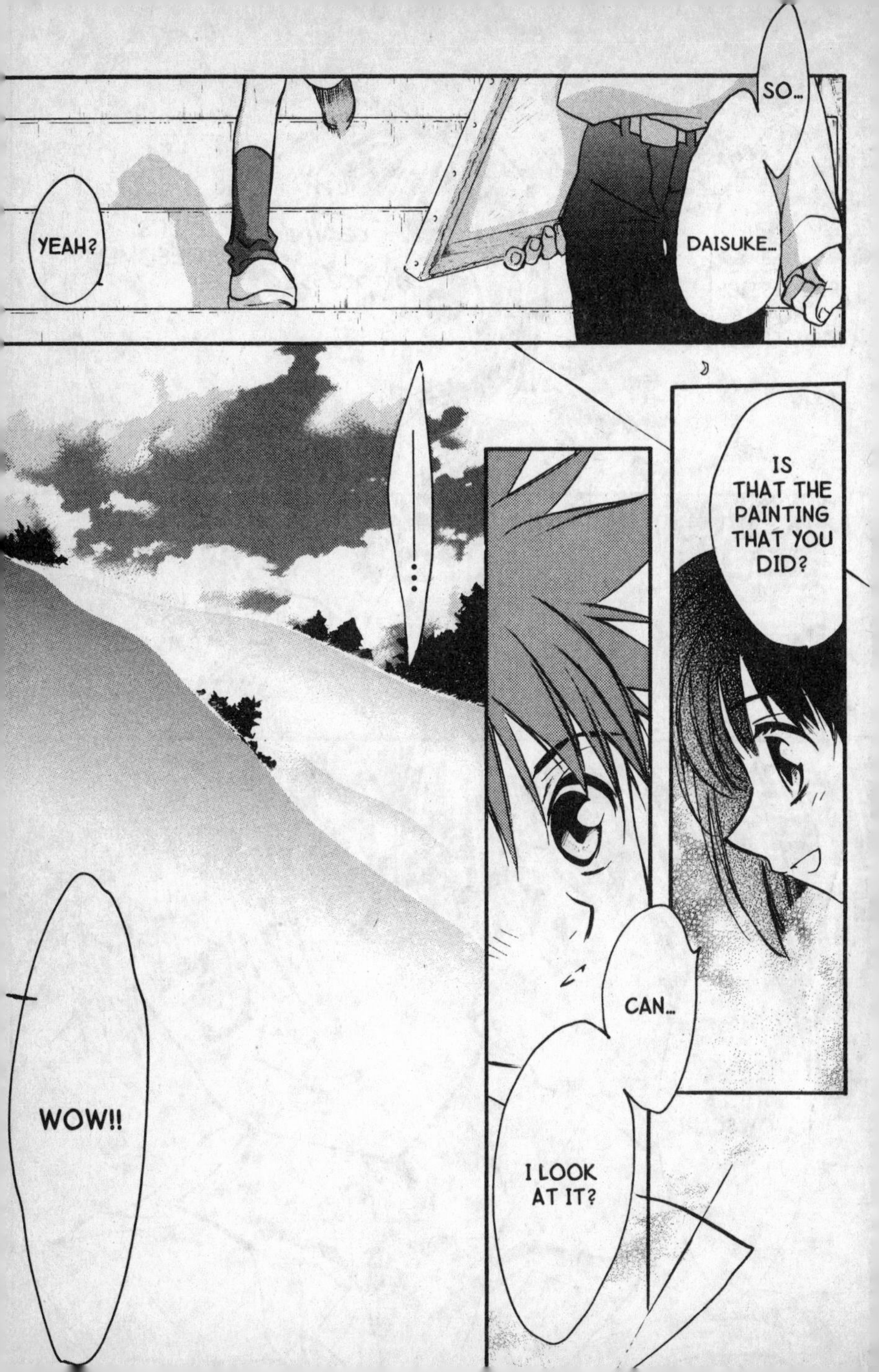
SO...
DAISUKE...
YEAH?
IS THAT THE PAINTING THAT YOU DID?
CAN...
I LOOK AT IT?
—...
WOW!!

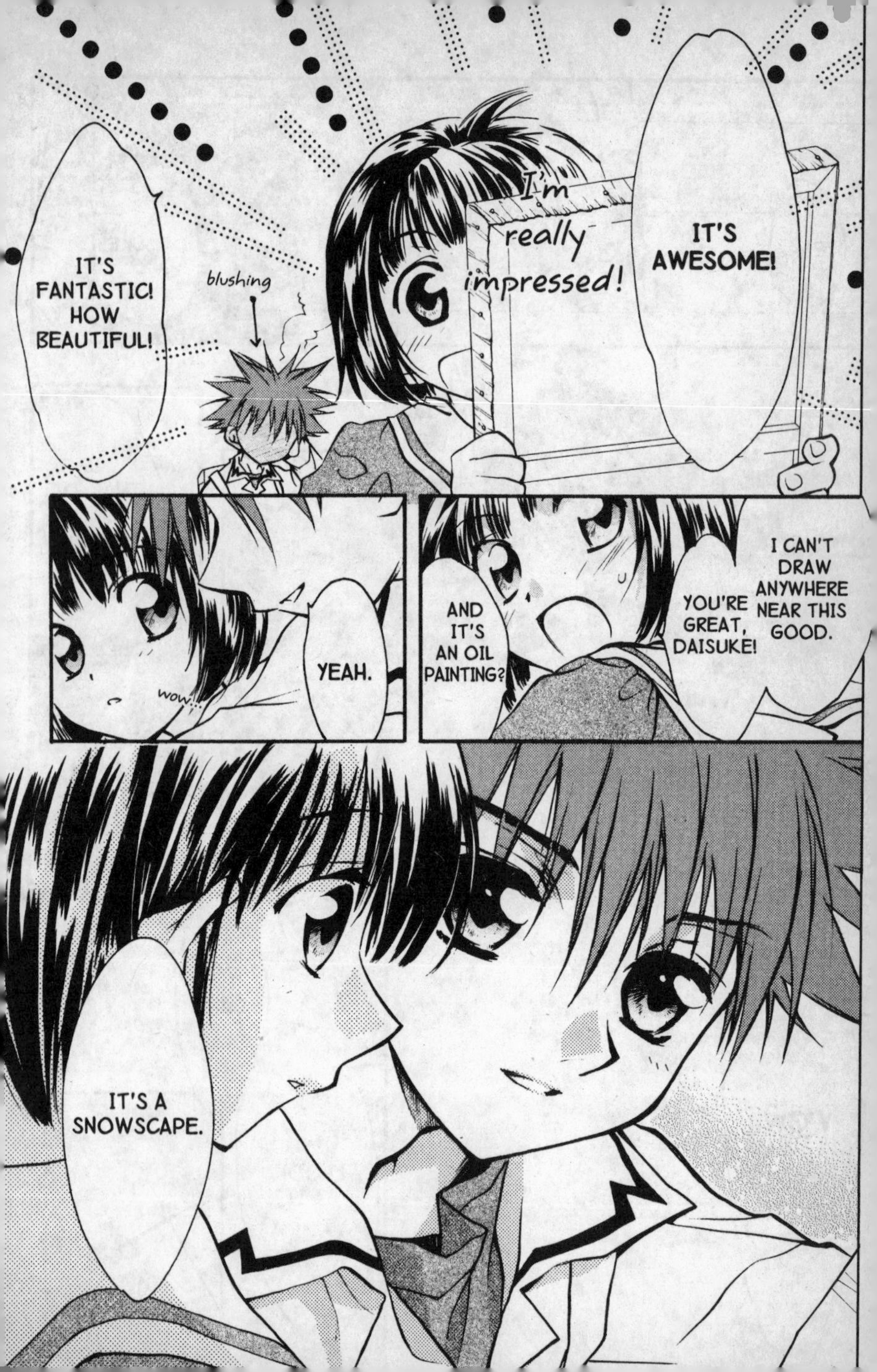
IT'S AWESOME!
I'm really impressed!
blushing
IT'S FANTASTIC! HOW BEAUTIFUL!
I CAN'T DRAW ANYWHERE NEAR THIS GOOD.
YOU'RE GREAT, DAISUKE!
AND IT'S AN OIL PAINTING?
YEAH.
wow...
IT'S A SNOWSCAPE.

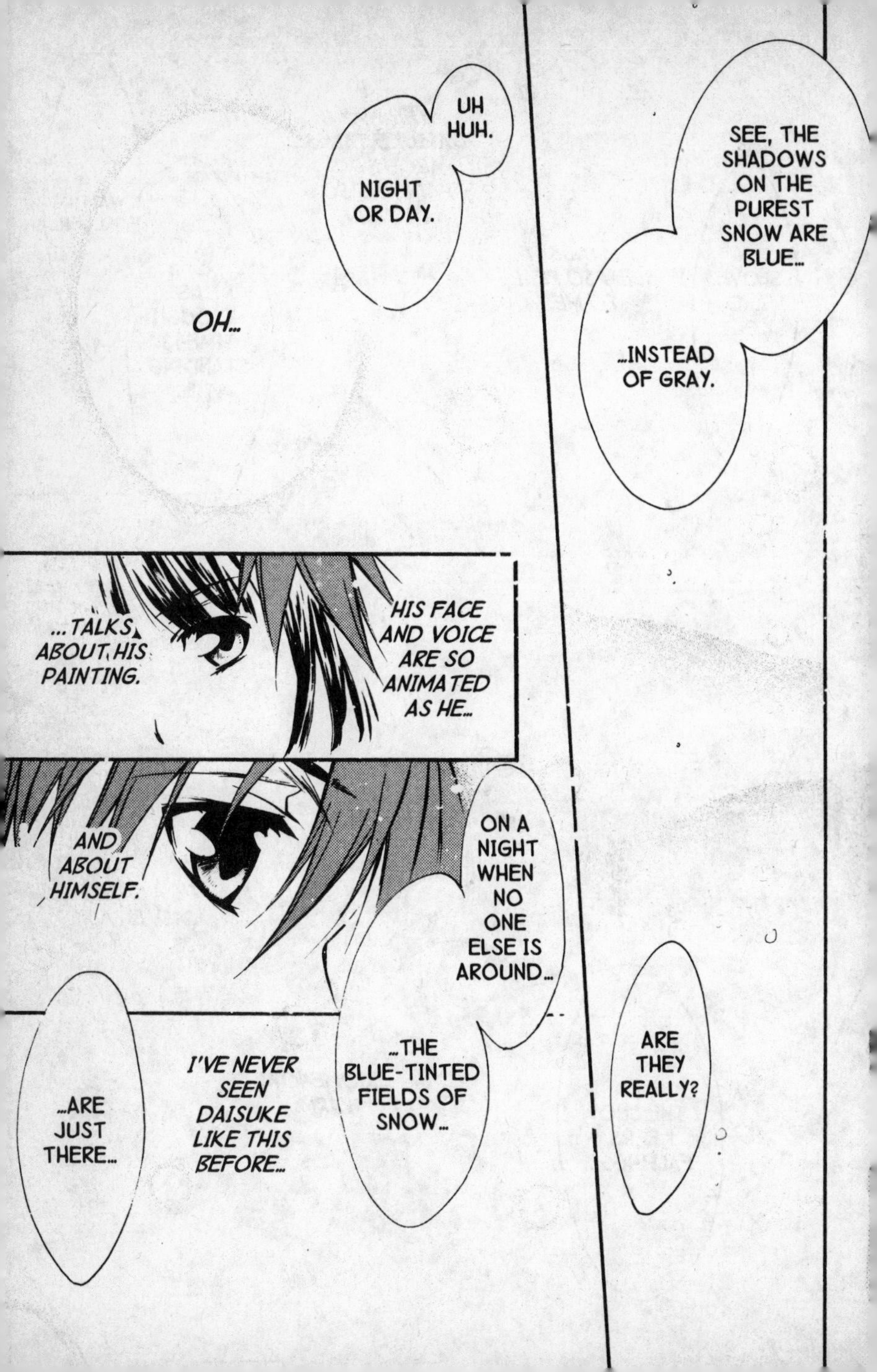
SEE, THE SHADOWS ON THE PUREST SNOW ARE BLUE...
...INSTEAD OF GRAY.
ARE THEY REALLY?
UH HUH.
NIGHT OR DAY.
OH...
HIS FACE AND VOICE ARE SO ANIMATED AS HE...
...TALKS ABOUT HIS PAINTING.
ON A NIGHT WHEN NO ONE ELSE IS AROUND...
AND ABOUT HIMSELF.
...THE BLUE-TINTED FIELDS OF SNOW...
I'VE NEVER SEEN DAISUKE LIKE THIS BEFORE...
...ARE JUST THERE...

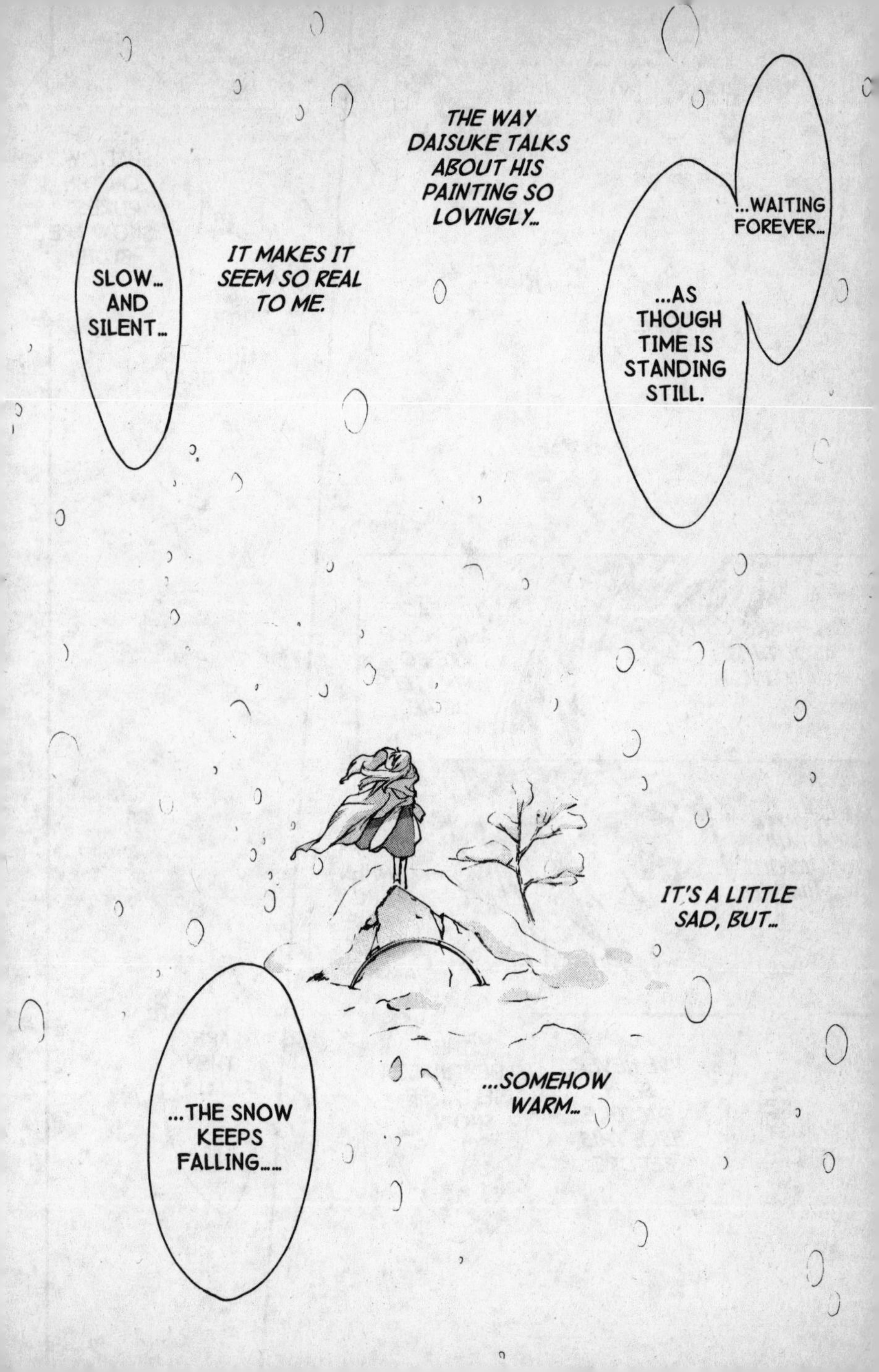
...WAITING FOREVER...
...AS THOUGH TIME IS STANDING STILL.
THE WAY DAISUKE TALKS ABOUT HIS PAINTING SO LOVINGLY...
IT MAKES IT SEEM SO REAL TO ME.
SLOW... AND SILENT...
IT'S A LITTLE SAD, BUT...
...SOMEHOW WARM...
...THE SNOW KEEPS FALLING.....

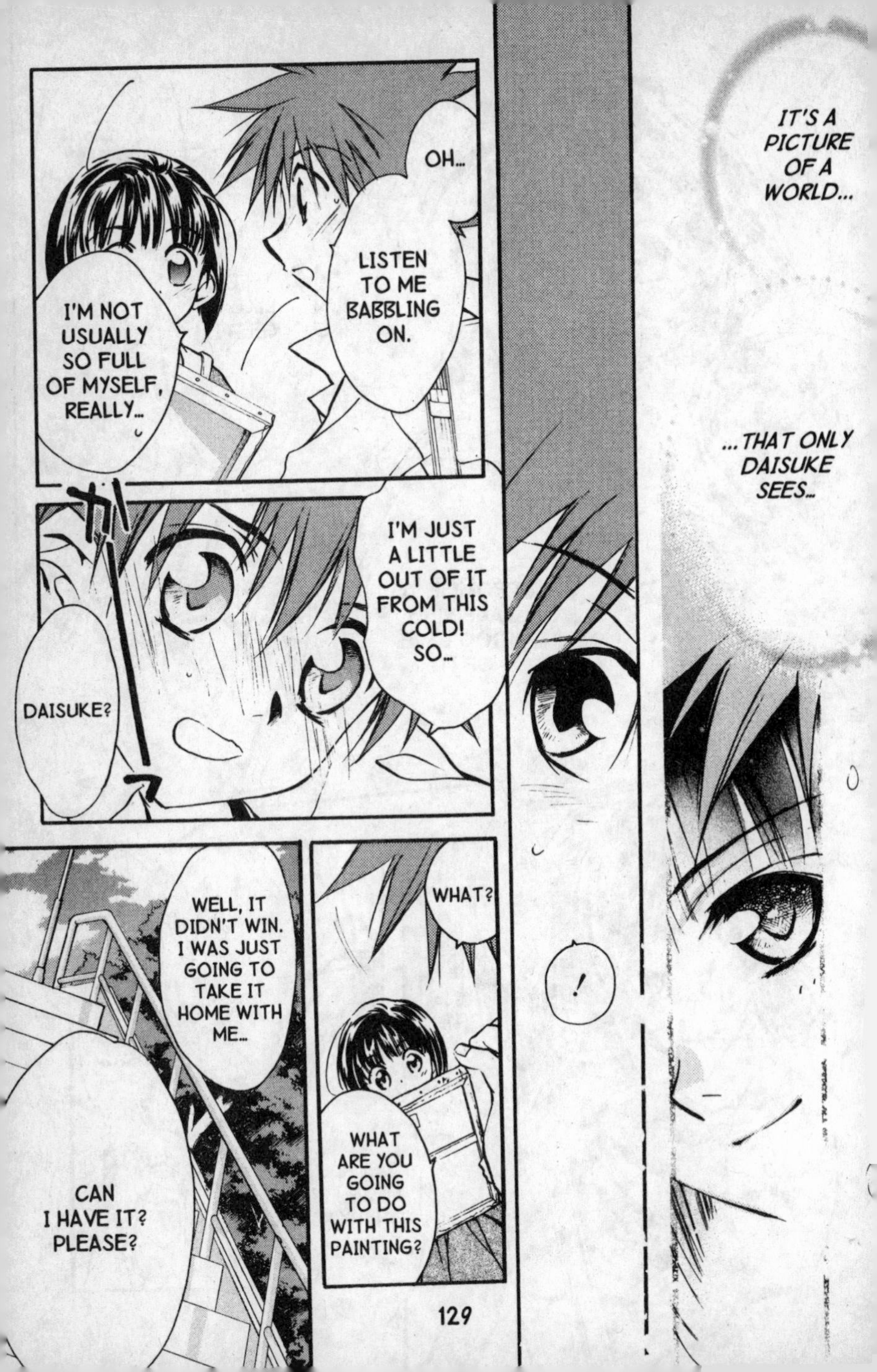
IT'S A PICTURE OF A WORLD...
...THAT ONLY DAISUKE SEES...
OH...
LISTEN TO ME BABBLING ON.
I'M NOT USUALLY SO FULL OF MYSELF, REALLY...
I'M JUST A LITTLE OUT OF IT FROM THIS COLD! SO...
DAISUKE?
!
WHAT?
WHAT ARE YOU GOING TO DO WITH THIS PAINTING?
WELL, IT DIDN'T WIN. I WAS JUST GOING TO TAKE IT HOME WITH ME...
CAN I HAVE IT? PLEASE?

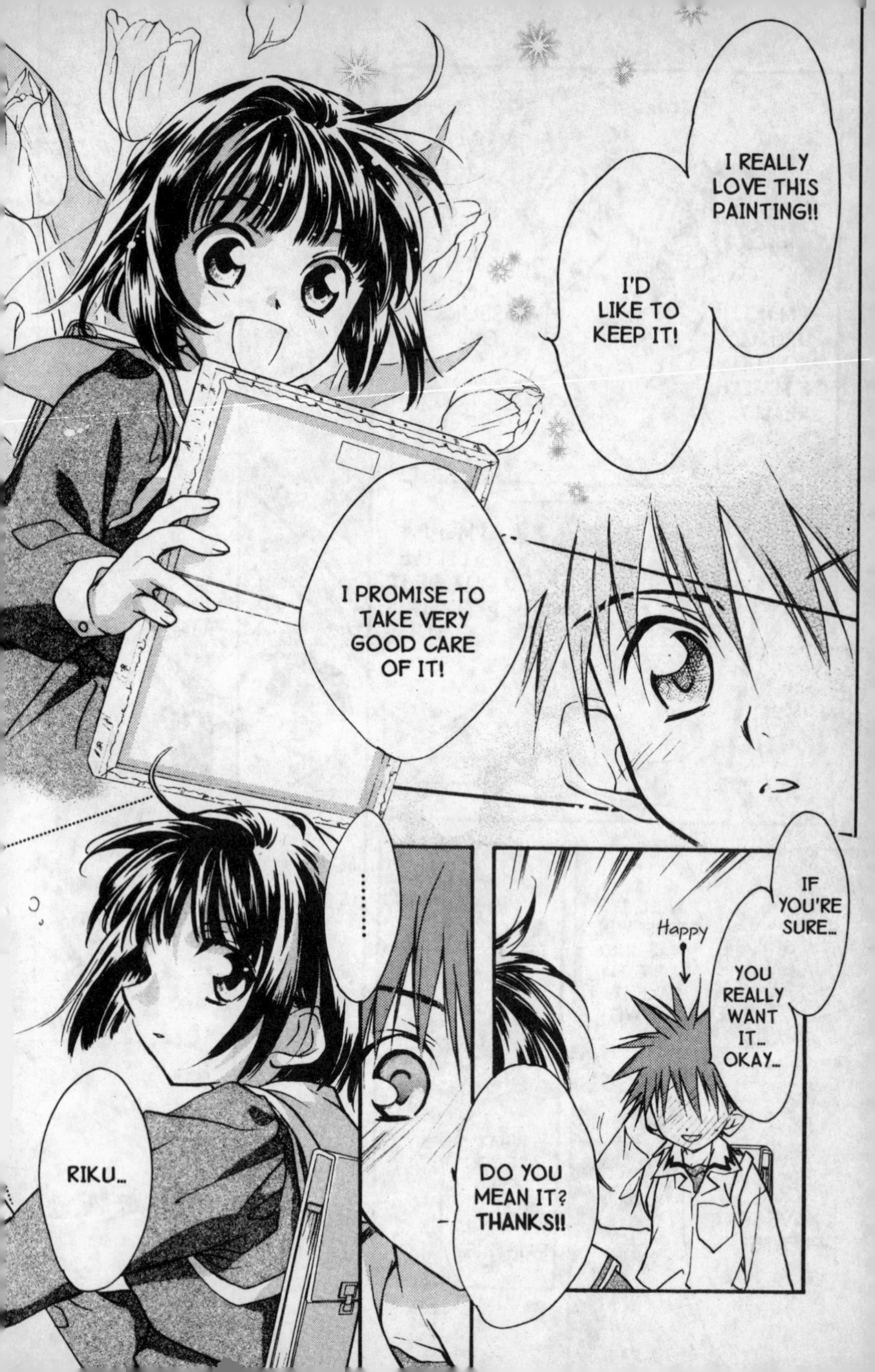
I REALLY LOVE THIS PAINTING!!
I'D LIKE TO KEEP IT!
I PROMISE TO TAKE VERY GOOD CARE OF IT!
IF YOU'RE SURE...
Happy
YOU REALLY WANT IT... OKAY...
DO YOU MEAN IT? THANKS!!
......
RIKU...

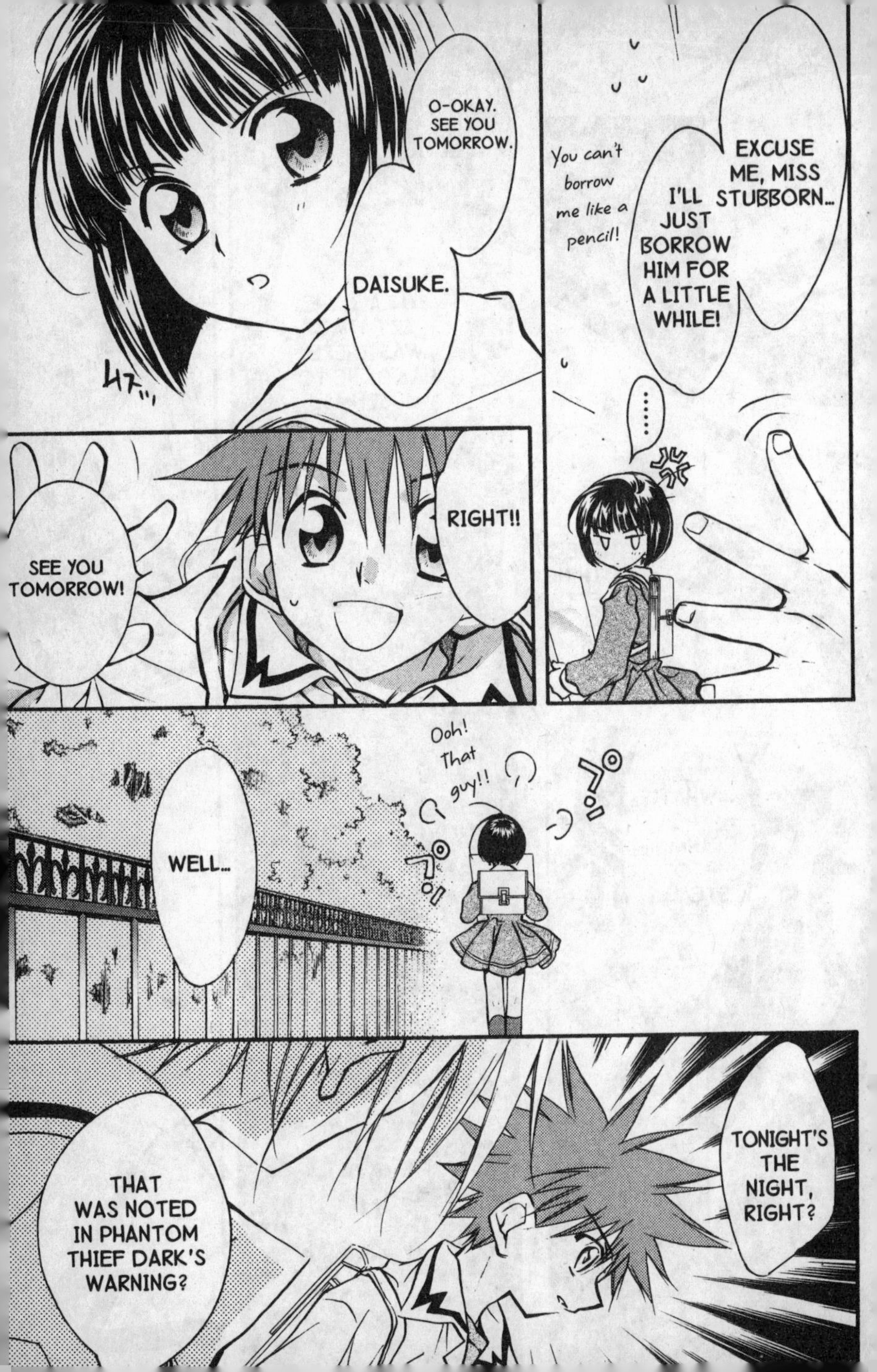
EXCUSE ME, MISS STUBBORN... I'LL JUST BORROW HIM FOR A LITTLE WHILE!
You can't borrow me like a pencil!
......
O-OKAY. SEE YOU TOMORROW.
DAISUKE.
RIGHT!!
SEE YOU TOMORROW!
Ooh! That guy!!
WELL...
TONIGHT'S THE NIGHT, RIGHT?
THAT WAS NOTED IN PHANTOM THIEF DARK'S WARNING?

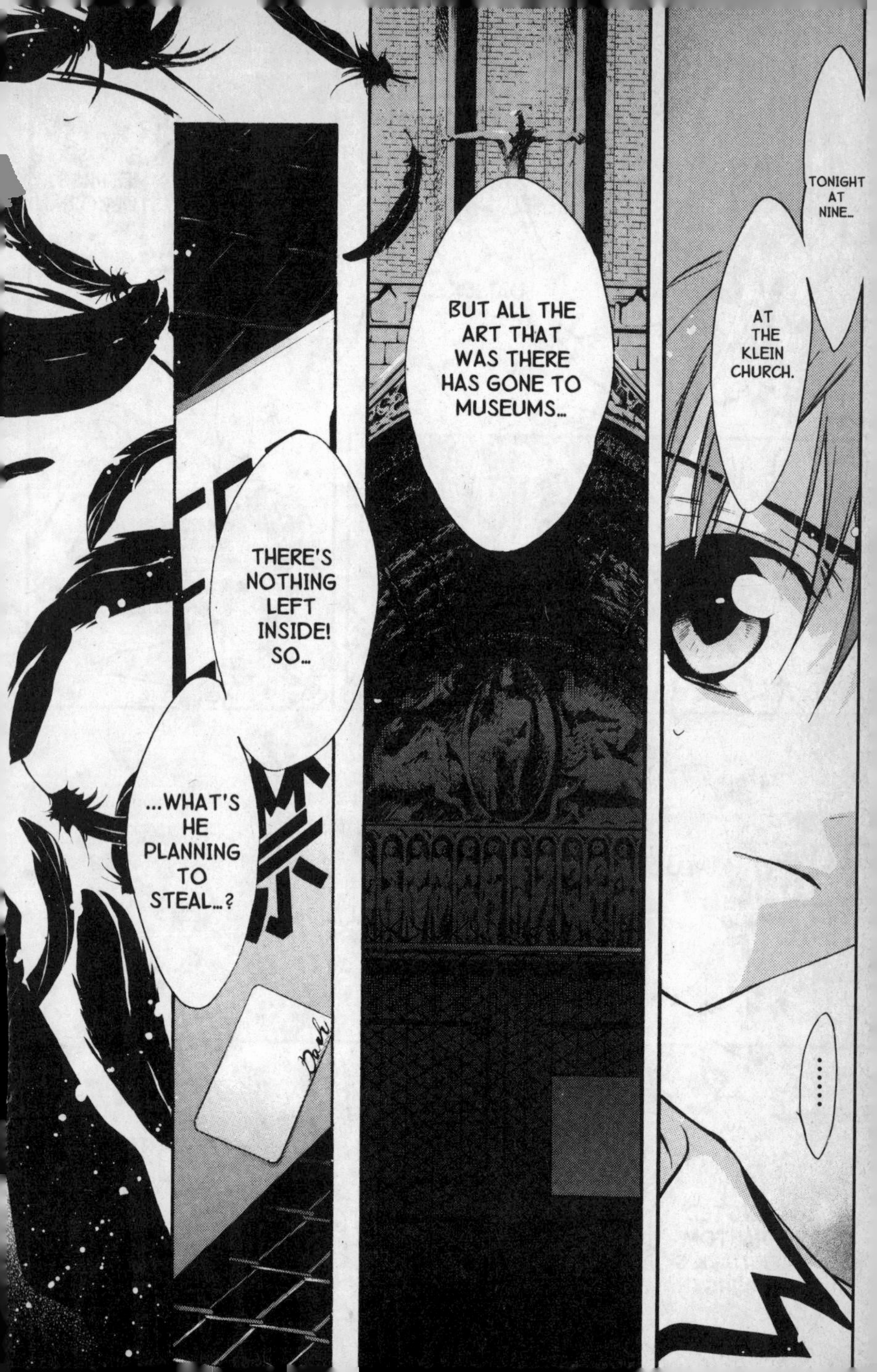
TONIGHT AT NINE...
AT THE KLEIN CHURCH.
......
BUT ALL THE ART THAT WAS THERE HAS GONE TO MUSEUMS...
THERE'S NOTHING LEFT INSIDE! SO...
...WHAT'S HE PLANNING TO STEAL...?

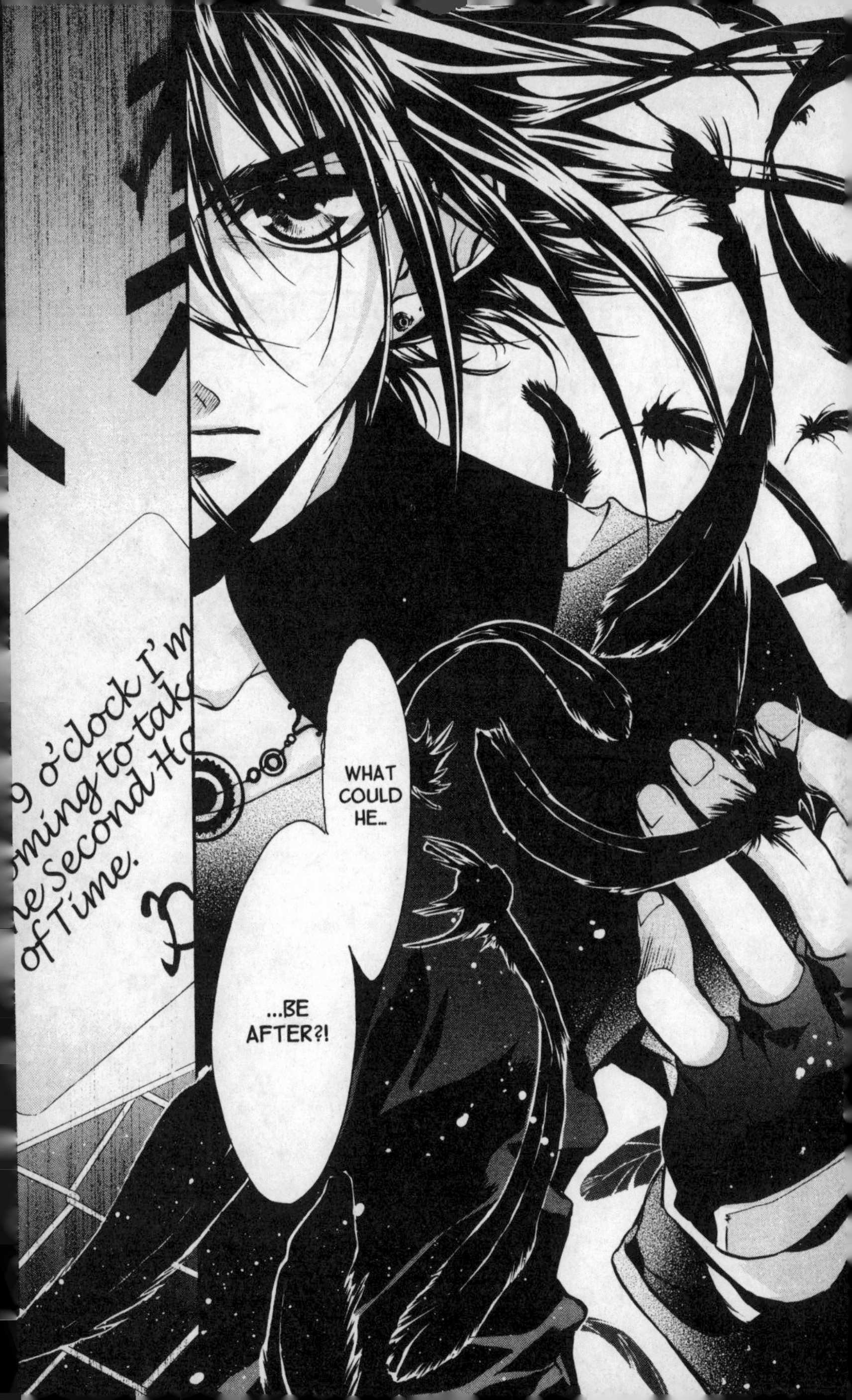
WHAT COULD HE...
...BE AFTER?!
9 o'clock I'm
oming to tak
he Second H
of Time.

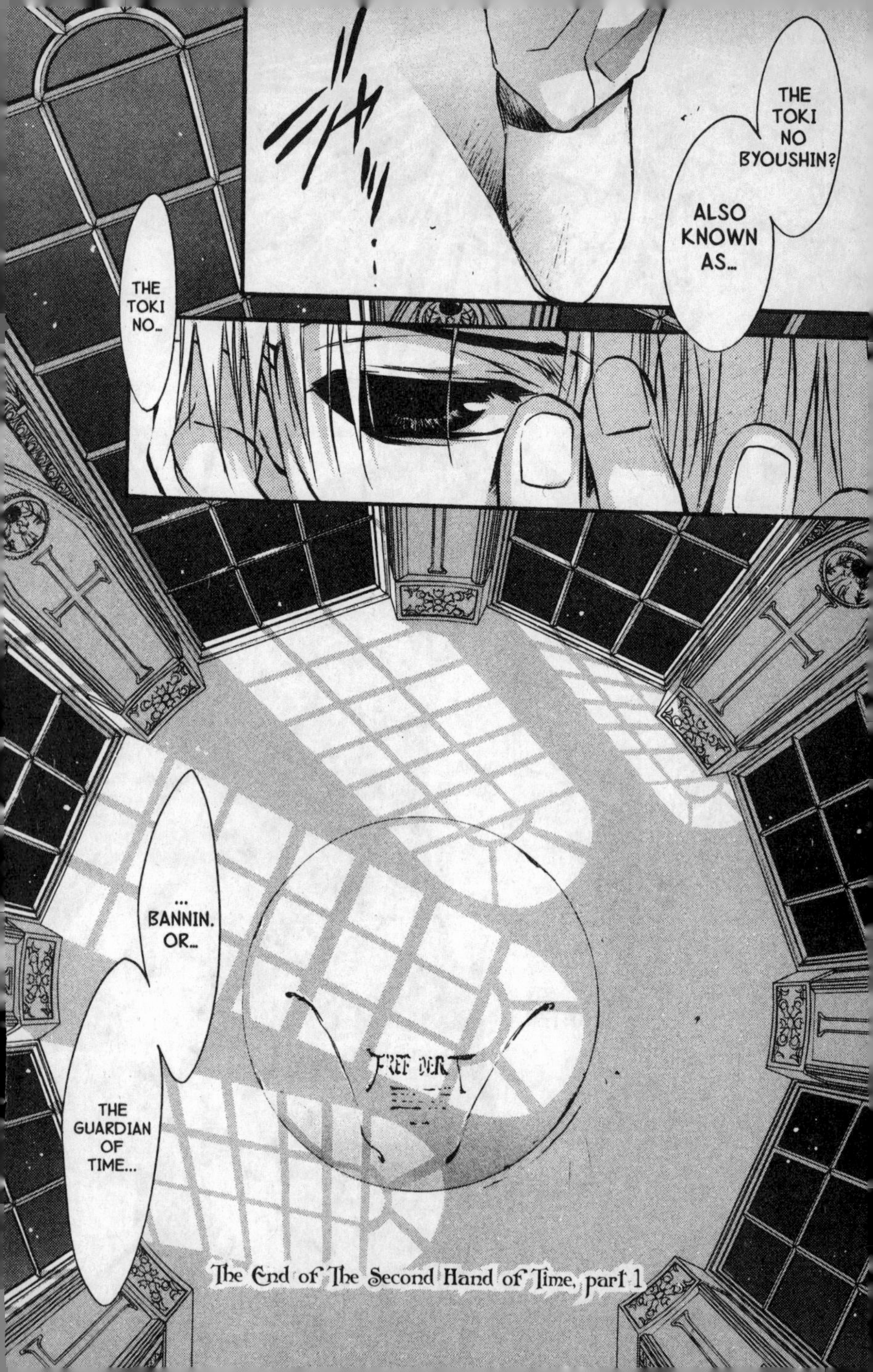
THE TOKI NO BYOUSHIN?
ALSO KNOWN AS...
THE TOKI NO...
...BANNIN. OR...
THE GUARDIAN OF TIME...
The End of The Second Hand of Time, part 1

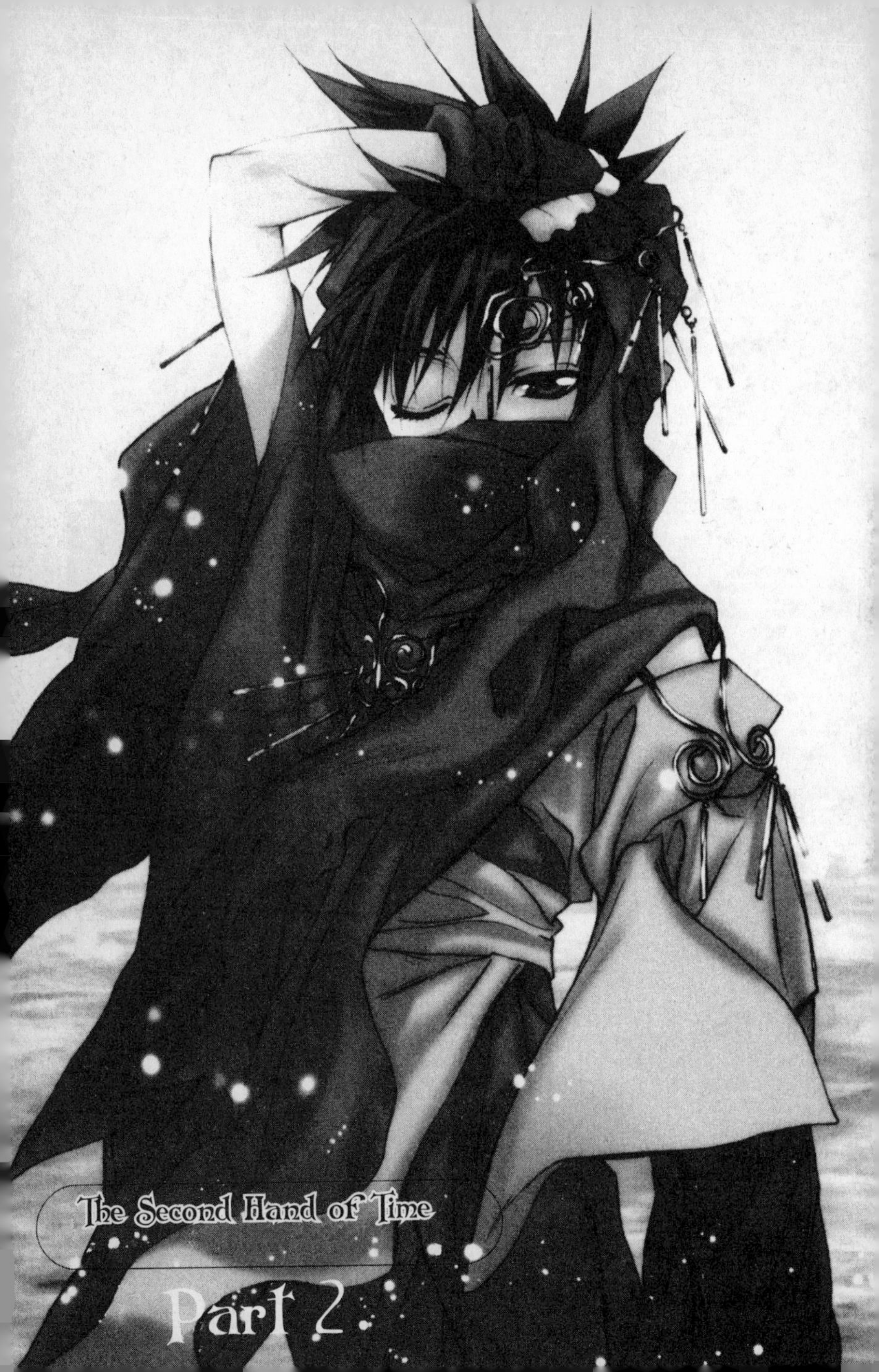
The Second Hand of Time
Part 2

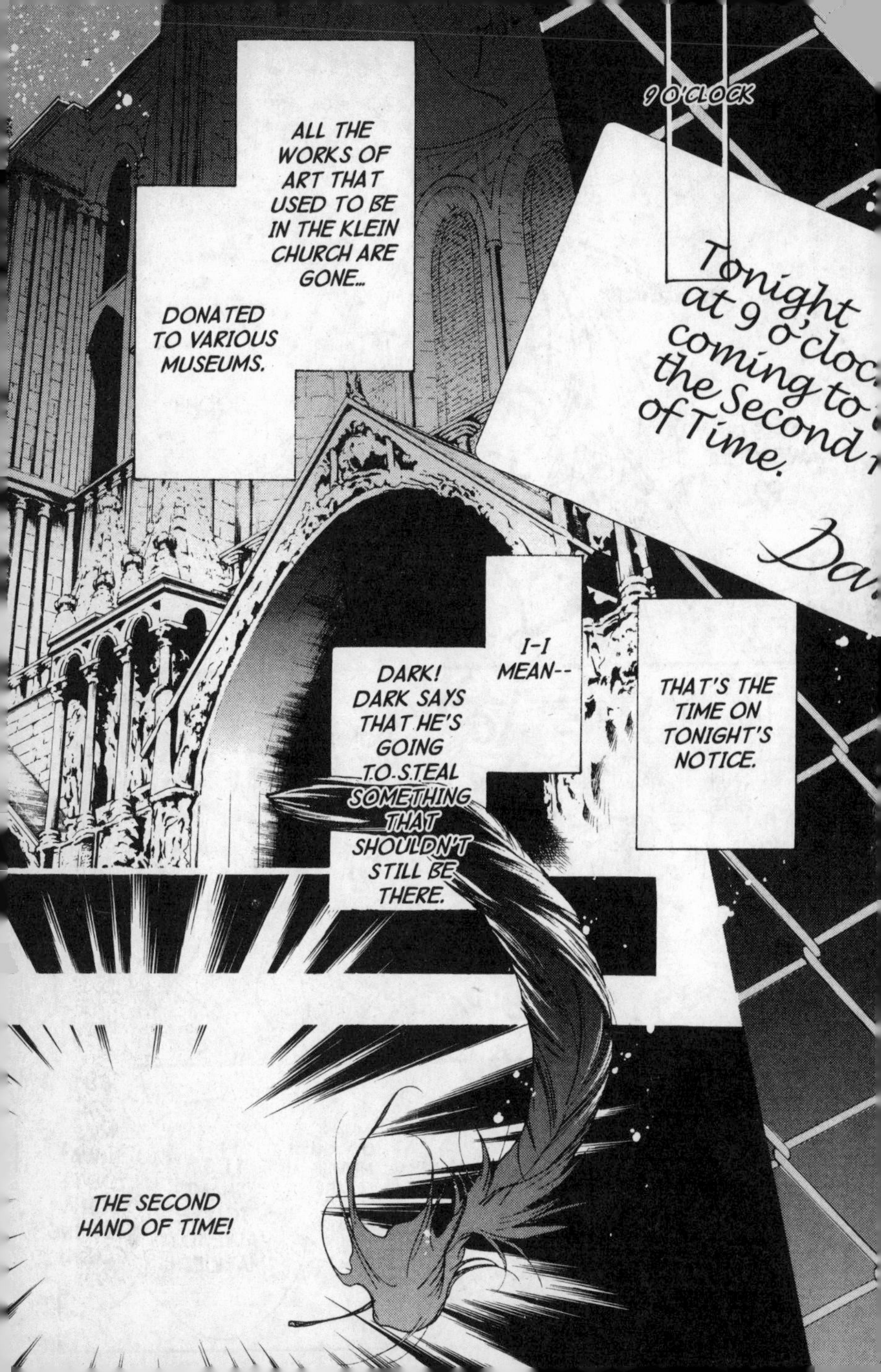
9 O'CLOCK
Tonight at 9 o'cloc coming to the Second of Time.
Da
ALL THE WORKS OF ART THAT USED TO BE IN THE KLEIN CHURCH ARE GONE...
DONATED TO VARIOUS MUSEUMS.
THAT'S THE TIME ON TONIGHT'S NOTICE.
I-I MEAN--
DARK! DARK SAYS THAT HE'S GOING TO STEAL SOMETHING THAT SHOULDN'T STILL BE THERE.
THE SECOND HAND OF TIME!

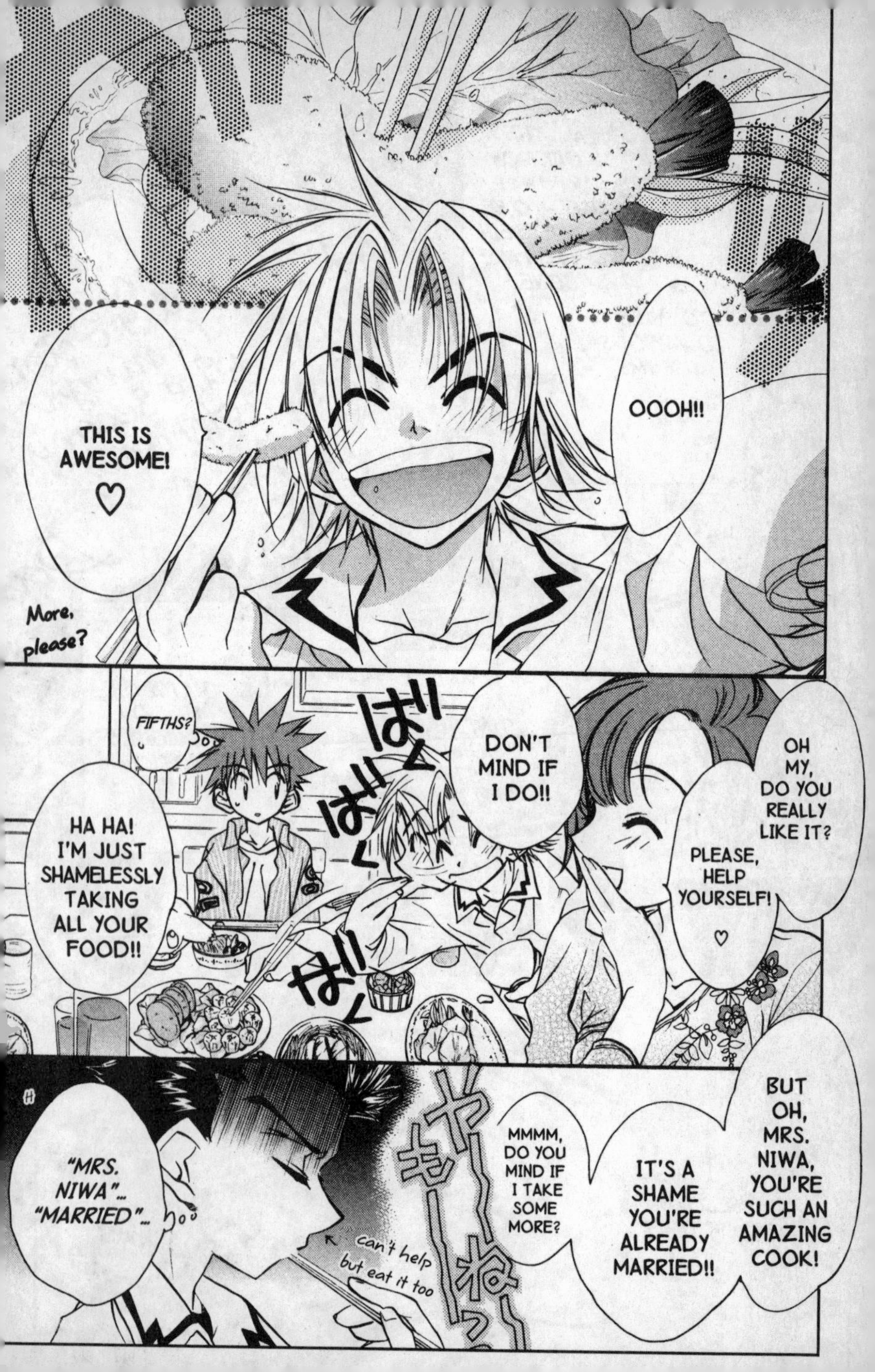
OOOH!!
THIS IS AWESOME! ♡
More, please?
OH MY, DO YOU REALLY LIKE IT?
PLEASE, HELP YOURSELF! ♡
DON'T MIND IF I DO!!
FIFTHS?
HA HA! I'M JUST SHAMELESSLY TAKING ALL YOUR FOOD!!
BUT OH, MRS. NIWA, YOU'RE SUCH AN AMAZING COOK!
IT'S A SHAME YOU'RE ALREADY MARRIED!!
MMMM, DO YOU MIND IF I TAKE SOME MORE?
can't help but eat it too
"MRS. NIWA"... "MARRIED"...

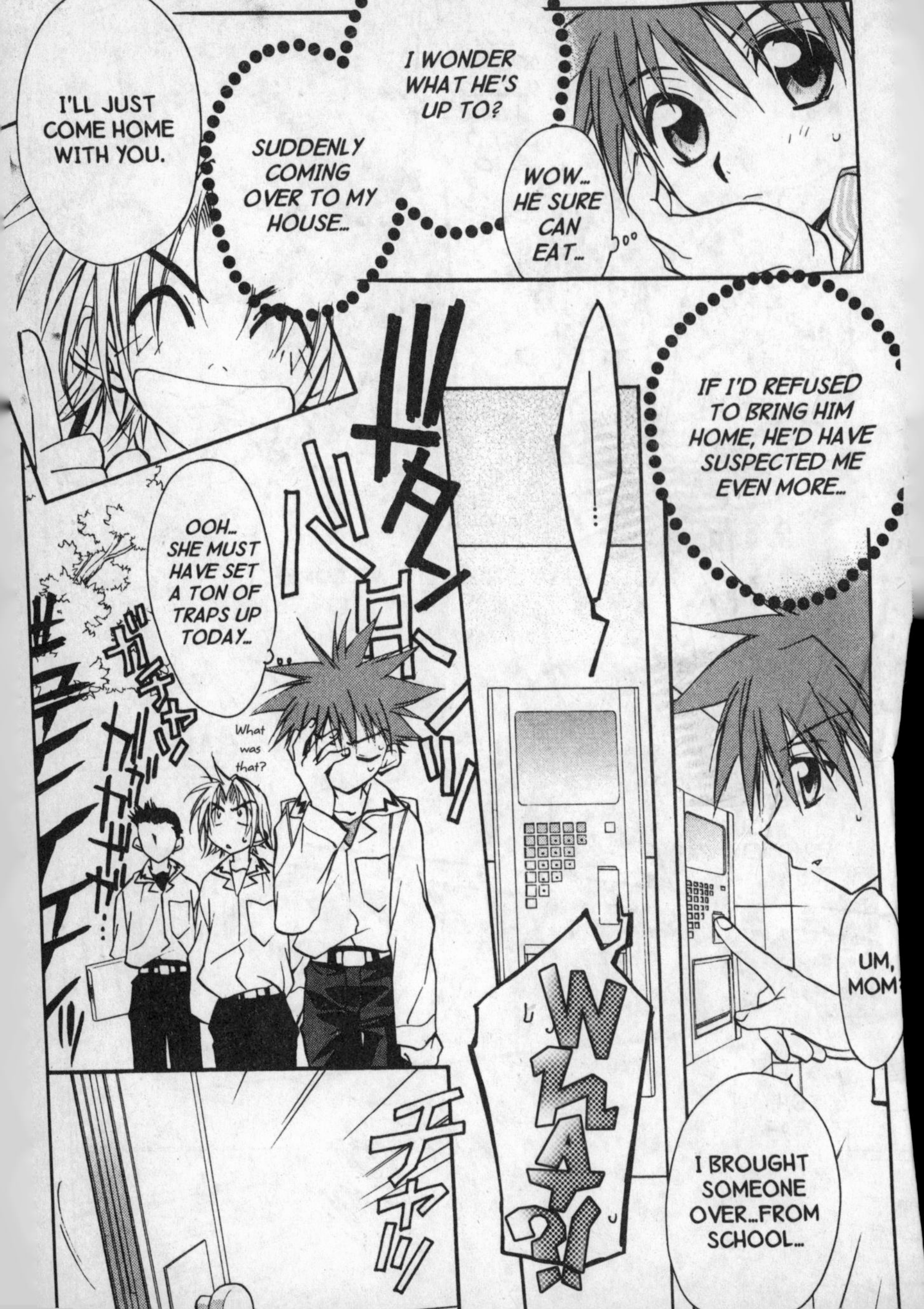
WOW... HE SURE CAN EAT...
I WONDER WHAT HE'S UP TO?
SUDDENLY COMING OVER TO MY HOUSE...
I'LL JUST COME HOME WITH YOU.
IF I'D REFUSED TO BRING HIM HOME, HE'D HAVE SUSPECTED ME EVEN MORE...
UM, MOM?
I BROUGHT SOMEONE OVER...FROM SCHOOL...
!
WHA?!
OOH... SHE MUST HAVE SET A TON OF TRAPS UP TODAY...
What was that?

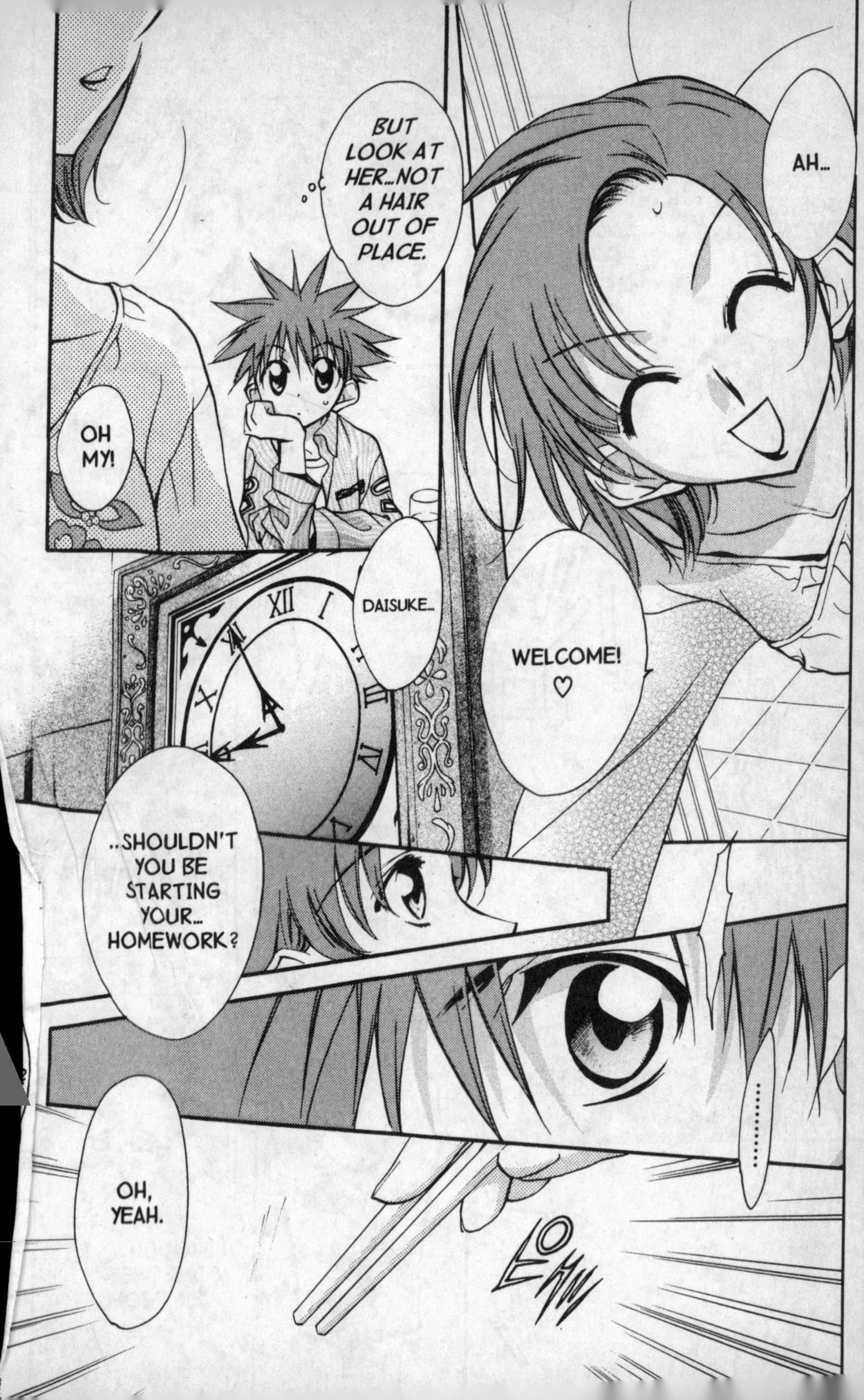
AH...
WELCOME! ♡
BUT LOOK AT HER...NOT A HAIR OUT OF PLACE.
OH MY!
DAISUKE...
...SHOULDN'T YOU BE STARTING YOUR... HOMEWORK?
......
OH, YEAH.

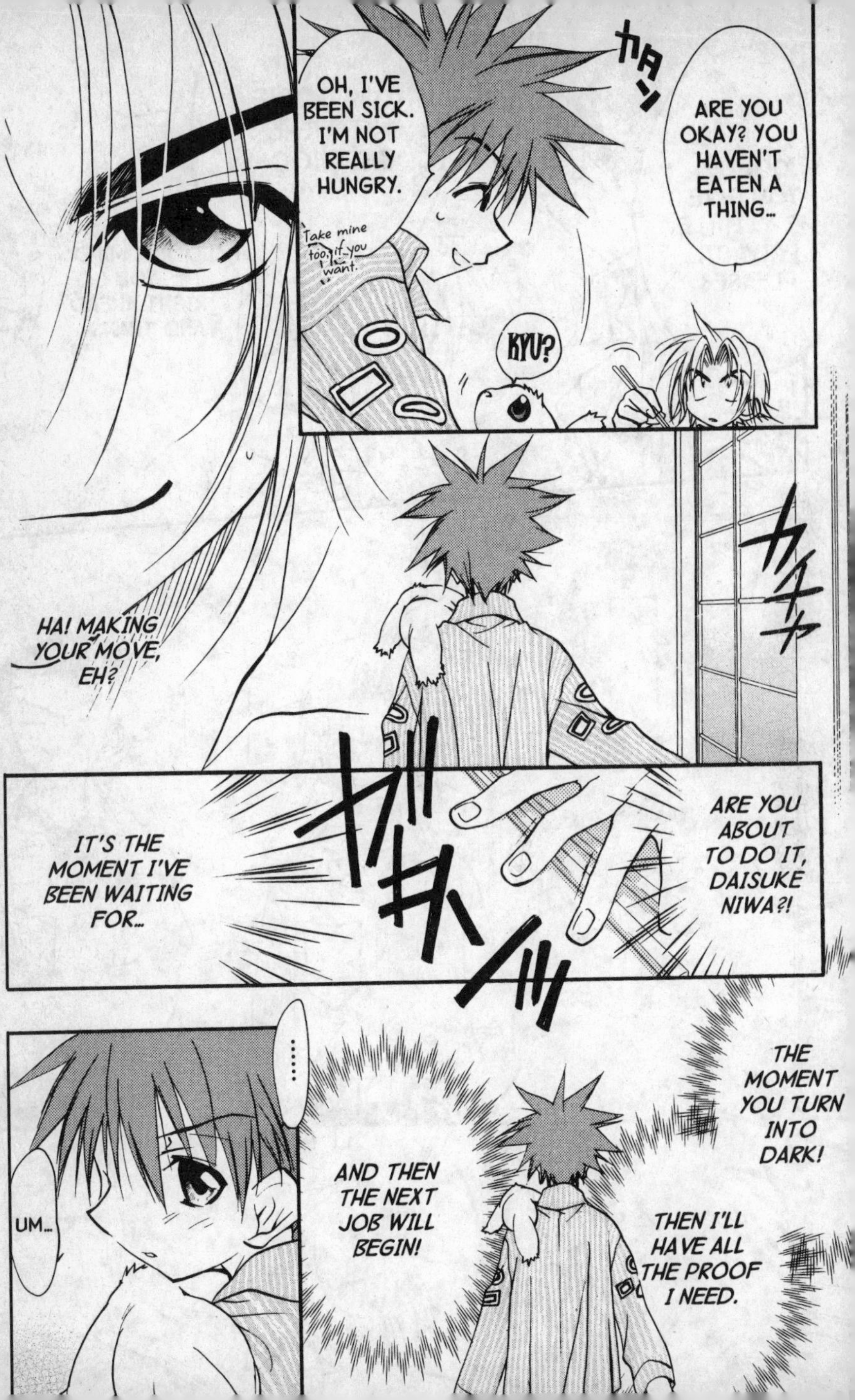
カタン
ARE YOU OKAY? YOU HAVEN'T EATEN A THING...
OH, I'VE BEEN SICK. I'M NOT REALLY HUNGRY.
Take mine too, if you want.
KYU?
HA! MAKING YOUR MOVE, EH?
ARE YOU ABOUT TO DO IT, DAISUKE NIWA?!
IT'S THE MOMENT I'VE BEEN WAITING FOR...
THE MOMENT YOU TURN INTO DARK!
THEN I'LL HAVE ALL THE PROOF I NEED.
AND THEN THE NEXT JOB WILL BEGIN!
......
UM...

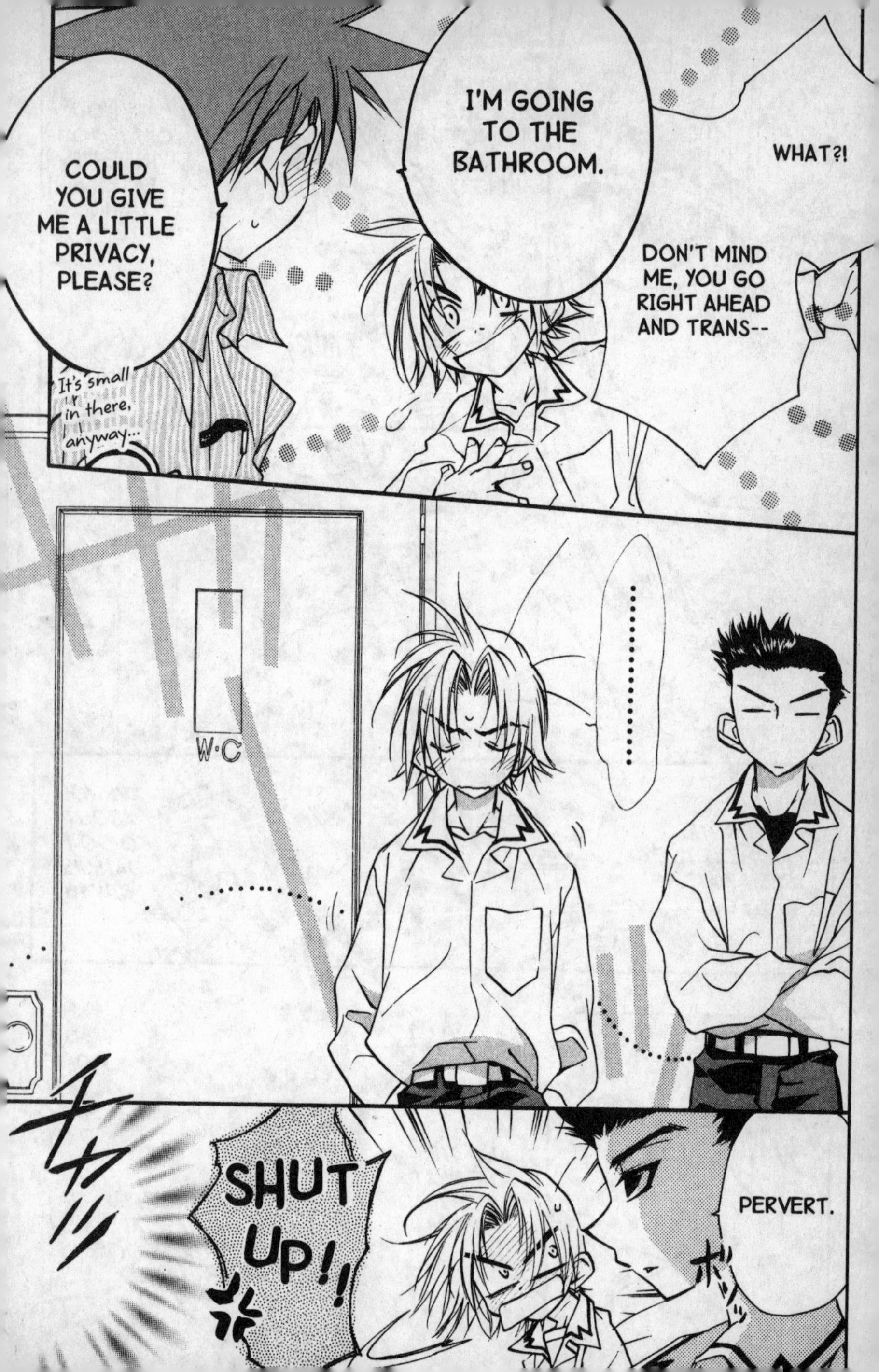
WHAT?!
DON'T MIND ME, YOU GO RIGHT AHEAD AND TRANS--
I'M GOING TO THE BATHROOM.
COULD YOU GIVE ME A LITTLE PRIVACY, PLEASE?
It's small in there, anyway...
W·C
......
PERVERT.
SHUT UP!!

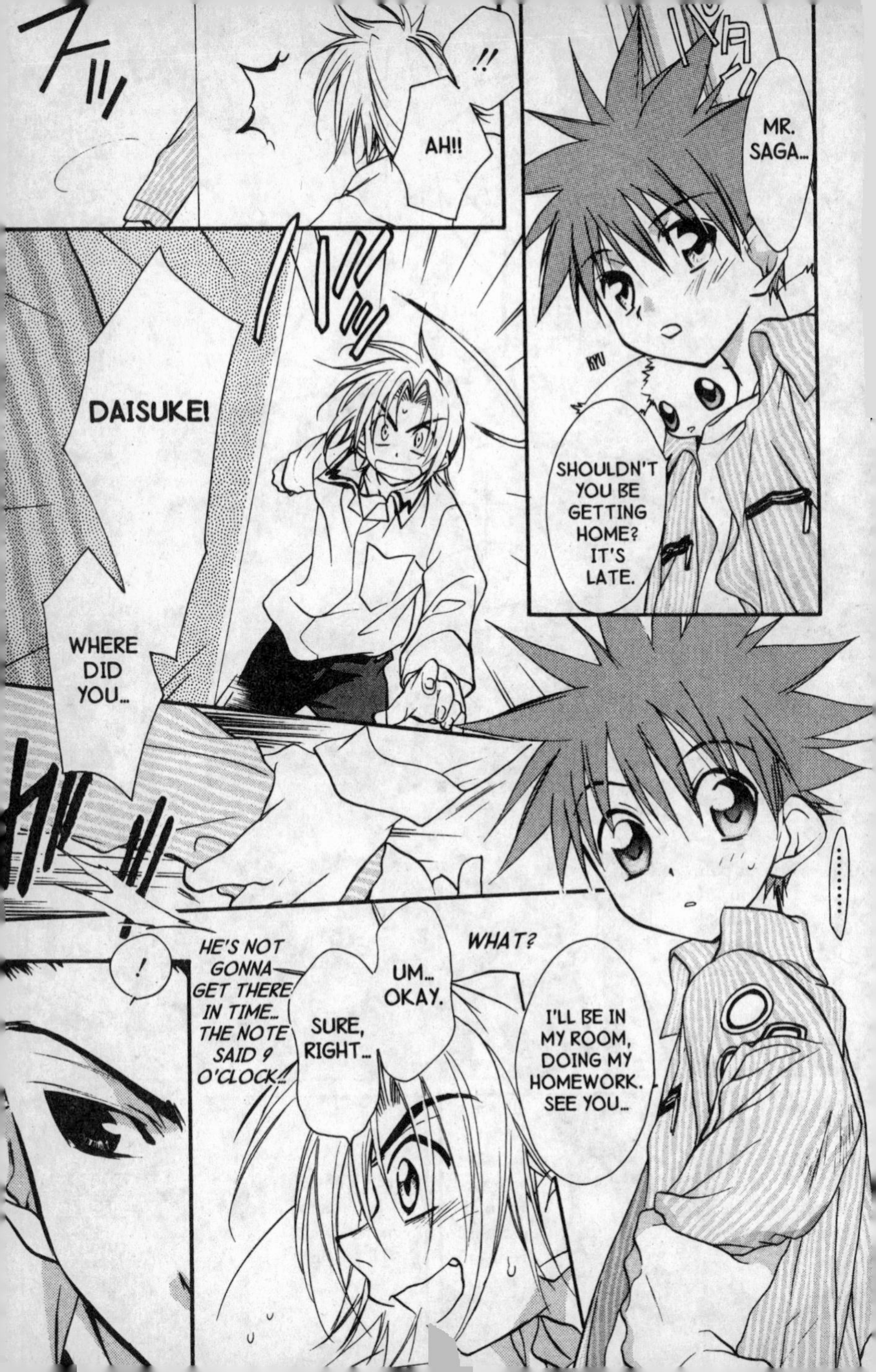
MR. SAGA...
KYU
SHOULDN'T YOU BE GETTING HOME? IT'S LATE.
!!
AH!!
DAISUKE!
WHERE DID YOU...
......
WHAT?
I'LL BE IN MY ROOM, DOING MY HOMEWORK. SEE YOU...
UM... OKAY.
SURE, RIGHT...
HE'S NOT GONNA GET THERE IN TIME... THE NOTE SAID 9 O'CLOCK...
!

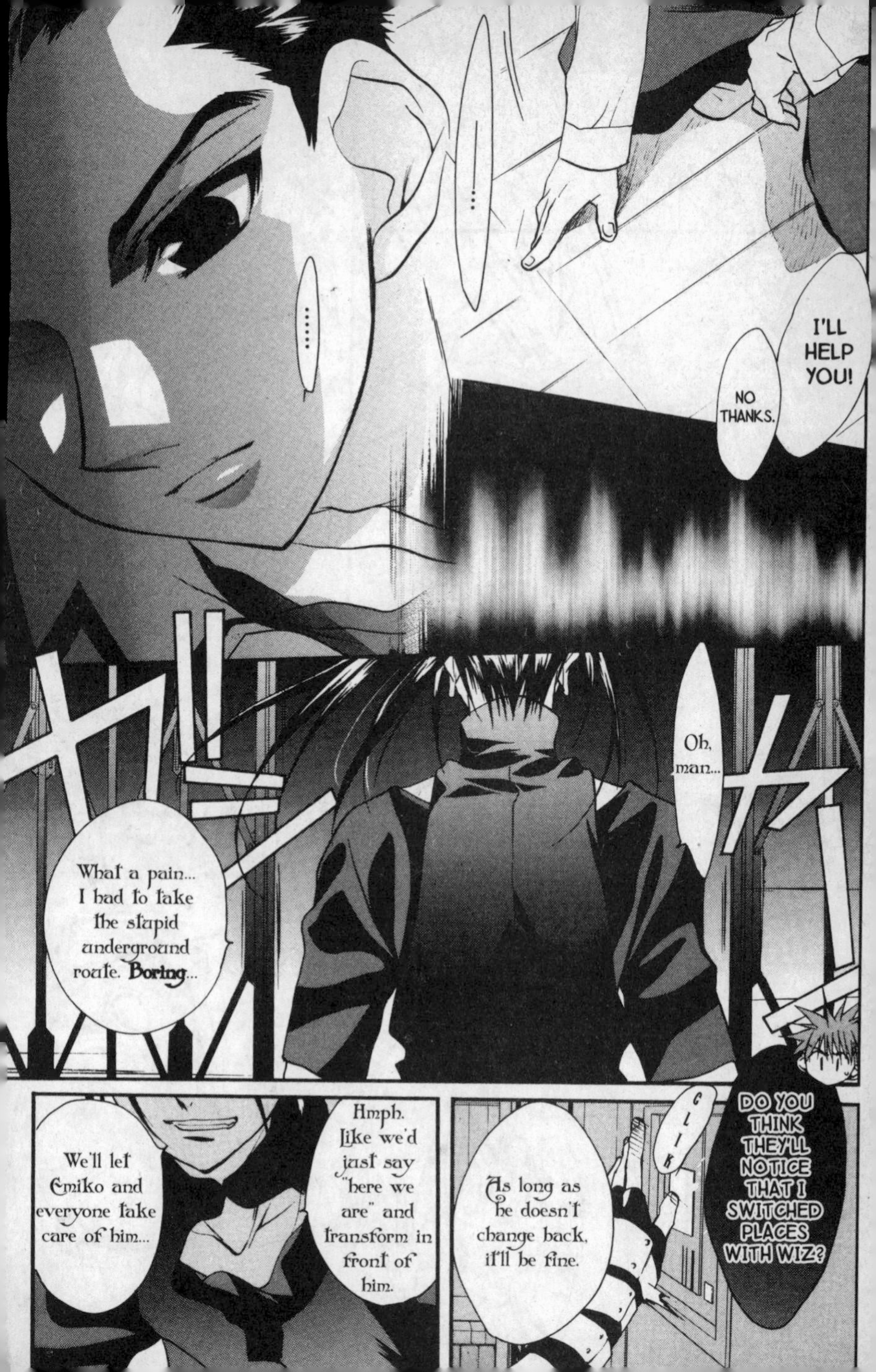
I'LL HELP YOU!
NO THANKS.
...
......
Oh, man...
What a pain... I had to take the stupid underground route. **Boring**...
DO YOU THINK THEY'LL NOTICE THAT I SWITCHED PLACES WITH WIZ?
CLIK
As long as he doesn't change back, it'll be fine.
Hmph. Like we'd just say "here we are" and transform in front of him.
We'll let Emiko and everyone take care of him...

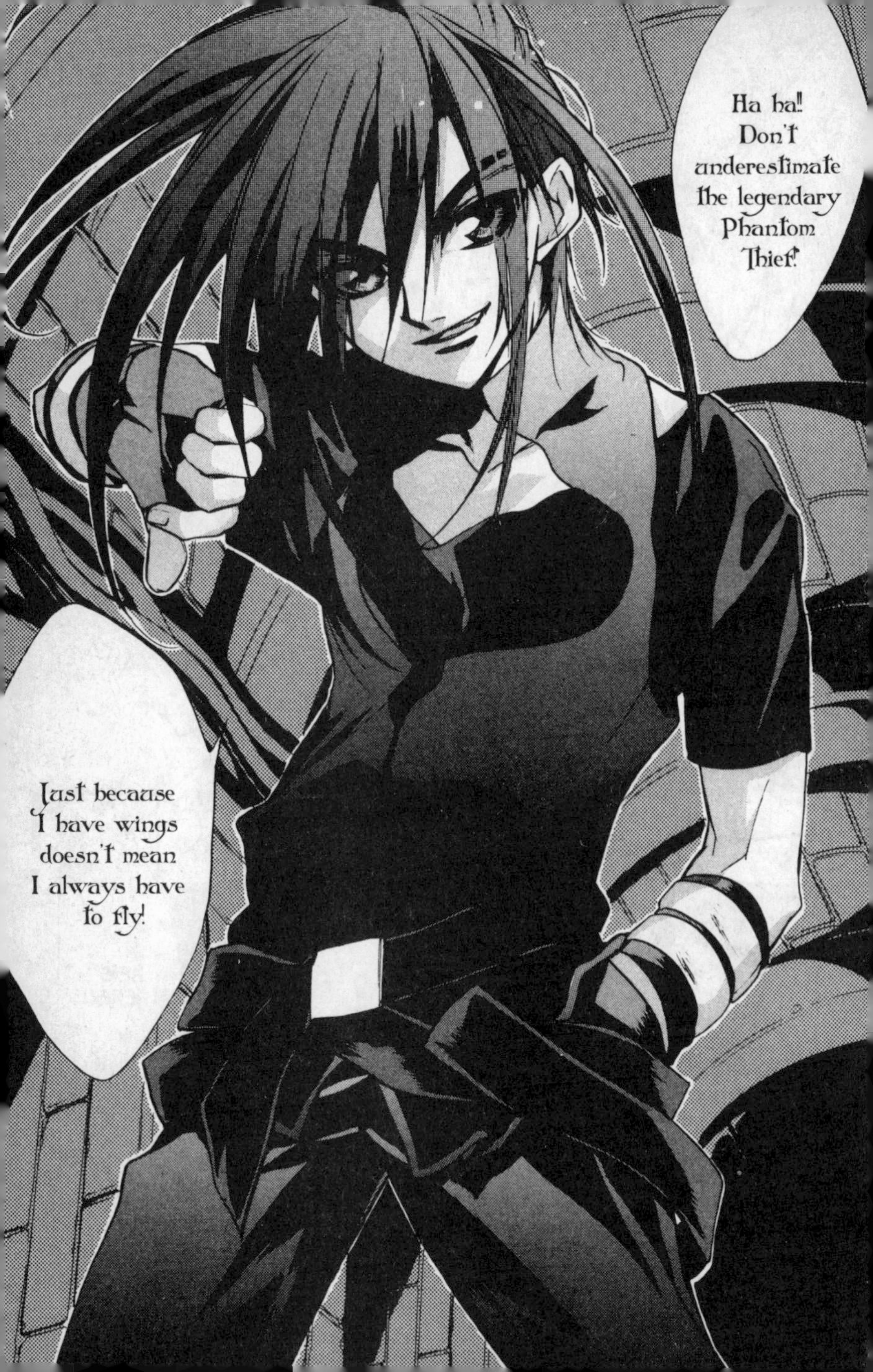
Ha ha!! Don't underestimate the legendary Phantom Thief!
Just because I have wings doesn't mean I always have to fly!

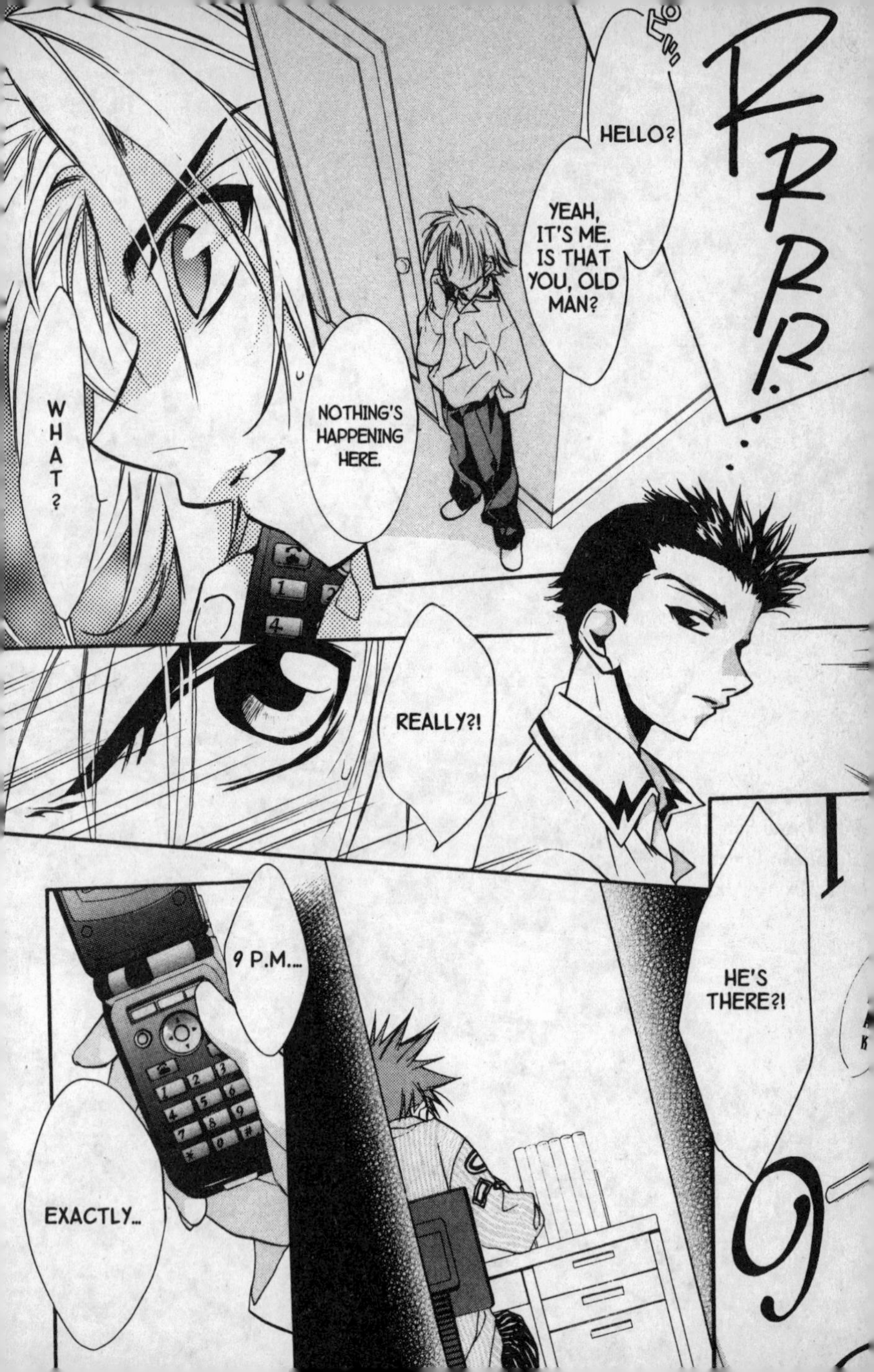
RRRR...
HELLO?
YEAH, IT'S ME. IS THAT YOU, OLD MAN?
NOTHING'S HAPPENING HERE.
WHAT?
REALLY?!
HE'S THERE?!
9 P.M....
EXACTLY...

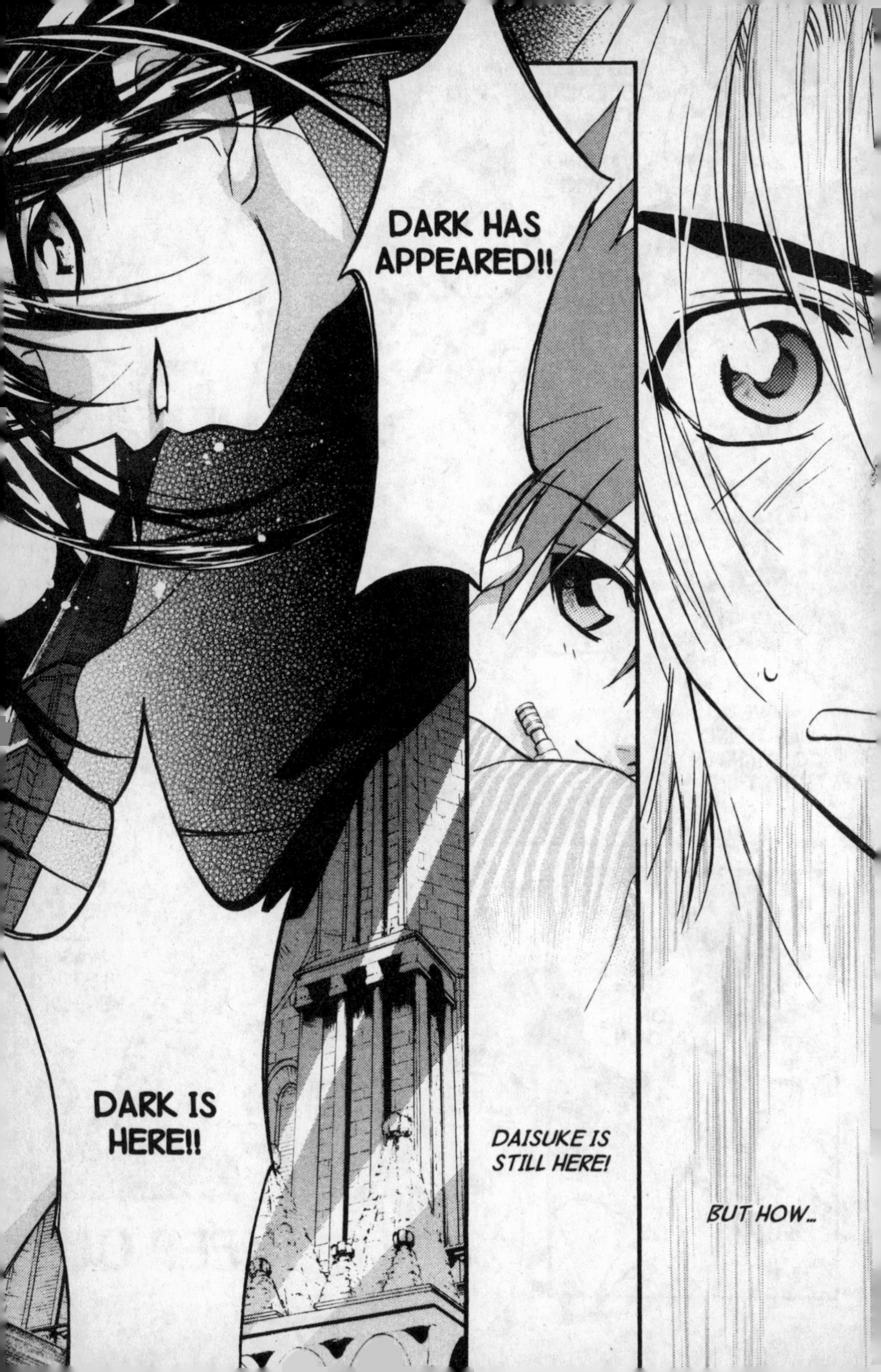
BUT HOW...
DAISUKE IS STILL HERE!
DARK HAS APPEARED!!
DARK IS HERE!!

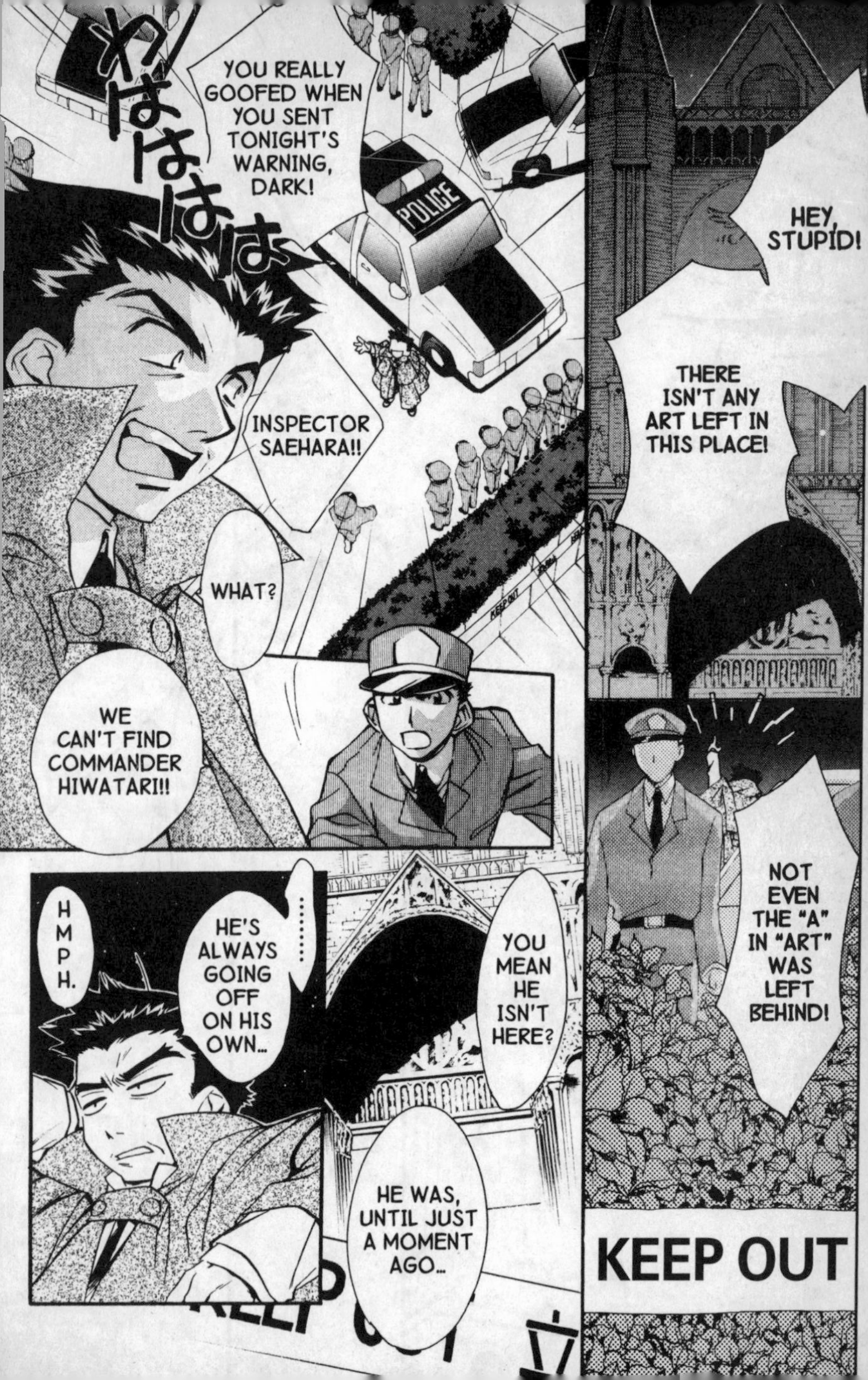

HEY, STUPID!
THERE ISN'T ANY ART LEFT IN THIS PLACE!
NOT EVEN THE "A" IN "ART" WAS LEFT BEHIND!
KEEP OUT
YOU REALLY GOOFED WHEN YOU SENT TONIGHT'S WARNING, DARK!
わははは
POLICE
INSPECTOR SAEHARA!!
WHAT?
WE CAN'T FIND COMMANDER HIWATARI!!
YOU MEAN HE ISN'T HERE?
HE WAS, UNTIL JUST A MOMENT AGO...
......
HE'S ALWAYS GOING OFF ON HIS OWN...
HMPH.

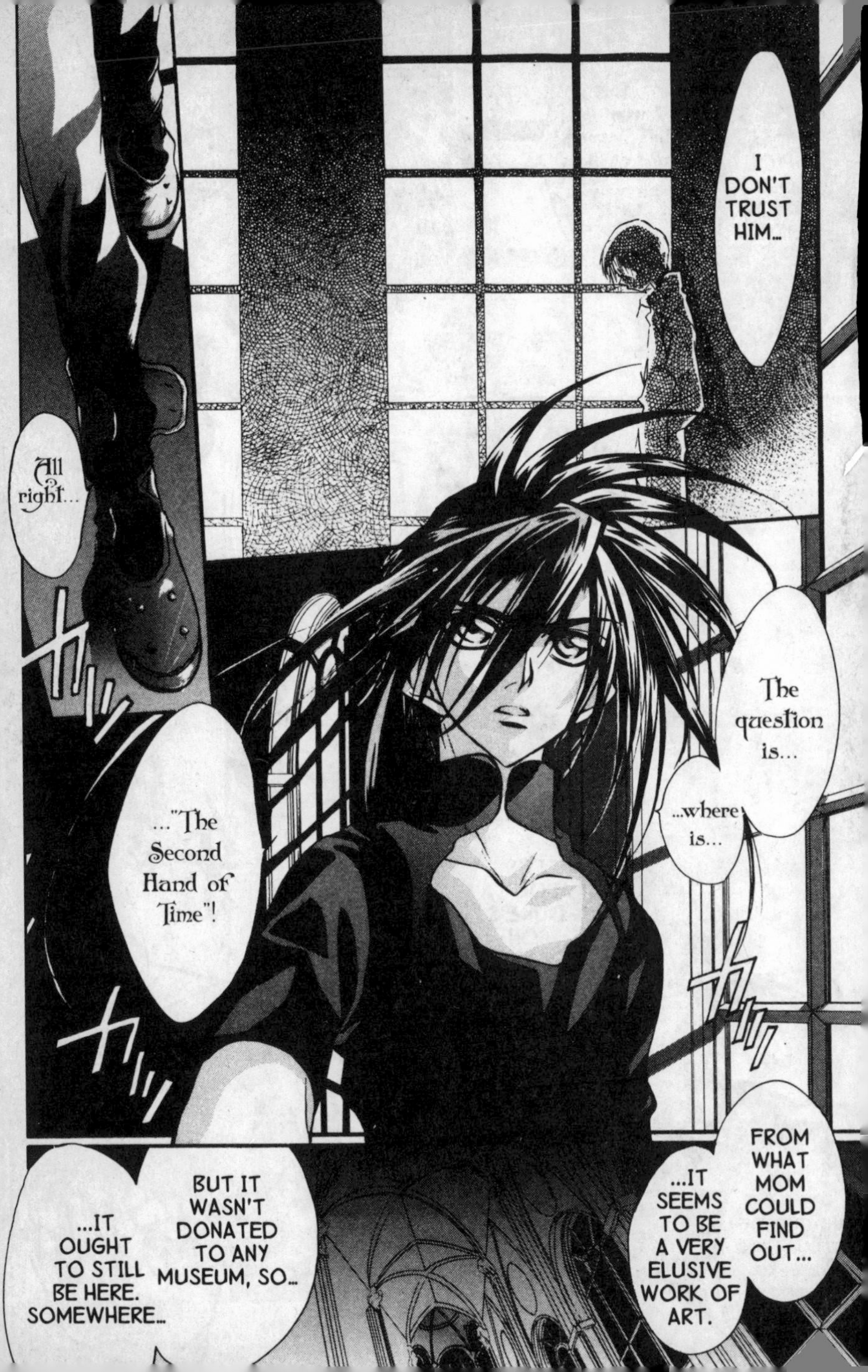
I DON'T TRUST HIM...
All right...
The question is...
...where is...
..."The Second Hand of Time"!
FROM WHAT MOM COULD FIND OUT...
...IT SEEMS TO BE A VERY ELUSIVE WORK OF ART.
BUT IT WASN'T DONATED TO ANY MUSEUM, SO...
...IT OUGHT TO STILL BE HERE. SOMEWHERE...

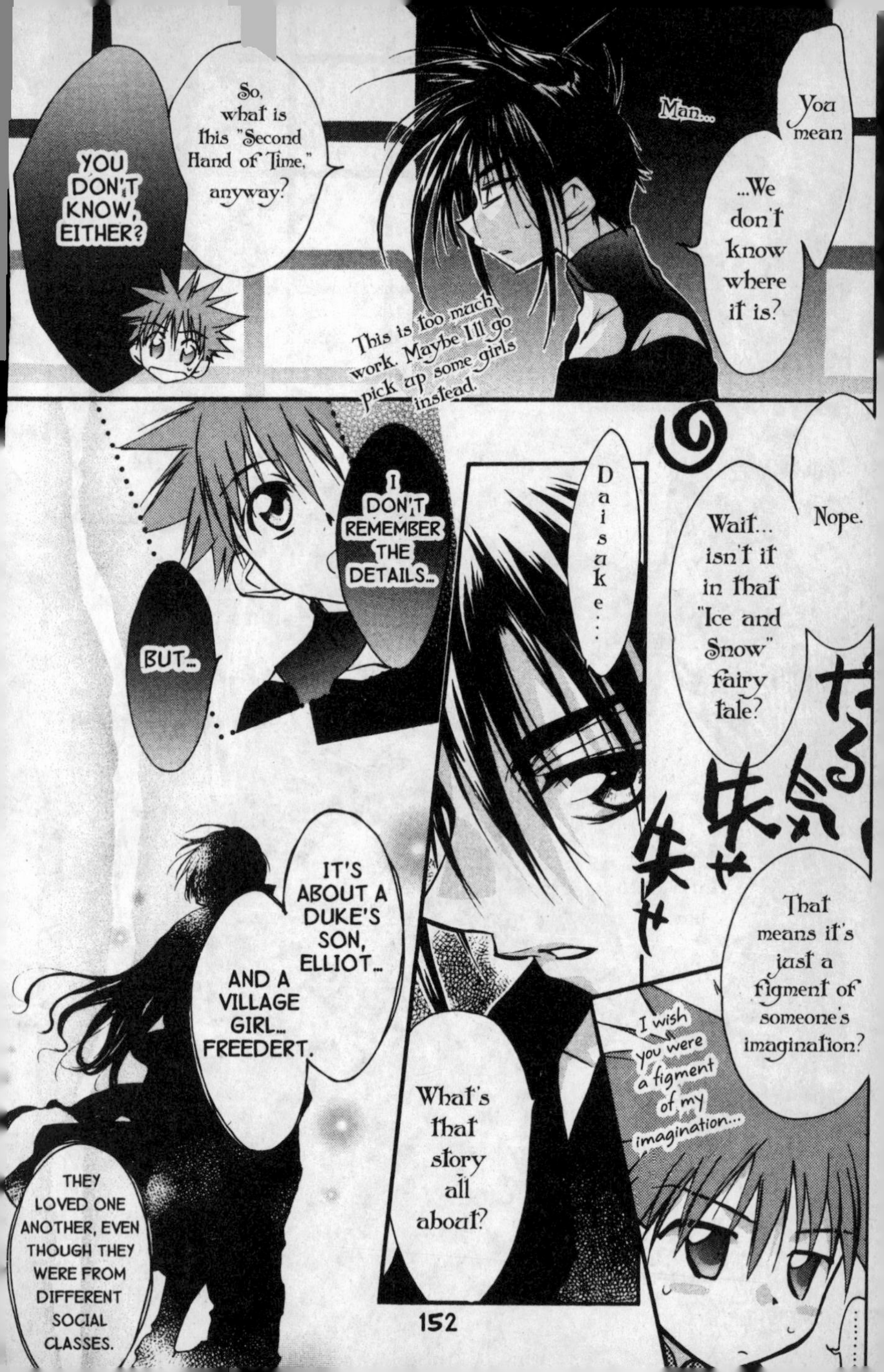
Man...
You mean ...We don't know where it is?
This is too much work. Maybe I'll go pick up some girls instead.
So, what is this "Second Hand of Time," anyway?
YOU DON'T KNOW, EITHER?
Nope.
Wait... isn't it in that "Ice and Snow" fairy tale?
That means it's just a figment of someone's imagination?
I wish you were a figment of my imagination...
Daisuke...
What's that story all about?
I DON'T REMEMBER THE DETAILS...
BUT...
IT'S ABOUT A DUKE'S SON, ELLIOT... AND A VILLAGE GIRL... FREEDERT.
THEY LOVED ONE ANOTHER, EVEN THOUGH THEY WERE FROM DIFFERENT SOCIAL CLASSES.

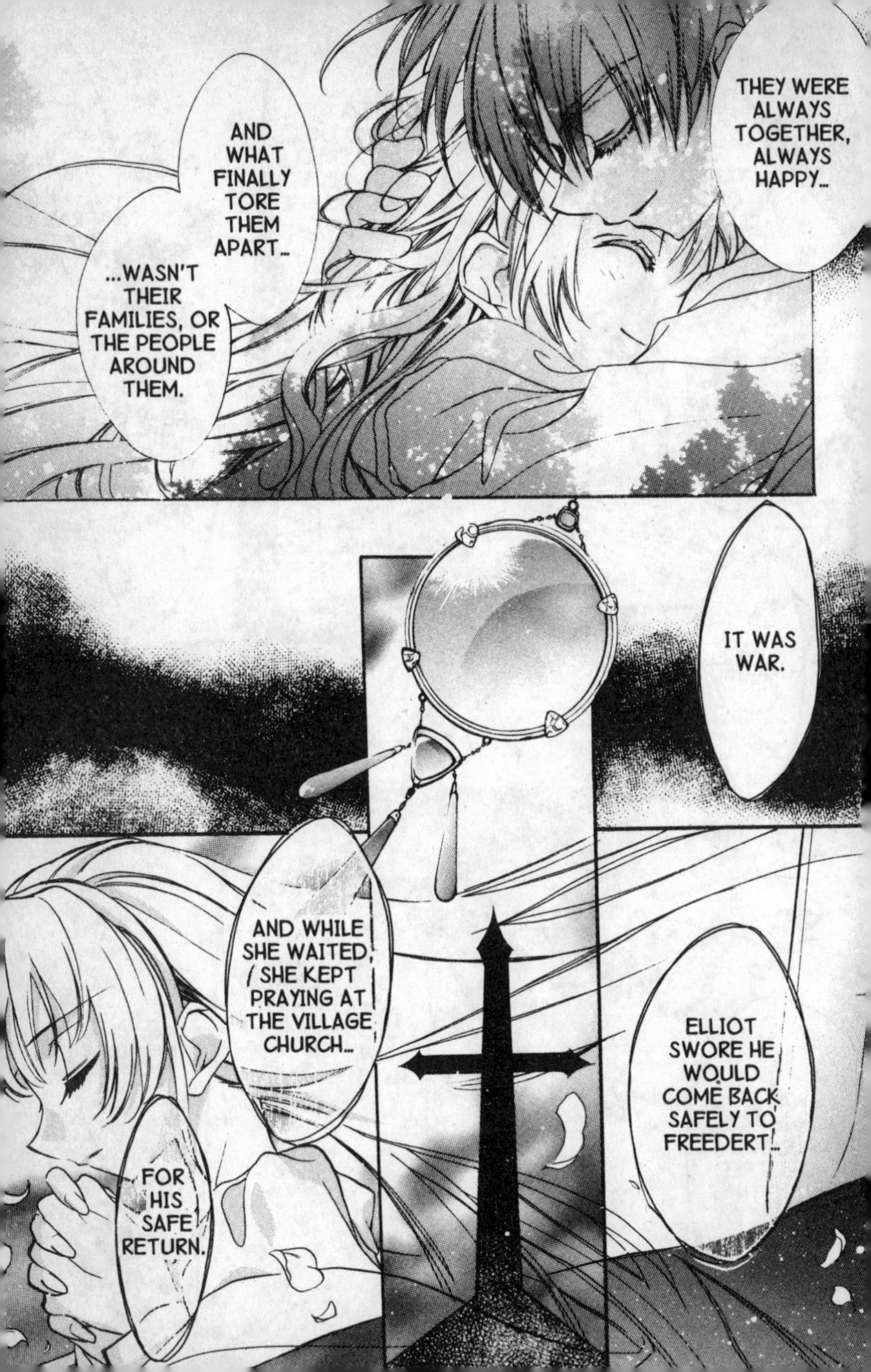
THEY WERE ALWAYS TOGETHER, ALWAYS HAPPY...
AND WHAT FINALLY TORE THEM APART...
...WASN'T THEIR FAMILIES, OR THE PEOPLE AROUND THEM.
IT WAS WAR.
ELLIOT SWORE HE WOULD COME BACK SAFELY TO FREEDERT...
AND WHILE SHE WAITED, SHE KEPT PRAYING AT THE VILLAGE CHURCH...
FOR HIS SAFE RETURN.

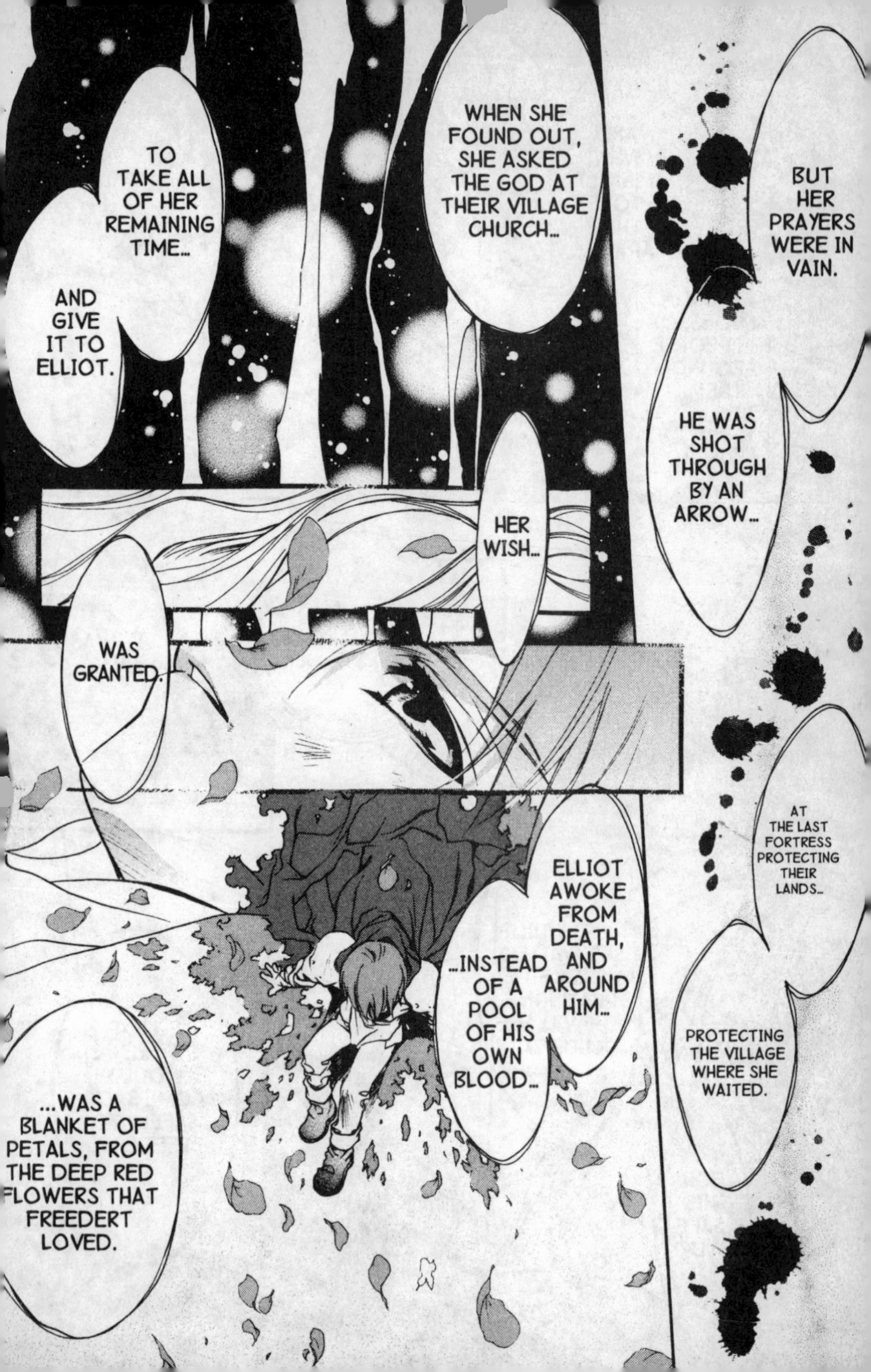
BUT HER PRAYERS WERE IN VAIN.
HE WAS SHOT THROUGH BY AN ARROW...
AT THE LAST FORTRESS PROTECTING THEIR LANDS...
PROTECTING THE VILLAGE WHERE SHE WAITED.
WHEN SHE FOUND OUT, SHE ASKED THE GOD AT THEIR VILLAGE CHURCH...
TO TAKE ALL OF HER REMAINING TIME...
AND GIVE IT TO ELLIOT.
HER WISH...
WAS GRANTED.
ELLIOT AWOKE FROM DEATH, AND AROUND HIM...
...INSTEAD OF A POOL OF HIS OWN BLOOD...
...WAS A BLANKET OF PETALS, FROM THE DEEP RED FLOWERS THAT FREEDERT LOVED.

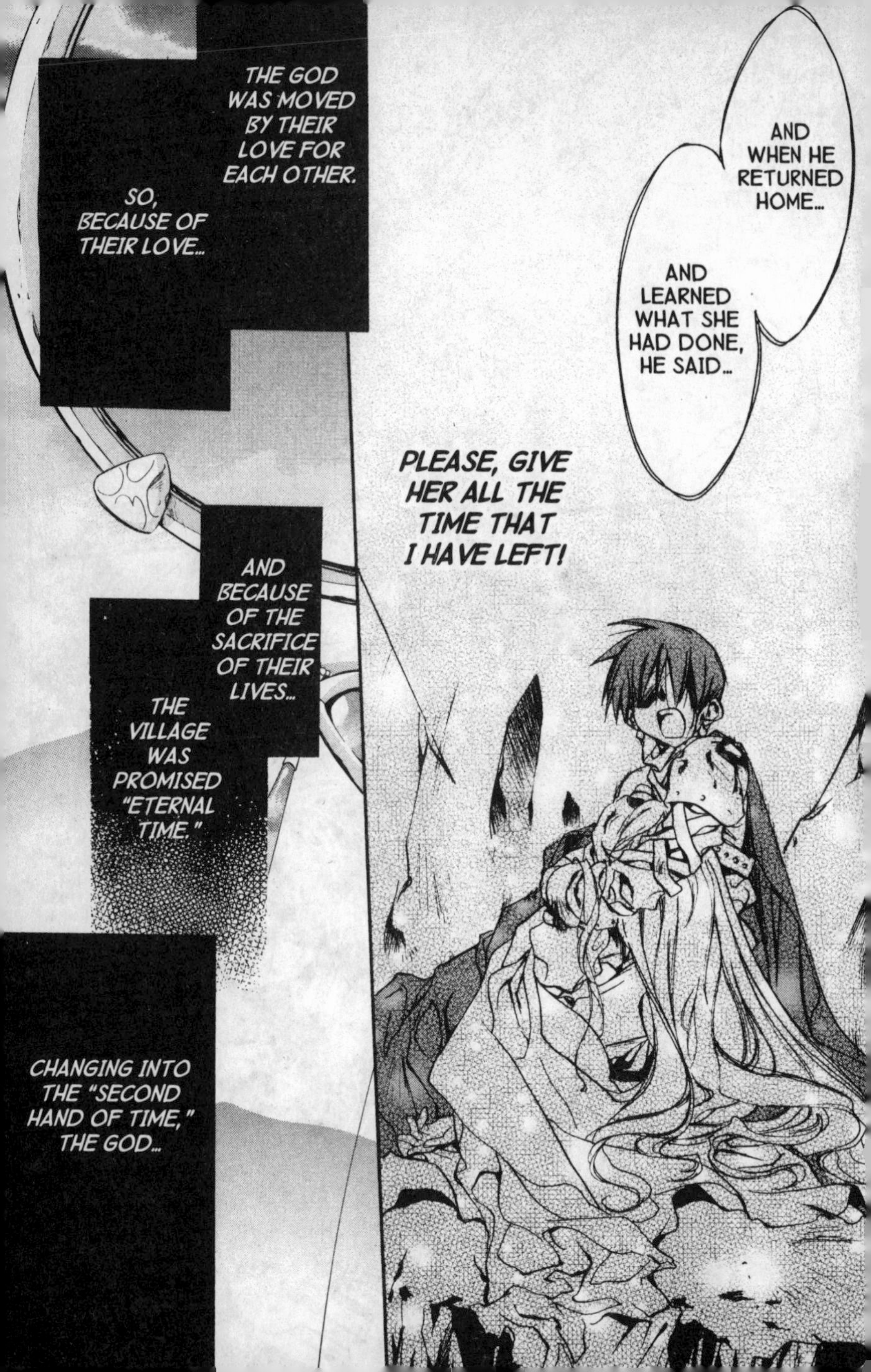
AND WHEN HE RETURNED HOME...
AND LEARNED WHAT SHE HAD DONE, HE SAID...
PLEASE, GIVE HER ALL THE TIME THAT I HAVE LEFT!
THE GOD WAS MOVED BY THEIR LOVE FOR EACH OTHER.
SO, BECAUSE OF THEIR LOVE...
AND BECAUSE OF THE SACRIFICE OF THEIR LIVES...
THE VILLAGE WAS PROMISED "ETERNAL TIME."
CHANGING INTO THE "SECOND HAND OF TIME," THE GOD...

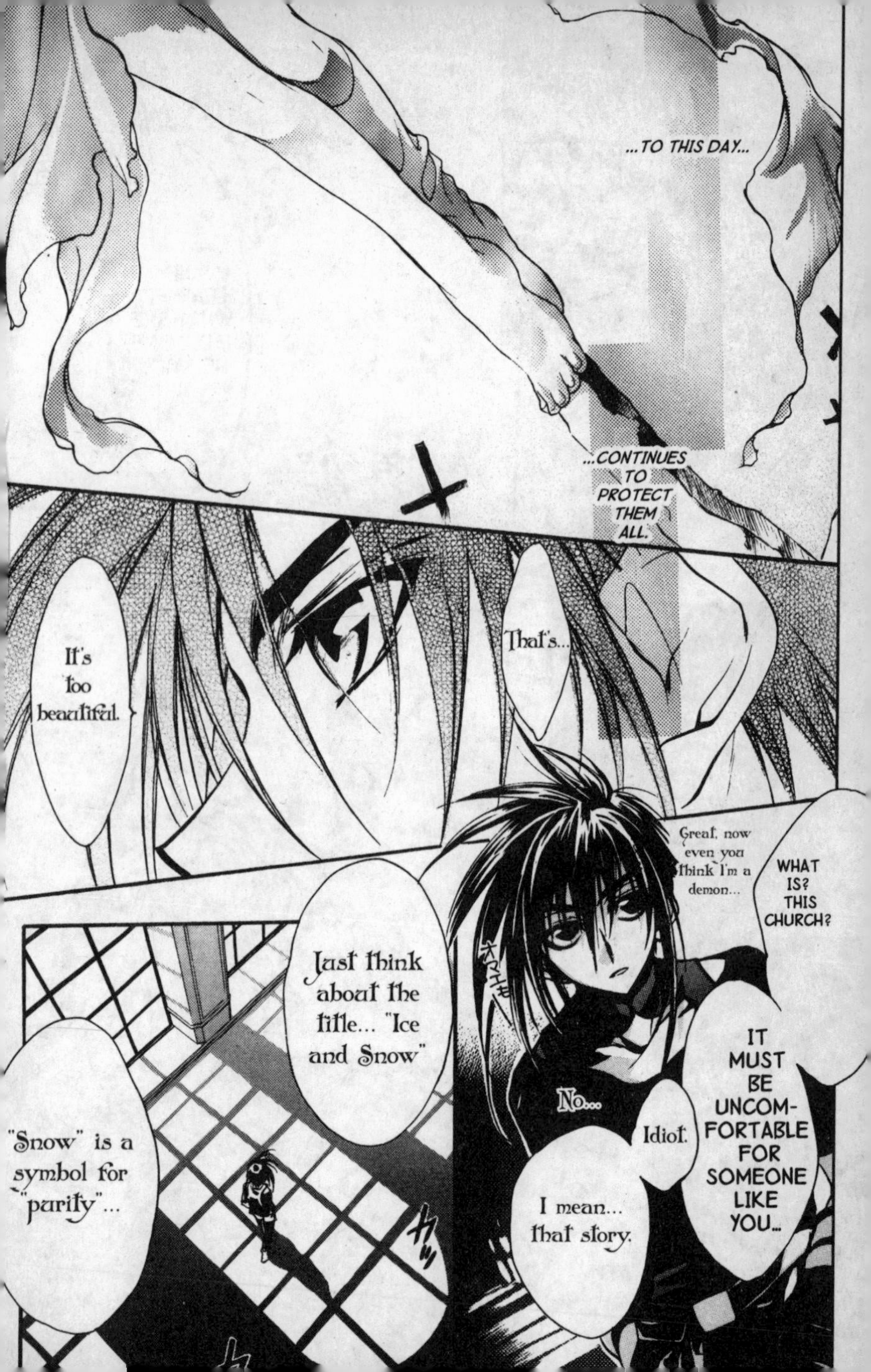
...TO THIS DAY...
...CONTINUES TO PROTECT THEM ALL.
That's...
It's too beautiful.
WHAT IS? THIS CHURCH?
Great, now even you think I'm a demon...
IT MUST BE UNCOM-FORTABLE FOR SOMEONE LIKE YOU...
Idiot.
No...
I mean... that story.
Just think about the title... "Ice and Snow"
"Snow" is a symbol for "purity"...

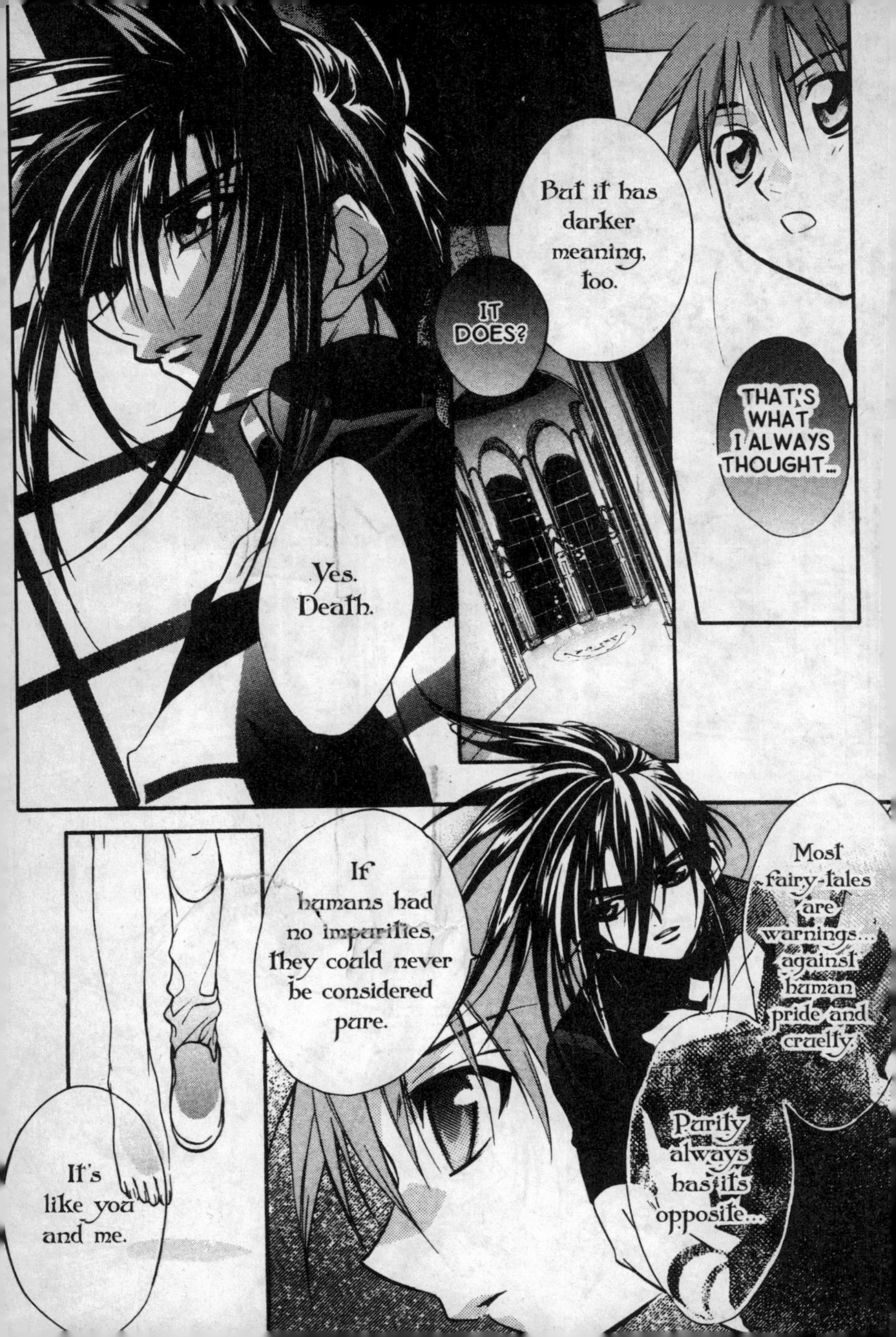
THAT'S WHAT I ALWAYS THOUGHT...
But it has darker meaning, too.
IT DOES?
Yes. Death.
Most fairy-tales are warnings... against human pride and cruelty.
Purity always has its opposite...
If humans had no impurities, they could never be considered pure.
It's like you and me.

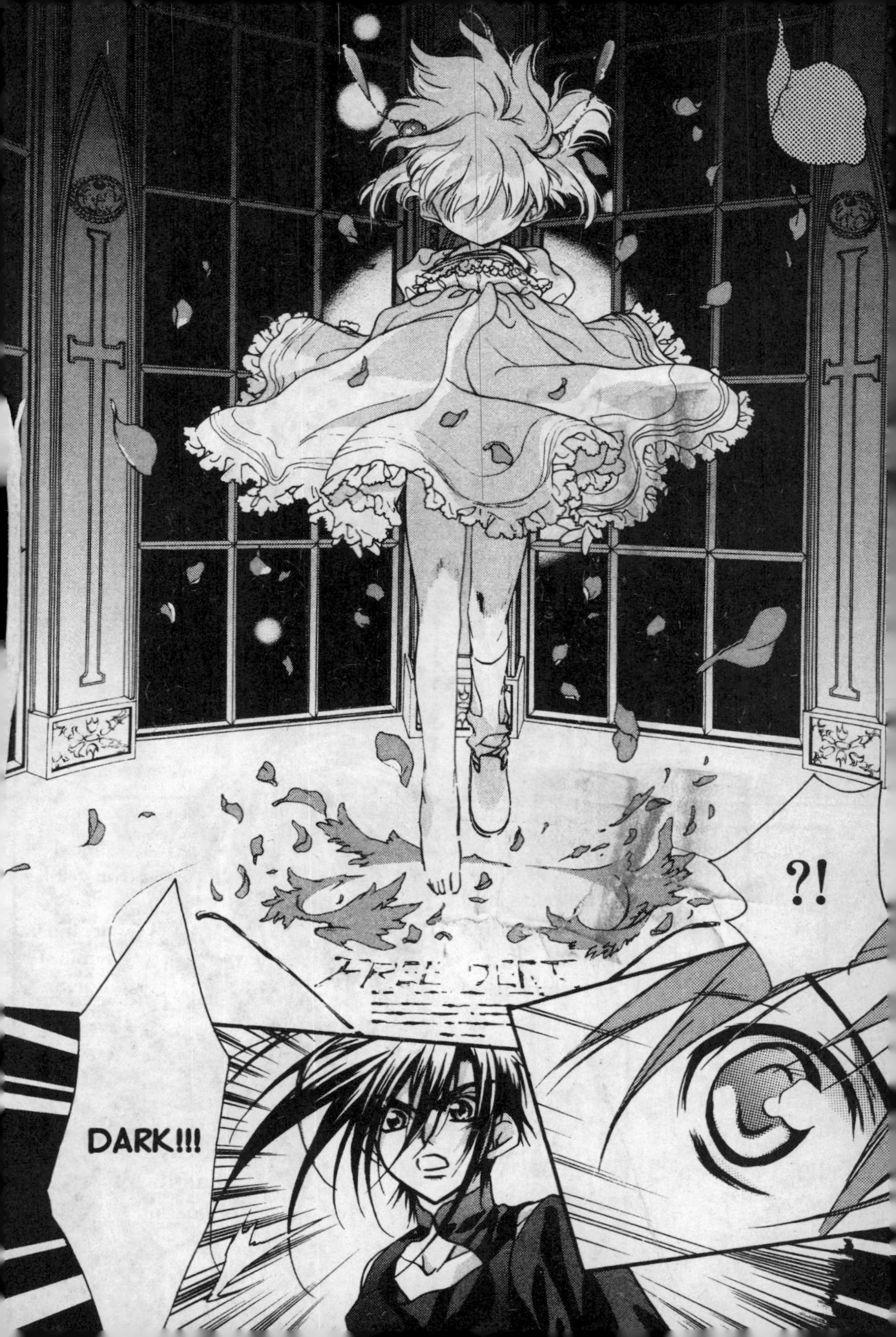
?!
DARK!!!

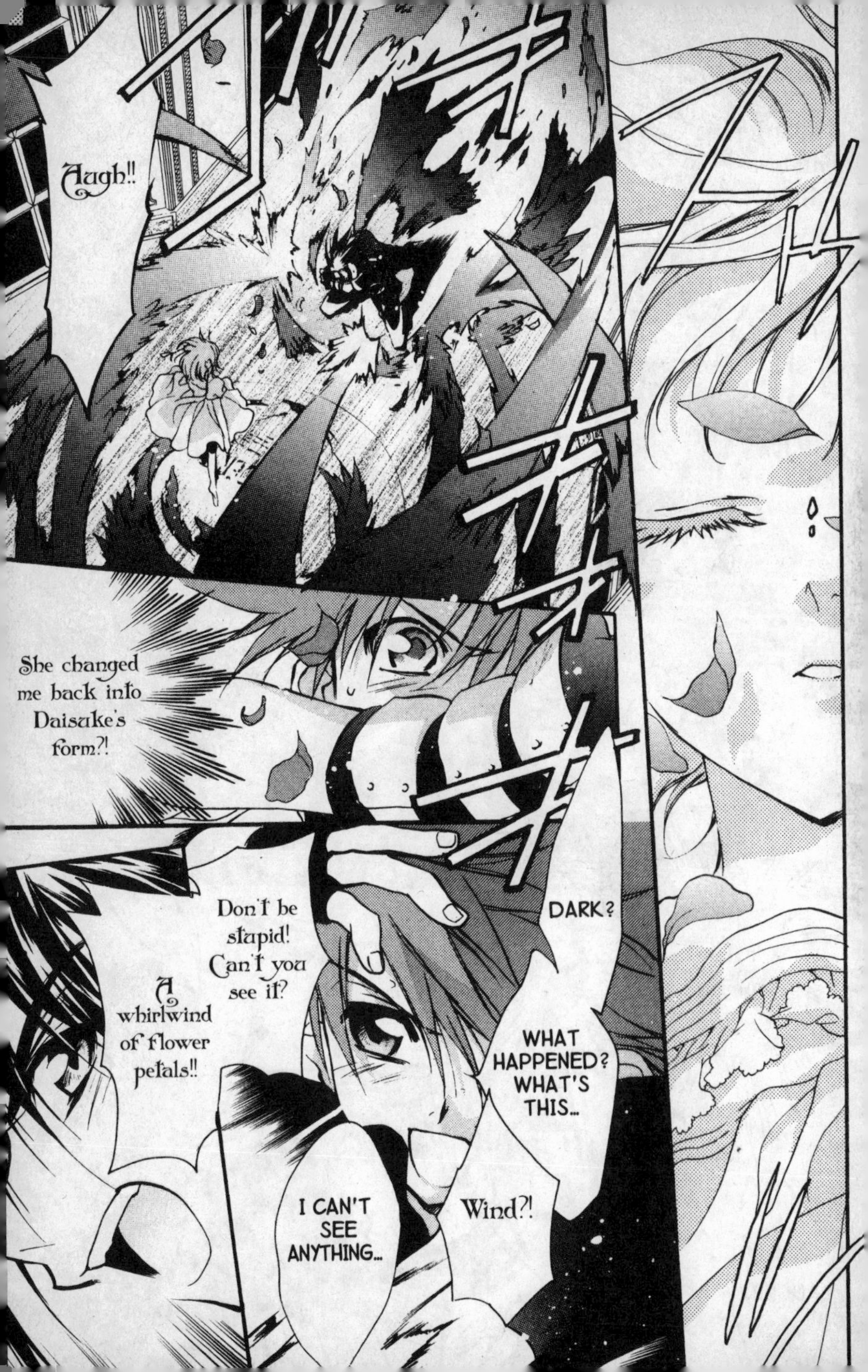
Augh!!
She changed me back into Daisuke's form?!
DARK?
Don't be stupid! Can't you see it?
A whirlwind of flower petals!!
WHAT HAPPENED? WHAT'S THIS...
Wind?!
I CAN'T SEE ANYTHING...

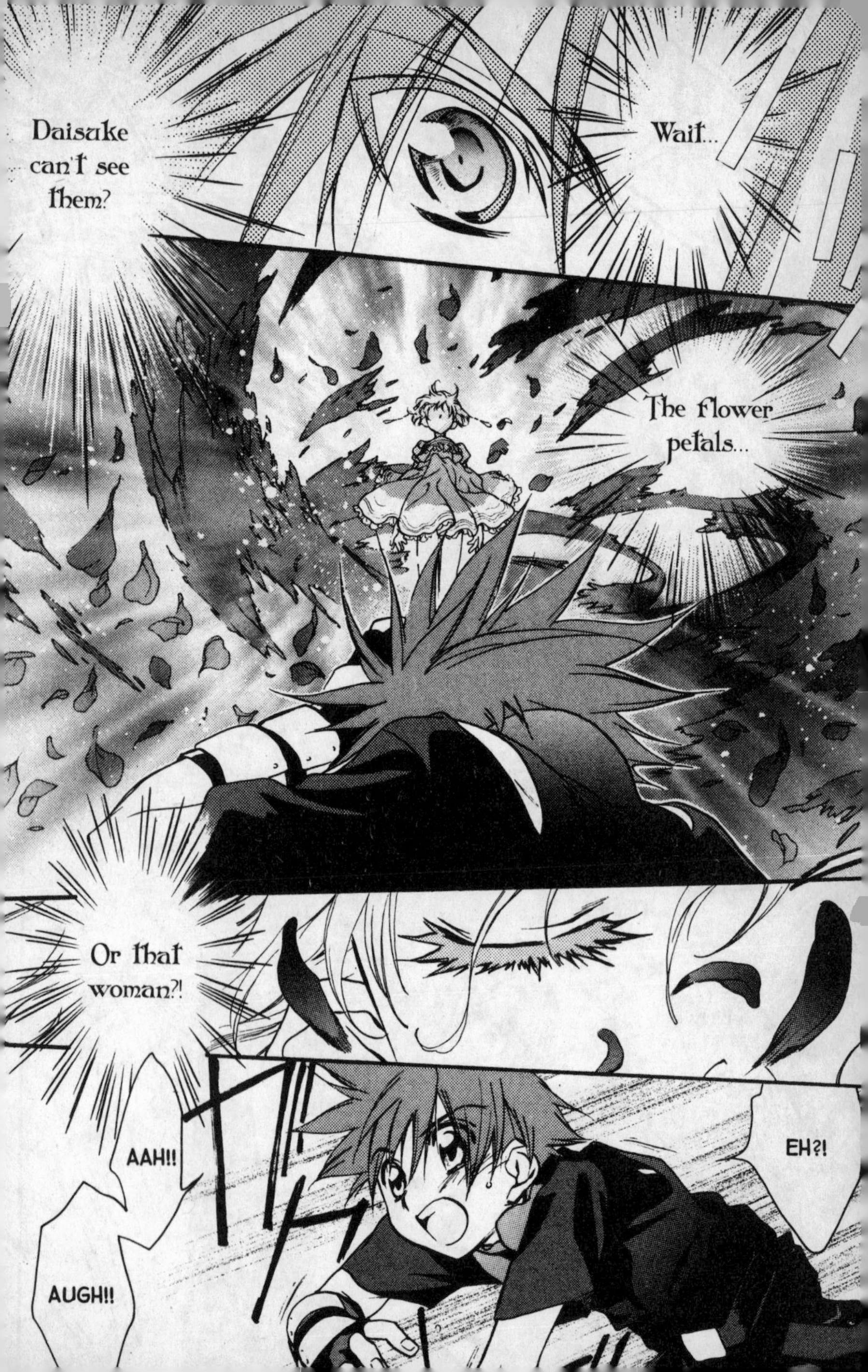
Wait...
Daisuke can't see them?
The flower petals...
Or that woman?!
EH?!
AAH!!
AUGH!!

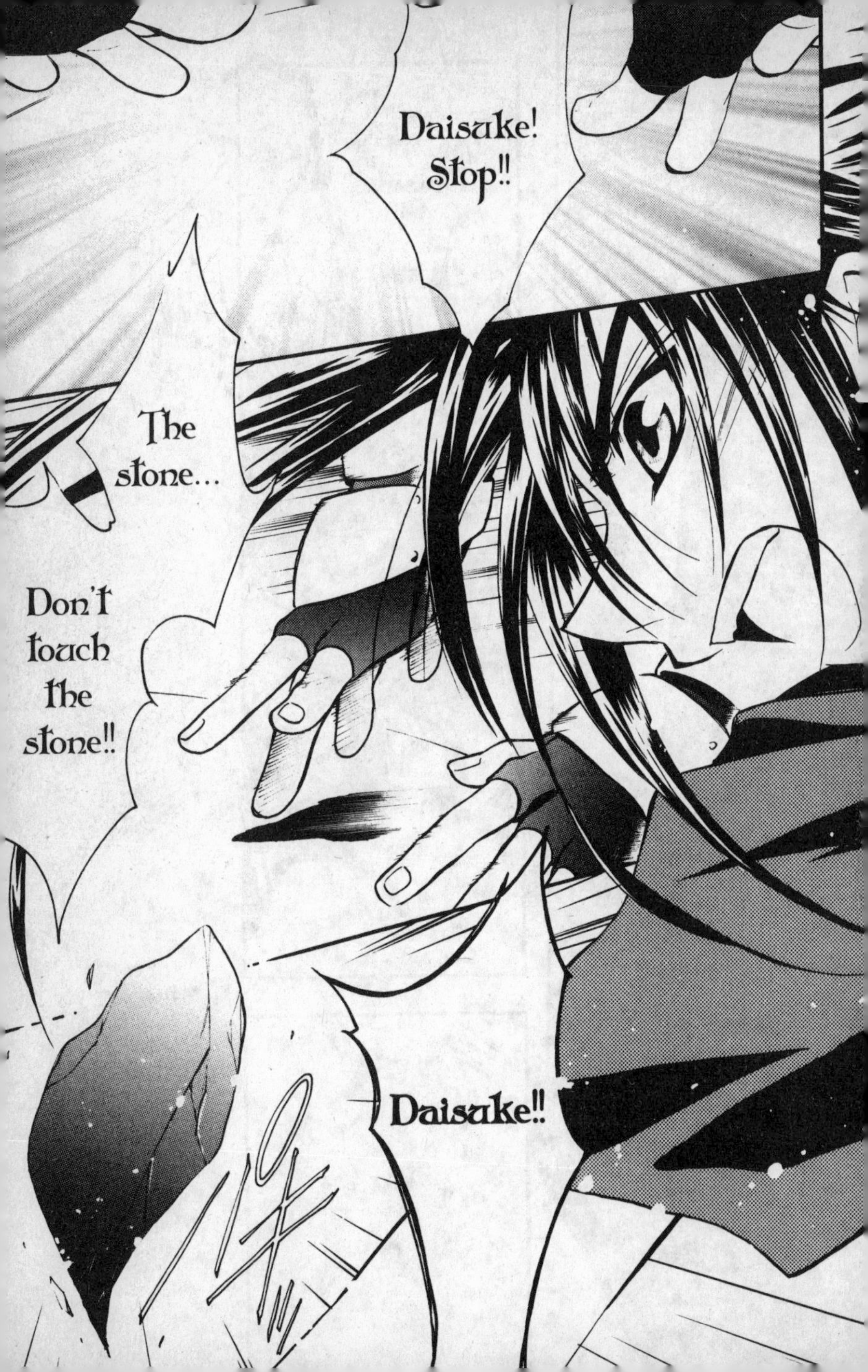
Daisuke! Stop!!
The stone...
Don't touch the stone!!
Daisuke!!

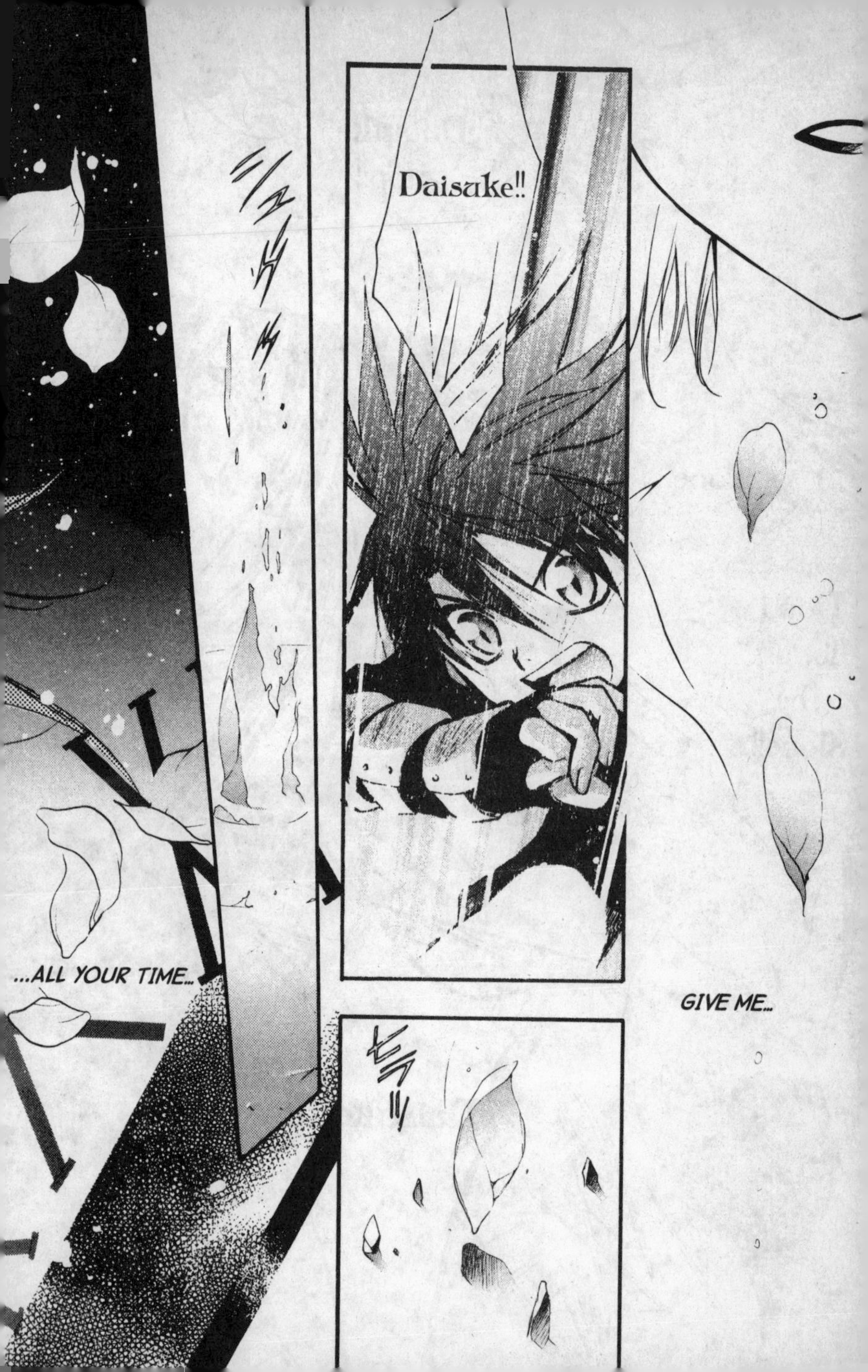
GIVE ME...
Daisuke!!
...ALL YOUR TIME...

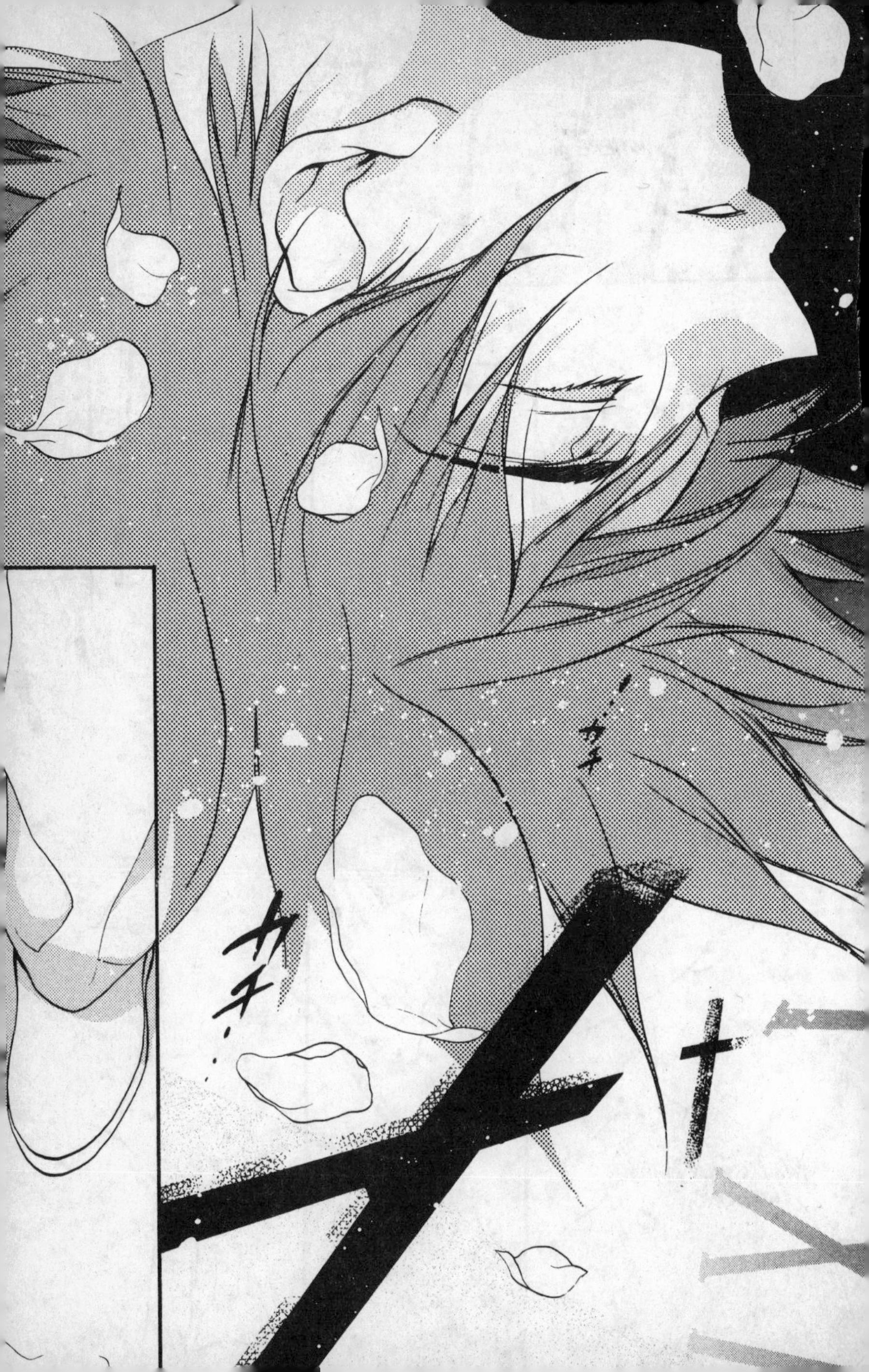
カチ
カチ…

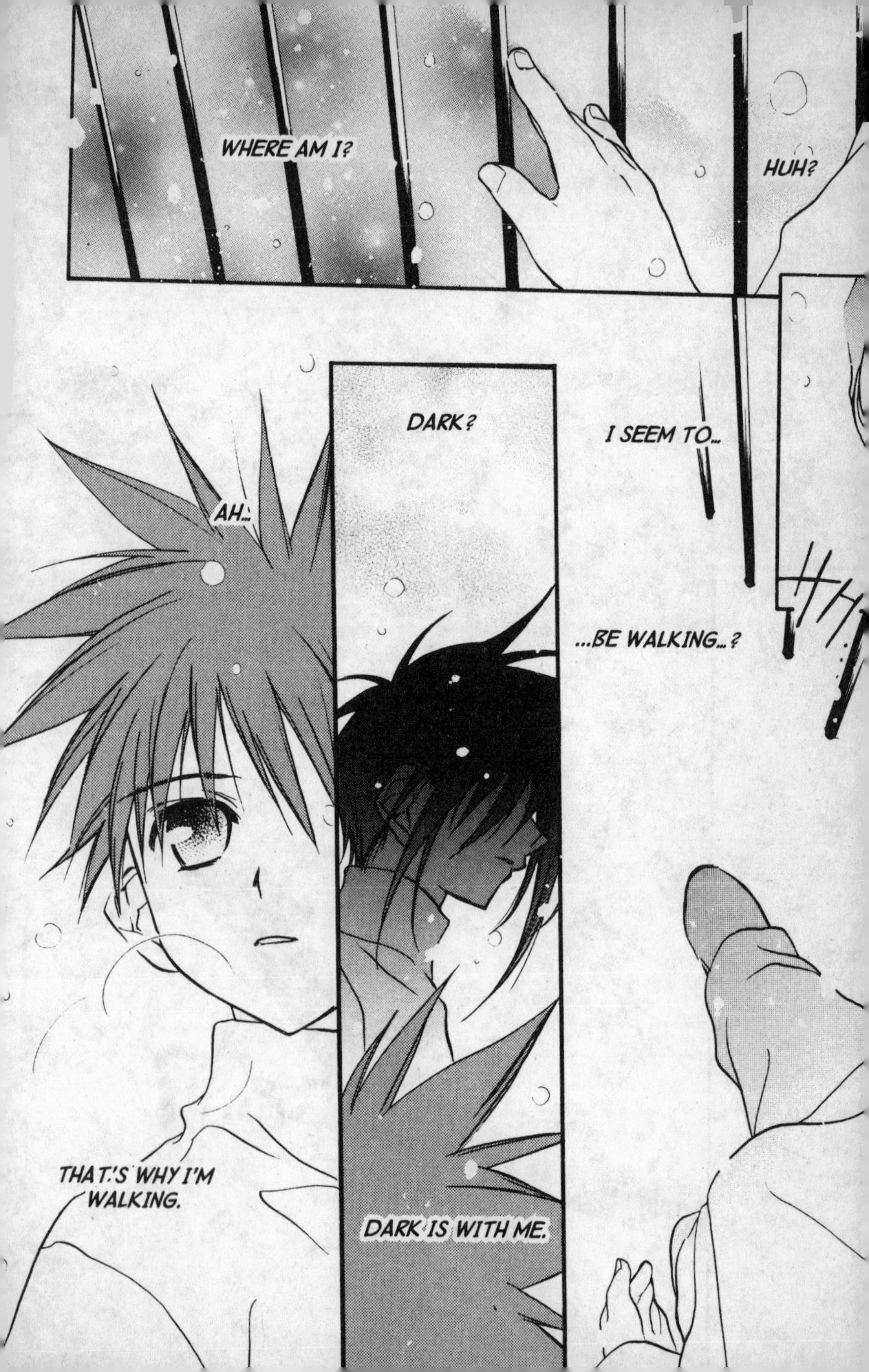
HUH?
WHERE AM I?
I SEEM TO...
...BE WALKING...?
DARK?
DARK IS WITH ME.
AH...
THAT'S WHY I'M WALKING.

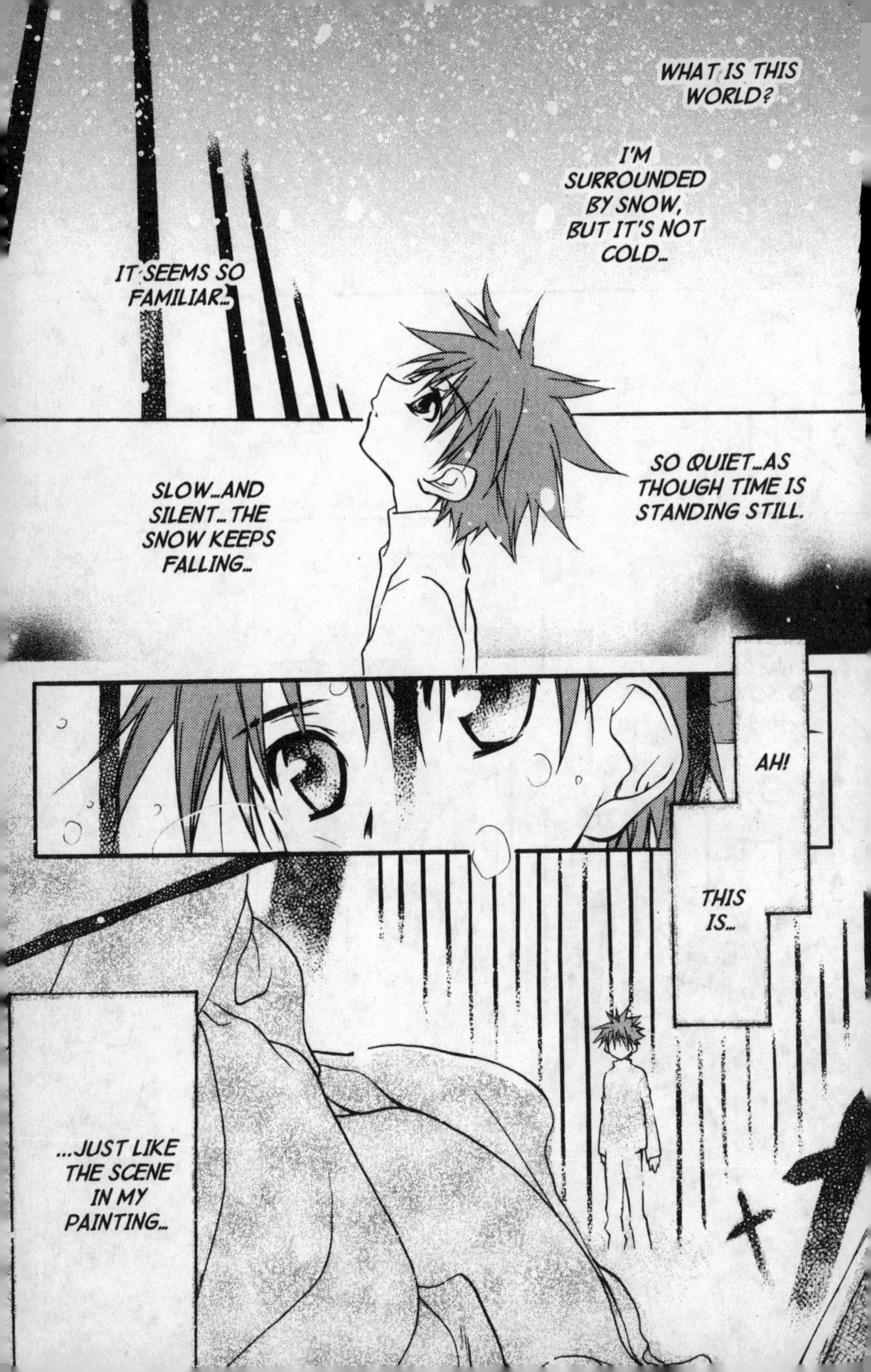
WHAT IS THIS WORLD?
I'M SURROUNDED BY SNOW, BUT IT'S NOT COLD...
IT SEEMS SO FAMILIAR...
SO QUIET...AS THOUGH TIME IS STANDING STILL.
SLOW...AND SILENT... THE SNOW KEEPS FALLING...
AH!
THIS IS...
...JUST LIKE THE SCENE IN MY PAINTING...

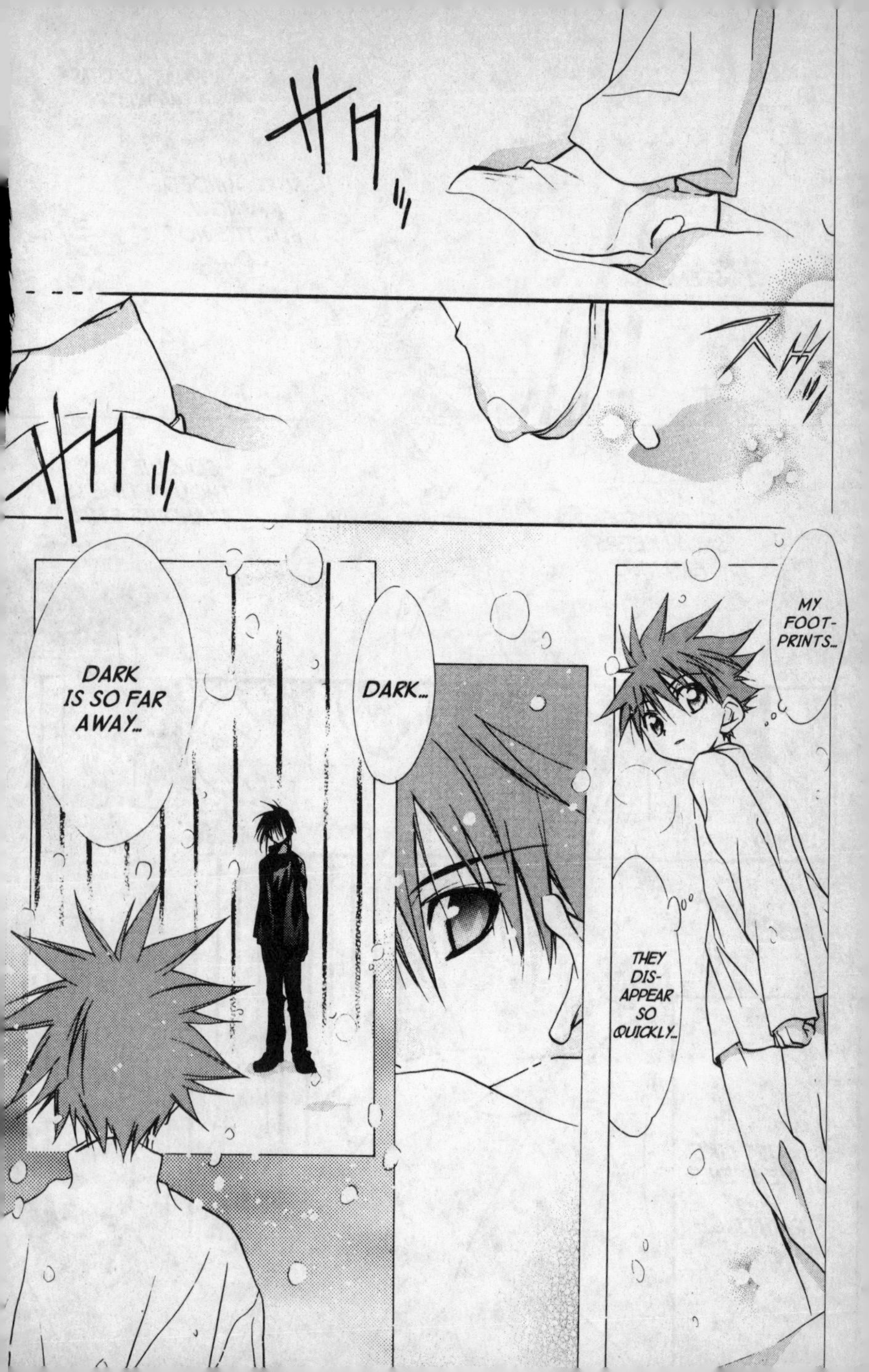
サクッ
MY FOOT-PRINTS...
THEY DIS-APPEAR SO QUICKLY...
DARK...
DARK IS SO FAR AWAY...

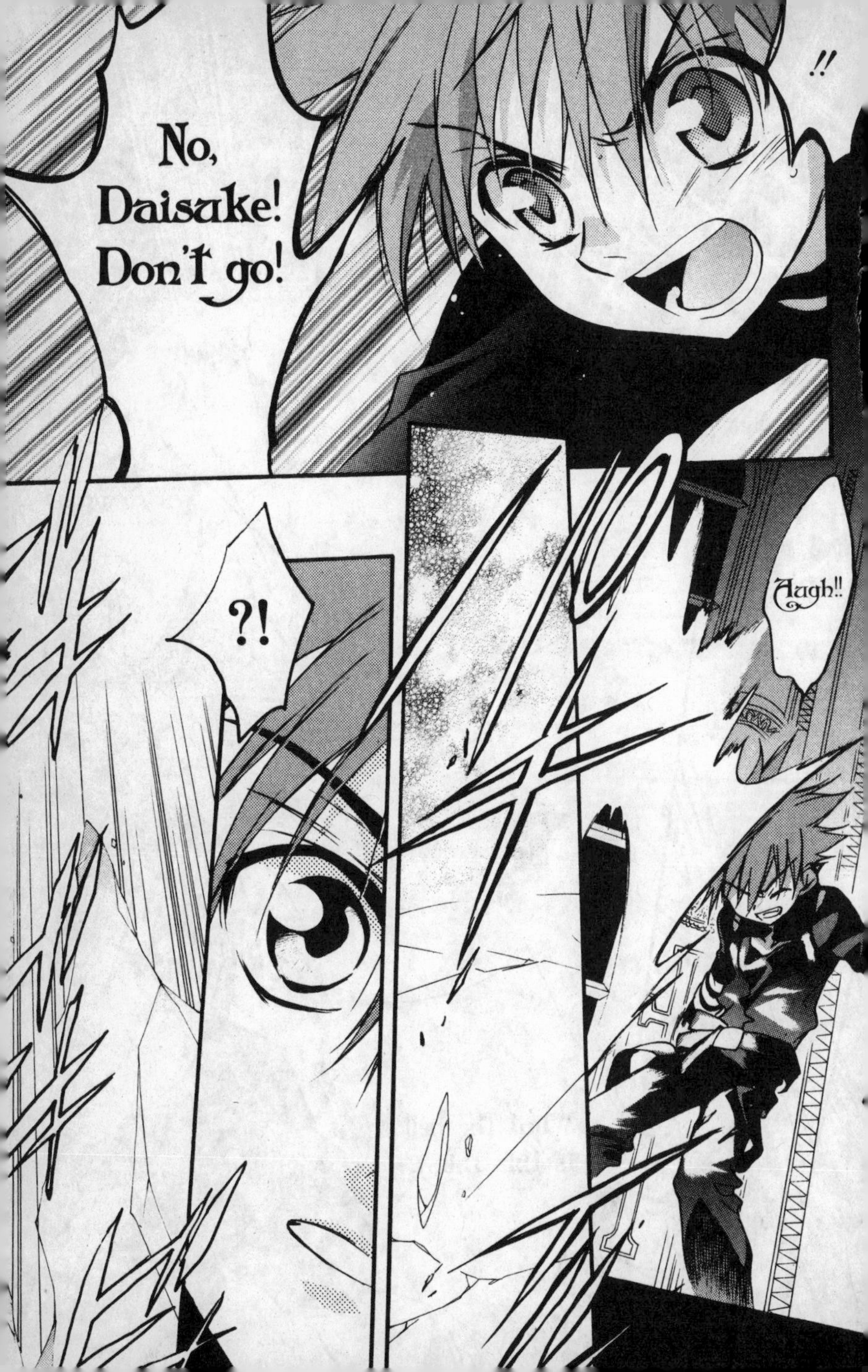
!!
No, Daisuke! Don't go!
Augh!!
?!

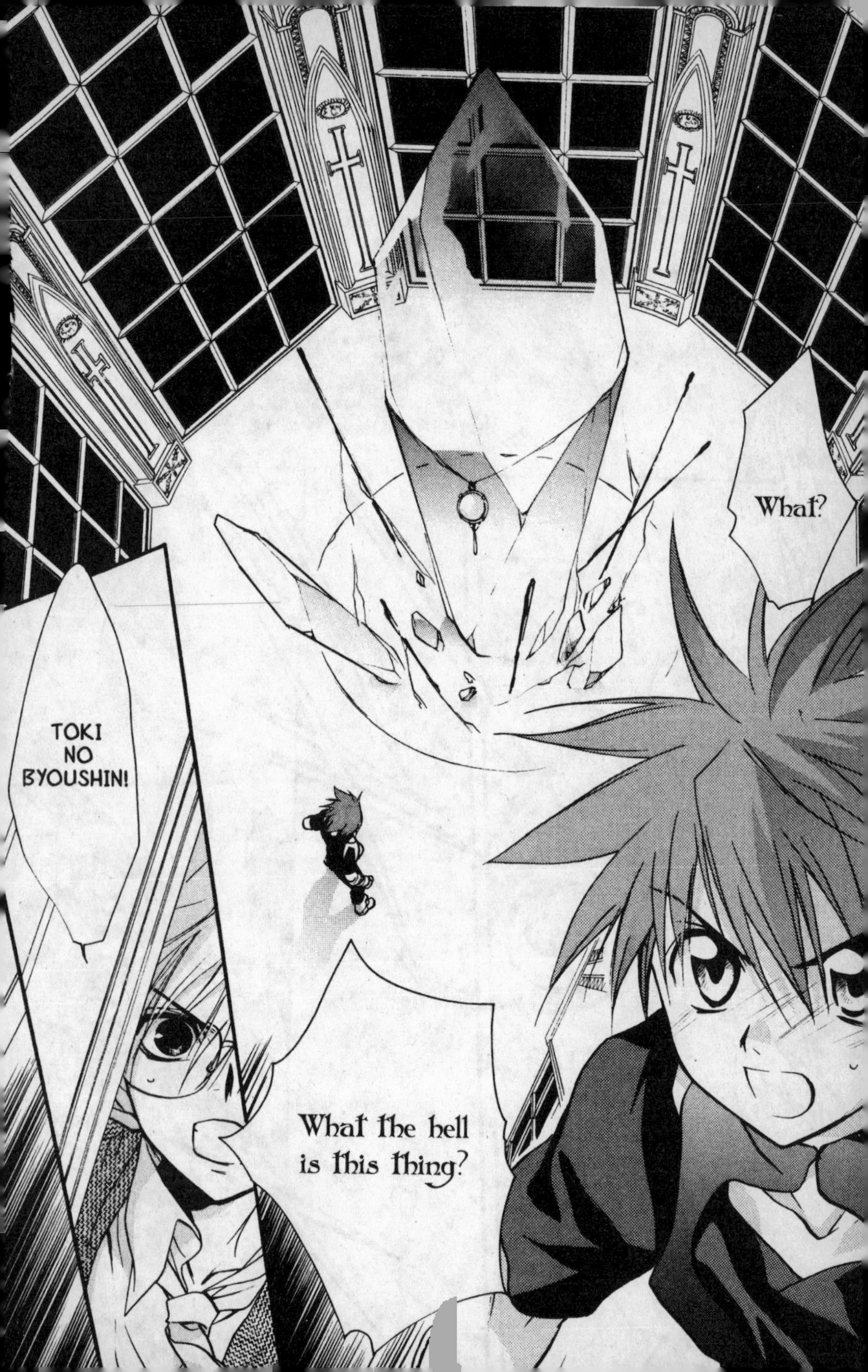
What?
What the hell is this thing?
TOKI NO BYOUSHIN!

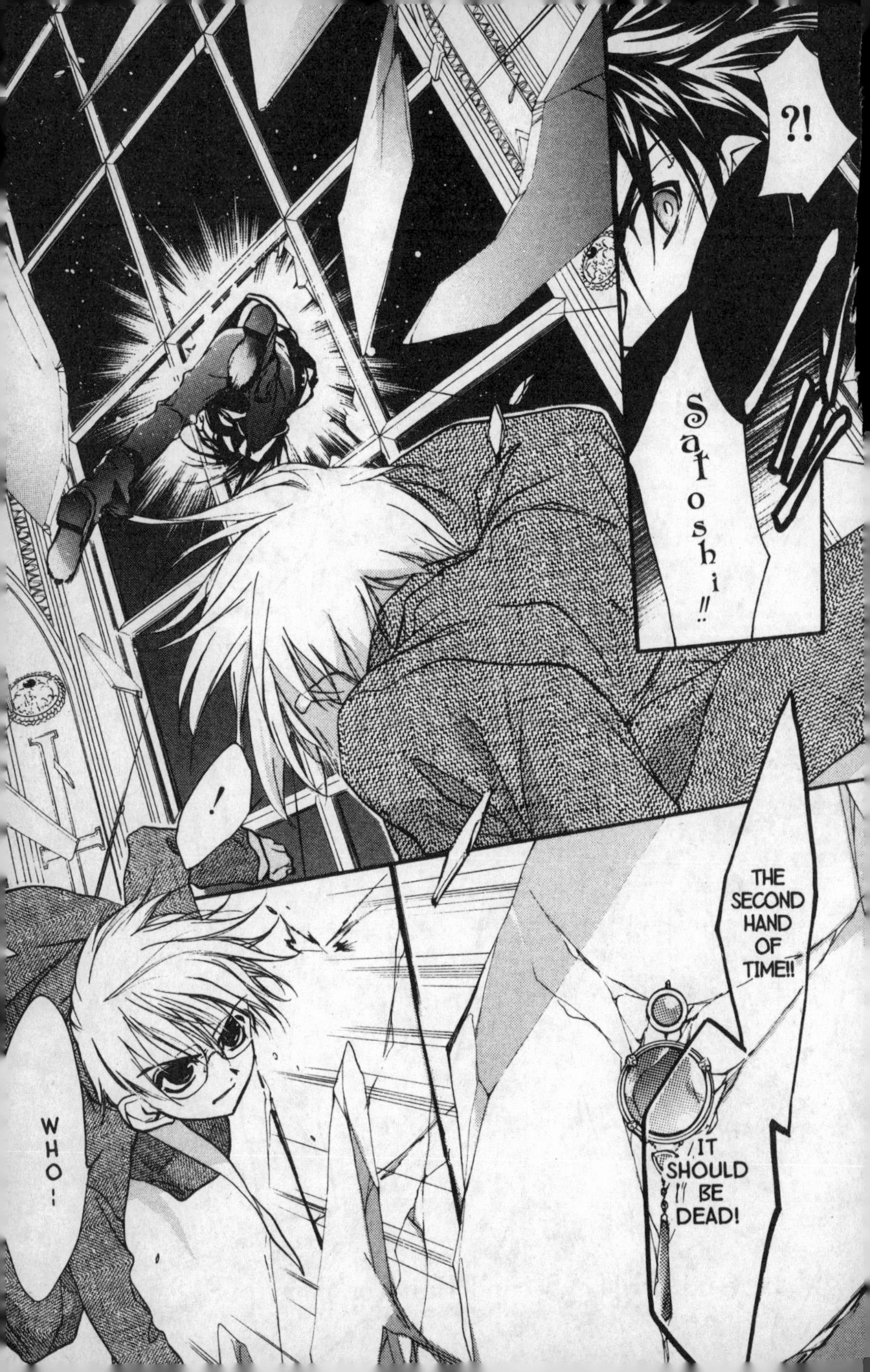
?!
Satoshi!!
!
THE SECOND HAND OF TIME!!
IT SHOULD BE DEAD!
WHO!

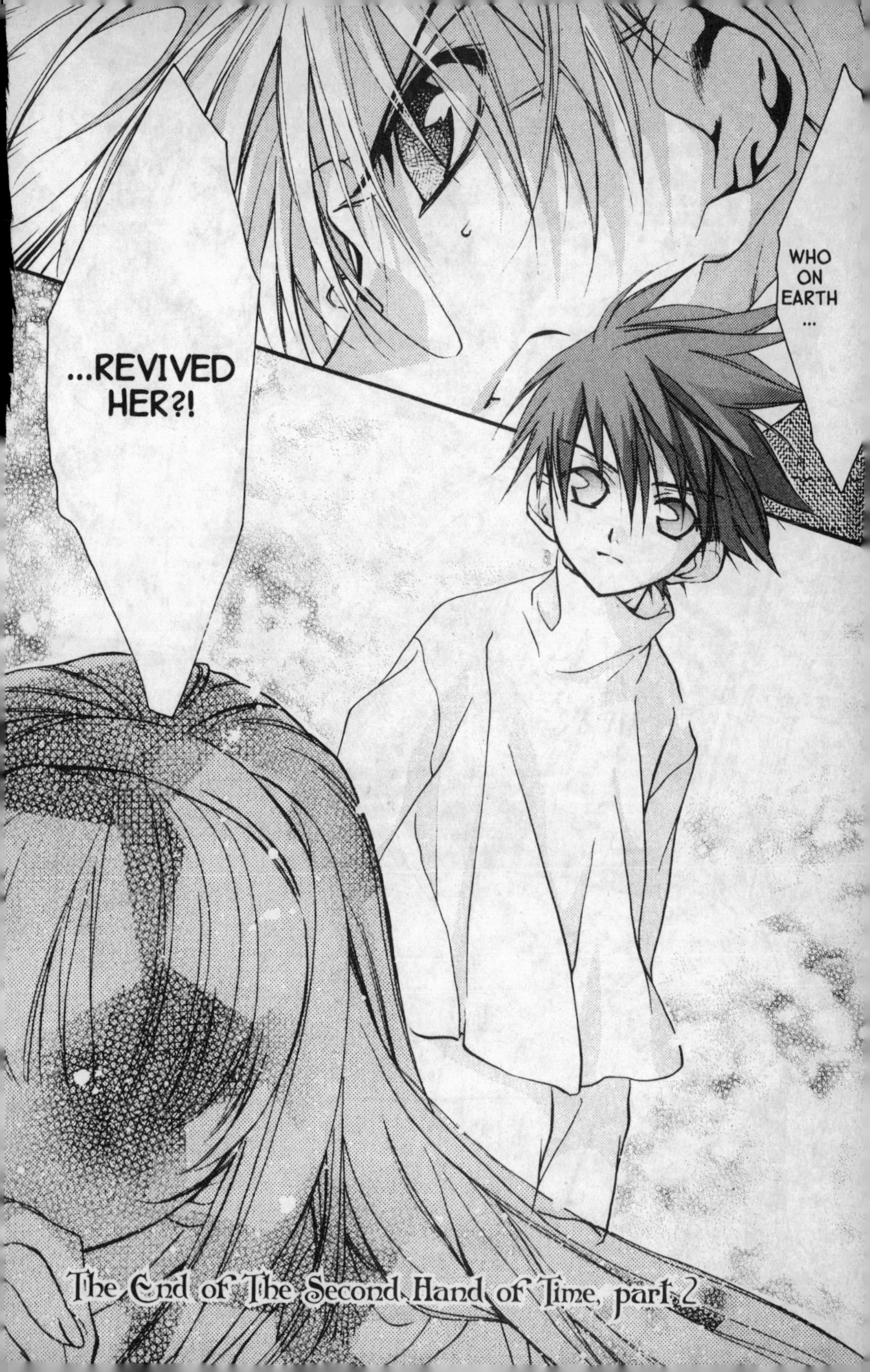
WHO ON EARTH ...
...REVIVED HER?!
The End of The Second Hand of Time, part 2

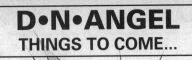

D•N•ANGEL
THINGS TO COME...

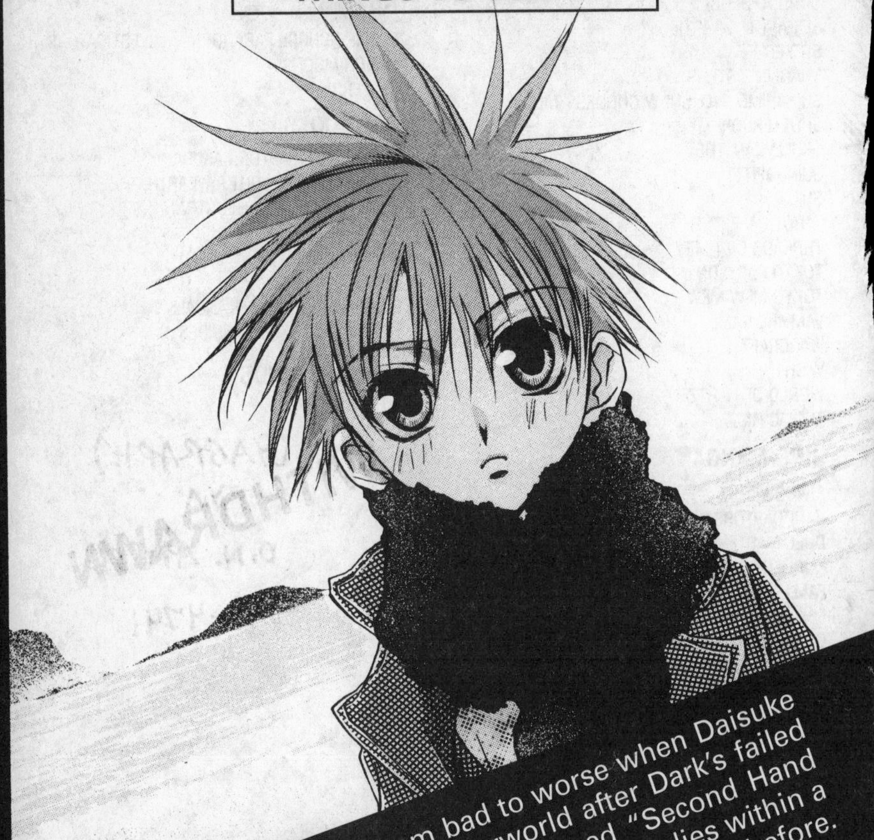

Things just keep going from bad to worse when Daisuke is taken away to a frozen netherworld after Dark's failed attempt at stealing the newly awakened "Second Hand of Time." The only remaining link to Daisuke lies within a drawing that he unwittingly gave to Riku the day before. Now Dark will have to impersonate Daisuke in order to retrieve the picture. But it won't be easy. It seems that Daisuke is participating in the school play, and the disappointed student body is slandering the good name of the Phantom Thief!

Be here for D•N•Angel Volume 7!

ALSO AVAILABLE FROM ☜TOKYOPOP®

WITHDRAWN (YAGRAPH)
D. N. YA
371-4741

10.19.04Y

ALSO AVAILABLE FROM ✪TOKYOPOP®

MANGA

.HACK//LEGEND OF THE TWILIGHT
ALICHINO
ANGELIC LAYER
BABY BIRTH
BRAIN POWERED
BRIGADOON
B'TX
CANDIDATE FOR GODDESS, THE
CARDCAPTOR SAKURA
CARDCAPTOR SAKURA - MASTER OF THE CLOW
CHRONICLES OF THE CURSED SWORD
CLAMP SCHOOL DETECTIVES
CLOVER
COMIC PARTY
CORRECTOR YUI
COWBOY BEBOP
COWBOY BEBOP: SHOOTING STAR
CRESCENT MOON
CROSS
CULDCEPT
CYBORG 009
D•N•ANGEL
DEARS
DEMON DIARY
DEMON ORORON, THE
DIGIMON
DIGIMON TAMERS
DIGIMON ZERO TWO
DRAGON HUNTER
DRAGON KNIGHTS
DRAGON VOICE
DREAM SAGA
DUKLYON: CLAMP SCHOOL DEFENDERS
ET CETERA
ETERNITY
FAERIES' LANDING
FLCL
FLOWER OF THE DEEP SLEEP
FORBIDDEN DANCE
FRUITS BASKET
G GUNDAM
GATEKEEPERS
GIRL GOT GAME
GUNDAM SEED ASTRAY
GUNDAM SEED ASTRAY R
GUNDAM WING
GUNDAM WING: BATTLEFIELD OF PACIFISTS
GUNDAM WING: ENDLESS WALTZ
GUNDAM WING: THE LAST OUTPOST (G-UNIT)
HANDS OFF!

HARLEM BEAT
HYPER RUNE
I.N.V.U.
INITIAL D
INSTANT TEEN: JUST ADD NUTS
JING: KING OF BANDITS
JING: KING OF BANDITS - TWILIGHT TALES
JULINE
KARE KANO
KILL ME, KISS ME
KINDAICHI CASE FILES, THE
KING OF HELL
KODOCHA: SANA'S STAGE
LAGOON ENGINE
LEGEND OF CHUN HYANG, THE
LILING-PO
LOVE OR MONEY
MAGIC KNIGHT RAYEARTH I
MAGIC KNIGHT RAYEARTH II
MAN OF MANY FACES
MARMALADE BOY
MARS
MARS: HORSE WITH NO NAME
MINK
MIRACLE GIRLS
MODEL
MOURYOU KIDEN: LEGEND OF THE NYMPH
NECK AND NECK
ONE
ONE I LOVE, THE
PEACH FUZZ
PEACH GIRL
PEACH GIRL: CHANGE OF HEART
PHD: PHANTASY DEGREE
PITA-TEN
PLANET BLOOD
PLANET LADDER
PLANETES
PRESIDENT DAD
PRINCESS AI
PSYCHIC ACADEMY
QUEEN'S KNIGHT, THE
RAGNAROK
RAVE MASTER
REALITY CHECK
REBIRTH
REBOUND
RISING STARS OF MANGA™,THE
SAILOR MOON
SAINT TAIL
SAMURAI GIRL™ REAL BOUT HIGH SCHOOL

10.19.04Y

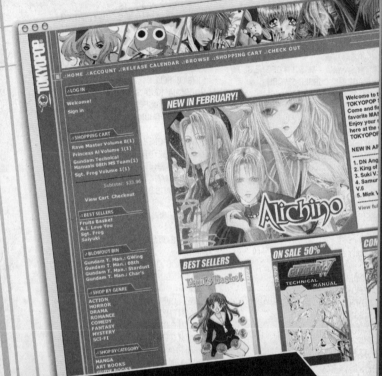

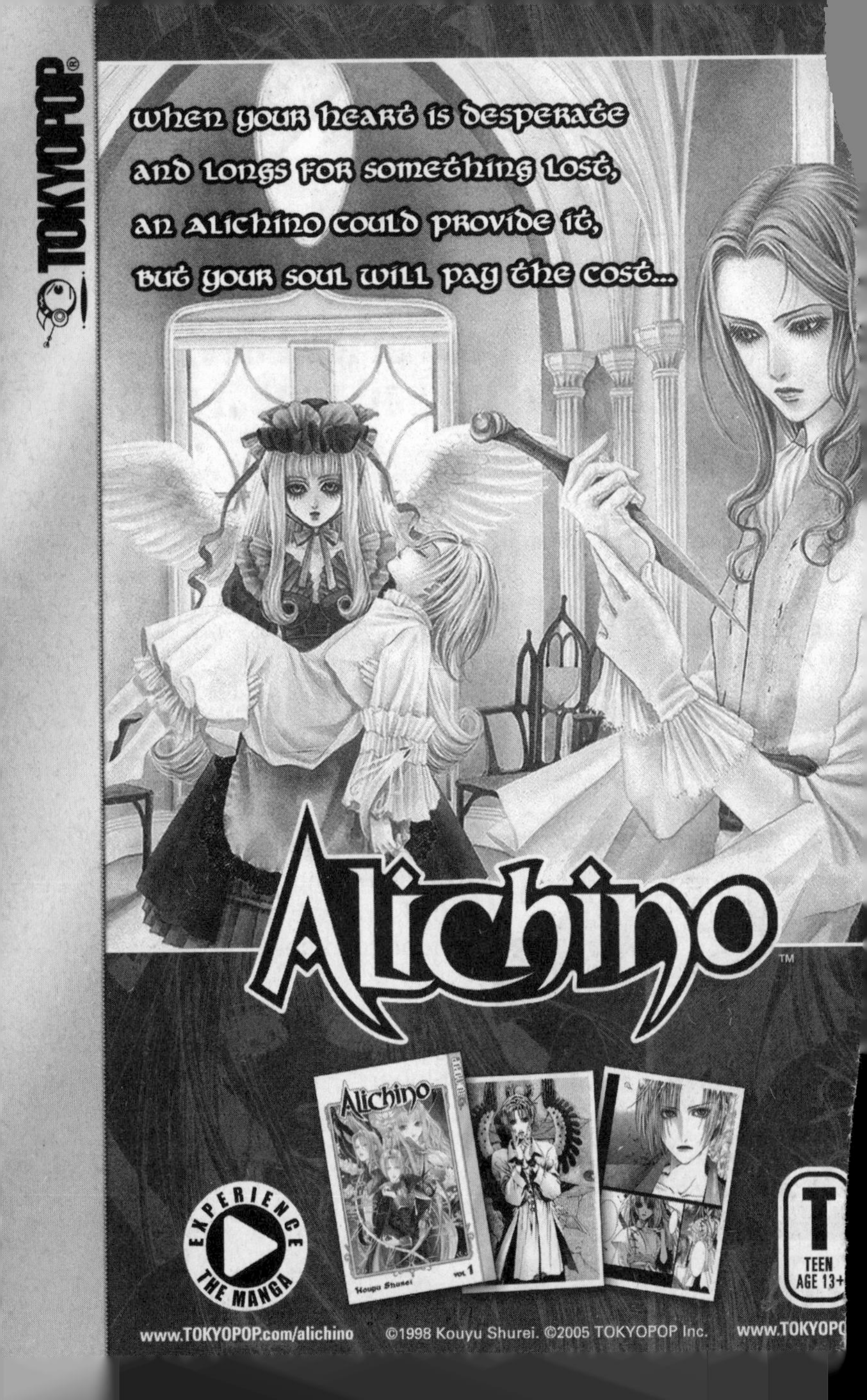
TOKYOPOP
when your heart is desperate
and longs for something lost,
an alichino could provide it,
but your soul will pay the cost...
Alichino™
Alichino
Kouyu Shurei
vol 1
EXPERIENCE THE MANGA
T
TEEN
AGE 13+
www.TOKYOPOP.com/alichino
©1998 Kouyu Shurei. ©2005 TOKYOPOP Inc.
www.TOKYOPO

STOP!

This is the back of the book.
You wouldn't want to spoil a great ending!

This book is printed "manga-style," in the authentic Japanese right-to-left format. Since none of the artwork has been flipped or altered, readers get to experience the story just as the creator intended. You've been asking for it, so TOKYOPOP® delivered: authentic, hot-off-the-press, and far more fun!

DIRECTIONS

If this is your first time reading manga-style, here's a quick guide to help you understand how it works.

It's easy... just start in the top right panel and follow the numbers. Have fun, and look for more 100% authentic manga from TOKYOPOP®!

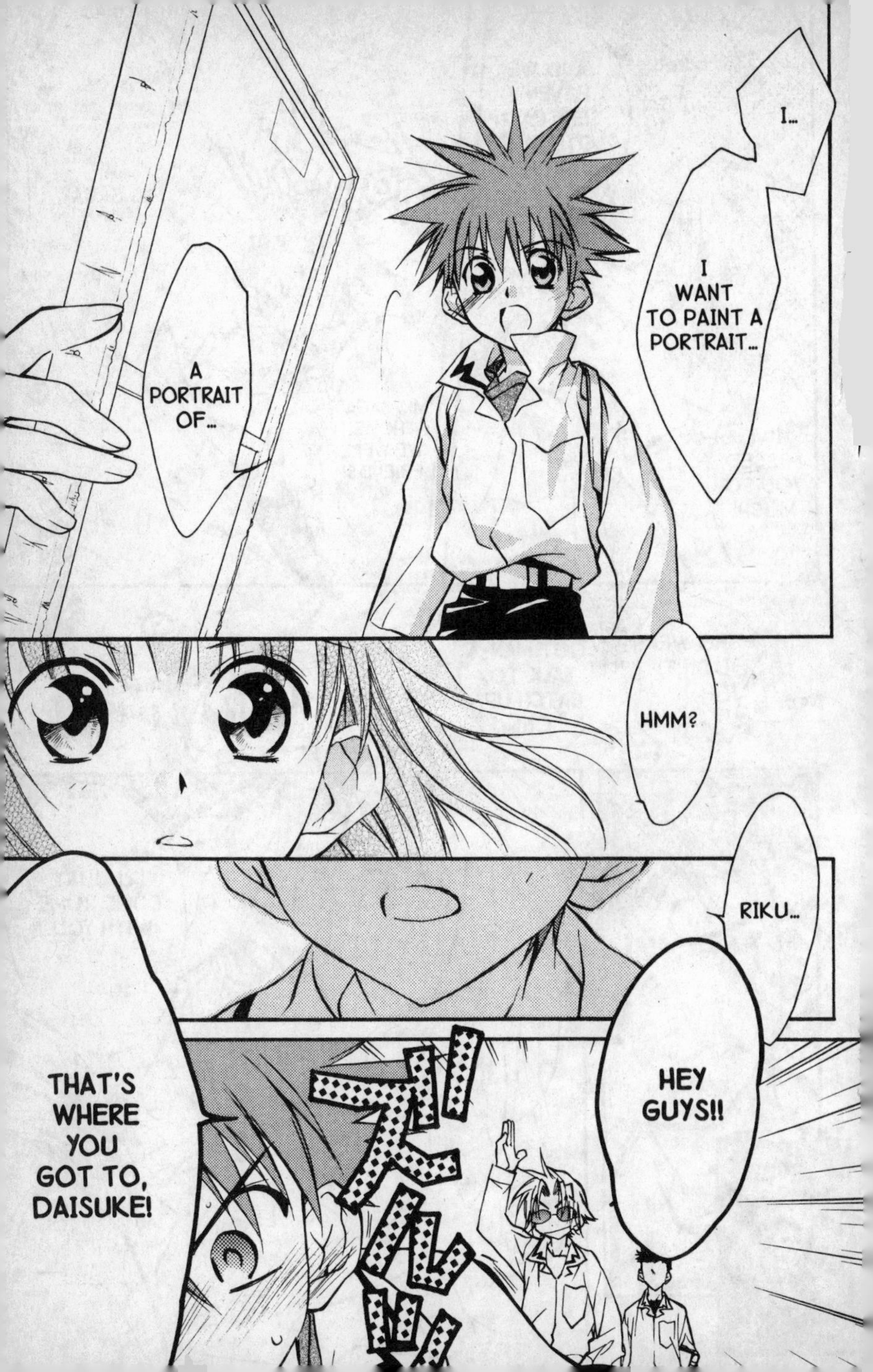
I...
I WANT TO PAINT A PORTRAIT...
A PORTRAIT OF...
HMM?
RIKU...
HEY GUYS!!
THAT'S WHERE YOU GOT TO, DAISUKE!

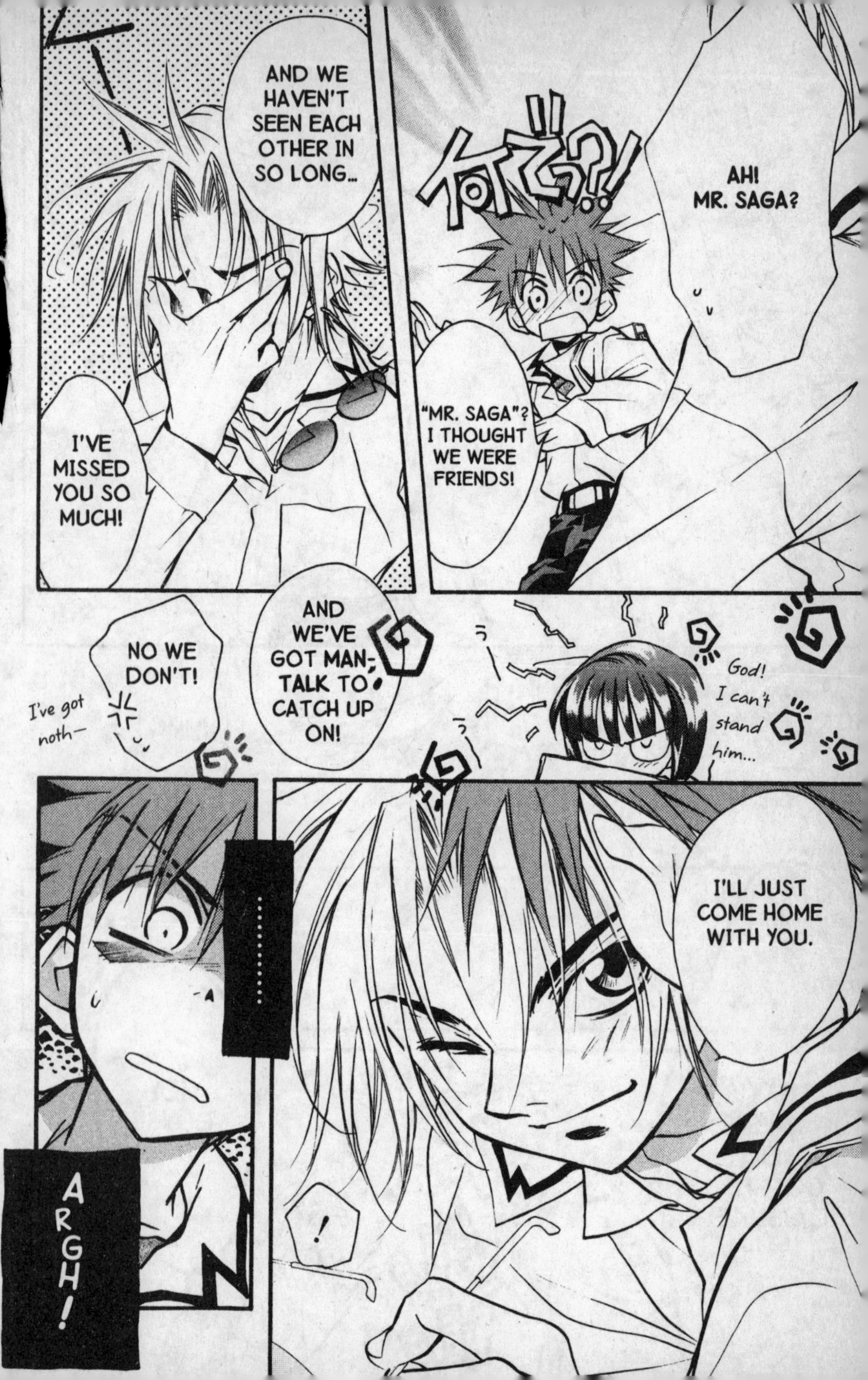
AH! MR. SAGA?
何でっ?!
"MR. SAGA"? I THOUGHT WE WERE FRIENDS!
AND WE HAVEN'T SEEN EACH OTHER IN SO LONG...
I'VE MISSED YOU SO MUCH!
God! I can't stand him...
AND WE'VE GOT MAN-TALK TO CATCH UP ON!
NO WE DON'T!
I've got noth—
I'LL JUST COME HOME WITH YOU.
!
....
ARGH!